Sunset
Gardener's
Answer Book

By the Editors of Sunset Books and Sunset Magazine

Lane Publishing Co. • Menlo Park, California

Sunset readers "outlined" this book

Western gardeners are great question-askers, and nobody knows and appreciates this as much as the garden editors of *Sunset Magazine* and *Sunset Books*. So, in a way, this book was "outlined" by our readers as much as by our editors. It serves as a book of ready answers for beginning gardeners as well as experienced green-thumbers, and also makes an excellent companion to the all-time best selling garden book for Westerners, the *Sunset New Western Garden Book.*

Most of the pages of this book (pages 49-146) are devoted to specific questions and answers, problems and solutions. The chapter is divided into seventeen separate subsections. Other primary chapters are the *Western Climate Guide* and *Regional Activities Calendars* which lead off the book, and the special 17-page section on pests and diseases, *Garden Troublemakers*, which begins on page 32.

We thank the many professional garden experts and Western garden club members who shared with us their experience, advice, and counsel. Our special thanks to Arthur L. Antonelli, Ph.D., Washington State University; Carlton S. Koehler, Ph.D., University of California; and Peter Sugawara, nurseryman, Los Altos, California.

Editor: David E. Clark
Supervising Editor: Marian May
Research and Text: A. Cort Sinnes
Contributing Editors: Joseph F. Williamson
Managing Editor, *Sunset Magazine*

Kathleen Norris Brenzel
Garden Editor, *Sunset Magazine*

John R. Dunmire
Associate Editor, *Sunset Magazine*

Illustrations: Sandra Popovich
Dennis Nolan (garden pests section)
Design Consultant: Alan May
Research Assistant: Donice Evans
Cover Art Director: Roger Flanagan
Cover Photograph: Steve W. Marley

Special Staff: Chuck Anderson, Phyllis Anderson, Michael Joseph Brozda, William Cheney, Barbara Criswell, Philip Edinger, Elizabeth Friedman, Sherry Gellner, Carol Bale Malcomb, Suzanne Mathison, Jim McCausland, Lynne Meyer, Sharon Symington Smorsten, Barbara Stacy, Peggy Kuhn Thompson, Susan Warton

First printing February 1983

TABLE OF CONTENTS

WESTERN CLIMATE GUIDE

Throughout this book you will find references to 24 climate zones. These are the zones that are mapped and described in the *Sunset New Western Garden Book.*

In the regional activities calendars on the following pages, the 24 zones are lumped together into 5 bigger climate groupings: mountains, west of the Cascades in Oregon and Washington, low elevations of northern California, deserts of the southwest, and the low elevations of southern California.

The West gets its diverse assortment of climates from several different physical facts and forces:

1. The farther from the equator a spot is, the longer and colder are its winters.

2. The greater a spot's distance upward from sea level, the longer and colder are its winters.

3. Areas with the most exposure to the ocean generally get the most influence from it—more moisture, cooler summers, milder winters.

4. Air masses from the continent make for colder winters, hotter summers, and summer precipitation.

5. Our mountains and hills funnel ocean and continental air masses into special patterns.

6. Warm air rises and cold air sinks. Hence hillside gardens may be more frost-free than valley-floor gardens a few miles away.

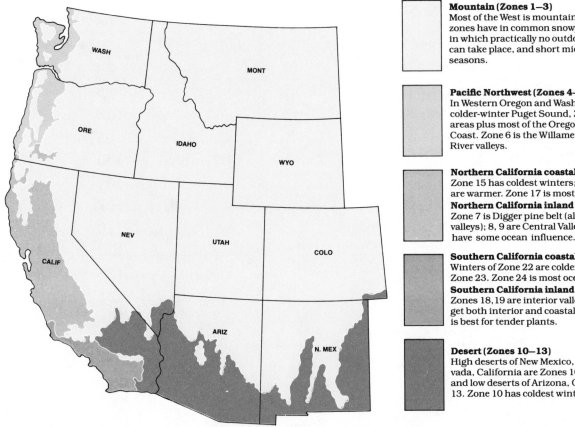

Mountain (Zones 1–3)
Most of the West is mountainous. The three zones have in common snowy, cold winters in which practically no outdoor gardening can take place, and short midyear growing seasons.

Pacific Northwest (Zones 4–6)
In Western Oregon and Washington: Zone 4 is colder-winter Puget Sound, Zone 5 is milder areas plus most of the Oregon-Washington Coast. Zone 6 is the Willamette and Cowlitz River valleys.

Northern California coastal (Zones 15-17)
Zone 15 has coldest winters; Zone 16 winters are warmer. Zone 17 is most ocean-influenced.
Northern California inland (Zones 7-9, 14)
Zone 7 is Digger pine belt (also southern Oregon valleys); 8, 9 are Central Valley; Zone 14 valleys have some ocean influence.

Southern California coastal (Zones 22-24)
Winters of Zone 22 are colder than those of Zone 23. Zone 24 is most ocean-influenced.
Southern California inland (Zones 18-21)
Zones 18, 19 are interior valleys. Zones 20, 21 get both interior and coastal weather; Zone 21 is best for tender plants.

Desert (Zones 10–13)
High deserts of New Mexico, Arizona, Utah, Nevada, California are Zones 10, 11. Intermediate and low deserts of Arizona, California are 12, 13. Zone 10 has coldest winters, 13 mildest.

IN WHICH GARDEN CLIMATE ZONE DO YOU LIVE?

To get the most from gardening information throughout this book, it is important that you know your individual Western gardening zone. The following list of Western cities and their zones will help you to locate yourself climate-wise.

If you don't find your home town listed, select the zone that is given for that city nearest to you.
To locate your zone more precisely, see the Climates section at the beginning of the *Sunset New Western Garden Book.*

CITY	ZONE
Aberdeen WA	5
Ajo AZ	12
Alamogordo NM	10
Alameda CA	17
Albany OR	6
Albuquerque NM	10
Alhambra CA	20
Alpine CA	18
Altadena CA	21
Alturas CA	1
Anaheim CA	23
Antioch CA	14
Arcadia CA	20, 21
Arlington WA	4
Aspen CO	1
Astoria OR	5
Atascadero CA	7
Auburn CA	9
Auburn WA	4
Baker OR	2
Bakersfield CA	8, 9
Banning CA	11
Barstow CA	11
Beaumont CA	18
Bellevue WA	5
Bellingham WA	4
Bend OR	1
Berkeley CA	16, 17
Beverly Hills CA	23
Billings MT	1
Bishop CA	11
Blythe CA	13
Boise ID	1, 3
Borrego CA	13
Boulder CO	1
Bozeman MT	1
Brawley CA	13
Bremerton WA	5
Brookings OR	17
Burbank CA	20, 21
Burlington CO	1
Burney CA	1
Burns OR	1
Butte MT	1
Caldwell ID	3
Camarillo CA	23
Carlsbad NM	10
Carmichael CA	9
Carson City NV	3
Casper WY	1
Castro Valley CA	15
Cedar City UT	2
Chatsworth CA	19
Chehalis WA	4
Cheyenne WY	1
Chico CA	8, 9
Chula Vista CA	24
Cle Elum WA	2
Clifton CA	10
Clovis NM	10
Coalinga CA	9
Coeur d'Alene ID	2
Colorado Springs CO	1
Colusa CA	8
Colville WA	1
Concord CA	14
Coos Bay OR	5
Corona CA	19
Corvallis OR	6
Covelo CA	7
Covina CA	21

CITY	ZONE
Crescent City CA	17
Culver City CA	22
Davis CA	14
Deming NM	10
Denver CO	2
Douglas AZ	10
Downey CA	22
Durango CO	1
El Cajon CA	23
El Centro CA	13
Elgin OR	2
Elko NV	1
Encinitas CA	24
Enterprise OR	1
Escondido CA	21
Eugene OR	6
Eureka CA	17
Everett WA	5
Fairfield CA	15
Farmington NM	2
Flagstaff AZ	1
Florence, OR	5
Ft. Bragg CA	17
Fremont CA	15, 16
Fresno CA	8
Gardnerville CA	15
Gilroy CA	14, 16
Glasgow MT	1
Glendale CA	20, 21
Glendive MT	1
Globe AZ	10
Gooding ID	1
Grand Junction CO	2
Grangeville ID	1, 2
Grass Valley CA	7
Grants Pass OR	7
Great Falls MT	1
Half Moon Bay CA	17
Havre MT	1
Healdsburg CA	14
Heber UT	1
Helena MT	1
Hemet CA	18
Hermiston OR	3
Hood River OR	3
Huntington Beach CA	24
Idaho Falls ID	2
Idyllwild CA	3
Indio CA	13
Ione CA	9
Irvine CA	22
Jackson WY	1
Jacumba CA	13
Jenner CA	17
Julian CA	3
Kennewick WA	3
King City CA	14
Kingman AZ	10
Klamath Falls OR	1
La Cañada CA	20, 21
Lafayette CA	14
La Grande OR	2
Laguna Beach CA	22–24
La Jolla CA	23, 24
Lake Arrowhead CA	3
Lakeport CA	7
Lakeside CA	21

CITY	ZONE
Lakeview OR	1
Lancaster CA	11
Laramie WY	1
Las Cruces NM	10
Las Vegas NV	11
Leavenworth WA	1
Lewiston ID	3
Livermore CA	14
Lodi CA	14
Logan UT	2
Lone Pine CA	11
Long Beach CA	24
Long Beach WA	5
Longview WA	6
Los Alamos NM	1
Los Angeles CA	22, 23
Los Banos CA	8
Lovelock NV	3
Madera CA	8, 9
Madras OR	1
Manteca CA	14
Mariposa CA	7
Martinez CA	15
Marysville CA	8
Marysvale UT	2
Medford OR	7
Menlo Park CA	15, 17
Merced CA	8
Middletown CA	7
Miles City MT	1
Mill Valley CA	15, 16
Milton-Freewater OR	3
Minden NV	3
Missoula MT	1
Moab UT	2
Modesto CA	8, 14
Monterey CA	17
Montpelier ID	1
Morro Bay CA	17
Moscow ID	2
Moses Lake WA	2
Mt. Shasta CA	1
Mt. Vernon WA	5
Napa CA	14
Needles CA	13
Newhall CA	18
Newport OR	5
Newport Beach CA	24
Novato CA	15
Oakdale CA	9
Oak Harbor WA	5
Oakland CA	17
Oceanside CA	23, 24
Ogden UT	2
Ojai CA	20
Olympia WA	4
Omak WA	2
Ontario OR	3
Orange CA	23
Oroville CA	9
Oxnard CA	24
Packwood WA	1
Page AZ	2
Palmdale CA	11
Palm Springs CA	13
Palo Alto CA	15, 17
Panguitch UT	1
Parker AZ	13
Pasadena CA	21
Paseo WA	3

CITY	ZONE
Pendleton OR	3
Perris CA	18
Petaluma CA	14, 15
Phoenix AZ	13
Placerville CA	7
Pocatello ID	1, 2
Point Reyes Station CA	15
Pomona CA	18
Port Angeles WA	5
Porterville CA	9
Portland OR	6
Portola CA	1
Port Townsend WA	5
Prescott AZ	2
Preston ID	2
Price UT	2
Prineville OR	1
Provo UT	2
Pt. Arena CA	17
Pueblo CO	2
Pullman WA	2
Puyallup WA	4
Ramona CA	20
Raton NM	2
Raymond WA	4
Red Bluff CA	9
Redding CA	9
Redlands CA	19
Redwood City CA	15, 17
Reno NV	3
Richmond CA	17
Ridgecrest CA	11
Rio Linda CA	14
Rio Vista CA	14
Riverside CA	19
Rock Springs WY	1
Roseburg OR	6
Roseville CA	9
Roswell NM	10
Sacramento CA	14
Safford AZ	12
St. George UT	10
Salem OR	6
Salinas CA	15
Salmon ID	1
Salt Lake City UT	2
San Bernardino CA	19
San Bruno CA	17
San Diego CA	24
San Francisco CA	17
San Fernando CA	18, 19
San Jose CA	15–17
San Luis Obispo CA	15, 16
San Mateo CA	16, 17
San Rafael CA	15, 17
Santa Ana CA	23
Santa Barbara CA	24
Santa Clara CA	15
Santa Cruz CA	15, 17
Santa Fe NM	2
Santa Maria CA	15
Santa Monica CA	24
Santa Paula CA	21
Santa Rosa CA	14
Sausalito CA	17
Searchlight NV	11
Seattle WA	5
Sebastopol CA	15
Sedona AZ	10

CITY	ZONE
Shelton WA	4
Sheridan WY	1
Silver City NM	2
Simi Valley CA	18
Sonora CA	7
Spokane WA	1
Steamboat Springs CO	1
Sterling CO	1
Stockton CA	14
Susanville CA	1
Tacoma WA	4, 5
Taft CA	8, 9
Tahoe City CA	2
Taos NM	1
Tehachapi CA	1, 7
The Dalles OR	3
Toledo WA	6
Torrance CA	22, 24
Trinidad CO	1
Tucson AZ	12
Tulelake CA	1
Turlock CA	8
Twentynine Palms CA	11
Twin Falls ID	2
Ukiah CA	14
Upland CA	19
Vacaville CA	8, 9
Vallejo CA	17
Van Nuys CA	20
Ventura CA	24
Victorville CA	11
Visalia CA	8
Vista CA	23
Walla Walla WA	3
Walnut Creek CA	14
Weaverville CA	7
Wenatchee WA	2
Whittier CA	23
Wickenburg AZ	12
Willits CA	14
Willows CA	9
Winnemucca NV	2
Winslow AZ	2
Woodland CA	8
Woodland Hills CA	18, 19
Woodside CA	14, 16
Yakima WA	2
Yreka CA	2
Yucca Valley CA	11
Yuma AZ	13

WESTERN CANADA
In British Columbia, Zone 5 covers the east shore of Howe Sound, all of Cortes and Redona Islands, and the south Vancouver Island coast from Sidney to Cape Cook. All remaining B.C. coastal areas are in Zone 4, while the rest of the province lies in Zones 1, 2, or 3. All of Alberta is Zone 1.

MOUNTAIN

Most of the Western United States is mountainous. In this region, the Sunset *New Western Garden Book* maps and describes climate Zones 1, 2, and 3. The three zones have in common snowy, cold winters in which practically no outdoor gardening can take place, and short midyear growing seasons.

SPRING

Springtime in the mountains starts when the snow melts and the soil becomes workable. For planting tender crops such as tomatoes, spring arrives when local authorities say the last frost has passed. One must be wary of the "last frost."

General garden care

Clean-up ● Leave pine needles and fallen leaves to help retain soil moisture during March's high, dry winds. However, in rainiest mountain areas, remove garden debris early in March so water and sunlight can penetrate soil.

● In April, give all gardens a good clean-up. Lightly cultivate partially rotted material, such as pine needles, into beds.

Fertilize ● In early spring, the growing season starts. Feed evergreen trees and shrubs with complete, water-soluble nitrogen fertilizer.

● Later, in April (prime growth time), all other plants will benefit from application of a complete fertilizer.

● In May, feed lawns with slow-release, high-nitrogen fertilizer; annuals and vegetables with complete food.

● Feed deciduous fruit trees while they are in bloom or shortly after with high-phosphorus complete fertilizer; bulbs after blooming with food high in phosphorus and potassium.

Mulch ● In arid mountain climates, mulches are a necessity. In May, put down organic mulches (pine needles, hay, straw, grass clippings). Use black plastic sheeting for heat-loving squash, corn, pepper, tomatoes. ● (See Mulches, pages 51–52, *Sunset New Western Garden Book*.)

Pests and diseases ● In March, while trees are dormant (before buds begin to swell), it is still safe to use dormant spray to ward off aphids, scale, mites. Follow label instructions carefully. Spray again if rain washes off first application. ● (See pages 32–48.)

● Dust roses, other plants susceptible to diseases such as rust or powdery mildew.

● (See Plant disease control, pages 63–66, *Sunset New Western Garden Book*.)

● Apply iron chelate or iron sulfate to lawns, trees, shrubs that show sign of chlorosis (recognized by leaves yellowing between the veins).

Prepare soil ● March is the last chance to get soil ready for spring planting (fall is *best* time). Spread organic material (compost, well-rotted manure, leaf mold, etc.). Cultivate amendments deeply into soil. ● (See Soils and planting mixes, pages 33–35, *Sunset New Western Garden Book*.)

Prune ● Best time to prune most woody deciduous trees and shrubs is March. Remove crossing branches, those growing toward center of plant, and those killed or damaged by frosts. ● Continue through spring to cut back uneven new growth.

● Wait until April to prune roses, vines, and grapes; finish pruning by early May.

● After new growth starts, remove frost-damaged or dead wood from tropical and subtropical plants, including citrus.

● Cut a few branches of flowering shrubs and trees for indoor display but save major pruning until bloom is over (usually by June).

● After bloom, cut back azaleas, camellias to encourage more flowering wood.

● Do *not* prune birch or maple trees until late summer when sap does not flow freely.

● In May, cut back raspberry canes to 4 or 5 feet.

● (See Pruning, pages 68–71, *Sunset New Western Garden Book*.)

Water ● When top 4 to 6 inches of soil thaws around evergreen trees and broad-leaf shrubs, water them early in day. Don't water enough to leave standing water to freeze over night. ● Drain hoses and sprinkler lines to prevent freeze damage.

● In May begin regularly to water lawns, ground covers, shrubs, trees, vegetable and flower beds, container plants.

● (See Watering, pages 48–52, *Sunset New Western Garden Book*.)

Annuals

● Prepare beds for summer annuals in March or April. ● Start seeds indoors (70°–75° F) for transplanting later. When seedlings show true leaves, move to cooler spot (60°–65° F) to harden off.

● In April or May, when danger of last frost is past, set out seedlings or transplants to garden locations.

● (See Annuals, pages 76–79, *Sunset New Western Garden Book*.)

Bare-root planting

● At end of March, nurseries should have bare-root deciduous fruit, nut, shade trees; roses; grapes; cane berries; rhubarb; asparagus. ● April is prime time for planting. ● (See Bare-root planting, pages 44–45, *Sunset New Western Garden Book*.)

Bulbs

● Plant cannas, dahlias, tuberoses, other summer bulbs in April. Plant in open ground any forced, potted spring bulbs you have after foliage dies back.

● Fertilize (see General garden care, preceding).

● Remove faded blooms, but allow foliage on spring-flowering bulbs to wither naturally.

● (See Bulbs, pages 75–77, *Sunset New Western Garden Book*.)

Herbs

● In May, plant these perennial herbs in full sun: chive, sage, lavender, spearmint, tarragon, thyme. Oregano is perennial in protected spots. ● Annual herbs also can be planted in sunny places: basil, borage, chervil, dill. ● (See individual plant listings in the encyclopedia section, *Sunset New Western Garden Book*.)

House plants

● At end of May, move tough house plants such as succulents and cactus outdoors to spots protected from sun and cold night temperatures; leave aloe, gesneriads, coleus, and caladiums indoors.

Lawns

● Rake lawns to expose lower parts of stems to sun and increase air circulation to eliminate diseases, especially snow mold.
● Fertilize (see General garden care, preceding).
● Apply herbicide to weeds in lawn.

Perennials

● Wait until after frosts to plant. ● Remove mulch from around crowns of established plants.
● Fertilize (see General garden care, preceding).

Vegetables

● In mid-March start seeds of broccoli, Brussels sprouts, cabbage, cauliflower, lettuce, okra, onions, spinach indoors in greenhouse, on sunny window sill, or in heated frame. ● At the same time, sow seeds of early cool-season crops, such as radishes and peas, directly outdoors in well-worked garden soil.
● Plant asparagus and rhubarb at end of March.
● In April, or when danger of last frost is past, sow seeds for root crops, such as beets and carrots, in well-worked soil. ● The end of April usually is a good time to sow seeds of mid-season cool crops, such as broccoli and cabbage, outdoors. ● Also start from seed late-season heat-loving crops, such as eggplants and tomatoes, in coldframe or greenhouse for transplanting when the weather warms.
● (For complete vegetable planting charts, keyed to all climate zones, see pages 82–84, *Sunset New Western Garden Book*.)

SUMMER

For mountain gardeners, summer is the time of most intense garden activity. Many flowers and vegetables must be brought to maturity and harvested during the comparatively brief growing season.

General garden care

Clean-up ● In mid-summer, pick faded blooms of roses, annuals, perennials,

ground covers to improve appearance and force new buds. Rake up pine needles so warmth and air can penetrate soil.

Fertilize ● Feed perennials with a complete fertilizer in early to mid-summer. July is a good time to feed established annuals with a complete fertilizer. ● Feed established lawns with high-nitrogen complete fertilizer. Use complete fertilizer for vegetables.
● Feed established fruit trees with high-nitrogen complete fertilizer (spread 2 to 3 pounds under each tree to dripline); water in deeply.
● Feed most vegetables with soluble complete fertilizer or a side-dressing of dry fertilizer in a trench alongside vegetable rows; water in deeply. Feed perennial vegetables (asparagus, rhubarb) with high-nitrogen complete fertilizer.
● As summer wanes, exercise caution with fertilizer. Starting in August withhold food from fruit or shade trees, azaleas, camellias, rhododendrons, roses and other woody plants in areas where early frost is a threat.

Mulch ● Early summer is the time to mulch around plantings to conserve water, hinder weed growth, and keep roots cool. Use organic mulch for most plantings, black plastic for tomatoes, peppers, eggplant, and squash. Newspaper is a good summer mulch; remove at end of summer as newspaper doesn't decay fast enough to be plowed under.
● (See Mulches, pages 51–52, *Sunset New Western Garden Book*.)

Pests and diseases ● Be on the lookout throughout summer for aphids, spider mites, thrips, caterpillars, grasshoppers, and other destructive garden insects. See pages 32 to 48.
● In July, prune old raspberry and boysenberry canes to improve air circulation and prevent mildew. (See page 41.) Control, with sevin or diazinon, borers that attack peach, prune, cherry trees.
● Throughout the summer, remove hornworms from tomatoes by hand; spray with *Bacillus thuringiensis* or sevin for severe infestations. Control spider mites (see page 35) and grasshoppers (see page 36).

Prune ● In early summer, conifers can be pruned to force denser growth. Remove no more than one third of the branches in one year. ● Trim ground covers to encourage new growth and bloom.
● Shape up boxwood, euonymus, yew, and other evergreen and deciduous shrubs. ● Suckers or vertical shoots on branches of crabapples, birches, hawthorns, maples, Russian olives, willows, and other trees should be pruned out in late summer.
● For larger fruit, thin fruit on trees, especially on limbs that may break.
● (See Pruning, pages 68–71, *Sunset New Western Garden Book*.)

Stake ● As dahlias, delphiniums, double peonies, gladiolus, peppers, and tomatoes put on rapid growth, stake them to reduce breakage and wind damage. Stakes should go 10 to 12 inches into the ground.

"Gardener's notepad"

Water • Plants are driest now—early summer. Deep water regularly during dry spells, paying special attention to new plantings.

• Continue to water most plants well throughout summer. Flowering plants, vegetables, lawns, fruit trees should receive especially deep waterings as summer comes to an end. • If early frost is a threat in your area, water woody plants less frequently in August. Build up mulch to conserve soil moisture.

• (See Watering, pages 48–52, *Sunset New Western Garden Book*.)

Weed • Weed your garden thoroughly in early summer. Weeding on a regular basis will prevent a take-over later in summer. Do not use harmful weed killers around vegetables and other edibles.

• (See Controlling weeds, pages 66–67, *Sunset New Western Garden Book*.)

Annuals

• In June, sow seeds of African daisy, bachelor's button, calendula, clarkia, cleome, godetia, linaria, lobelia, pansy, snapdragon, sweet alyssum, sweet William, verbena, viola. Plant when danger of frost is past.

Bulbs

• When foliage browns, dig, dry and store spring-blooming bulbs for fall planting. • Tulips can be kept in ground or stored until October or November. • Dig and divide overcrowded clumps of daffodils; replant or store until September.

• For summer bloom, plant gladiolus, montbretia, tigridia, peacock orchids, dahlias in June.

• In August, dig, divide, store summer-blooming bulbs too tender to survive winter: amaryllis, caladium, calla, canna, dahlia, gladiolus, lilies, tuberous begonia.

• (See Bulbs, pages 75–77, *Sunset New Western Garden Book*.)

Lawns

• August is the best month for starting new lawns from seed or sod. • Reseed or patch bare spots in established lawns. Keep new plantings well watered.

• (See Lawns, pages 85–88, *Sunset New Western Garden Book*.)

Permanent planting

• During early and midsummer, plant hardy container-grown or balled-and-burlapped (B&B) trees and shrubs.

• (See Planting balled and burlapped trees, pages 45–46, *Sunset New Western Garden Book*.)

Strawberries

• Plant strawberries from sixpacks or pots in June if you missed the spring bare-root season. They prefer rich, well-drained soil, full sun, ample water. Mulch with hay, straw, pine needles, sawdust.

Vegetables

• In June, sow seeds of beans, corn, cucumber, squash, pumpkin, watermelon. Sow successive crops of beets, bush beans, corn, chard, carrots, radishes.

• Set out transplants of eggplant, tomato, pepper (they will also do well in containers against heat-retaining walls).

• Thin vegetables, leaving the hardiest plants. Apply a complete fertilizer after thinning, and apply once again as vegetables mature.

• Mulch, using organic material for most crops, black plastic for tomatoes and squash.

• Early to mid-July, sow seeds or set out transplants of cabbage, cauliflower, kale, spinach. Make a second planting of beets, fast-maturing varieties of beans and corn (in mild areas), mustard, radishes, Swiss chard, turnips, winter squash.

• Plant winter squash among spinach to take over when spinach is harvested.

• In milder areas, succession-plant early this month for harvest into fall.

• Harvest early vegetables: sugar peas, lettuce, spinach, broccoli in July. To keep broccoli producing all summer, cut main head above side buds, then feed and water thoroughly. • To blanch immature cauliflower, tie leaves up around young heads that have reached golf-ball size.

• Harvest other fruits and vegetables in August, checking daily for produce at peak of flavor: beets, broccoli, bush beans, cauliflower, corn, new potatoes, raspberries, strawberries, summer squash, tomatoes, zucchini.

• (See Vegetables, page 81–84, *Sunset New Western Garden Book*.)

FALL

In the fall, mountain gardening slows down noticeably week by week. It's time to harvest and store end-of-season crops, set out a few hardy plants, work the soil, and clean up the garden before winter sets in.

General garden care

Clean-up • Pick up fallen leaves, grass clippings, spent blooms, pots, sticks, trimmings. Dig spent vegetable plants. • Add undiseased organic material saved from clean-up to compost pile.

• (See Garden sanitation, page 96, *Sunset New Western Garden Book*.)

Frost protection • In September, mulch beds of bulbs, annuals, perennials, and other tender plants for frost protection. Pick or protect tomatoes, pepper, eggplant, and other tender produce. • Harvest peaches, plums before frost.

• Return most house plants indoors before temperatures fall below 50° F. • Water woody plants generously before expected frost so plant tissues won't need to seek moisture from frozen soil. Apply tree wrap to trunks of these young trees—apple, elm, hard or sugar maple, linden, poplar, willow. Their bark is susceptible to frost cracking. • Provide protection for all tender plantings.

Pests and diseases • Use least toxic effective treatment for common garden pests. (See Garden troublemakers, pages 32 to 48.) • Burn fallen leaves of plants affected by virus or fungus infection; *do not add to your compost.*

Propagate • Take tip cuttings of geraniums, fuchsias before frost; root and grow indoors until spring. • Lift, divide, and store dahlia tubers.

Prune • Cut out dead sections of shrubs or trees killed by insects or disease. Burn or throw away prunings; *do not compost.* • Do not prune in freezing weather. • Do not prune deciduous plants; wait until early spring when buds begin to swell.

• (See Pruning, pages 68–71, *Sunset New Western Garden Book*.)

Soil preparation • Work organic matter into garden soil; leave soil in big clods; they will break during winter. • Wait until spring to add fertilizer; it will only leach out in the heavy rains and snows over winter.

Water • Don't water deciduous shrubs and trees until leaves fall; then water thoroughly. Water conifers deeply so they'll enter winter with leaves filled with water. • Irrigate only when temperature is above freezing; don't water so much that water stands. • Drain hoses and sprinkler lines after watering. • Continue to deep-water lawns regularly.

• (See Watering, pages 48–52, *Sunset New Western Garden Book*.)

Weeds • In September, remove weeds one last time before winter sets in. Especially attack annual weeds (dock, lambsquarter, pigweed, polygonum, wild lettuce) that scatter seeds everywhere. Remove perennial grasses and dandelions that creep in and take over flower beds and rock gardens.

• (See Controlling weeds, pages 66–67, *Sunset New Western Garden Book*.)

Annuals

• Through September, remove spent blooms of over-the-hill annuals for more flower production and a neater-looking garden. Later, take out plants when they finish blooming.

Bulbs

● September starts bulb-planting season: plant daffodils, tulips, iris, crocus, hyacinth, narcissus, scillas, snow drops. Water thoroughly and mulch for winter protection.

● After first frost, lift cannas, dahlias, gladiolus; let dry for 1 week to 10 days and store in moist sand or perlite at 35° to 50° F. Lift begonia tubers and store dry at same temperature.

● Lily bulbs mail-ordered last summer may not arrive until November. However, prepare beds in September. Cover beds with thick mulch or layers of newspaper to keep soil from freezing.

● (See Bulbs, pages 75–77, *Sunset New Western Garden Book.*)

● To force bulbs to bloom indoors (crocus, daffodil, hyacinths, tulips), plant in pots of damp aquarium gravel, then refrigerate or store in garage at 40° to 45° F. until the top growth is 1 to 1½ inches high.

Evergreens

● The second best time to transplant evergreens is in September, after the leaves of the deciduous trees fall. The *best* time is in early spring. Plant juniper, pine, yew, arborvitae. Water well, especially during winter dry spells.

● (See evergreen tree list for your zone, pages 99–101, *Sunset New Western Garden Book.*)

Fruit trees

● Light frost shouldn't hurt apples or pears, but you should pick peaches and plums before frost. Pick and discard all wormy or diseased fruit on trees or ground—throw in garbage or bury deeply.

Lawns

● Early fall (mid-August to mid-October) is the best time to seed or sod new lawns, or to reseed or sod spots in existing lawns. Water 3 or 4 times daily with fine spray. ● (See Lawns, pages 85–88, *Sunset New Western Garden Book.*)

Perennials

● Lift and divide spring-blooming and late-blooming plants (no later than early September)—ajuga, bleeding heart, campanula, cerastium, daylilies, delphinium, peonies, poppies, phlox, Shasta daisies, vinca. Divide roots at crown or "eye"; replant and mulch well to protect from winter frost.

● (See Perennials, pages 74–75, *Sunset New Western Garden Book.*)

Protect shrubs and trees

● Protect the trunks of young trees and shrubs from frost. Apple, elm, hard or sugar maple, linden, poplar, and willow are susceptible to winter sunburn. Cover trunks with burlap, commercial tree wrap, or heavy cloth.

● (See Winter-long protection, pages 95–96, *Sunset New Western Garden Book.*)

Vegetables

● Start lettuce, spinach in coldframes (grow them in as cold a temperature as possible). ● Leave carrots, turnips, and beets in the ground until snow threatens (they'll last longer); feed twice a month with complete fertilizer. ● If necessary, lift and divide asparagus, horseradish, rhubarb; mulch generously.

Wildflower seeds

● Broadcast seed over rock gardens, hillsides, or fields for spring bloom. Check nurseries, mail order companies for availability of bulk seeds.

WINTER

For many people in the mountains, there is little or nothing to do in the garden from the first freeze or snow of late fall until spring. During periods when there is not a continual snow cover, and when drying winds blow, be sure to water evergreens. For greenhouse owners, winter offers opportunities to start seeds of annuals, perennials, and vegetables; start cuttings; overwinter tender plants; and (if you are a hobbyist) grow "specialties" such as orchids and tropical plants.

"Gardener's notepad"

PACIFIC NORTHWEST

In Western Oregon and Washington are located *Sunset New Western Garden Book* climate Zones 4, 5, and 6. Zone 4 is the colder-winter portions of Puget Sound. Zone 5 is the milder areas of Puget Sound plus most of the Oregon-Washington Coast. Zone 6 is the Willamette and Cowlitz River valleys.

SPRING

Seems like there's never enough time to do all the things that spring offers—planting, feeding, pruning, shearing, weeding, etc. It helps if you get some dry weekends in which to keep up with all the opportunities.

General garden care

Compost ● As the weather warms and fresh organic material is added to compost pile, speed decomposition by turning with a pitchfork twice monthly until June. ● (Also see Compost, page 35, *Sunset New Western Garden Book.*)

Dormant spray ● Early March is the last chance before leaf buds open to spray deciduous trees with dormant spray for controlling pests and diseases such as mites, fungus, scale. Direct spray away from walls, walks, and fences; some sprays stain.

Fertilize ● In early spring, feed established strawberries, caneberries, and roses (not newly planted roses), and ground covers with a complete fertilizer.

● Feed all deciduous fruit trees with a complete fertilizer; pay particular attention to those that did not bear profusely last year.

● Right after bloom, at which time rhododendrons are starting to initiate new growth, is the time of year they need nitrogen most; this is a good time to feed them, since they may need a supplement to the nitrogen that is available naturally.

● Most established plantings will benefit from a feeding in mid-spring; they're putting on their new spring growth.

● Continue to feed bulbs after blooms fade.

● Begin a lawn-feeding program (see Lawns, later in this section).

● Start fertilizing house plants as soon as hours of daylight start to exceed hours of darkness.

Pests and diseases ● Cut colonies of tent caterpillers out of trees (use long tree pruners); destroy them by burning, or dunking them in diesel oil.

● Watch carefully for aphids active this time of year in attacking new spring growth, especially on fruit trees.

● Removing garden debris is one of the best defenses against slugs and snails. Bait, spray, or hand-pick snails or slugs, especially around coldframes, seedbeds, newly planted seedlings, leaf crops, and primroses. (Also see page 34.)

Prepare soil ● When soil where you want to plant is dry enough, dig in compost, manure, or other soil amendments. (Also see Soil amendments, page 33, *Sunset New Western Garden Book.*)

● Before they set seed, turn under cover crops (such as clover, fava beans, alfalfa, or winter rye) that you may have grown during winter to keep soil from eroding during heavy rains. These crops make good organic fertilizer.

Prune ● When forsythia, plum, and quince bloom in March, cut flowered branches for display indoors. This is a form of pruning. Remove flowered branches with sharp shears just above the growth buds or branching joints; don't leave stubs.

● In early spring, cut back clematis varieties that bloom only in summer to within a foot of the ground, to encourage new growth and heavy summer bloom.

● Prune dormant deciduous fruit trees and shrubs before buds swell.

● Clip ground covers for neat summer appearance.

● In March, in mild-weather areas, trim ragged deciduous hedges. Cut back old, weak stems to the ground. Trim broad-leafed evergreen hedges. (In colder areas, wait until April to prune.)

Water ● If there isn't enough spring rain, water everything regularly, especially new plantings, blooming rhododendrons. Remember plants under overhangs and in containers—they need water, too.

Weed ● Warmer weather means weeds. Hoe or hand weed them regularly, particularly when they're young.

Annuals

● Where soil is workable, sow summer-blooming annuals in late March: bachelor's button, calendula, clarkia, cosmos, larkspur, annual phlox, Shirley poppy, scarlet flax, snapdragon, and sweet alyssum.

● (Also see Annuals, pages 76–79, *Sunset New Western Garden Book.*)

Bare-root plants

● Mid-March is the last chance for planting bare-root roses, flowering trees, and shrubs. Buy early while nurseries still have a good supply.

Berries

● In earliest spring, set out bare-root cane berries in well-cultivated soil in full sun. Give plenty of growing space. Don't expect berries until summer of the following year.

● Fertilize (see General garden care, preceding).

● There's still time in April to plant blueberries, currants, gooseberries. Plant in full sun and keep well watered this first season. ● Do not plant gooseberries or currants near five-needle pine trees; they can infect each other with white pine blister rust.

● Weed strawberry patches carefully; watch out for their shallow roots.

Bulbs

● Weed and fertilize beds of bulbs, corms, tubers. In mild-winter areas, plant in March: *Acidanthera,* callas, montbretia, ranunculus, *Tigridia* in late March.
● Set out gladiolus corms at 2-week intervals for continuous summer bloom.
● In cold-winter areas plant callas in containers to move outdoors later.
● In mid-spring, pick faded blooms, but allow foliage to wither naturally before removing it (foliage supplies bulb with energy for next year).
● Check stored dahlia tubers for rot or damage.
● Divide overgrown winter iris by midspring. Order rhizomes of later-flowering iris for midsummer planting.
● (Also see Bulbs, pages 60–67 and 75–77, *Sunset New Western Garden Book.*)

Conifers

● In early spring, pinch tips to limit growth. Sheared with a hedge trimmer, cut ends are soon covered with new growth.
● Prune off unwanted branches to improve shape. ● (Also see Pruning, pages 68–71, *Sunset New Western Garden Book.*)

Ground covers

● In early spring, clip back established ground covers such as ivy and winter-blooming heather to encourage dense growth. ● Tear out dead patches, work amendments (compost, ground bark, wood shavings, peat moss) into soil, replant bare areas with healthy divisions from outer edges of ground cover. ● (Also see Division, pages 74–75, *Sunset New Western Garden Book.*)
● Sift soil, compost, or thoroughly aged manure into ground covers and feed lightly with a complete fertilizer to encourage rooting of runner or surface stems.

Hedges

● Prune evergreen hedges so that bottom is wider than top, and the whole hedge can get maximum light and water. ● In April, in cold weather areas, trim deciduous hedges.
● (Also see Shearing, page 69, *Sunset New Western Garden Book.*)

Lawns

● Grasses grow actively through spring. March means the beginning of regular mowing. ● Dethatch, edge, and weed as needed. ● Rake up bare spots to expose the soil; resoil and reseed.
● Water lawns deeply and regularly, when rain doesn't do it for you.
● For really green grass, feed with high-nitrogen fertilizer or ammonium sulfate April through September. Use a spreader to apply fertilizer evenly.
● (Also see Lawns, pages 85–88, *Sunset New Western Garden Book.*)

Perennials

● You'll find more perennials at nurseries or garden centers in April than any other time: asters, bleeding hearts, columbine, delphiniums, dianthus, evergreen candytuft, peonies, poppies, Shasta daisies, and violas.
● Divide crowded plants now for better blooms: daylilies, hostas, Michaelmas daisies, phlox, winter iris. Lift old root clumps, divide new growth, and transplant the divisions.

Rock gardens

● As early as spring weather permits, remove weeds and debris from your rock garden. Cut back dead, leggy, and winter-damaged growth; thin out dense plantings. Add soil where winter rains have washed it away; replant.

Vegetables

● In mild-weather areas, March is the time to plant seeds of beets, broccoli, cabbage, carrots, cauliflower, lettuce, peas, radishes, spinach. Also, set out onion seedlings and perennial vegetables such as artichokes, asparagus, horseradish, rhubarb.
● In March and April, plant warm-season vegetables indoors for transplanting outdoors in May: cucumbers, eggplant, melons, peppers, squash, tomatoes. Peppers need 8 weeks for maturing to transplanting size; tomato and eggplant need 6 weeks; and squash family members need 3 weeks. ● In early May, sow seeds of warm-season vegetables outdoors in full sun. ● (Also see Summer-fall vegetable list, pages 82–83, *Sunset New Western Garden Book.*)
● Plant lettuce at 2-week intervals for long harvest. Cover tomato seedlings with hotcaps or cloches until weather warms up. ● To reduce shade problems, plant taller vegetables to the north side of shorter ones. ● Sow cabbage seeds indoors for planting late summer or fall.

SUMMER

Now, when your weather really mellows, comes the time when you can enjoy your garden—and meanwhile keep it growing and bountiful. The long evenings give you time to experiment and try new plants and techniques.

General garden care

Clean-up ● Throughout summer, pick up leaves, faded flowers, garden debris to eliminate hiding places for slugs and snails.

Compost ● Moisten compost regularly.
● Organic debris such as grass clippings packs down and encourages fly breeding, unless you turn it often.

Fertilize ● Fuchsias and begonias need high-nitrogen fertilizer; use every 2 weeks or as often as specific product recommends on label. ● Feed azaleas, camellias, rhododendrons with an acid-type fertilizer during June and July. ● Feed chrysanthemums with complete fertilizer every 3 weeks throughout the summer until buds begin to show color.
● Broadcast fertilizer over ground covers at least once during the summer, or as condition dictates. ● Keep house plants and outdoor container plants well fed and watered generously.
● (Also see Fertilizing your garden, pages 52–55, *Sunset New Western Garden Book.*)

Mulch ● Mulch deeply (2 or 3 inches) around rhododendrons and azaleas. Both have shallow feeder roots and don't like hot weather; mulching keeps roots cool.

Pests ● Control slugs and snails and earwigs (see pages 34 and 36).
● In mid- to late summer, spray for mites (see page 35) and aphids (see page 34).

Propagate ● Make softwood cuttings during June: azalea, barberry, camellia, clematis, daphne, dogwood, filbert, forsythia, fuchsia, heather, holly, hydran-

gea, kinnikinnick, magnolia, mahonia, maple, nandina, passion flower, photinia, rhododendron, rose, wisteria.
● (Also see Softwood cuttings, page 38, *Sunset New Western Garden Book*.)

Prune ● Pinch summer-blooming annuals for bushy growth, more flowers, before they begin flowering. ● Cut back faded flowers on spring-blooming perennials. ● Remove suckers from trees and shrubs as they appear.
● After bloom, cut back old flowering wood from such deciduous shrubs as weigela, kerria, kolkwitzia, philadelphus.
● Prune heather after bloom. ● In July, remove suckers from roses, azaleas, camellias, rhododendrons.
● Cut summer-blooming perennials almost to the ground, leaving some foliage. Pinch back chrysanthemum tip growth.
● In late summer, remove old berry canes that have borne fruit. ● Disbud and prune roses lightly for better air circulation. ● Cut back shoots of wisteria and pyracantha.
● In August, prune leggy perennial herbs such as tarragon, thyme, and marjoram, almost back to the ground.
● (Also see Pruning, pages 68–71, *Sunset New Western Garden Book*.)

Water ● Water according to the weather and needs of individual plants. Give special attention to container plants, raised beds, and areas in direct sun.
● Deep water lawns, trees, shrubs to encourage deep rooting.
● During dry spells, mist-spray foliage of shrubs and trees. Don't allow rhododendrons and azaleas to dry out; next year's blooms will be damaged.
● Reduce watering of cabbages to prevent heads from maturing too fast and splitting.
● Rebuild watering basins around trees, shrubs; mulch.

Weed ● Hand-pull, hoe, or use herbicides to kill weeds before they mature and go to seed.

Annuals

● Buy transplants early from nurseries; avoid leftovers. Plant seeds of marigold, nasturtium, portulaca, zinnia.
● Keep soil moist (especially for new plants); mulch. Feed with high-nitrogen fertilizer every 2 weeks until buds form, then switch to fertilizer high in phosphorus and potassium. ● To keep plants productive, pick flowers regularly.
● (Also see Annuals, pages 76–79, *Sunset New Western Garden Book*.)

Berries

● If necessary, cover vines with nylon netting to protect crops from birds.
● Mulch to 2 inches under cane and bush berries (raspberries, blackberries, blueberries). ● Keep bearing canes moist through the summer.

● After harvest, cut to the ground canes that have fruited. Remove weak, undersized canes at the same time. Leave healthy canes that haven't fruited to bear next year.
● Weed around plants; be careful of shallow, easily damaged roots.
● Set out strawberries as soon as available in August. ● Water blueberries, currants, gooseberries, strawberries often during hot weather. ● Cut back fruit-bearing canes of raspberries, blackberries, boysenberries after harvest; water deeply, cultivate, fertilize.

Bulbs

● Water bulbs until foliage dries; then pull off dead leaves. ● Dig and divide narcissus bulb clumps on which blooms have started to diminish; store for replanting in fall.
● Mail order hard-to-find varieties for fall planting.
● In August, set out winter aconite, colchicum, erythronium, glory-of-the-snow. ● Sow seeds of cyclamen in flats.
● Dig and divide crowded bearded iris rhizomes; replant in full sun in fast draining soil. ● Lift, dry, store anemone and ranunculus.
● (Also see Bulbs, pages 75–77, *Sunset New Western Garden Book*.)

Container plants

● Water daily or as needed, and feed every two weeks during summer. ● Flush containers with water once during the summer to leach out salt deposits that cause foliage burn.
● (Also see Container gardening, pages 79–81, *Sunset New Western Garden Book*.)

Fruit trees

● Prop fruit-heavy limbs to prevent breaking. Pick up fallen fruit.

Fuchsias

● During summer months, fuchsias may need daily watering (especially those in containers) and weekly feeding with half-strength complete fertilizer (liquid or soluble). ● Pick faded flowers (and the attached fruits) to force more bloom.
● Control aphids by washing them off with hose water; or spray (see page 34).

Hedges

● Shear hedges; new shoots will branch before fall. ● Mulch to keep soil moist.
● (Also see the charts of recommended hedges, pages 103–107, *Sunset New Western Garden Book*.)

Herbs

● Before they bloom, usually by midsummer, harvest herbs after morning dew dries: basil, marjoram, mint, rosemary, sage, savory. ● Spread herbs in a cool place to dry or use leaves fresh.
● Prune (see General garden care, preceding).

● (Also see Herbs, pages 321–322, *Sunset New Western Garden Book*.)

House plants

● Keep plants well rotated, watered, fertilized. ● Watch carefully for mealybugs, scale, and other pests that attack plants from flowers or soil brought indoors from the garden.
● Cut back damaged or faded leaves.
● Water regularly and hose dust off leaves of house plants.
● (Also see pages 79–81, *Sunset New Western Garden Book*.)

Lawns

● Water lawns deeply. ● Mow higher to shade grass roots from heat. Use grass clippings as mulch or add to compost pile (except clippings treated with weed killer). ● Apply complete fertilizer after mowing.

Perennials

● Pick blooms for continued flower production. ● Pinch tip growth in June to force branching.
● Stake and tie tall, top-heavy perennials; water and fertilize regularly.
● After flowering, cut summer-blooming perennials almost to the ground; leave some foliage.
● Plant rooted chrysanthemums for bloom this fall.
● Dig up and divide overcrowded root clumps of irises after bloom.

Primroses

● Dig up and divide overcrowded clumps after bloom. Keep well-watered after replanting.
● Plant spring-blooming kinds in August (except *Primula alpicola, P. florindae, P. sikkimensis*) for good bloom next year.

Rhododendrons, azaleas

● Pick rhododendron trusses as they fade; don't break off tender new buds. Prune straggly growth now to avoid sacrificing next year's bloom. Mulch and keep well watered. Feed with acid-type fertilizer immediately before or after bloom.
● Prune to take cuttings of rhododendrons and azaleas until mid-July (later cutting will sacrifice next year's bloom). Root cuttings in peat moss and sand; keep moist until cuttings root in 6 weeks to 6 months, depending on variety. ● Keep ground around established plantings well mulched to protect shallow feeder roots.

Roses

● In June, feed roses with complete fertilizer (don't let it touch the plant base); water in well. ● Watch carefully for pests and diseases such as aphids, mildew, and black spot. Spray or dust as necessary. (See pages 34, 41, and 42.)
● Keep beds well weeded. Mulch, water, and remove faded blooms just above

5-leaflet leaves throughout the summer.
● After bloom, feed roses again with complete fertilizer.
● As summer begins to wane in August, water plants in early mornings to prevent mildew. ● Apply last feeding of complete fertilizer. ● Pick faded flowers to encourage a final bloom season.
● (Also see rose care, pages 450–453, *Sunset New Western Garden Book.*)

Shrubs

● Thoroughly water broad-leafed evergreen shrubs such as rhododendrons, azaleas, camellias that are setting flower buds now for next year's bloom. (Lack of water now can ruin next year's bloom.)

Strawberries

● As berries begin to ripen in June, protect them from birds; cover plants with bird netting. ● Watch for aphids, spider mites, slugs, snails, beetles *(do not control with chemicals if fruit is set).* ● Feed with complete fertilizer when growth starts late in spring and early summer; again after first crop.

Vegetables

● June is the last month to plant these warm-season vegetables and expect good results: (seed) beans, summer squash; (plants) cucumber, eggplant, melon, pepper, squash, tomato.
● Sow leaf lettuce in August for fall harvest.
● Slow down on watering cabbage to prevent heads splitting.
● Harvest corn when husk fits tightly around ear. To be sure corn is just right, you may want to pull back husk (just a little), and pop a kernel or two with your thumbnail; watery juice, too early; milky juice, just right; thick cream, over mature.

Fall is the season for harvesting and for some planting. It's also when you begin to put your garden to bed for the winter.

General garden care

Clean-up ● As you harvest fruit, flowers, vegetables, clean up the planting areas. After killing frost, pull up annuals; rake up leaves, blooms, fruit. Compost all disease-free organic refuse.

Fertilize ● Reduce feeding house plants as days get shorter and weather gets

cooler. ● Fertilize annuals lightly to keep blooming until frosty weather arrives.
● Fertilize roses lightly in September to prolong bloom another month.
● Feed lawns for the final time this season in earliest fall.
● Add compost and fertilizer to beds for winter and spring planting.
● (Also see Fertilizing, pages 52–55, *Sunset New Western Garden Book.*)

Frost protection ● Put frost-tender container plants in a protected place for winter. Mulch heavily around tender plants that can't be moved.
● (Also see Frost protection, pages 94–96, *Sunset New Western Garden Book.*)

Pests and diseases ● Spray or dust rose foliage to discourage formation of mildew, rust.
● When leaves fall from fruit trees, apply a dormant spray to reduce overwintering pests and fungus diseases (see page 14).
● Spray for holly twig-blight if your evergreen hollies are starting to become defoliated; use a solution of maneb and zinc.
● Spray for peach leaf curl if your trees were victims this year; use fixed copper, Bordeaux solution, or lime sulfur spray immediately after leaf drop and again when buds swell in spring.

● Bait for slugs and snails (see page 34).

Prune ● Thin dense trees and shrubs in fall so that wind can flow through later in winter. ● Prune vines, summer-blooming heather; remove lilac and quince suckers.
● (Also see Pruning, pages 68–71, *Sunset New Western Garden Book.*)

Water ● Continue watering lawns, trees, shrubs, vines and all new plantings until rains take over.
● Don't forget to water plants under eaves and in other sheltered areas. ● Soak conifers and broad-leafed evergreens if soil is dry.
● Well-watered plants survive freezing temperatures better than dry ones.

Annuals

● Keep marigolds, petunias, snapdragons blooming until frosty weather—feed, water, pick faded blooms.
● Sow annuals so they'll bloom earlier next spring—baby blue eyes, bachelor's button, calendula, candytuft, clarkia, forget-me-not, larkspur, snapdragon, stock, sweet alyssum.

Azaleas, rhododendrons, camellias

● To force camellias to branch, pinch out slender center leaf buds in September.

● October, November, and March are best months to plant azaleas, rhododendrons, camellias and other hardy broadleafed evergreens.

● Water plants well; they are setting buds for bloom next spring.

Berries

● Plant bare-root caneberries, currants, and gooseberries as soon as they show up in nurseries (as early as late November). To multiply your caneberries, divide kinds that sucker freely and ground layer those that don't. You *must* tip layer thornless berries to preserve their thornless character.

● After harvest, cut (to the ground) canes of blackberries and once bearing raspberries that bore fruit. On everbearing raspberries, cut back only the part of each cane that produced berries.

Bulbs

● Be ready when the shipments of crocuses, daffodils, irises, freesias, hyacinths, and tulips arrive at nurseries in September. Early shopping guarantees best selections. Plant immediately.

● In early October, lift and store begonias, dahlias, gladiolus. Mark dormant bulbs so they won't be destroyed when ground is prepared for spring planting (see page 60).

● (Also see Bulbs, pages 60–67 and 75–77, *Sunset New Western Garden Book.*)

Chrysanthemums

● Stake heavy-flowering plants to prevent breakage from wind, rain, water. ● Pick faded flowers. After bloom, trim plants back to 5 or 6 inches.

● (Also see chrysanthemum care, page 241, *Sunset New Western Garden Book.*)

Greenhouse activity

● Prepare greenhouse for winter gardening: clean glass, disinfect flats and pots. Strip moss off wood; organize tools. Make sure vents, heaters, irrigation systems work satisfactorily. ● Replace planting soil if your plants had diseases last season.

Ground covers

● Plant flat and slightly sloped areas with ground cover in September so roots will get a head start before winter. Do not plant *steep slopes;* rains will wash plants away.

● In October, cut back ground covers that spread out of bounds. Start from cuttings: heather, heaths, Japanese spurge, kinnikinnick, vinca.

House plants

● Before bringing indoors, examine all plants that have been summering outside. Hose off leaves, wash off outside of containers. As days grow shorter, reduce feeding and watering. Plants may be left out until first frost threatens, usually late in October.

● As winter approaches, house plants get less light; move plants closer to a window. Cluster sun-sensitive plants around north- or east-facing windows.

Iris

● Plant or transplant Dutch, English, Spanish irises. They'll establish before winter and produce more flowers in summer.

Lawns

● Inland, lawns will slow down in September, but may continue to need mowing. Feed lightly for the last time late in September. ● Sow seeds for new lawns in early fall. September is a good month for dethatching.

Perennials

● In late September, lift and divide plants that have bloomed. ● Enrich beds with organic soil amendment. ● Sow seeds of alyssum, arabis, armeria, aster, coreopsis, dianthus, English daisy, helianthemum, hollyhock, leopard's bane, Oriental poppy, rudbeckia, Shasta daisy, snow-in-summer, viola.

● October is the best month to transplant most perennials. ● Divide, replant daisies, callas, daylilies, marguerites every few years for best bloom. ● Shelter frost-tender plants or overwinter cuttings.

● (Also see Perennials, pages 74–75, *Sunset New Western Garden Book.*)

Permanent planting

● Plant or transplant broad-leafed evergreens, conifers, ground covers, vines, trees. *Do not* plant or transplant frost-tender plantings such as tropicals, subtropicals.

Strawberries

● Set out during fall rains for fruit next June. If planted in spring, plants won't bear well until the following year.

Vegetables

● In early September, plant asparagus and rhubarb from root divisions. ● Sow seeds for winter harvest—Chinese cabbage, lettuce, mustard, roquette, spinach. ● Harvest kale and parsnips after frost for sweeter flavor. ● Store carrots in ground only in well-drained soil.

● By mid-October, or if frost is predicted, pick all tomatoes, ripe or not. Refrigerate ripe ones, wrap the greens ones, or hang entire plants (with unpicked fruit) upside down from garage rafters.

● In November, cut asparagus stalks to the ground, mark the location, mulch 3 to 4 inches.

● Prepare vegetable beds in October for next season; remove all debris.

WINTER

In this section you'll find the things you can do when it's dry enough to work in the garden—and a number of ways to get ready for next year's garden on days when the rains keep you indoors.

General garden care

Fertilize ● Scatter fertilizer under rhododendrons in early winter. It will be washed in deep by winter rains. ● Also spread it around other spring-blooming broad-leafed evergreens such as azaleas and camellias.

● Apply aged manure or a commercial acid-type fertilizer to Japanese iris.
● On lilacs, scratch a complete fertilizer into the soil around the base of the plants in late February. ● Also feed primroses that are in the ground now with complete fertilizer. Give strawberries a complete fertilizer.

Frost and snow damage ● Renew mulches to keep soil from heaving and tearing roots during cycles of freezing and thawing. ● Heavy snow can bend or break branches; sweep it off with a broom before it builds up.

● Look over plants that have been damaged by the cold, but wait until well into spring, when buds and leaves have popped out, before you cut off damaged wood. What looked quite dead may be alive after all.

Order seeds ● Have fun poring over the seed catalogs. Then order vegetable, annual, and perennial seeds in time for spring planting.

Pests and diseases ● Spray peach trees for peach-leaf curl. Between mid-January and the end of the month, apply a dormant spray such as lime sulfur, fixed copper, or Bordeaux mixture to other fruit trees. Spray on a dry, windless day when the temperature is above freezing.

Prune ● Any fruit tree can be pruned in January if temperatures are above freezing. ● Summer and fall-flowering shrubs, such as hydrangea and abelia, can also be pruned now. ● Don't prune spring-flowering shrubs though, or you'll lose this year's bloom.

● After a wind or snow storm, inspect trees and shrubs for broken branches. Cut off cleanly as close to trunk or main branch as possible.

Stored produce ● Get rid of any stored bulbs, fruits, or vegetables that are starting to rot. If dahlia tubers or gladiolus corms look withered, sprinkle them with a little water to plump them up.

Weeds ● Start hoeing or pulling weeds in February, and avoid the rush later. Most will come out of soggy ground with no more than a gentle tug.

● (Also see the special section on weeding tools, page 92, *Sunset New Western Garden Book.*)

Annuals

● Where ground is workable in February, sow seeds of sweet peas (run rows north-south to give vines maximum sun later).

● For spring color, frame sweet peas in snapdragons.

● Check seed catalogs and nursery racks for new garden additions. Indoors, start seeds of ageratum, asters, candy-tufts. Outdoors you can sow some seeds now in sunny, open ground: sweet alyssum, bachelor's button, calendula, clarkia, godetia.

● (Also see Annuals, pages 76–79, *Sunset New Western Garden Book.*)

Asparagus and rhubarb

● Give asparagus beds a light covering of well-rotted manure, rich compost, or commercial high-nitrogen fertilizer in January. Also use a small amount of fertilizer around the base of rhubarb plants.

Bare-root plants

● When soil is diggable, plant bare-root cane fruits, grapes, currants, fruit trees, deciduous ornamentals, and strawberries.

● If you wait until March or April, when nurseries must put all unsold bare-root trees into cans, you'll pay a lot more.

● (Also see Bare-root planting, pages 44–45, *Sunset New Western Garden Book.*)

Berries

● In February, apply a complete fertilizer between rows of strawberries and raspberries.

● Plant bare-root bush and cane berries. Be sure supports will be able to bear the weight of new growth that is coming.

Fuchsias and geraniums

● Plants being overwintered indoors should be kept dry but not bone dry—they need an occasional sprinkling of water.

● Fertilize geraniums starting in February. Give overwintered plants a feeding with half-strength fertilizer. Then put them in a sunny, protected place such as a porch or sunroom.

Greenhouse activity

● Plants in bloom or about to bloom (gardenias, orchids, African violets, citrus) should be fed at 2-week intervals with half-strength liquid fertilizer. ● If leaves on gardenias and citrus look pale, add some iron to soil.

House plants

● Tender indoor plants near windows can be nipped by cold night air. Pull shades or curtains to protect them; don't let leaves touch the window pane. ● Don't feed nonblooming plants during the dead of winter; water sparingly.

Hydrangeas

● Prune hydrangeas at the same time you do roses.

● If your big-leaf hydrangea blooms red or pink, you can turn the flowers blue by supplementing fertilizer with 1 tablespoon of aluminum sulfate per gallon of water. Feed hydrangeas when you prune.

Lawns

● Keep lawns raked—many broad-leafed evergreens drop more leaves in January and February than at any other time. ● If the grass gets too long, mow it.

● Lawns that appear yellow may need nitrogen. Apply ammonium nitrate (it works even in cold weather) at about 1½ pounds per 1,000 square feet of grass.

Primroses

● If January produces enough balmy days to cause primroses to send up buds and leaves, mulch with straw to keep later freezes from cutting them down.

● Also bait for slugs after March 1; they love to hide in mulches.

Roses

● In February, gardeners should remove woody old canes that didn't produce well last year. Cut healthy, vigorous canes back by about a third.

● You can also set out plants in February. Bare-root bushes will be on sale, as well as roses in cans.

Shrubs

● Even during the wet winter, shrubs protected from rain by overhangs may need soaking once a month. Water their roots on days when the temperature is well above freezing.

Vegetables

● You can start seed for broccoli, Brussels sprouts, cabbage, cauliflower, tomatoes in February. When they are seedling size, transfer to flats or individual pots.

"Gardener's notepad"

NORTHERN CALIFORNIA

The low elevations of northern California and southwest Oregon include seven *Sunset* climates: Zone 7 is southern Oregon valleys plus California's Digger pine belt; Zones 8 and 9 are the Central Valley; Zone 14 has the valleys that get some ocean influence; 15, 16 and 17 are coastal climates.

SPRING

In most years spring offers many chances (i.e., dry weekends) to plant flowers and vegetables for spring, summer, and fall. But in some years the rains force you to wait for weeks and then do it all in a short space of time.

General garden care

Compost ● Save lawn clippings, leaves, and other garden refuse for compost. With warmer weather, these materials will break down faster. Turn pile with a spading fork, and water if it begins to dry. ● (Also see Compost, page 35, *Sunset New Western Garden Book*.)

Fertilize ● Fertilize lawns, ground covers, trees, vines, and shrubs as well as citrus, roses, and other plants in spring to support vigorous new growth. ● Feed tender subtropicals such as hibiscus and bougainvillea once warm weather arrives.
● Generally, lawns and citrus need high-nitrogen fertilizer. ● Azaleas, rhododendrons, and camellias prefer an acid fertilizer. ● Most permanent landscape plants take an all-purpose, complete fertilizer. ● Feed fuchsias and annuals with a low-nitrogen complete fertilizer at 3–4 week intervals. ● Feed container plants once a month (or half-strength feeding every 2 weeks).
● Plants with leaves that turn yellow while veins remain green may not need fertilizer, but iron chelate or iron sulfate to correct chlorosis (caused by lack of iron). ● (Also see page 34, *Sunset New Western Garden Book*.)

Mulch ● A 2- to 3-inch layer of mulch (such as compost, ground bark, or leaf mold) around shrubs, trees, and annuals will discourage weeds, conserve moisture, and help keep roots cool. Renew mulches around roses, keeping mulch away from base stems to reduce chances of crown rot.

Pests and diseases ● Watch for aphids on new growth (see page 34).
● Keep boards, pots, and other garden debris off the ground to eliminate hiding places for slugs and snails. Bait or handpick regularly around favorite feeding places such as near tender new plants and leafy ground covers. (Also see the special section on snails and slugs, page 34.)
● Protect seed beds and seedlings from hungry birds by covering area with netting draped over short stakes.

Propagate ● Spring is an excellent time to start new plants from softwood cuttings. Some easy-to-propagate choices are carnations, chrysanthemums, dianthus, fuchsias, geraniums, ivy, lavender, pelargoniums, marguerites, and roses. Take tip cuttings 2 to 6 inches long and root them in a damp medium such as sand or potting soil. Dip cut ends in rooting hormone to speed root development. ● (Also see Cuttings, page 38, *Sunset New Western Garden Book*.)

Prune and groom ● Wait until new growth starts as weather warms to prune frost-damaged branches on trees and shrubs.
● Tip-pinch fuchsias, geraniums, marguerites to encourage new side shoots ● Cut off old rhododendron and iris blooms; prune lanky camellias to promote denser growth. ● Remove withered fern fronds. ● Tie up vines and stake tall-growing flowers such as delphiniums, lilies, and stocks.

● (Also see Pruning, pages 68–71, *Sunset New Western Garden Book*.)

Water ● Build up watering basins.
● Mulch and water deeply all shrubs, trees, fast-growing flowers, vegetables.
● (Also see Watering, pages 48–52, *Sunset New Western Garden Book*.)
● Water container plants attentively.
● Set up drip irrigation to ease watering chores and conserve water. ● (Also see Drip irrigation, page 52, *Sunset New Western Garden Book*.)

Weeds ● Hoe, or pull out weeds in spring before they go to seed. Moistening soil slightly before removing weeds will help get roots, too.

Annuals

● Prepare beds for summer annuals as soon as soil can be spaded. Work organic amendments and fertilizer into top 6 inches of soil; rake smooth, water thoroughly.
● In *mild coastal areas*, you can plant both spring- and summer-flowering annuals in early spring: ageratum, cinerarias, lobelia, marigold, nemesia, pansy, petunia, schizanthus, snapdragon, stock, and viola. Wait until the weather warms up to plant the real heat lovers such as portulaca and zinnias.
● *Inland*, cool-season spring flowers put out in March will give you instant color until hot weather arrives. Start seeds of marigolds and other summer-blooming annuals indoors in March to set outdoors in a month or two.
● When transplanting bedding plants, pinch off tips and flower buds to encourage compact, bushy growth. Protect from intense sun for 2 weeks; feed with complete fertilizer low in nitrogen once plants are established and growing. ● (Also see lists of annuals, page 79, *Sunset New Western Garden Book*.)

Bulbs

- In early spring, plant these for summer and fall blooms: calla, canna, dahlia, gladiolus, tuberose, tuberous begonia.
- Save some bulbs to plant 3 or 4 weeks later for longer bloom display. • Established bulbs demand regular watering.
  - If you didn't plant ranunculus and anemones last fall, you can get seedlings at some nurseries for planting in March. They'll bloom in April or early May.
  - Spring-flowering bulbs you want to save for bloom again next year: remove faded flowers, fertilize, and water until foliage withers; then cut foliage to the ground.
  - (Also see Bulbs, pages 75–77, Sunset New Western Garden Book.)

Camellias

- After bloom, prune leggy camellias back to branch swellings that mark the end of last year's summer growth; this forces dense new growth.

Fruit trees

- Check fruit size at end of April. Thin fruit when it is marble size or smaller.
  - Thin apricots 3 to 6 inches apart; thin apples, peaches, Japanese plums, and nectarines 6 to 8 inches apart.

Fuchsias

- Feed fuchsias with complete fertilizer (liquid or soluble) when leaves begin to appear. Give light dosages every 10 to 14 days or label-recommended feedings monthly to keep plants growing and to bring on maximum bloom.
  - After chance of frost is past, carefully pinch and train to desired shape.
- Locate plants under overhanging eaves or under lath structures to protect from an unexpected late frost, and provide shade from summer heat. • (Also see Fuchsias, pages 304–305, Sunset New Western Garden Book.)

Lawns

- Cool-season grasses (bent, bluegrass, rye, and fescue) grow rapidly from March until May. Mow, weed, fertilize, and water regularly. Reseed bare spots. • Spring, when chance of last frost is past, is good time to start new lawn. Lay sod, or start from seed when soil is dry enough to work.
  - May is a good time to start new dichondra lawns. Sow seeds, or set out dichondra from flats.
  - Feed established lawns with high-nitrogen fertilizer; begin regular mowing. • Reseed bare spots in established lawns. Clear off thatch, dead grass, roots in area to be replanted.
  - Aerate and dethatch lawns to help air and water to penetrate and encourage deep roots.
  - (Also see Lawns, pages 85–88, Sunset New Western Garden Book.)

Perennials

- In cool-summer areas, early spring is a good time to plant summer-flowering perennials: coreopsis, pansy, penstemon, poppy, primrose, Shasta daisy, stock, viola. • Where summers are hot, plant petunias; in mild coastal areas, you can also plant cineraria.
  - To keep them flowering abundantly, divide summer- and fall-flowering perennials in early spring when they are still semidormant: campanula, daylily, dianthus, garden phlox, yarrow, Shasta daisy, and aster.
  - Propagate chrysanthemums by stem cuttings or by pulling rooted new shoots from outside edges of old clumps. • (Also see Propagation, pages 35–44, Sunset New Western Garden Book.)
  - Perennials are available in March at nurseries in six-packs; they'll be more expensive later.

Permanent planting

- March and April are second only to October for landscape planting—ground covers, trees, shrubs. • Wait until danger of frost is over to put out tender plants such as avocado, bougainvillea, and citrus.

Roses

- Rebuild watering basins around established rose bushes; renew mulches 2 to 3 inches deep. To prevent crown rot don't pile mulch around main stem of bush.
  - Fertilize established roses monthly; water deeply. If you water overhead, do it before noon to give foliage a chance to dry off before evening.
  - May is peak blooming month in most areas. To keep flowers coming, cut plenty of long-stemmed blossoms, and remove dead blooms. • (Also see Rosa, pages 450–455, Sunset New Western Garden Book.)

Vegetables

- In early spring, you can sow seeds for cool-season vegetables: beets, carrots, lettuce, onions, peas, radishes, spinach, Swiss chard. Set out broccoli, cabbage, celery, cauliflower seedlings, and potato and Jerusalem artichoke tubers. • Use mesh or temporary collars to protect seedlings from birds.
  - Indoors or in a greenhouse, sow seeds in early spring for hot-weather vegetables such as eggplants, peppers, tomatoes, and summer herbs (basil, dill, marjoram, oregano, parsley).
  - By April, you can sow seeds of summer crops in the ground. Sow seeds of beans, beets, carrots, corn, cucumbers, melons, squash, Swiss chard, and herbs. Set out seedlings of eggplant, peppers, tomatoes, herbs.
  - Stagger planting of crops that have a short producing period: beets, beans, carrots, and corn (2- to 6-week intervals). For corn, you can plant early, midseason,

and late varieties to mature at different times during summer. • (Also see Vegetables, pages 81–84, Sunset New Western Garden Book.)

SUMMER

> The farther your garden is from the summer fog banks, the more you must water. If you live in or near the foggy areas, watering is not such a chore and you can do a lot more puttering than your friends in the interior valleys.

General garden care

Clean-up • Pick up and destroy dry or rotting vegetables and fruit on the ground and in trees; they draw flies, yellow jackets, and cause diseases.
  - (Also see Garden maintenance, pages 89–96, Sunset New Western Garden Book.)

"Gardener's notepad"

_____
_____
_____
_____
_____
_____
_____
_____
_____
_____
_____
_____
_____
_____
_____
_____
_____

Fertilize ● During summer, feed fast-growing vegetables, begonias, fuchsias, annuals, perennials, container plants, and other top summer performers with diluted dosages of complete liquid fertilizer.

● For best flower production, alternate feedings of fish emulsion or other complete fertilizer with 0-10-10 formula. ● Feed citrus, roses, warm-season grasses with high-nitrogen fertilizer.

● In August, give azaleas, camellias, rhododendrons a last dose of acid plant food. ● (Also see Fertilizing, pages 52–55, *Sunset New Western Garden Book*.)

Mulch ● Mulch to 3 inches, especially around shrubs, young vegetables, bedding plants, azaleas, camellias, rhododendrons, roses. If you use grass clippings as mulch, spread thinly (less than 1 inch deep) so clippings dry like straw and don't breed flies. ● Don't pile mulch around main stalk of plants; it will cause crown rot.

● (Also see Mulches, pages 51–52, *Sunset New Western Garden Book*.)

Pests and diseases ● High humidity, crowding, poor air circulation, and too much shade can cause powdery mildew on foliage of apple, begonia, crape myrtle, dahlia, rose and zinnia. ● You can achieve some measure of control by doing any overhead watering before mid-day. For chemical control advice, see page 41.

● Bait for slugs, snails or handpick in the evening when they are most active. ● Trap or bait for earwigs. ● Control aphids with effective insecticides, hose water, soapy water. ● Spray or dust if diabrotica, red spider, or thrips are a problem on roses, citrus, other ornamentals.

● Watch for gophers that can destroy garden crops and lawns; trap or bait with poison.

● Water lawns early in the morning to discourage fungus diseases.

● (See pests section on pages 32–48.)

Propagate ● In June, take tip cuttings of azaleas, chrysanthemums, camellias, carnations, ericas, evergreen candytuft, fuchsias, geraniums, hydrangeas, marguerites. Lift and divide crowded root clumps of bearded iris in July or August. In hottest areas, wait until September.

● (Also see Cuttings, page 38, *Sunset New Western Garden Book*.)

Prune ● Tie runners of vines and remove surplus new growth. ● Tip-pinch annuals to force bushier growth.

● Cut back spring-flowering perennials such as basket-of-gold, alyssum, dianthus, foxglove, penstemon; they'll flower again in August or September. ● Lightly prune rose bushes as you remove flowers.

Stake ● Stake and tie tall dahlias, delphinium, gladiolus, tomatoes, vines.

Sun protection ● Plant in late afternoons or evenings to avoid hot mid-day sun that can wilt new plantings. ● In hot weather, shade new plants with shade cloth, shingles, cardboard, or lath for about 10 days after planting; mulch and keep soil moist.

● Cover exposed trunks and branches of citrus trees to prevent damage from sunburn.

● (Also see Heat, shade, and humidity, page 96, *Sunset New Western Garden Book*.)

Water ● Keep roots of surface feeders—azaleas, camellias, rhododendrons—moist; mulch, water often. They're forming next year's flower buds. ● Water lawns, shrubs, trees, other plantings deeply to encourage deep rooting. ● Construct soil basins to hold water around the base of plants.

Weed ● Hoe or hand pull weeds before they go to seed. If you use chemical weed killers on lawn, apply according to manufacturer's directions; water in thoroughly. (*Do not* compost these clippings.) ● Mulch thickly to retard weed growth around plantings. ● Ground covers, annuals, perennials, vegetables planted closely together help to shade out weeds.

● (Also see weeding tools, page 92, *Sunset New Western Garden Book*.)

Annuals

● In June, you can still plant these and other annuals: Full sun—cosmos, dwarf dahlia, marigold, petunia, portulaca, scarlet sage, sweet alyssum, verbena, *Vinca rosea*, zinnia. Shade—coleus, begonia, impatiens, lobelia. Grow quickly from seed—cosmos, marigold, portulaca, sweet alyssum, zinnia. Require little water—celosia, Gloriosa daisy, Madagascar periwinkle, petunia, sweet alyssum, verbena. ● In mild coastal areas, many annuals will keep blooming through October.

● In August, sow seeds of winter-bloomers to transplant in 4 to 8 weeks: calendula, candytuft, fairy primrose, forget-me-not, nemesia, pansy, snapdragon, stock, viola. ● Feed with complete fertilizer.

● (Also see individual listings, pages 161–505, *Sunset New Western Garden Book*.)

Berries

● In July, tie this year's canes to a trellis or fence; next year's crop will be easy to reach. ● Cut 2-year canes to the ground; keep suckers pulled.

Bulbs

● In August, set out colchicum, autumn crocus, daylily, iris. Plant cyclamen varieties while tubers are still dormant. ● In *coastal areas*, set out rhizomes of bearded iris; in *hotter areas*, wait until fall. ● Divide crowded iris rhizomes. ● (Also see Bulbs, pages 75–77, *Sunset New Western Garden Book*.)

Citrus

● In June, prune floppy citrus trees. Don't remove much lower growth; most fruit develops there. ● Provide sun protection, especially for new trees; cover exposed trunks and limbs with white latex paint, whitewash, burlap, commercial tree wrap. ● Water established trees every 15 to 20 days in clay soil; 7 to 10 days in sandy soil. Water new trees once or twice weekly.

● Feed established citrus with high-nitrogen fertilizer or citrus food monthly, through summer. ● If leaves are yellowing and dropping, supply in-ground citrus with fertilizer containing iron sulfate or iron chelate.

● (Also see Citrus, pages 243–245, *Sunset New Western Garden Book*.)

Fruit trees

● To protect fruit from birds, use plastic netting especially made for fruit trees. ● Throughout summer, regularly collect fallen stone fruit (apricots, peaches, plums) and brown or rotted fruit still hanging in trees to help prevent spread of brown rot. Dispose of fruit in plastic bags; *don't* compost.

● Thin developing apples, peaches, pears if trees seem overloaded; prop up sagging branches with sturdy posts 2 inches wide or wider.

Fuchsias

● Shelter both container plants and plants in ground from direct midday sun and wind. ● Keep well watered and fertilized. ● Watch for pests. Control aphids, whiteflies, spider mites (see pages 34 and 35). To prolong bloom, remove spent flowers and yellow leaves; pinch tips of branches to force side branching.

● (Also see Fuchsia, pages 304–305, *Sunset New Western Garden Book*.)

Herbs

● You can still plant herbs from seed or transplants in June. Marjoram, rosemary, sage, savory, thyme thrive in relatively poor, well-drained soil. Basil, chive, coriander, parsley prefer richer soil. Plant in full sun and hold off on fertilizing.

House plants

● In June, house plants may be moved to a patio or protected area outdoors for the summer. ● Wash dusty foliage, scrub crusty pots, flush the soil to remove harmful salt deposits, remove yellowing leaves.

Lawns

● In June, plant dichondra from seed or sod; hybrid Bermuda and other subtropical grasses from stolons or sod. ● Mow other warm-season subtropical grasses (Bermuda, St. Augustine, zoysia) to at least 1 inch; feed with high-nitrogen fertilizer.

• Water established lawns deeply early in the morning so grass dries by evening; this reduces chances of fungus infection. • (Also see Lawns, pages 85–88, *Sunset New Western Garden Book*.)

Perennials

• From June to August, as they finish flowering, cut back flower stems on the following perennials to 6 inches to encourage repeat blooming in the fall: coreopsis, delphinium, penstemon, Shasta daisies, yarrow. • Sow seeds in August for transplanting later: basket-of-gold *(Aurinia saxatilis)*, columbine, coreopsis, dianthus, gaillardia, geum, heuchera, Iceland and Oriental poppies, polyanthus primrose, Shasta daisy, wallflower.
• (Also see individual plant listings, pages 161–505, *Sunset New Western Garden Book*.)

Roses

• In early summer, lightly prune and shape bushes as blooms are picked. Pruning out crossing branches in the center of the bush increases air circulation and discourages mildew. Save major pruning until dormant period in January. • Remove faded flowers, dead wood, unwanted suckers. Water, feed with rose food or other complete fertilizer, mulch.
• (Also see *Rosa*, pages 450–455, *Sunset New Western Garden Book*.)

Vegetables

• In most areas, fall planting begins in July. Start seeds of broccoli, cabbage, leeks, lettuce in flats to set out later.
• In *mild coastal areas* of northern California, wait until August to start fall crops. • Plant a late crop of cucumbers, summer squash from seed, or tomatoes from transplants.

• In the *interior valleys*, plant in August for early winter harvest: beets, carrots, cauliflower, Chinese cabbage, kale, lettuce, radishes, spinach.
• Tie heavy tomato clusters, trellis-train cucumbers and melons. • Pick fruit as soon as it ripens to encourage more fruiting.

FALL

For gardeners, fall comes almost exactly on September 15. That's when longer nights begin to give heat-worn gardens a break—and when you can go into action with fall planting; lawns, flowers, vegetables, shrubs and trees.

General garden care

Clean-up • Remove and destroy dried or rotted stone fruit in trees or on ground to prevent brown rot. • Rake and destroy camellia blooms regularly to discourage petal blight. • Clean up grass clippings, leaves, spent blooms, vegetables, weeds.
• Stake up chrysanthemums and other tall, top-heavy plants.

Compost • Add garden debris to compost pile for spring. Chop up bulky debris —woody sticks and slow-to-decompose material—and cover chopped matter with a thin layer of soil. Keep it moist; turn often.
• (Also see Compost, page 35, *Sunset New Western Garden Book*.)

Fertilize • Feed late summer-blooming begonias, fuchsias, annuals, perennials every 2 weeks with complete fertilizer.

• Stop feeding chrysanthemums when buds show color. • Feed flowers and vegetables with a complete fertilizer a week or two after planting, then once or twice a month. • Feed citrus for the last time this season in mild-winter areas only (do not feed if frost is expected). • Fertilize fall-planted trees, shrubs, ground covers one month after planting; do not repeat until spring. • Mid-September to early October, feed cool-season lawns (bent, bluegrass, fescue, rye), now beginning their full growth cycle.
• Apply a complete fertilizer to winter annuals, perennials, vegetables after planting and then again once a month. • Feed roses in mid-October then wait until March to feed again.
• (Also see Fertilizing, pages 52–55, *Sunset New Western Garden Book*.)

Frost protection • Lift and store bulbs in late fall. • Do not fertilize tropicals, subtropicals and other frost-tender plants.
• (Also see Frost protection, page 94, *Sunset New Western Garden Book*.)

Pests and diseases • Mites, mildew are problems in autumn months. For control, see pages 35 (mites) and 41 (mildew).
• Clear out garden debris to eliminate nesting places for snails, slugs, earwigs, millipedes, cutworms, and other pests; bait or spray.
• Apply dormant spray to leafless peach, ornamental peach and nectarine trees between mid-November and mid-December to prevent fungus infection and overwintering insects; drench branches thoroughly with lime sulfur, zineb, ziram, or Bordeaux solution. Repeat spraying late December or January before trees flower.

Propagate • Take tip cuttings of fuchsias, geraniums, hydrangeas, ivy, mar-

---

"Gardener's notepad"

---

guerites, pelargoniums; root in mixture of peat moss and perlite. Late October, transplant to containers. • Divide and replant perennials—agapanthus, basket-of-gold, alyssum, bearded iris, bergenia, coral bells, daylily, rudbeckia, Shasta daisy, yarrow. • (Also see Propagating, pages 35–44, *Sunset New Western Garden Book*.)

Prune • Remove dead or diseased wood on roses, in trees. • Cut back and shape up leggy geraniums, pelargoniums, marguerites, ground covers, ivy, baccharis, lantana, santolina. Prune oleander after bloom. • Thin crowded buds on camellias to encourage larger bloom.

Soil preparation • After mid-September, plant landscape plants; prepare soil in planting beds, improve drainage. • Install or repair sprinkler or drip irrigation systems.

Water • Azaleas, fuchsias, hydrangeas, rhododendrons show stress from lack of water; mulch thickly and water frequently as needed. • In *mild-weather areas*, summer flowers will produce into October with deep watering. Daily water seedlings and container plants. • Hold off watering dahlias, gladiolus, tuberous begonias when leaves yellow.
• (Also see Watering, pages 48–52, *Sunset New Western Garden Book*.)

Weed • Remove weeds going to seed immediately; *do not compost*. • Weeds and invasive grass flourish in late fall; remove early when roots are shallow, young and tender.

Wind protection • Thin wind-exposed evergreens and large shrubs to allow air to flow through. • Stake and tie young trees, shrubs, vines, and tall plants.

Annuals

• Sow seed in October, for winter-spring color: bachelor's button, calendula, California poppy, annual candytuft, clarkia, dimorphotheca, forget-me-not, linaria, lobelia, sweet alyssum, sweet pea. • Or, set out young transplants: calendula, dianthus, Iceland poppy, pansy, snapdragon, stock, viola. • Provide sun protection, water plantings often.
• (Also see lists of Annuals, page 79, *Sunset New Western Garden Book*.)

Bulbs

• Buy spring bulbs as soon as they are available. Major planting should be in October and November, but in late September plant Dutch and autumn crocus, daffodils, Dutch iris, freesia, grape hyacinth, leucojum, scilla, sparaxis, tritonia, watsonia.
• Keep bulbs you don't plant right away in a cool, dry place. Refrigerate tulips, hyacinths for 6 weeks before planting to assure strong stems and blooms (see page 65).
• Dig, dry and store cannas, dahlias,

begonias, gladiolus in November. Cut cannas and dwarf dahlia stalks to the ground; they'll survive winter in the ground in mild areas.
• (Also see Bulbs, pages 75–77, *Sunset New Western Garden Book*.)

Cane berries

• In October, cut off old canes that bore berries last summer; also weak canes and suckers.

Chrysanthemums

• For large blooms, remove all but one bud per stem; stop feeding when buds show color. • Stake tall stems to keep from toppling; avoid overhead watering. • Remove spent blooms to force more flower production.
• Keep plants moist until they finish blooming, then cut stems 3 inches from ground.
• (Also see pages 239–241, *Sunset New Western Garden Book*.)

Lawns

• Plant cool-season lawns—bent, bluegrass, fescue, rye—from mid-September through October. • Late September and early October, reseed bare spots, aerate, feed with complete fertilizer, water deeply.
• (Also see Lawns, pages 85–88, *Sunset New Western Garden Book*.)

Perennials

• Plant from nursery selection available in six-packs: campanula, candytuft, carnation, columbine, coral bells, daylily, delphinium, dianthus, English daisy, nierembergia, penstemon, primrose, Shasta daisy, yarrow. • Lift and divide early-blooming perennials in October (late-summer and fall-blooming kinds in spring).
• (Also see Perennials, pages 74–75, *Sunset New Western Garden Book*.)

Permanent planting

• Late September through November, put in landscape plants: trees, shrubs, herbaceous plants, vines, ground covers.
• Wait until spring to put in frost-tender plants. • Wait until winter for bare-root planting.

Pumpkins

• To prevent rot, stop watering when pumpkin leaves first begin to yellow.
• Harvest when vines are withered, leaving 3-inch stem when you cut. • (Also see Pumpkin, page 435, *Sunset New Western Garden Book*.)

Roses

• Prune plants lightly in September to reduce mildew and encourage October bloom. (Also see advice for controlling mildew, page 41.) • Remove spent flowers, feed with rose food or complete fertilizer every 2 weeks.

• Feed roses for the last time by mid-October for bloom by Thanksgiving. Don't feed again until February. • Continue deep watering.
• (Also see *Rosa*, pages 450–455, *Sunset New Western Garden Book*.)

Strawberries

• Plant bare-root strawberries up to mid-October for early spring harvest. • (Also see Strawberry, pages 475–476, *Sunset New Western Garden Book*.)

Vegetables

• From coast to Central Valley, plant cool-season crops in September: beets, broccoli, Brussels sprouts (coast only), carrots, celery, chard, chives, garlic, leeks, lettuce (head or loose-leaf), onions, parsley, peas, radishes, spinach, turnips.
• Stagger sowing of lettuce and radishes every 2 weeks from September to December.
• (Also see Vegetables, pages 81–84, *Sunset New Western Garden Book*.)

Wildflowers

• Sow seeds in November for bloom next spring or summer: baby blue eyes, forget-me-nots, California poppies, godetia, larkspur, linaria, lupine. Keep soil moist.

WINTER

The planting opportunities that come with fall continue into December and January—as long as the soil remains dry enough. Later on in the dead of winter, and into early spring, comes the time for planting roses and fruit trees.

General garden care

Clean-up • Rake up fallen leaves from the lawn so grass doesn't yellow beneath.

Fertilize • In February, feed lawns and spring-blooming annuals and perennials. • Give azaleas, camellias, and rhododendrons a complete acid-type fertilizer after they finish blooming (read label for full instructions). • Deciduous fruit trees should have a high-nitrogen feeding 2 to 3 weeks before blooming. • Fertilize other established trees and shrubs as new growth starts.
• (Also see Fertilizing, pages 52–55, *Sunset New Western Garden Book*.)

Frost protection • Move tender, container-grown plants to a protected spot.
• Cover plants in the open ground with burlap, plastic, or other material draped over a frame that prevents the covering from touching the plants. Cover smaller

plants with aluminum foil, cardboard, or several thicknesses of newspaper; remove coverings in the morning after the temperature rises above freezing.

Pests and diseases ● When temperatures rise above 40°, snails and slugs stir from hibernation. Hand-pick them in the evening when they come out of hiding, or bait.

● Apply dormant spray now to fruit trees, roses, and other deciduous trees and shrubs to control overwintering pests and disease organisms. Peaches and nectarines need early *and* late winter spraying for adequate protection from peach leaf curl. Apply lime sulfur, zineb, ziram, or a Bordeaux solution in December; repeat before buds open in February. Keep spray off neighboring evergreens.

Prune ● Deciduous fruit trees, cane berries, grapes, wisteria, and roses need to be pruned while they are still dormant. ● Hold off on pruning fuchsias until mid-February. ● Major pruning of deciduous ornamentals—such as crabapples, deutzia, forsythia, plums, quince, spiraea, and weigela—should be delayed until after bloom.

● (Also see Pruning, pages 68–71, *Sunset New Western Garden Book.*)

Soil preparation ● Apply organic material, such as compost or nitrogen-stabilized bark, to any beds where you intend to plant in the spring, as well as around established plantings. ● If soil is too wet to work, lay amendments 3 inches deep over the top. Dig into the top 9 inches of soil as soon as ground is workable. ● (Also see Soils, pages 33–35, *Sunset New Western Garden Book.*)

Water ● If winter rains are skimpy, water plants regularly. Don't forget container plants under eaves or overhangs—they may still be dry even after a rain.

Weed ● Hoe or pull out young weeds sprouting up in gravel paths, driveways, and in the open ground, as soon as you spot them.

● (Also see Controlling weeds, pages 66–67, *Sunset New Western Garden Book.*)

Annuals

● In winter, you can set out bedding plants, including Iceland poppy, nemesia, English and fairy primroses, pansies, schizanthus, sweet William, and viola.

● In January, sow seed of these annuals indoors or in a greenhouse for an early start: cineraria, dianthus, impatiens, lobelia, nemesia, petunia, and schizanthus.

● Seeds of any of the summer annuals can be sown indoors to set out in March. ● Feed spring-blooming annuals, since they'll start their main show in a few weeks. ● If you live near the coast, later in February you can set out cineraria, nemesia, and schizanthus. It's too

early to plant them inland, where you'll risk frost burn.

● (Also see Annuals, pages 76–79, *Sunset New Western Garden Book.*)

Azaleas and rhododendrons

● February is the best month to shop because nurseries should be well stocked. Azaleas have started blooming and rhododendrons should show fat, ready-to-open buds. Many come balled and burlapped and are available only at this time of year.

Bare-root planting

● Berries, grapes, roses, some shrubs, deciduous fruit and ornamental trees, and some vegetables are available bare root in January. Shop now to find the year's best selection and prices.

● (Also see Bare-root planting, pages 44–45, *Sunset New Western Garden Book.*)

Bulbs

● Plant spring and summer bulbs and bulblike plants in February: amaryllis, anemones, callas, cannas, gladiolus, lilies, ranunculus, and tuberous begonias. ● Plant at 2- to 3-week intervals for a succession of bloom. ● Prepare soil for dahlias to be planted after danger of frost is past.

● (Also see Bulbs, pages 75–77, *Sunset New Western Garden Book.*)

Camellias

● Shop for camellias in February—many of the japonicas are at the height of bloom, and you can see what you are buying.

Lawns

● Keep off lawns when they are wet or frosty; they'll damage easily then. ● Feed lawns in February to help them get a head start against weeds.

Roses

● Prune as buds begin to swell. Remove dead or damaged wood, and branches that cross or rub on other canes.

● All climbers should be left unpruned for the first 2 to 3 years after planting. Then, prune the repeat bloomers at the same time you prune shrub roses. Those climbers that bloom only once in the spring should be pruned soon after flowering.

Vegetables and berries

● In January, nurseries offer many bare-root vegetables—artichokes, asparagus, rhubarb—as well as cane berries and strawberries. ● Sow seeds of cool-season crops directly in the ground: beets, carrots, chard, lettuce, onions, peas, radishes, spinach, and turnips. ● Cover these with a glass or plastic cover for protection and a faster start. ● Indoors, you can start seeds to set out in early spring.

"Gardener's notepad"

DESERT

High deserts of New Mexico, Arizona, Utah, Nevada, and California are in Zones 10 and 11. Intermediate and low deserts of Arizona and California are Zones 12 and 13. Zone 10 has the coldest winters (up to 100 nights below freezing); Zone 13 is mildest (10 freezing nights).

SPRING

In the low and intermediate deserts, now is the time to maintain and enjoy what you planted in the fall, and —perhaps—to plant some more. In high deserts, early spring is a good time to plant so you can maintain and enjoy in later spring.

General garden care

Fertilize ● Stimulate spring growth of trees, shrubs, vines, vegetables, and flowering plants with complete fertilizer. ● Begin feeding established roses regularly with rose food. ● Feed citrus and flowering stone fruits when fruit is about marble-size.

● Try to keep spring annuals going as long as possible; feed them and vegetables at least once a month with complete fertilizer.

● Use iron chelate or iron sulfate to correct chlorosis—leaves yellowing between veins—on roses, pyracantha, bottlebrush, gardenias, geraniums, and citrus. ● (Also see Chlorosis, page 34, *Sunset New Western Garden Book*.)

● Apply high-nitrogen complete fertilizer to trees, shrubs, lawns, foundation plantings.

● When palms, hibiscus, Natal plum, bougainvillea, lantana, other subtropicals begin to put on new growth, feed with complete fertilizer.

Mulch ● Apply 2 to 3-inch layer of organic mulch (shredded bark, peat moss, wood shavings) around trees and shrubs to conserve moisture, prevent weed growth and keep soil cooler.

● For vegetables, mulch with heavy-duty, black plastic sheeting. Remove plastic once daytime temperatures warm up.

● To keep lightweight mulches from blowing away during high winds, cover with layer of coarse bark chunks or gravel. ● (For more information on mulches, see pages 51–52, *Sunset New Western Garden Book*.)

Pests and diseases ● Aphids feast heavily on new spring growth, especially citrus and roses. Repeatedly attack aphids with a blast of water from the hose, applications of insecticidal soap spray, or a chemical insecticide.

● Check pyracanthas for fireblight, which causes black stems and leaves and dieback. Fireblight usually occurs during the spring flowering season when insects transmit the disease (see page 43).

● Spray for mites, thrips. Plants have mites if leaves are stippled with tiny red, yellow, or green specks. Thrips cause twisted flowers, leaves. For controls, see page 35 (mites), page 38 (thrips).

Prune ● By April, it's safe to prune frost-damaged wood from bougainvillea, citrus, hibiscus, lantana, thevetia, and other tender plants when new growth appears.

● Trim overgrown juniper, pyracantha, and xylosma. ● Thin out olive trees and evergreen elms. Spray olive trees with a solution of naphthalene acetic acid to help prevent messy fruit. ● Cut back new tip growth ("candles") of pines to keep them compact. ● Trim dying *Washingtonia* palm fronds.

● In high desert areas, prune spring-flowering shrubs such as forsythia, spiraea, and weigela after bloom.

● Morning hours are best for watering lawns and most other plantings. ● Water deeply to leach out harmful salt deposits from plant roots and encourage plants to develop deep roots. ● Because they dry out faster, water container plants more frequently than others; flush out containers with repeated applications of water at least once a month to reduce harmful salt deposits.

● To prevent wasteful runoff, build basins around plantings. (See Soaking, pages 50–51, *Sunset New Western Garden Book*.)

● Mulching around plantings holds moisture in the ground longer.

Annuals

● *Low and intermediate desert:* in March plant summer-blooming annuals: castor bean, coreopsis, cosmos, four-o'clock, gaillardia, globe amaranth, Gloriosa daisy, lobelia, marigold, nasturtium, phlox, portulaca, salvia, scarlet sage, and strawflower.

● Mid-March, plant heat-loving Madagascar periwinkle, nasturtiums, nicotiana, petunias, portulaca, zinnias in open ground.

● *Cooler, high desert elevations:* in mid-April or May, plant heat-loving annuals: candytuft, pansies, painted daisy, petunia, snapdragon, strawflower, stock, sweet alyssum, violas.

● *At all elevations,* protect young seedlings from hot sun for a week or two after planting. ● Thin seedlings before they become crowded.

● End of April, replace withering spring annuals with summer annuals.

● *Low and intermediate desert:* set out small plants you've started or purchased from a nursery: coreopsis, cockscomb, dwarf marigold, portulaca, strawflower, Madagascar periwinkle, zinnia. ● Sow seeds for transplanting into flower beds later: bachelor's button, calendula, clarkia, cleome, godetia, linaria, lobelia, marigold, pansy, petunia, snapdragon, sweet alyssum, verbena, viola.

● *High desert:* plant seeds for fast-growing sweet alyssum, amaranthus, cosmos, kochia, larkspur, portulaca, snapdragon, zinnia. Set out plants of ageratum, China aster, Gloriosa daisy, larkspur, lobelia, nasturtium, phlox, sweet alyssum, verbena.

● (Also see special section on annuals, pages 76, 78, 79, *Sunset New Western Garden Book*.)

Broad-leafed evergreens

● In mild weather areas, plant tender subtropical broad-leafed evergreens: bougainvillea, calliandra, Natal plum, ficus, hibiscus, thevetia, citrus. ● (See Planting techniques, pages 44–48, *Sunset New Western Garden Book*.)

Bulbs

● *Desert areas below 1,100 feet:* make March plantings of canna, dahlia, zephyranthes in sunny spots; agapanthus and tuberose in shade.

● *High desert areas:* plant ranunculus from flats or pots.

● For healthy spring-flowering bulbs, water steadily during growing and blooming periods, but decrease when foliage starts to yellow; feed with complete fertilizer; pick off faded flowers. Do not remove foliage until completely dry.

● For bulbs to be left in the ground, apply complete fertilizer after bloom while leaves are still green; soak ground after feeding.

● Feed gladiolus with a complete fertilizer every 3 to 4 weeks before bloom; don't feed while in bloom.

● (Also see Bulbs, pages 75–77, *Sunset New Western Garden Book.*)

Chrysanthemums

● Make tip cuttings or divide rooted new growth from old clump. ● (See Division, Cuttings, pages 37–38, *Sunset New Western Garden Book.*) ● Set out rooted cuttings in May; keep shaded for 2 or 3 weeks. ● Pinch off tips to encourage bushier growth. ● (See Chrysanthemum, page 239, *Sunset New Western Garden Book.*)

Citrus

● *Low desert areas,* March and April are best times to plant citrus. *Intermediate and high desert,* wait until danger of frost is past.

● Protect young citrus plantings from sunburn or frost by painting exposed trunks and limbs with white latex paint, or using commercial tree wrap or burlap.

● Water established citrus deeply. Start watering basins about 6 inches from trunk base to keep trunk as dry as possible; this helps to prevent gummosis, a disease which causes plants to exude a gummy substance. ● Prune frost-damaged branches and suckers of established trees. ● Feed with citrus food after last frost. ● If there are signs of chlorosis, also feed with iron chelate after last frost. ● Watch for aphids that come out in full force now. ● (Also see citrus care, page 243, *Sunset New Western Garden Book.*)

Container plants

● Move all but the most heat-resistant container plants away from intense sun and wind. ● When possible, plant in wooden hanging baskets, which absorb less heat, hold moisture longer.

Deciduous fruit trees

● Thin crop on deciduous fruit trees to get larger fruit; this also helps prevent limb breakage. Thin apricots, plums, peaches when fruit is ½ to ¾ inches in diameter. Thin apricots and plums 4 to 6 inches apart; allow 6 to 10 inches between peaches.

Herbs

● In mid-spring, set out perennial herbs from small pots or bands for fast growth. ● Divide and replant perennials. ● *Higher elevations:* sow seeds of basil, marjoram, oregano, parsley, sage.

Lawns

● Winter annual rye grass usually will begin to die out in March and April, and warm-season Bermuda grass lawns take over. Do not feed or water until warm-season grasses are growing well. Then resume feeding with a complete fertilizer and water deeply.

● Prepare soil to plant new warm-season lawns such as Bermuda, dichondra, St. Augustine, zoysia, and ground covers, but delay planting until night temperatures remain above 60° to 65° F.

● *High desert areas:* wait until May to plant warm-season lawns. Plant lippia to get established before summer weather.

Palms

● May is an excellent time to plant or transplant. Back-fill rooting hole with mixture of equal parts native soil and nitrogen-treated organic amendment. ● Water deeply and keep wet during summer. ● Keep outer leaves tied together at top for 4 to 6 weeks to shade center bud.

Permanent planting

● Milder air and soil temperatures make April a good month to do most major landscape planting, so roots can establish before summer.

● Nursery-grown desert native plants are easy to grow: plant them in a large hole with 1 part organic amendment to 3 or 4 parts native soil. They require excellent drainage.

Perennials

● *Low, intermediate, high desert areas:* plant carnation, chrysanthemum, columbine, coral bells (in shade), pelargonium, Gloriosa daisy, Transvaal daisy, nierembergia, Shasta daisy, sweet William, verbena.

● Chrysanthemum, carnation, daylily, garden phlox, Michaelmas and Shasta daisies don't flower well when crowded. Divide clumps; also make stem cuttings.

● Feed established perennials lightly with iron-chelate enriched fertilizer.

Grapes

● *High desert areas:* In March, finish pruning grapevines. ● To control mildew, dust with sulfur or spray with lime sulfur when new shoots are 5 to 8 inches long. Repeat the application three or four times, 10 to 14 days apart. ● Water grapevines deeply and regularly during active growth.

Roses

● *Low desert areas:* In March, roses are preparing to bloom. Apply organic mulch around bushes to keep soil moist.

● *High desert areas:* March is the best time to prune roses that are coming out of dormancy.

● *Low and intermediate desert areas:* roses (especially hybrid teas), come into peak bloom in April. Water them deeply regularly; mulch to keep roots cool and retain soil moisture. ● To encourage larger blooms, remove spent flowers and feed with a complete fertilizer or rose food after the blooming period. ● When you cut spent blooms, leave plenty of foliage to protect canes from the sun.

● Leaves yellowing between veins mean chlorosis; treat with iron chelate or iron sulfate.

Vegetables

● *Low desert areas:* In March, sow seeds of bush beans, cucumber, eggplant, melon, squash, and sweet corn. Set out young pepper and tomato seedlings.

● *High desert areas:* In March, plant cool-season vegetables such as broccoli, Brussels sprouts, cabbage, radish, beet, onion, carrot, spinach, peas. Delay planting warm-season vegetables until end of April.

● *Low desert areas:* plant vegetables by March 15; *intermediate desert areas:* plant from mid-March to early April; *high-desert areas:* plant in May.

"Gardener's notepad"

SUMMER

In low and intermediate deserts, the only comfortable time to work in the garden in summer is in the very early morning or in the evening. There is some planting that can be done if you wish, but summer gardening is mostly maintenance.

General garden care

Fertilize ● Most plants, but not cactus and desert natives, will benefit from a June feeding. ● Feed summer annuals, vegetables, fast-growing subtropicals with complete fertilizer; hardy shrubs, ground covers, lawns monthly or bi-monthly with complete fertilizer. ● After bloom feed roses with rose food or any complete fertilizer.

● Container plants and plants that are watered often need frequent light applications of fertilizer. ● Don't feed frost-tender plants after mid-August. ● Apply fertilizer containing iron chelate or iron sulfate to chlorosis-susceptible bottle-brush, citrus, pyracantha, roses, xylosma.

● (Also see Fertilizing, pages 52–55, *Sunset New Western Garden Book*.)

Mulch ● Apply a 2-inch-thick mulch around trees, shrubs, vines, annuals, perennials, vegetables. Organic mulches break down and improve soil. Cover light-weight mulches with pea gravel or other heavier material to prevent high winds from blowing it away. ● Keep mulches away from tree trunks.

● (Also see Mulches, pages 51–52, *Sunset New Western Garden Book*.)

Pests and diseases ● In early morning, spray or dust to control insects and mildew. ● Bait for snails near leafy plantings. ● Water lawns early so grass dries before evening; this can prevent fungus diseases.

● Control aphids with a spray of water from the hose or with soapy water.

● Start watering basins a few inches from tree trunks to prevent gummosis.

● (Also see special chapter on pests, pages 32–48.)

Prune ● In June, prune azaleas, hibiscus, privet, pyracantha. ● Cut off frost-damaged wood of tender subtropicals—bougainvillea, citrus, lantana. ● Prune low-growing branches of fast-growing trees that interfere with walks or driveways. ● Remove spent blooms from flowering plants, trees, shrubs to encourage additional bloom.

● Prune excess growth and lower branches of fast-growing trees and shrubs to increase air circulation and minimize wind damage. ● Cut off dead fronds from those palms that need it.

● (Also see Pruning, page 68–71, *Sunset New Western Garden Book*.)

Water ● Flower beds, lawns, new shrubs and trees need watering at least every 4 to 5 days all summer. ● Water established citrus every 12 to 14 days. Mulch heavily (2 to 4 inches).

● If the lawn takes up water slowly, sprinkle briefly, then sprinkle again later.

● Construct tree watering basins from a few inches away from the trunk to the dripline, sloping away from trunk. Fill basins twice when watering.

● Water and feed container plants at least twice as often as those planted in the ground. ● Flush container plants monthly to leach out harmful mineral deposits. ● (Also see Container gardening, pages 79–81, *Sunset New Western Garden Book*.)

● Water fast-draining granite soils more frequently.

Weed ● Immediately attack weeds that sprout after summer rains. ● Hoe where damage to other roots is not a risk; pull by hand from beds and planted areas; use weed killer carefully on lawns. ● (Also see Controlling weeds, pages 66–67, *Sunset New Western Garden Book*.)

Annuals

● In *low desert areas*, limit July planting to heat-resistant varieties that bloom late summer until fall: globe amaranth, cockscomb, cosmos, Gloriosa daisy, tithonia, vinca, zinnia.

● In July in *high desert areas*, plant for bloom in late summer through fall: balsam, celosia, cosmos, dahlia, lobelia, marigold, petunia, nasturtium, verbena, zinnia. ● (Also see individual plant listings, pages 161–505, *Sunset New Western Garden Book*.)

● Shade new plantings from sun; water as often as twice a day.

Bulbs

● Autumn crocuses and spider lilies are available in August at nurseries. ● Lift and divide crowded iris rhizomes older than 3 years.

Cactus and succulents

● Let soil dry out between waterings. ● Feed occasionally with bone meal (1 tablespoon per 6-inch pot) or liquid fertilizer when plants are actively growing, especially during bloom period—May to August. ● Keep succulents well shaded. ● (Also see Cactus, page 211, and Succulent, page 477, *Sunset New Western Garden Book*.)

Chrysanthemum

● Stop pinching tips at end of July to ensure fall bloom. ● Feed plants two or three times during growing season; make last application not less than 2 weeks before bloom. ● Stake chrysanthe-mums upright. ● Watch for and control aphids (see page 34).

Citrus

● In early summer, pinch tips of fast-growing shoots to force fuller growth. ● During summer, water young trees twice weekly; water established trees deeply every 10 to 14 days, depending on soil type and tree size.

● Maintain water basins to driplines of trees. Start basins a few inches away from trunks to prevent rot.

● Feed once in May with a complete fertilizer. ● Prune sucker growth that sprouts from below the bud union.

● Control spider mites (see page 35) and snails (see page 34). ● Treat chlorosis with iron chelate or iron sulfate.

● Protect new plantings from sun.

● (Also see Citrus, pages 243–245, *Sunset New Western Garden Book*.)

Container plants

● In June, move container plants (including sun-loving ones) into light shade temporarily. ● Do not place container plants near wall or paving that reflects heat. ● Watch for soil dryness; water generously. ● Monthly, flush containers with water to leach salt deposits. ● Apply half-strength doses of complete fertilizer twice as often as directed, or apply diluted dosages each time you water.

Fruit and shade trees

● Thin fruit of citrus and deciduous trees not only to produce larger fruit, but also to prevent breaking and rotting of limbs, and to improve air circulation.

● Adjust ties on fast-growing young trees such as ash, locust, mulberry, and willow to prevent bark damage. ● Prune low branches that interfere with traffic.

● Protect trunks of trees from extreme sun; cover with burlap or manufactured tree wrap.

Iris

● Prune faded flowers; remove dead foliage. ● Burn diseased leaves and rhizomes affected by rot. ● Water iris deeply two or three times during the hot season.

● In *low desert*, wait until early fall to lift and divide crowded clumps that are 3 or 4 years old. ● In *high desert*, divide and replant early in July so iris will establish strong roots before cold weather. ● (Also see Iris, pages 332–334, *Sunset New Western Garden Book*.)

Lawns

● Hot weather turf plants can still be planted in June—Bermuda, dichondra, St. Augustine, zoysia. ● Keep soil of new lawns moist; water two or three times daily or as needed.

● Established hot-weather lawns need deep watering twice weekly, and monthly feeding with high-nitrogen complete fertilizer. ● If yellowing occurs and growth slows, feed with iron chelate or iron sulfate.

Perennials

● In *high desert,* plant these perennials in July: achillea, bearded iris, candytuft, columbine, coral bells, daylily, hardy aster, violets.

● In *low desert areas,* plant campanula, evergreen candytuft, chrysanthemum, dianthus, dusty miller, gazania, geranium, Gloriosa and Michaelmas daisies, lantana, marguerite, nierembergia, pelargonium, Shasta daisy. Shelter from extreme sun the first few weeks after planting.

● (Also see individual listings, pages 161–505, *Sunset New Western Garden Book.*)

Permanent planting

● In *high desert,* July is the best time to plant trees, shrubs, vines, ground covers; roots will develop by fall. ● Add plenty of organic matter to soil before planting. ● Construct a water basin to outer edge of rootball; mulch. ● Water to keep soil moist.

Roses

● Remove faded blooms, pruning as necessary, but leave enough foliage to shade stems. ● Feed with complete fertilizer monthly; replenish mulch. ● Water deeply; in early morning (to avoid sunburn), hose off foliage to remove dust, aphids, spider mites. ● Dust or spray with fungicide as needed to control mildew (page 41), rust (page 42), and black spot (page 42).

Vegetables

● In June in the *high desert,* where the growing season is short, plant fast-maturing vegetables from flats or nursery packs—beans, corn, cucumber, eggplant, melon, pumpkin, squash, tomato.

● In *intermediate* and *low desert,* plant beets, cantaloupe, carrots, corn, cucumber, endive, lettuce, parsnip, radish, rutabaga, squash, watermelon. ● Plant pumpkin seeds late June or early July for harvest before Halloween.

● In *high desert,* start fall crops from late July through mid-August: beets, cabbage, carrots, cauliflower, chard, lettuce, radish, spinach, turnip; by mid-August: beans, broccoli.

● In *low* and *intermediate desert* elevations, sow seeds of fall and winter vegetables by end of August: broccoli, Brussels sprouts, bush beans, cabbage, cauliflower, chard, cucumber, endive, garlic, kale, kohlrabi, leeks, lettuce, spinach, corn, turnip.

● (See individual vegetable listings, pages 162–505, *Sunset New Western Garden Book.*)

FALL

What springtime is to the eastern states, fall is to the low and intermediate deserts. It's the season for starting new gardens and redoing old ones—in short, it is the best possible planting time for just about everything.

General garden care

Clean-up ● Avoid a build-up of leaves, dead fruit and other debris that could harbor insects and fungus diseases. Rake every few days, then compost disease-free material. ● Pull out any remaining summer annuals; cut back perennials.

● Add to your compost pile organic material from garden and kitchen—leaves, pine needles, fruit, grass clippings, faded blooms. Keep pile moist and turn it often. ● Add bulky, woody material only in small amounts. ● (Also see Compost, page 35, *Sunset New Western Garden Book.*)

Fertilize ● Most ground covers, shrubs, trees should be fertilized at least once during fall. ● Feed citrus with complete fertilizer or ammonium sulfate where winters are mild. *Do not* feed citrus in cold-winter areas.

● In November, fertilize evergreen shrubs and trees with low-nitrogen, high-phosphorus, high-potassium fertilizer. ● Avoid feeding frost-tender shrubs such as bougainvillea, citrus, hibiscus, lantana, Natal plum, poinsettia.

Frost protection ● November and December bring the first frosts. ● Move tender container plants indoors or under shelter. Use plastic film, cardboard, newspaper, garbage bags over a frame or supports to cover other tender plants in case of sudden frost. ● Stop feeding frost-tender plants with nitrogen, cut back on water, but give them a soaking just before a predicted hard frost to reduce cold damage.

Pests and diseases ● In September, spray or hose off foliage of arborvitae, Arizona and Italian cypress, juniper, pyracantha, roses to control spider mites. ● Watch for grasshoppers (see page 36 for control).

● Watch for aphids in November on tip growth and undersides of leaves (see page 34 for control). ● In late November, apply dormant spray to deciduous trees that have dropped their leaves to control overwintering pests; drench trees thoroughly.

Prune ● Delay pruning deciduous fruit and shade trees until leaves have dropped. ● In *low desert,* prune bougainvillea, lantana, oleander, pyracantha, star jasmine in September only to remove dead or storm damaged limbs. ● Lightly prune roses to remove dead wood, suckers, faded blooms.

● Before strong November winds, thin out fan palms, Brazilian pepper, evergreen pear, and other top-heavy evergreens.

● In September, water deeply and infrequently, allowing soil to dry between times.

● Flood container plants several times every second or third time you water to flush out accumulated salts. ● Lawns and new shrubs need watering once a week. ● Irrigate established trees every 15 to 20 days, young trees every 7 to 10 days. Extend water basins to dripline of new growth.

Soil preparation ● Prepare soil in flower and vegetable beds for spring planting; add amendments and till or dig in. ● Dig and prepare planting holes for bare-root plants if heavy soil is a problem.

● Also see Soils, pages 33–35, *Sunset New Western Garden Book.*)

Water ● As the weather cools in October and November, cut back on watering. ● In *high desert,* water in morning or mid-day so excess water will evaporate by dusk. ● Winter vegetables will not produce if allowed to dry out. ● Water half as often as before for evergreens; water deciduous trees and shrubs even less. ● Water non-woody perennials just enough to prevent wilting.

Weed ● Pull and destroy puncture vine and tumbleweed before they go to seed in September. ● Remove Bermuda grass runners in flower beds. ● Hoe weeds, turn them under, or spray with a weed killer.

"Gardener's notepad"

_____
_____
_____
_____
_____
_____
_____
_____
_____
_____
_____
_____

WINTER

There is considerable busy work and a fair amount of planting to be done in the low and intermediate deserts during the winter months. In the high deserts, gardening is pretty much limited to the dormant season basics.

Annuals

• In *low and intermediate desert areas*, start planting spring-blooming annuals when cool weather comes, usually toward the end of September. (Don't buy frost-tender leftovers from summer—marigolds, portulaca, zinnias.) • In *high desert* areas, plant winter annuals by mid-October.

    • Sow seeds of African daisy, ageratum, calendula, California poppy, candytuft, coreopsis, clarkia, Iceland poppy, larkspur, lobelia, lupine, pansy, petunia, nasturtium, phlox, Shirley poppy, snapdragon, stock, sweet alyssum, verbena, viola. • In October, sow seeds or plant seedlings of spring-flowering sweet peas. • Provide screen or netting for support and protect seedlings from birds.

    • Protect seedlings from hot sun at first and keep well watered.

Bulbs

• In *low and intermediate desert areas*, September is still too warm to plant spring-blooming bulbs—but buy bulbs as soon as they appear in nurseries to get the best choices. Look for anemone, crocus, daffodil and other narcissus, Dutch iris, freesia, ranunculus, scilla, tigridia, and others. Store bulbs in cool, dry place; plant when weather cools in October or November.

    • Store hyacinth and tulip bulbs in refrigerator (40° to 45° F.) 6 weeks before planting. • Gladiolus planted in early September will bloom by Thanksgiving in low and intermediate elevations.

Citrus

• In September, feed citrus for the last time this year. • As the weather cools, water less frequently, but don't let trees dry out. Young trees need water once every other week, established trees need monthly watering. • Protect trees from frost; construct a temporary overhead shelter or frame covered with plastic. Wrap trunks of young citrus trees to protect from winter damage. • (Also see Frost protection, page 94, *Sunset New Western Garden Book*.)

Date palms

• Spray date palms with malathion to kill dried fruit beetle. Keep fallen dates cleaned up. • (For more information on date palms see *Phoenix*, page 405, *Sunset New Western Garden Book*.)

Iris

• September is the last chance to get spuria irises in nurseries this season. • Before mid-October, divide and replant spuria and bearded irises in *low and intermediate desert*. Plant in fast-draining soil; don't overwater while rhizomes are becoming established.

    • (For illustrated information on dividing iris, turn to page 63.)

Lawns

• To keep Bermuda grass green later, dethatch in early fall, water regularly and feed monthly with high-nitrogen fertilizer. • Or, overseed Bermuda with winter grass when the Bermuda goes dormant. • Sow new lawns of cool-season annual grass (rye, fescue). • Remove spotted spurge and other lawn weeds before they scatter seeds.

Perennials

• In early fall, lift and divide overcrowded perennials and take tip cuttings. • In *mild-winter areas*, plant in sunny locations: carnation, dianthus, gaillardia, hollyhock, lavender, penstemon, Shasta daisy, sweet William, verbena. In shade, plant columbine, coral bells, phlox, violets.

    • (Also see Perennials, pages 74–75, *Sunset New Western Garden Book*.)

Permanent planting

• September and October are best months to put in permanent landscape plants. You can plant almost anything except bare-root plants and frost-tender subtropicals. • In *low desert areas*, prune oleanders in September to allow time for regrowth while weather is warm. If you prune later, new growth won't start until spring.

Roses

• October begins one of the best seasons for roses—they'll flower again. For blooms until Christmas, water deeply, weed regularly, remove faded blooms and hips. • Trim suckers coming from below the bud union, but leave heavier pruning until plants go dormant in winter.

Tropical plants

• As long as warm weather continues, tropicals and subtropicals will bloom (bougainvillea, Natal plum, hibiscus, yellow oleander). • Prepare them for colder weather by cutting back on water and fertilizer.

Vegetables

• In *low and intermediate desert areas*, start winter vegetables in late September: sow seeds of beets, carrots, kale, kohlrabi, lettuce, mustard, parsley, peas, radish, spinach, Swiss chard; plant transplants of cabbage, broccoli, Brussels sprouts, cauliflower. • Plant tomatoes and peppers; provide frost protection.

    • In *high desert areas*, in September, plant spinach and kale—they survive light frost. (It's too late to start other vegetables.) • Mulch vegetables with hay or straw.

Wildflowers

• Sow wildflower seeds; rake in lightly, and keep soil moist until seedlings are established.

General garden care

Clean up • To keep plants neat and encourage more blooms, pick dead flowers off cool-season annuals, particularly pansies. • Dispose of leaves and debris under deciduous fruit trees and roses.

Fertilizing • Feed winter rye grass lawns with high-nitrogen fertilizer in January. • Unless you provided your fall-planted annuals with a long-season, slow-release fertilizer, feed them in January with complete fertilizer. It will help them grow and set buds for their coming performance. • Give shade trees, deciduous fruit trees, shrubs, and hedges an application of high-nitrogen fertilizer in February to help them get off to a fast start when warm weather arrives. However, wait to feed citrus until March.

    • (Also see Fertilizing, pages 52–55, *Sunset New Western Garden Book*.)

Pests and diseases • December begins the year's most important spray season. • To control scale insects, over-wintering mite and insect eggs, and many kinds of fungi, spray with a combination insecticide-fungicide, such as oil mixed with lime sulfur or fixed copper. To control peach leaf curl, spray with lime sulfur once just after leaf drop, again in midwinter, and again just as buds begin to swell. Mix spray material exactly as label instructions recommend. Drench all branches, limbs, trunks, and the ground under plants.

    • (Also see special chapter on pests, pages 32–48.)

Plant • Plant or transplant deciduous and hardy evergreen shrubs, trees, and vines in December. • You can move deciduous plants without soil on the roots in December. • January is the best month to plant bare-root shade trees, fruit trees, shrubs, grapes, and cane berries.

    • Plant strawberries in February. Set plants in a spot with rich, porous soil and filtered shade. Keep crowns at soil level. • Hardy evergreen plants are about as dormant as they will ever be; move them with as much soil around the roots as you can handle. Water well. • In *low and intermediate desert areas*, gardeners can set out plants of annuals: sweet alyssum, calendula, lobelia, pansies, petunias, annual phlox, snapdragons, and stock in February. ● Wait until March before planting the heat-lovers: periwinkle, marigold, and zinnia. In *high desert areas*, start these seeds indoors in February.

Prune ● December is the time to shape and thin out conifers and broad-leafed evergreen trees to open up dense growth and prevent winter storm damage. Use the trimmings for holiday decoration. ● In the *high desert*, begin to prune deciduous fruit trees; elsewhere, wait until January. ● In *low and intermediate desert areas*, prune deciduous trees and shrubs after their leaves have fallen. In the high desert, prune near end of dormant season. ● Cut out congested growth of hardy evergreen trees and shrubs. ● Prune roses as soon as buds begin to swell—about January 15 in the *low desert*, about March 1 in the *high desert*. ● This is also the time to prune grape vines and cane berries. ● In the *high desert*, wait until March or April to prune most shrubs and trees. ● (Also see Pruning, pages 68–71, *Sunset New Western Garden Book*.)

Watering ● It's especially important to water permanent plants thoroughly in winter to encourage deep root systems. Water about half as frequently as you did in summer, but soak deeply.

Weed ● Remove weeds and spread a thick layer of organic mulch to conserve soil moisture and reduce future weed problems. ● If tumbleweed was a problem last summer, apply a pre-emergent herbicide to destroy tumbleweed seeds as they sprout. ● To help control crabgrass on bare ground, treat the soil in late winter or early spring with a pre-emergent weed killer. In a lawn, use a pre-emergent labeled for lawn use. Since crabgrass produces so many seeds that remain dormant for several years, it may take two or three annual treatments to control it. ● (Also see Controlling weeds, pages 66–67, *Sunset New Western Garden Book*.)

Winter protection ● Wind and high light intensities dry out plants rapidly. ● Mulch newly planted roses and other deciduous plants. Without such protection, buds may not open. ● When frost is predicted for the next morning, cover young plants that might be damaged: bauhinia, bougainvillea, citrus, and hibiscus. (Use a card table, box, or suspended sheet just above the plant.)

Annuals

● Plants set out in October should be blooming soon. To keep them healthy, water regularly and give a light monthly feeding. ● Pinch back spindly stems of petunia, snapdragon, and stock to make them branch.

● Pinch off faded blooms to keep new ones coming.

Bulbs

● You can continue to plant spring-blooming bulbs in December as long as they are in good condition. ● Plant tulips and hyacinths after they have been stored in a refrigerator for 6 weeks. ● In *mild-winter desert areas*, this is the best time to plant gladiolus.

● Nurseries have pony packs of already-started ranunculus as well as ranunculus tubers. The started ones will give equally large flowers—and with slightly less risk. ● In the *low desert*, plant amaryllis in February. Plant bulbs with the tops barely exposed, 12 to 24 inches apart in a spot in filtered sun.

Citrus

● To protect young citrus trees from severe frosts, wrap trunks from the ground to limbs with several layers of burlap, newspaper, narrow strips of cloth, or carpet. ● Leave wrapping on until danger of frost is over. ● In cold weather, water deeply but less often. ● In all desert areas wait until frosty weather is over before planting new citrus.

● In *low desert areas*, you can start feeding citrus with high-nitrogen fertilizer at the end of February. Mature trees (5 years or older) need from 1 to 3 pounds of actual nitrogen per year. Younger trees (second, third, and fourth growing seasons) need ¼, ½, and ¾ pound, respectively, of actual nitrogen per year.

● (Also see Citrus, pages 243–245, *Sunset New Western Garden Book*.)

Fruit trees

● In late winter, feed with nitrogen well before spring growth, to make up for nutrients washed away by rains. Trees deficient in nitrogen will produce small, poor-quality fruit, yellow-green leaves, and slow growth. In fertile desert soils, use about 1 pound actual nitrogen per year for mature trees, about 0.2 to 0.4 pound per 100 square feet for dwarf or young trees.

Lawns

● Water winter rye grasses regularly to keep them green as long as possible. ● Don't feed rye lawns in late winter—the fertilizer makes them too competitive for emerging Bermuda. ● If spurge was a problem in your Bermuda lawn last summer, turn to page 44 for control measure. ● Avoid walking on frosted dichondra—the crushed leaves turn black.

Perennials

● If you missed the fall perennial planting season, February is the month to catch up. Set out asters, blue marguerites, coreopsis, feverfew, gaillardia, gerbera, hollyhocks, pelargonium, Shasta daisies, statice, and tritoma. (See individual listings, pages 161–505, *Sunset New Western Garden Book*.)

Roses

● For better flowering and more attractive shape prune roses in January (low desert), March (high desert). ● Roses in mild-winter areas respond better to moderate pruning than severe cutting back. Remove old canes, dead wood, and weak or crossing branches.

Vegetables

● In the *low desert*, you can sow vegetable seeds of such warm-season crops as beans, cucumbers, melon, and squash in February. ● Also set out young plants of eggplant, peppers, and tomatoes.

● In the high desert, start seeds of *warm-season* crops indoors.

● Bare-root perennial vegetables also are available: artichoke, asparagus, horseradish, rhubarb.

● Water fall-planted crops heavily between rains. Thin beets, carrots, lettuce, spinach. ● There is always a danger of frost, so be prepared to give plants protection with paper caps or other devices.

"Gardener's notepad"

SOUTHERN CALIFORNIA

South of the Tehachapis and west of California's deserts lie the gardening climates that *Sunset* recognizes: Zones 18 and 19, interior valleys; Zones 20 and 21, areas that get both interior and coastal weather; Zones 22 and 23, coastal weather most of the time; and Zone 24, the beaches.

SPRING

The early part of spring is often rainy. By May it's getting warmer and the weather for days and weeks is the famous "late night and early morning low clouds, clearing in afternoon." Boring for people but good for planting.

General garden care

Clean-up ● Remove weeds, leaves, and other debris from your garden. Rake up fallen camellia blossoms to prevent the spread of petal blight. ● Wait to cut off the foliage of daffodils and other bulbs until it withers naturally. The leaves strengthen the bulbs for the next season's growth; remove flowers as they fade.

Fertilize ● Feed all lawns in March with a fast-acting, high-nitrogen fertilizer.
● Feed established citrus trees.
● Most plants will benefit from a feeding in March. Apply complete fertilizer to established flowers, vegetables, trees, and shrubs.
● If plants show signs of iron deficiency (yellowing leaves with green veins), feed with iron chelate or iron sulfate, following the label instructions for application rates.
● (Also see Fertilizing, pages 52–55, *Sunset New Western Garden Book.*)

Pests and diseases ● Watch citrus and roses for aphids. ● Bait for snails, slugs, especially around young plants. Treat roses with a fungicide to control mildew before it becomes established.
● As weather warms, mites may in-

fest citrus trees, causing the leaves to look silvery and stippled. For identification and control, see page 35.

Prune ● Give frost-damaged plants plenty of time to show signs of new growth before pruning them. Wait until well after the danger of frost has passed, the damage may not actually be as bad as it looks in early spring.
● (See Pruning, pages 68–71, *Sunset New Western Garden Book.*)

Water ● If spring rains are inadequate you may need to water container plants. Water newly planted citrus and subtropicals, and anything else that needs it. Established trees and shrubs should be all right for the next couple of months or so.
● *Do not water* California native oak trees or other established natives; they shouldn't get any more water than nature provides.
● (See Watering, pages 48–52, *Sunset New Western Garden Book.*)

Weed ● Remove weeds while they're small, before they set seed; you'll save yourself a lot of work this summer. If you use herbicides, check labels first for proper application rates.
● (See Controlling weeds, pages 66–67, *Sunset New Western Garden Book.*)

Annuals

● Spring flowers planted in March *inland* areas still have time to perform before summer heat. On the coast, some kinds last into summer—try anemones, calendulas, pansies, Iceland poppies, primroses, ranunculus, stocks, sweet alyssum. Start these bulblike plants: gladiolus, hippeastrum, tuberose.
● Wait until April or later to plant most warm-weather annuals.
● May's the time to remove fading spring-bloomers and replace them with summer-flowering plants. Plant ageratum, alyssum, aster (Callistephus), bachelor button, cockscomb, coleus, coreop-

sis, cosmos, dwarf dahlia, gaillardia, hollyhock, lobelia, marigolds, morning glory, nasturtium, nicotiana, nierembergia, portulaca, salvia, verbena, vinca rosea, and zinnia.
● Apply a light mulch and if possible, shelter newly transplanted seedlings from the sun for the first two or three days; water regularly.

Azaleas

● Shop for azaleas in bloom at nurseries in April to get the colors you want.
● When you plant, add 50 percent organic material such as ground bark or leaf mold to the backfill soil or to the mix for the planting container.
● After bloom apply an acid fertilizer according to label instructions. As the days heat up, keep soil around plants slightly damp. Mulch the soil beneath plants heavily.

Bulbs

● April is the time to buy and plant summer-flowering bulbs. Plant cannas, dahlias, and (in shade) tuberous begonias.
● Most spring-flowering bulbs like daffodils and freesias will have finished blooming by May; don't remove the foliage until it dies. After foliage has dried, if you wish, you can lift bulbs to store or divide them. Store lifted bulbs in dry sawdust during the summer, replant in October.

Camellias

● After plants finish blooming, feed them with an acid fertilizer; apply according to label instructions.
● (See Camellias, pages 216–219, *Sunset New Western Garden Book.*)

Citrus

● Citrus planting season starts in March. Scout nurseries for best varieties.
● Protect trunks of young citrus from sunburn by using a commercial

tree wrap, or painting with white latex paint or whitewash. *Hot inland areas:* If possible, shelter newly planted trees for about a month with shade cloth.

● Established citrus trees need their first big feeding in March—apply a fast-acting, high-nitrogen fertilizer.

● If leaves are yellowish with green veins, work iron chelate or iron sulfate into the soil beneath the tree.

● Prune frost-damaged wood after new growth starts.

● Lemon trees may need a heavy pruning; cut back long, straggly branches.

● Closely watch new, tender growth for aphids (see page 34).

● (For details on citrus care, see pages 243–245, *Sunset New Western Garden Book.*)

Fuchsias

● You find a large supply of fuchsias at nurseries in April. Plant them now so they become established before hot weather arrives.

● (See Fuchsias, pages 304–305, *Sunset New Western Garden Book.*)

Lawns

● Cool-season turf grasses grow fast in early spring. Give bluegrass, rye, and fescue grasses a dose of fast-acting, high-nitrogen fertilizer now.

● Bermuda grass and other warm-season grasses (St. Augustine, zoysia) should begin growing rapidly in March; feed them with a high nitrogen fertilizer. It's still a bit early to plant Bermuda; wait until April or May.

● This is a good time to reseed sections of your lawn that look spotty. Before sowing rake out all thatch in areas to be replanted.

● April is the last good month before fall to plant a new cool season lawn.

● (See Lawn care, pages 85–88, *Sunset New Western Garden Book.*)

Perennials

● Established perennials begin their yearly growth cycle in March—feed them now with complete fertilizer. Water them as often as necessary through the summer.

Permanent Planting

● March is the second best time of the year to plant evergreen shrubs, ground covers, trees, perennials, and vines (October is the best month). March or April is the best time to plant tropical or subtropical plants.

Roses

● Roses leaf out in February and March, and produce their first big bloom in April. Aphids may appear on new growth —hose them off or squish them by hand.

● Feed established rose bushes now, but wait until next month to fertilize new roses.

● Renew mulch around bushes. To stimulate quick repeat bloom, remove dead flowers, fertilize with a complete fertilizer or special rose food, water regularly, and remove weak, inward growth and suckers that won't bloom. Pinch off side buds of hybrid tea roses for extra large blooms. If necessary spray or dust roses with a fungicide to prevent mildew.

● (See *Rosa*, pages 450–455, *Sunset New Western Garden Book.*)

Vegetables

● In March sow seeds of these summer vegetables: beets, carrots, cucumbers, kale, lettuce, parsley, radishes, squash. Start eggplant, melons, peppers, and tomatoes indoors; and wait for more warmth in April or May to sow outdoors or set out plants.

● Coastal areas, last chance to plant winter vegetable seedlings: broccoli, Brussels sprouts, cauliflower, celery, spinach, Swiss chard.

SUMMER

June continues the day-after-day "late night and early morning low clouds, clearing in afternoon." But in July and August the inland areas get many days in the 80's and 90's— there the primary summer gardening activity is watering.

General garden care

Compost ● Add organic kitchen and garden remains to pile. Turn often, add small amounts of soil and nitrogen fertilizer occasionally, and keep moist. Avoid adding chunks of wood, heavy prunings, weed grasses, common Bermuda lawn clippings, and morning glory that has gone to seed, to the pile; send these out with your trash.

● (Also see Compost, page 35, *Sunset New Western Garden Book.)*

Fertilize ● Feed vegetables, summer annuals, and other spring-planted flowers with a low-nitrogen fertilizer once or twice in May. Feed leafy vegetables (lettuce, for instance) with a high-nitrogen fertilizer.

● Feed established hibiscus, bougainvillea, and other subtropicals with a citrus food; feed Bermuda, dichondra, St. Augustine and other subtropical lawns with high-nitrogen fertilizer; and feed azaleas and camellias with a final dose of acid fertilizer in August. Feed roses monthly with rose food or other complete fertilizer.

Garden preparation ● Prepare bulb beds for fall planting. ● Start fall-winter annual and vegetable seeds in containers for planting out in late September. ● Order any special trees, shrubs, ornamentals so they'll arrive before fall planting time.

Mulch ● Spread organic mulches of straw, ground bark, and compost, for instance, several inches deep around garden to help retain moisture around roots.

Pests and diseases ● Bait for snails and slugs around new plantings. Pick up anything they could hide under during the day. ● Blast aphids and mites off foliage

"Gardener's notepad"

with hose water or soapy water. White-flies begin in summer and they are tricky; see page 35.

Pinching/pruning ● Some perennials, annuals, and small shrubs may benefit from light trimming now. ● Remove sucker growth from permanent plants. ● Cut chrysanthemums back to about a foot tall to encourage bushiness. ● Remove canes of berries that have finished fruiting; tie up new canes that will produce next year's crop.

Water new plantings and container plants as often as necessary. ● Deep water fruit and shade trees monthly. ● Water azaleas, camellias, and other moisture-lovers when soil beneath them dries completely; mulch to conserve moisture.

Weed ● Bermuda grass, oxalis, crabgrass, spotted spurge spread like wildfire (see pages 43 and 44).

Fuchsias

● Feed fuchsias in June to encourage more flowering. Watch foliage for aphids, whiteflies and mites; control by spraying with water jet or effective insecticides (see pages 34 and 35).

Lawns

● Plant warm-season lawns (Bermuda, St. Augustine, zoysia) through the summer; water established lawns deeply and infrequently to encourage deep rooting. Feed monthly with high-nitrogen fertilizer.
● Hold off feeding cool-season lawns (bluegrass, perennial rye, fescue) until fall. Also, wait until fall to plant cool-season lawns, it's too hot during the summer.
● Aerate to improve air circulation around roots and aid water penetration.

Perennials

● Plant daylilies, dianthus, ivy geraniums, Shasta daisy now for summer and fall bloom; keep well watered. Pinch tip growth occasionally to force branching. Start new plants from stem cuttings.

Tropicals and subtropicals

● Plant tropicals and subtropicals now so they'll be established before cool weather arrives. In this category: citrus, bougainvillea, hibiscus, lantana, Natal plum, palms. Build generous watering basins under plants, mulch, water frequently. If possible, shade plants from sun for the first two weeks.

Vegetables

● Near the coast you can still plant cool-season vegetables such as lettuce and cauliflower in May. Inland gardeners can plant beans, beets, carrots, corn, cucumbers, eggplant, melons, okra, peppers, pumpkin, radish, squash, and tomato.

● In July, plant seeds of these vegetables for harvest from September to December: beans, beets, carrots, chard, cucumber, radish, squash. Set out seedlings of corn, pepper, tomato.
● Harvest crops often to keep plants producing. As you harvest tomatoes, tie up fruit-laden branches. Pick off and step on hornworms.

FALL

This is the Santa Ana season—those hot, dry winds are tough on gardens, but after they are over the weather is nice. Do all the planting you can do—it's the very best season of the year to plant everything except frost-tender items.

General garden care

Clean-up and remove weeds, leaves, grass clippings, dead plants, fallen fruit.

Compost all organic garden and kitchen debris; keep pile moist and well turned.

Fertilize ● In October stop feeding woody plants to allow them to harden up before cold weather arrives.
● Feed junipers and other conifers with slow-release fertilizer. ● Feed roses if you want continued bloom until December. ● Feed cool-season grasses in October. ● Mix superphosphate or bonemeal into the soil beneath bulbs as you plant them.

Wind protection ● Santa Ana winds whip up suddenly; stake new trees, tall plants. Thin out inner branches on established trees to allow wind to pass through.

Annuals

● Plant these seedlings in early October for winter and spring flowers: calendula, candytuft, Canterbury bells, carnation, cineraria, columbine, delphinium, dianthus, dusty miller, English daisy, English primrose, foxglove, Iceland poppy, lobelia, nemesia, pansy, penstemon, phlox, Shasta daisy, snapdragon, stock, sweet alyssum, sweet pea, sweet William, violas.
● For quick color by Thanksgiving, in early fall plant these from 4-inch or larger pots: calendula, chrysanthemum, dianthus, Iceland poppy, lobelia, nemesia, pansy, snapdragon.

Bulbs

● Plant these spring bulbs in September or October: allium, anemone, daffodils, Dutch iris, freesia, ixia, oxalis, scilla, spider lily, watsonia.

● Buy tulips, hyacinths, and crocus now; store them in your refrigerator's vegetable crisper for 6 weeks before planting. Plant ranunculus and anemones when soil has cooled, around Thanksgiving.

Chrysanthemums

● After blooming, cut plants back to 6 inches tall. Dig up and divide overcrowded clumps.

Camellias

● Give camellias a final disbudding in November.

Ground Covers

● Plant spring-blooming ground covers in early fall so they'll be established before winter arrives: gazania, ice plant, ivy geranium, and trailing African daisy, among others.

Lawns

● Sow cool-season lawns (bluegrass, rye, fescue) in October or early November.
● Feed established cool-season lawns monthly, mow when necessary. Hold off feeding warm-season grasses (Bermuda, St. Augustine, zoysia) until February.

Perennials

● Lift and divide clumps of over-crowded perennials. November is a good time to plant carnations, columbine, coral bells, delphinium, foxglove, marguerites, and other spring bloomers.

Permanent planting

● Plant most trees, shrubs, ground covers, and California natives—everything except frost-tender plants—in fall. Plant roses and deciduous fruit and shade trees during the winter dormant season —January and February.

Tuberous begonias

● When leaves and stems dry up, lift tuberous begonias; remove soil from roots and dry tubers in the shade for several days. Store tubers in sawdust in a cool, dark spot until March.

Vegetables

● As summer vegetables finish, remove plants and prepare soil for winter crops.
● In September or October, sow seeds or set out plants of beets, broccoli, Brussels sprouts, cabbage, cauliflower, celery, chives, collards, endive, kale, kohlrabi, lettuce, onions, parsley, parsnips, peas, radishes, spinach, Swiss chard, turnips.

Wildflower seeds

● Any time in the fall, sow wildflower seeds. After scattering, rake the area lightly to insure that they contact the soil. Give them a sprinkling; later, let winter rains do the watering.

WINTER

Southern California's winters are justifiably famous. (Where else can roses bloom on New Year's Day?) Hope that the winter will bring you lots of rain—and in between times, when it's dry, get your dormant season planting and chores done.

General garden care

Clean-up • Remove withered plants, dead branches, palm fronds, grass clippings, leaves, other garden debris as necessary.

Compost • Add complete fertilizer to your compost pile. Turn it regularly and keep it moist. Avoid adding diseased or woody material to the pile.
• (See Compost, page 35, *Sunset New Western Garden Book*.)

Fertilize • Give established cool-season lawns a monthly feeding with high-nitrogen fertilizer.
• Give winter and spring-blooming annuals and bulbs a complete fertilizer in February. Water it in well.
• When camellias and azaleas near the end of their bloom season, fertilize with acid food.
• Fertilize established fruit trees before they bloom.

• Toward the end of February, feed fall-planted trees and shrubs. Feed bare root plants six weeks after planting.
• (See Fertilizing, pages 52–55, *Sunset New Western Garden Book*.)

Pests and diseases • Midwinter spraying is one of the safest and most effective ways of knocking out mite and insect eggs, scale, and some kinds of fungus (such as peach leaf curl) on deciduous woody plants. Use a combination insecticide–fungicide such as oil and lime sulfur, or oil and fixed copper. Drench the trunks, main branches, and soil beneath the plants, but try not to let spray hit evergreens; if it does, just wash it off.
• Use snail and slug bait or spray containing mesurol or metaldehyde around newly-planted seedlings.
• (See the chapter on garden troublemakers, pages 32–48.)

Prune • January is the time for the year's heaviest and most important pruning.
• This includes all deciduous fruit trees, berries, and grapes. You can also prune other leafless plants, but not those valued for spring blossoms. Generally, wait until after they bloom.
• Prune dormant summer-blooming shrubs early in February, before they begin to leaf out. • You still have a little time to cut back late-budding roses. • Cut back fuchsias at the end of February.
• (See Pruning, pages 68–71, *Sunset New Western Garden Book*.)

Soil preparation • Prepare for bare-root planting by digging holes; add compost or another organic amendment to the backfill material if soil is heavy.
• (See Bare-root planting, pages 44–45, *Sunset New Western Garden Book*.)

Water • If rains are inadequate, water any plants that need it.

Wind protection • Stake and tie newly planted shrubs and trees to protect against strong winds. Replace worn or tight ties.

Bare-root planting

• Deciduous fruit and shade trees, cane berries, and roses arrive at nurseries in late December. Shop early to get choice plants; if you are unable to plant immediately, heel bare roots into damp soil, sawdust, wood shavings, or sand.

Impatiens

• Coastal gardeners who have impatiens growing in their gardens should cut them back fairly hard in December or January, removing all lanky stems. By mid-February to March, new leaves should have sprouted. Feed plants then.

Vegetables

• In February you can sow seeds of beets, cabbage, carrots, celery, endive, kale, kohlrabi, mustard, onions, parsnips, radishes, spinach, and turnips.
• Sow eggplant, peppers, and tomatoes indoors. • As early as they're available, plant these bare-root: artichokes, asparagus, horseradish, rhubarb, and strawberries.

"Gardener's notepad"

GARDEN TROUBLEMAKERS

On these pages, you can read how to contend with the West's 36 worst garden troublemakers: insects, mites, diseases, weeds, snails and slugs, even animals and one bird.

The map on the facing page shows where those 36 make trouble. The facts were gathered by *Sunset* from 56 garden clubs in the eleven Western states. The garden clubs told us what the big troublemakers were—and universities and extension services told us about the ways you can lessen the damage or the troubles the organisms bring on.

As you will see, different climates foster different problems. In some cases, a "bad guy" would make the list of leading pests in one or more regions and be down among the also-rans (or not listed) in others.

The things you should know about the organisms—how they live, what they do to garden plants, how your plants can live with them, how you can temporarily get rid of them—are all spelled out, one troublemaker at a time, in this chapter. The troublemakers appear by category in order of their badness here in the West, as determined by our garden club survey. The ones that are most widespread—and got the most votes from the garden clubs—appear first in each category.

Gardeners and farmers have learned that they can seldom control outdoor pests to the point of getting rid of them completely and permanently. In total, the pests' survival systems are so strong that the best we can do is to make them go away for awhile or to limit their numbers to a tolerable level—until we get the crop harvested, until next week, or perhaps until the same time next year.

The impossibility of banishment is why you now see the term "pest control" less used than in other years. Instead, you see and hear of "pest management." In most cases, we can *manage* the troublemakers—helping nature, using common sense, using physical means, and using purchased biological or chemical controls when necessary.

Below is an alphabetical index to the 15 pages of pests. There are more than 36 names because some troublemakers are known by several names; we have included all the commonly used ones.

THE WEST'S MAJOR CLIMATES AND THE WORST PESTS IN EACH

Pacific Northwest (West of the Cascades)
Slugs, root weevils, aphids, moles, mildew,
mites, blackberry, dandelion, cutworms,
crows, black spot, deer, gophers

Northern California—Coastal
Slugs and snails, mildew, gophers, earwigs,
aphids, whiteflies, oak moth, mites, rust,
mealybugs, deer, moles, cutworms

Northern California—Inland
Slugs and snails, aphids, mites, Bermuda grass,
mildew, crabgrass, whiteflies, geranium budworms,
field bindweed, earwigs, scale, oxalis, rust

Southern California—Coastal
Mildew, whiteflies, gophers, slugs and snails, rust,
aphids, oxalis, scale, Bermuda grass, thrips, sowbugs
and pillbugs, geranium budworms, mealybugs

Southern California—Inland
Grasshoppers, whiteflies, mites, aphids, mildew,
slugs and snails, oak root fungus, squirrels,
earwigs, moles, roof rats, cutworms, crows

Mountain
Slugs, aphids, mites, grasshoppers, mildew,
leaf rollers, fireblight, gophers, crabgrass,
earwigs, cutworms, leaf-cutting bees, field bindweed

Desert
Aphids, mites, whiteflies, grape-leaf skeletonizers,
grasshoppers, spotted spurge, leaf-cutting bees,
slugs, mildew, squash bugs

*By the colors on this map,
you can find the seven major
climate zones of the West
and the worst troublemak-
ers that home gardeners
must contend with in each
climate. The pests were
named by garden clubs
within the climate zones.*

SLUGS & SNAILS

That's a slug at left, a snail at center, and the kind of leaf damage that they both do at right. In daytime they hide in dark, damp places. They feed at night and during dull, rainy days.

Slugs and snails (a slug is just a snail without a shell) rank as the West's overall worst garden pest—number 1 in four regions, and in the top 10 in the other three.

Nobody ever gets rid of slugs or snails for good. You can combat them to the point where you may not have any for a season or two, but they'll come back—from neighbors' lots, on new plants, or even as eggs in soil that you bring in. Always watch for those eggs and destroy them when you see them (under rocks, boards, and pots): they look like ⅛-inch pearls in clusters.

The most popular controls are packaged baits containing metaldehyde or mesurol in pellets, meal, or emulsion form. If you use the pellets, scatter them on the ground so there's space between them—don't pile them up. Be careful using the material where dogs live or visit. Some dogs eat it; it can poison them.

An easy control for snails (but not for slugs) is hand-picking. Go out in the garden after 10 P.M. with a flashlight and a container. Pick up the snails and destroy them however you wish. They can be prepared as the delicacy escargot but it takes some time and trouble.

A useful trap: attach a pair of 1½-inch wooden strips to the sides of a 12-inch-wide plank (any length) or to a piece of plywood. Squash a slug or snail on the underside of it. This acts as a "starter" to attract other slugs or snails. Put the traps in an infested area and clean them off each morning.

APHIDS

Aphids are fairly easy to deal with: wash them off with a blast of water from the hose. Or wash them with a mixture of insecticidal soap and water. The soap can kill aphids that you don't see or that hang on through your blasting.

Numerous creatures continually keep aphid populations in check. In Southern California's Huntington Botanical Gardens, the rosarian has recorded 12 creatures that regularly eat the aphids on the rose plants: two species of parasitic wasps, adult and larval lacewings, syrphid fly larvae, adult and larval ladybird beetles, native praying mantis, lizards, bushtits, house finches, yellow warbler, Townsend's warbler, and Wilson's warbler. The gardeners at Huntington never spray their roses for aphids. If they did spray with an insecticide, it would probably kill the first six predators on the list, along with the aphids.

Aphids that make trouble are those that can hide from your hose and from their natural enemies by curling leaves around them or staying in protected places (as within a head of cabbage). The only way to control these involves anticipating them. If they came last year, expect them again this year and blast them off or spray when the aphid colony is young and leaves are still open. On ornamental plants (but not edibles) you can kill aphids without harming predators and parasites by using disyston or other systemic insecticide.

Ants often maintain aphids, fighting off parasites and predators in order to eat the honeydew the aphids exude. They do this with several other sucking insects; for details, see scale insects on page 36. Control ants with diazinon or dursban granules, which don't harm aphid predators, and you'll help control aphids.

If an aphid infestation is bad enough that you need to kill them with a chemical regardless of what happens to the aphid-killing creatures, use diazinon, malathion, or orthene (the latter on non-edibles only).

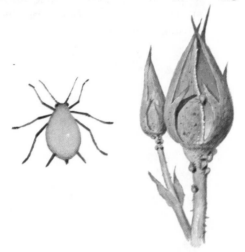

Aphids come in many shapes and colors, with and without wings. Here you see a single small green rose aphid (left) and a pair of rosebuds with a colony of them sucking sap.

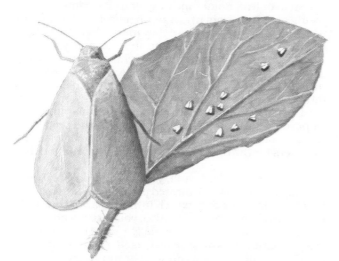

Spider mites rank in the top 10 home garden pests throughout the West and are in the top 3 in interior regions.

As the illustration and caption at left tell you, the first and sometimes the only sign of mite damage is yellow stippling of leaves. The trouble is, yellowing leaves can come from many causes. To confirm that it's mite damage, hold a piece of white paper beneath the branch and give the main stem a sharp hit. If there are mites, the blow will knock some onto the paper. They will look like tiny moving specks. With some mites on some plants, you also see fine, spider-like webbing across the leaves and around the stems.

By the time you see the stippling damage, it's generally too late to do anything about it—for the current year. The next year, however, you can watch the leaves closely (use a hand lens) and go into action when you first see mites. Then, if it's a small plant, jet it thoroughly with water from the hose to wash off the mites, the webbing, and the dust that has fallen on the leaves since the last rain—dust seems to make mite infestations worse.

If you can't wash off the plant, or if washing is not effective, the most effective chemical product is kelthane. If the infestation is severe, apply it a second time 7 to 10 days after the first application.

Many natural predators keep mites in check most of the time. Some of the predators—lacewing larvae and five different species of predatory mites—are bred and sold by biological control companies.

Typical mite damage—stippled yellow. To the naked eye, mites look like dust specks. At upper left, much enlarged, is a two-spotted mite, a common type.

WHITEFLIES

These annoying creatures made the top 10 in every part of the West. In recent years, whiteflies have definitely become more widespread and more troublesome in home gardens. But their significant life cycle and their tricky built-in defenses remain defiantly the same.

Nature keeps whiteflies in check most of the time by a number of tiny wasp species that parasitize the nymphs and pupae and by some predatory bugs that also feed on them. When you spray with a chemical, you can kill the parasites and predators and thereby increase the whitefly infestation. So, before you apply a chemical, consider:

- You could just eliminate the highly susceptible plant(s) from your garden.
- On a plant such as squash, get rid of old, nonproductive yellow leaves near the center. They carry the most whitefly eggs, pupae, and nymphs.
- Try hosing off the infested plants, hitting both sides of all leaves. Water doesn't get the flying adults but it can wash off and destroy immature crawlers (nymphs). Do it every few days. To put more authority in your hydraulic killing, use a solution of insecticidal soap; it is less harmful to natural enemies than conventional insecticides.

You can buy and release in your garden a commercially reared natural parasite; *Encarsia* wasps. They will parasitize greenhouse whitefly (that's a species) in a greenhouse or outdoors. There are some less-widespread whitefly species that *Encarsia* do not kill.

Yellow cards or stakes covered with sticky stuff and placed next to plants, attract the adults and kill them.

If you decide to make the insecticide commitment, be sure to spray at 4-to-6-day intervals (every Saturday won't work). For nonedibles, use these chemicals: cygon, orthene, resmethrin, dursban; for edibles: pyrethrins, malathion.

At left, adult whitefly enlarged—in real life it's about ⅛ inch long. On the leaf underside are 10 more of them. More advanced colonies also contain eggs, nymphs, and pupae.

This is a grass-hopper nymph —no wings yet. May to October, this kind inhabits grasslands (and sometimes gardens) in Colorado, New Mexico, Arizona.

GRASSHOPPERS

Grasshoppers own the West except where coastal weather is felt.

When you are cultivating in fall, winter, and early spring, watch for and destroy their egg clusters: up to 75 cream to yellow eggs shaped like grains of rice.

In spring and early summer, when the newly hatched grasshoppers are still young, they are most vulnerable to chemicals and baits. Use malathion, diazinon, sevin, dursban, or bran-and-sevin baits.

Nosema locustae, a commercially packaged disease-producing organism, works on grasshoppers in large applications (ranches) but not in small plots (gardens).

In summer, when the grasshoppers get bigger and less vulnerable, hand-pick adults, fling them to the ground, and stomp on them.

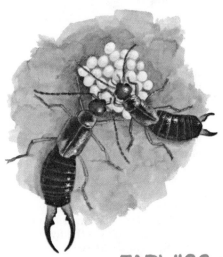

Earwig couple at their nest: male with long forceps, female with short. They use the forceps mostly to do earwig things and can't pinch you hard with them.

EARWIGS

Gardeners in all climates except the desert complained about earwigs. In the San Francisco Bay Area and along the northern California coast, they are garden damager number two.

In small numbers, earwigs do trifling damage to plants, and they do eat aphids and other pests but if they damage your plants and flowers, go after them. Earwigs feed at night and hide by day; they like their hiding places snug. At night put rolled-up newspapers, rolls of corrugated cardboard, or short sections of garden hose on the ground. In the morning, dump their earwig contents into kerosene or hot water. Or try earwig bait—the killing ingredient is baygon or sevin (carbaryl). If the attractant is fish oil, which can attract pets, be careful.

A capital H mark on its back identifies this as black scale—it's on the branches and leaf backs of an olive tree. These are adults; they lay eggs and hatch young under their shells.

SCALE INSECTS

Scale insects abound in the West; the only places where they didn't make the top list were in desert areas. There are hundreds of kinds, but the common ones divide into two classes: armored and soft. One big difference: soft scales produce honeydew (sticky stuff that falls on surfaces below and often turns black), armored scales do not.

Baby scale insects hatch beneath the stationary mother, stuck for its life (usually one year) to its place on the stem or leaf. Sometime in spring or summer, the young crawl out from under mother and move to another position on the plant where they insert their sucking mouth and begin to become big and stationary.

If you must spray scale with a chemical insecticide, do it when crawlers might be out. Generally the recommendation is diazinon, malathion, or orthene in spring; oil spray or oil spray plus malathion or diazinon in winter. Don't spray for scale unless a valuable plant is in jeopardy—naturally occurring parasites and predators usually control scale insects or keep them in low enough numbers for the host plant to survive and function in good health.

In dry, dusty California, you can help nature. Frequently wash off scale-infested plants with hose and water to get rid of the dust which inhibits parasites and predators (there are many). Also, you can buy and release aphytis wasps, commercially-reared natural parasites of some kinds of scale insects. Keep ants out of plants with diazinon or dursban granules, by banding the trunks with bands of sticky ant barrier, by putting a ring of silica powder around the base of the trunk, or by using poison ant sticks. Ants tend and protect scale insects just as they do aphids.

At lower left, a pillbug walking. At lower right, a pillbug in the pill position. At top, the close relative, the sowbug.

At top, a cutoff seedling and the cutworm that did it (a nighttime scene you'd see with flashlight). Lower right, a cutworm curls up as you'd find him in his daytime hiding place.

SOWBUGS & PILLBUGS

Sowbugs and pillbugs didn't make the top 10 anywhere in the West, but they got enough votes everywhere except western Oregon and Washington to make the West's top 36.

Mostly these creatures eat decaying vegetation. But they can eat seedlings and also overripe vegetables and berries after some other agent has broken the skin. If they bother your garden, apply sevin to the seedlings or to the ground where they are active. Also, keep your compost—which sowbugs love—as far as possible from vegetables and berries. Also keep surfaces raked clean.

CUTWORMS

There are many kinds of cutworms: they all work at night or on overcast days, and most can cut off young plants at the ground—hence their name. In the daytime they hide in the ground, curled up as shown.

Once you lose certain kinds of seedlings to cutworms, you should thereafter protect those kinds of seedlings, physically if possible. Put a barrier around each seedling the day it sprouts or the day you plant it. One easy barrier is a cutoff milk carton sleeve with 1 inch below soil level, 2 inches above, and with at least an inch between the sleeve and the plant. As an extra, put petroleum jelly or sticky ant barrier along the upper edge.

Some cutworms crawl up into plants and eat buds, leaves, and fruit. One way to keep them out is with the sticky ant barrier spread around base of the trunk.

Either barrier system is easy with just a few plants, impossible with great numbers. If you can't put up barriers, try hand-picking by night with a flashlight.

Many cutworm species prefer weeds as hosts, but when the weeds dry up they move to garden plants.

Cutworms in lawns are another matter. They hatch from eggs that the moths laid there—so there's no excluding them. What you see in the daytime, in grass or dichondra, are small bare patches that get bigger fast, day by day. If you are in doubt whether or not it's cutworms in your lawn, go out several hours after sunset and examine the lawn with a flashlight. To whatever degree possible, hand-pick and destroy the worms.

Chemicals do not work very well on large (mature) cutworms, but they can be effective on young ones. For lawn cutworms, apply diazinon according to label instructions. For seedling-eating cutworms you can try dusting the ground with sevin where they live and feed.

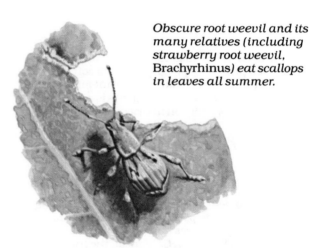

Obscure root weevil and its many relatives (including strawberry root weevil, Brachyrhinus) eat scallops in leaves all summer.

ROOT WEEVILS

More than a dozen root weevils are found in western Oregon and Washington and northern California. Flightless adults eat U-shapes from leaves of many plants, especially azaleas, rhododendrons, roses, viburnums, from June through fall. Larvae eat roots mainly in spring.

To control adults (shown above), which only feed at night, apply orthene. To control the pinkish or whitish-bodied, tan-headed larvae, treat soil with caterpillar nematode (*Neoaplectana carpocapsae*). The nematodes (too small to see) are packaged in a paste or in shavings. You apply them on the soil; they can also kill other soil-dwelling larvae. No home garden chemical product can kill root weevil larvae.

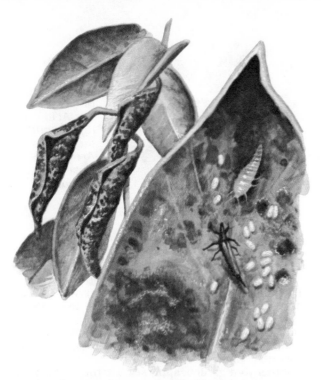

Little white eggs, tan nymphs, black adults, curled-up leaves—it's Cuban laurel thrips, a pest in Southern California. It's darker and twice as big as the more widespread kinds.

Cottony tuft near undersides of leaf joints is mealybug. Much-enlarged inset of body, with waxy, mealy fuzz scraped off, shows a soft-plated oval underneath.

THRIPS

On the Southern California coast, thrips were cited as serious garden pests. They feed by rasping soft flower and leaf tissue and then drinking the plant juices that come forth. Overall effect on most plants is a silvery or tan cast to leaves, a distortion or discoloration of flower parts, and a distortion of fruit. The species shown above is unusual in the noticeable curl it puts in the leaves of its host plant, Indian laurel fig *(Ficus microcarpa)*.

Many kinds of thrips spend spring on weeds and native plants and, when these plants dry up in late spring and summer, move to garden plants. They breed fast. They can be a problem starting in May and increasing as the season goes on. Thrips are notorious on the flowers of white and light pink roses and on the leaves and flowers of gladiolus. In Southern California, the trick is to do all your gladiolus planting from October to January and enjoy the flowers from January to April. Then, by the time thrips season comes in May, it's "sorry, guys, no glads left."

Cuban laurel thrips were first found in Southern California in 1959. They never destroy the host trees, but can make them look bad. Best control is the systemic insecticide meta-systox-R. On roses, gladiolus, and other ornamental hosts, malathion and orthene also work—use them if the infestation reaches an intolerably damaging level. On edible plants, use malathion. Natural enemies of the ficus thrips have been imported from Cuba for study and may ultimately be released in Southern California. The natural enemies of flower thrips are numerous, including ladybird beetles and larvae, green lacewing larvae, some parasitic wasps, and predaceous thrips.

MEALYBUGS

A close relative of scale insects, the mealybug plagues coastal and southern inland portions of California. Unlike scale, it can move around at a very slow crawl. It sucks plant juices, causing stunting or death. Often, a black sooty mold grows on the honeydew excreted by mealybug colonies.

Untouched mealybugs look woolly. If you remove the "wool" and see a flattish creature like the one in the drawing, you've got mealybugs.

The mature males are tiny, winged, and about the size of an adult whitefly. During mating, from sunset to dusk on warm days, the males hover around plants infested by the females. A female deposits about 300 orange or yellow eggs in clusters on the host plant. In 10 days, the eggs hatch; smooth-bodied, immature mealybugs crawl freely on the plant.

Although we speak of them here as outdoor pests, mealybugs are also one of the prime house plant pests. For any infestation indoors or for a minor infestation outdoors, daub mealybugs with a cotton swab dipped in rubbing alcohol; the white tufts turn light brown and the insects die. Outdoors hose with jets of water every two to four weeks to remove mealybugs and their eggs as well as dust, which deters beneficial insects. As with aphids, scale, and whiteflies, controlling ants is important; the ants maintain the mealybugs.

Natural predators such as ladybird beetles can help keep mealybugs in check: commercially available predators and parasites also do away with mealybugs: lacewing larvae and Cryptolaemus beetles. Before your plants get too weak from mealybug feeding or too coated with honeydew, spray with malathion or diazinon.

The geranium budworm takes on the color of what he just ate. At center of flower cluster is a big green worm; he just ate green tissue. The reddish one at lower right just ate some red petals.

C-shaped leaf cutout and body shape (sway-backed from side view) identify leaf-cutting bee. It's beneficial even though it cuts rose leaves like this and carries cutouts to its nest.

GERANIUM BUDWORMS

In the 1960s and '70s, the geranium budworm ballooned from complete obscurity to first-rank garden pest in California gardens. It is closely related to another familiar garden troublemaker, the corn earworm. Both are heliothids and members of the noctuid family—adults are stout-bodied, dull-colored, night flying moths.

Geranium budworm overwinters in soil as a pupa. In late April or May, it emerges as a gray, nightflying moth and lays eggs on geranium buds, one per bud. The eggs are a translucent green, about the size of sugar grains.

From these eggs hatch very small worms that enter and feed upon geranium buds (also petunias). Once you see a hole in such a bud, pick the bud and throw it away. It contains a young larva, it can't bloom, and you'll be destroying one larva with each such bud. The larvae in the picture above are further advanced; they have emerged from the buds.

The best control for budworms is *Bacillus thuringiensis*. Dusting each bud head with sevin seems to prevent eggs from being laid there.

Geranium budworm also resembles corn earworm in reproductive habits—both mate and lay eggs according to a definite moon pattern (see page 58 of the *Sunset New Western Garden Book*).

A biological control product especially for control of heliothids has been in development in recent years. It is elcar, a microbe that attacks these larvae and no other organisms. Its chief use is in cotton and other farm crops on which the heliothids are troublesome, but it should become available to home gardeners during the mid-1980's.

LEAF-CUTTING BEES

Even though the leaf-cutting bee is definitely a beneficial insect, the garden clubs in Phoenix, Tucson, and several other Arizona towns voted to put the creature on their lists of top garden troublemakers. The trouble is that its benefits go mostly to farmers and not to home gardeners. The bee is extremely efficient at pollinating the flowers of alfalfa that is being grown for seed. Arizona and Nevada growers put old refrigerators, old cars, and lean-tos in their fields to serve as shelters for opened packages of soda straws or boards with holes drilled in them in which these bees can lay their eggs in their own peculiar fashion.

A typical nest tube consists of alternative layers of foliage discs, bee eggs, and pollen to serve as food for the soon-to-hatch larvae.

Leaf-cutting bees seem to prefer rose leaves and bougainvillea leaves for lining their nests. The bees also cut discs from developing rose buds, making holes in the flowers later.

In nature, leaf-cutting bees lay and wrap the eggs in hollow stems. At the rose plant, the bee quickly cuts out a circular piece of leaf or flower, rolls it up, and flies it back to its nest, where it uses the piece as a wrapper or lining around each egg it lays.

Here's a case where you shouldn't put out chemical controls, even if there were any that were effective (there aren't). Be philosophical: take pleasure in the knowledge that your scalloped rose leaves or flowers are helping to produce more pollinating insects—nowadays the plant world seems continually to need more of them. Healthy rose plants almost always live through the depredation no matter how severe.

In real life you wouldn't see this scene. The leaf roller larva stays rolled up in his leaf all day. If you unrolled it, you'd find a larva like the one protruding at left.

LEAF ROLLERS

This member of the butterfly-and-moth order was voted into the top bracket in the mountainous West. The eggs are laid in Fall; the larvae hatch and overwinter in cracks in the bark of their host tree. The larvae grow and eat—the bigger they grow, the more they eat. For the first few weeks, while the larvae are about the size of long rice grains (but green), they eat day and night.

After they get about half-grown, they begin to hide in daytime by folding leaves together, as illustrated. At night they crawl out of their folded leaves and feed elsewhere on the plant.

Even at maturity the leaf rollers are not very big—about ½-inch long. When disturbed, leaf roller larvae thrash about violently.

The two commonest kinds are the fruit-tree leaf roller and the oblique-banded leaf roller. The latter feeds on more than 40 kinds of domestic plants; the fruit-tree species pretty much limits its diet to fruit trees.

After a while, the larvae pupate; the pupa is a light brown or green segmented cylinder within the rolled-up leaf. From it emerges the moth. The females lay flat clusters of eggs which they cover with a waterproof cement. From those clusters, the tiny larvae emerge to start the cycle again. The oblique-banded leaf roller goes through two such generations a year; the fruit-tree kind goes through just one.

Leaf rollers are subject to a number of parasitic insects. Light infestations are easy to take care of physically (just pick off and destroy rolled leaves).

Use chemical controls when leaf rollers' numbers are such that you believe you'll lose a crop or a plant. The favorite spray control for leaf roller seems to be *Bacillus thuringiensis*. The surest chemical sprays are diazinon, sevin and orthene (for nonedible plants only). Don't use any of the chemical sprays if the bees are out.

Deeply veined wings distinguish an oak moth; real damagers are the black-and-yellow-striped caterpillars. You may find the pupae (at top) hanging from leaves, limbs, and fences.

OAK MOTHS

California oak moth is big enough to rank as a major pest in coastal California, mostly in the San Francisco and Monterey bay areas.

The tan, inch-wide moths lay eggs in live oak trees twice a year (three times if winters are unseasonably mild). The first generation of larvae hatch in November and overwinter on live oak leaves, growing and eating more as weather warms in March and April. Full-size worms are about an inch long and look like the one pictured above, with bulbous brown heads and distinct black and olive or yellow stripes. Their pupae emerge as fluttery moths in June and July, and their offspring eat leaves again from late July to October. The worms aren't a problem every year; big outbreaks occur in cycles. Populations may get heavy enough to defoliate trees for two or three years in a row, then almost disappear for several years.

In late March or April, look for little green pellets (droppings of feeding larvae) falling from live oaks. Even if the population is heavy (a pan under the tree is a good gauge), trees can get by without treatment. However, if the loss of shade or the messy droppings raining on patios, walks, and people can't be tolerated, you can have the tree sprayed.

Spray operators use three controls: BT *(Bacillus thuringiensis)*, sevin, and orthene. BT won't harm natural predators and parasites (oak worms have many). BT needs to be applied as soon as worms are big enough to eat through leaves completely. As worms grow larger, they're more difficult to kill with BT.

Sevin and orthene kill all sizes of worms quickly. Both are highly toxic to bees.

At left, the 1-inch-long moth that lays the eggs, at lower right a typical colony of the skeletonizers, at upper right a damaged grape leaf—eaten down to the leaf's "skeleton."

GRAPE-LEAF SKELETONIZERS

This creature in some recent years has become a rather serious pest of grape vines in the low deserts and in California's San Joaquin Valley.

If you find colonies of skeletonizers on just one or two grape leaves, pick and destroy those leaves and larvae immediately. To prevent a heavy infestation, put on the insecticide cryolite in May, at grape blooming time. Get it onto *all* surfaces, top and bottom. The important thing is to apply the cryolite when the first brood is out laying eggs. Call your county agent or farm advisor to get best timing for this year's brood in your area.

The color, the size (⅝ inch long), and the shape identify this as an adult squash bug. It completely wilts squash and pumpkin leaves and damages the fruit. It emits a bad odor, too.

SQUASH BUGS

This creature makes the top 10 in the high deserts. It feeds only on squash-family plants. In spring, adults lay eggs on squash or melon leaves—if you find a mass of dark orange eggs crowded together on a leaf underside, destroy it. The bugs spend nights under flat objects, so put boards out in evening; in early morning, flip them over and kill the squash bugs. Three chemicals will work but they are hazardous to bees: sevin, diazinon, malathion. Rotenone dust works and is safe around bees.

Powdery white patches sapped these rose leaves of nutrients, distorting them. Mildew also attacks stems; note white patches on thorns.

POWDERY MILDEW

A fungus that is notorious on roses but also has forms that attack calendula, dahlias, and certain other plants, powdery mildew is the third worst pest in the West, according to our survey; it ranked among the top four in all areas except coastal Southern California.

Mildew thrives in inland areas, in foggy coastal areas, and in overcrowded plantings in damp, shady gardens where air circulation is minimal. But it needs dry leaves to become established. On many kinds of plants, powdery mildew is evident when days are warm and nights cool; shorter days when the amount of sunshine declines also encourage powdery mildew.

The disease first appears as small circular patches on plant tissue. These develop into powdery areas of fungus filaments laden with spores that spread rapidly, covering leaves, stems, or buds—or all of these depending on the type of mildew. Infected leaves become crumpled and distorted as fungus saps nutrients from the plant and injures the cells.

Powdery mildew generally attacks young growth of woody plants such as roses, and older, more mature leaves of nonwoody plants such as dahlias. But one type attacks both new and old leaves of tuberous begonias.

Some rose varieties are more susceptible to mildew than others; kinds with leathery, glossy leaves are much less mildew-prone than dull, soft-leaved kinds. Ask your nurseryman for help in choosing the most mildew-resistant varieties.

The best cure is prevention. Start with a program of early spraying and dusting. Before new growth appears, spray plants and soil with a dormant season spray of oil and lime sulfur. Phaltan and triforine (Funginex) can also help prevent spores from germinating. Grow susceptible plants in warm, sunny areas (except those that might discolor or burn in intense sun). Put them far enough apart to allow free air circulation among them. To help keep foliage spore-free, hose off plants with strong jets of water in the early morning.

If mildew appears, treat infected plants early with triforine, acti-dione PM, or karathane. Remove diseased stems. To prevent the disease from overwintering to infect next year's growth, rake up and destroy fallen leaves.

Orange pustules on rose leaf's undersides spell signs of this fungus disease.

Conspicuous fringed dark spots are easy-to-identify symptoms of black spot, a disease that attacks roses.

BLACK SPOT

This disease thrives in high humidity and in areas where summer rainfall is common; gardeners in the Northwest reported it especially troublesome. Dark spots on the foliage are usually circled with yellow; in severe cases, entire leaves yellow and fall off.

Spores live through winter in cane lesions and on old leaves on the ground. They germinate in spring and are carried to new leaves by splashing water.

Keep dead leaves picked up. Apply sulfur dust, captan, benomyl, wettable sulfur, triforine (Funginex), or phaltan spray to new foliage.

RUST

Gardeners in coastal Southern California rank this fungus disease among the top 10 pests. Winter rains, moist summer fogs, favorable temperatures, and cool nights—combined with heavy dew that lingers on the foliage well into morning—favor its growth (leaf surfaces must be continuously wet for 4 hours for spores to germinate). Rust sometimes disappears during summer hot spells; spores can't survive temperatures in excess of 80° much longer than a week.

Although primarily a rose pest, rust has different strains that attack hollyhocks, snapdragons, and certain other plants (One strain of rust is such a pest on snapdragons that some gardeners avoid growing these plants). On roses, the disease usually appears in late spring as small, roughly circular rusty orange spots on leaf undersides; these enlarge to thick, powdery masses of orange spores as yellow blotches (sometimes bordered with light green) appear on the leaf surface. Stem lesions are long and narrow; leaf lesions are slightly cup-shaped.

In rust's advanced stages, entire leaves yellow and fall off. Shoots may be deformed. In cooler areas during late summer, orange spores may develop into blotches of black spores that can survive over the winter. Insects, rain, or wind spread the disease; spores germinate on damp fallen leaves.

Basic good gardening practices help control rust. At first signs of the disease, pick off and destroy infected leaves before they fall to the ground. Clean up leaves and debris around rose bushes where spores can overwinter. Prune and destroy infected stems. To avoid spreading the disease to neighboring plants, don't water leaves of infected bushes.

Early in the growing season, treat plants with sulfur, triforine (Funginex) or phaltan (follow directions on labels). Where rust is a severe problem, spray dormant canes and soil with oil or lime sulfur; this will destroy many of the other organisms, including mildew and black spot, that might otherwise live over the winter.

Oak root fungus (Armillaria) mushrooms are tan with stem ring, gills joining stem.

OAK ROOT FUNGUS

Oak root fungus attacks many trees and woody plants in the low elevations of California (but not in the desert).

Winter symptom is clusters of mushrooms growing on or near the plant. The tree dies back, but leaves may hang on for months. If you think one of your trees has it, peel bark in several places at soil surface. Just under the bark, flat, white, creamy layers of mycelium indicate the disease.

In summer, avoid watering close to trunks of susceptible trees and shrubs. The only treatment: uncover the infected root crown and leave it exposed to air.

Fireblight, a bacterial disease that hits plants in the rose family. Stems quickly wilt, curl, darken and dehydrate as shown.

Wiry, jointed stolons of this grass may run out several feet from the crown, rooting where they touch soil. Thin, claw-like seed head, at left, has 5 spikes (3 to 5 are typical).

FIREBLIGHT

Although it occurs in many places, fireblight made the list of top troublemakers only in the high elevations. In the mountains—especially the eastern slope of the Rockies—the disease can be vexatious indeed.

Plants that get it include apple, cotoneaster, crabapple, flowering quince, hawthorn, mountain ash, pear, pyracantha, quince, and other members of the rose family *(Rosaceae)*.

In spring, the disease can be carried from previously diseased branches to flowers by insects, and from the flowers the disease moves into the plant tissue. Splashy rain can also spread the disease. Warm temperatures (above 60° daily average), combined with wet weather, favor fireblight's development.

For trees and shrubs that regularly get this disease in spring, it's wise to spray every four to seven days during the flowering season—if temperatures are warm—with a copper based spray (can cause minor blemishes on developing pears) or streptomycin. The more it rains during the blooming season the more frequently you should apply it.

Infections can also enter the tree through any kind of fresh wound in the bark or foliage, including pruning cuts or hailstone bruises.

If at any time during the year you see a branch that looks like the one shown above, quickly remove and dispose of it. Look for healthy bark and leaves below the infected area and make your cut well into healthy tissue with no symptoms of disease. On a small branch, you might make the cut 4 inches into healthy tissue, but on a big branch, 12 to 18 inches would be better.

If you are going to make more than one cut, disinfect the shears so you won't introduce the bacteria elsewhere. Dip the shears for 20 to 30 seconds in rubbing alcohol or a 10 percent solution of household bleach. If you use the bleach, wash and dry the blade afterward —bleach solution can corrode steel shears.

BERMUDA GRASS

This fine-textured perennial is a well-established lawn grass and the second most difficult garden weed in low elevations of California, Arizona, and New Mexico. A fast-growing native of warm, Old World areas, Bermuda grass spreads by seeds, underground by rhizomes, and aboveground by stolons. If not carefully confined, roots invade shrubbery and flower beds and can be difficult to eradicate once established.

If stray clumps do turn up in flower beds, pull or hoe them before they form sod. Be sure to remove all of the underground stem; otherwise, it can start new shoots. Or spray isolated patches with glyphosate. Where patches are too big to hoe out of a lawn, apply glyphosate in fall as common Bermuda slows its growth (avoid desirable plants nearby). Repeat applications may be necessary. To get rid of an entire Bermuda grass lawn, see page 124 for methods.

As a lawn, Bermuda grass has its drawbacks: it turns brown when frosted (even in frost-free areas, it turns a scruffy combination of brown and dull green in winter), it grows poorly in shade, and it builds up a thatch of old stolons unless you follow a thatch-removal program. During summer, it produces unsightly seed heads three days after mowing.

But common Bermuda can make a decent lawn (tough underfoot, heat tolerant, relatively unthirsty, pest- and disease-free) if you understand its needs and are willing to tolerate its drawbacks.

Mow the lawn often enough to keep seed heads from forming (twice a week in hot weather). To keep runners from invading flower beds, edge the lawn each time you mow. Water lawn deeply and regularly (about once a week) and dethatch lawn every October. To dethatch, rough up stolons with a thatch-cutting machine (you can rent one) or a rake for small areas, then mow closely to remove them. Fertilize with a high-nitrogen fertilizer every month from early spring (or whenever grass starts to green up) until November (except July and August when growth is robust enough).

For winter color in the lawn, overseed common Bermuda with a cool season grass. Hybrid Bermudas can crowd out common Bermuda in time (a plus since they're finer in texture and better in color than the common kind), but they are harder to overseed.

Three heart-shaped lobes make up this perennial weed's clover-like leaves, sometimes tinged red.

Spotted leaves identify this prostrate weed. Seed capsules (between leaves) burst in hot weather.

YELLOW OXALIS

This aggressive weed thrives throughout the West in sun or shade; gardeners in central and southern California rated it especially troublesome. It grows mainly in lawns and greenhouses, spreading quickly by seed. Yellow flowers are followed by pointed seed capsules that open like popcorn as they dry and shoot seeds as far as 6 feet. In mowed lawns, clumps stay low and tight. In flower beds, they grow rangier and tangle up with desirable plants.

Seedlings start out from a single taproot that soon develops into a shallow, spreading, knitted root system.

Control is difficult. Dig out small plants, or carefully spot-treat isolated plants with glyphosate. In lawns, 2,4-D or a combination of 2, 4-D, MCPP, and dicamba provide some control.

A vigorous, well-fertilized lawn provides tough competition for oxalis. Frequent surface watering encourages the shallow-rooted weed; water the lawn less frequently and more deeply.

SPOTTED SPURGE

A demon in hot weather, this aggressive summer annual was put at the top of the list in inland areas of Southern California and the desert. It grows from a shallow taproot in exposed areas such as sparse lawns, garden walks, and flower beds. It spreads fast; in as little as a month each plant can produce several thousand seeds in clusters of tiny pinkish seed capsules. Oblong, ¼- to ⅜-inch leaves have reddish green undersides. Cut stems exude a milky juice. Plants turn red-orange and decline in fall (especially noticeable in lawns) as temperatures drop. Seeds germinate as early as January in Palm Springs, and seedlings start active growth when temperatures warm up in spring.

Control is difficult. Hoe out isolated plants early before they produce seed, or spray them with glyphosate. On lawns (except dichondra), use a pre-emergent broadleaf herbicide such as DCPA (dacthal). Watch for small plants in areas that have been problems in past years. A vigorous, well-fertilized lawn provides tough competition for spurge.

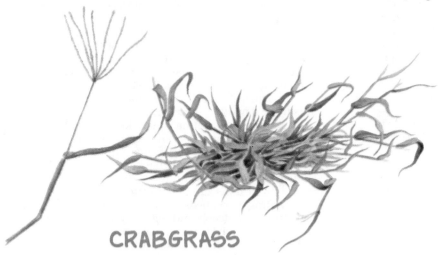

These crabgrass leaves are hairy (some kinds have smooth leaves). Spikes on the seed head (shown close up) can develop from a central point, as shown, or from different points.

CRABGRASS

The infamous summer annual grows well in hot, damp areas; most votes for its pest status came from garden clubs in California's Central Valley and southern interior. A shallow-rooted weed, it thrives in lawns that get frequent surface watering, in underfed lawns, and in poorly drained fields.

Seeds germinate in early spring in Southern California, later in northern California. As the plant grows, it branches out at the base; stems can root where they

touch the soil. Seed heads form in mid- to late summer. As crabgrass declines in fall, it turns purplish, becoming especially noticeable in lawns.

In flower beds, pull up crabgrass before it makes seeds. Keep lawns well fertilized and vigorous to provide tough competition for weeds; to dry out crabgrass roots, water lawns deeply and less frequently. Control in spring with a granular pre-emergent such as DCPA applied with a fertilizer spreader. Otherwise, apply DSMA or MSMA.

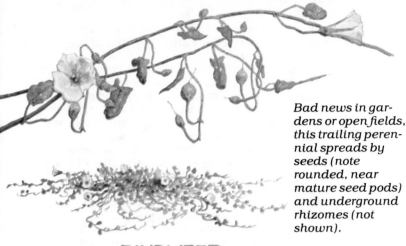

Bad news in gardens or open fields, this trailing perennial spreads by seeds (note rounded, near mature seed pods) and underground rhizomes (not shown).

BINDWEED

Also called wild morning glory, bindweed grows in open, exposed areas—usually in loam to heavy clay soils—throughout the West, but in our survey gardeners in the Northwest, northern California, and mountain states indicated it as a troublemaker. Bindweed crawls over the ground and twines over and around other plants, competing with them for nutrients and light. Pale, white to pink funnel-shaped flowers appear in late summer or early fall before the plant goes dormant for winter.

When you pull it, stems break off but the frequently deep roots and underground stems are left. The more you break it, the more it sprouts. If allowed to go to seed, bindweed becomes nearly impossible to control: hard-coated seeds can lie dormant in the soil for years.

In midsummer, at plant's peak growth but before seeds are set, spray isolated patches with 2,4-D or glyphosate; repeat applications may be needed. If bindweed is intertwined with desirable plants, dig up roots where possible.

Devilish thorns on woody stems make this vigorous, fast-growing vine unfriendly when allowed to ramble out of control in a garden. Oval leaves are divided like a fan, with small but prickly thorns along the spines.

Golden flowers, seed-bearing puffballs make this perennial easy to identify. Toothed leaves, 2 to 12 inches long, form rosette at plant's base.

DANDELION

A familiar lawn weed throughout the West, dandelion got the most votes in Northwest and mountain states. It grows from a deep, fleshy taproot that breaks (and can regrow) when you try to pull the plant out. It spreads by wind-borne seeds and sprouting root crowns. Flowering begins in spring and often continues until frost; in mild weather, seeds can germinate year-round.

Pull out young plants before the taproot has a chance to grow much. On lawns, apply 2,4-D in spring and fall. Spray isolated plants with glyphosate, 2,4-D, or other herbicide for broad-leafed weeds.

BLACKBERRY

Of the three commonest blackberry varieties in the Northwest, 'Himalaya' is predominant. It grows wild in pastures and along highways, thriving in the mild, moist climates of western Oregon and Washington (where gardeners named it as a top pest). It can turn up in flower beds, gravel paths, or lawns.

The roots are perennial, but canes are biennial: they grow one year and flower and fruit the next. Blackberry spreads rapidly by underground runners and seeds; birds eat the ripe, shiny black berries in late summer and scatter the seeds willy-nilly across the landscape.

Pull out young plants in spring before feeder roots develop. Cut back established plants during the summer growing season when foliage is green (it's easier to dispose of fresh than dry); wear heavy gloves. Use a pick and shovel to dig up as many roots as possible.

Paint fresh shoots with glyphosate when 6 to 12 inches tall (spray only in isolated areas). Retreatment is usually necessary to control plants coming from dormant seeds, old and incompletely killed roots, and root crowns.

POCKET GOPHERS

Pocket gophers are troublesome in many areas of the West, but in coastal California they rank among the top three garden pests.

Like little bulldozers, these furry creatures dig a network of tunnels—usually 6 to 12 inches below the surface—with strong, clawed forefeet and powerful shoulders. Tunnels near the surface are for gathering food; deeper ones are for sleeping, storing food, and raising young. Gophers eat roots, bulbs, and sometimes plants. Well suited to burrow life, they have small eyes and ears that don't clog with dirt, sensitive whiskers and tail to guide them forward or backward through a dark tunnel, and small hips that allow them to turn around in tight spaces. Their long teeth can bite off chunks of hard earth or roots when the burrowing gets tough.

Trapping is the most widely used and efficient method of catching gophers; see page 62 of the *Sunset New Western Garden Book* for trap-setting guidelines.

Clobbering a gopher with a shovel can work after the victim has been flushed from his tunnel by flooding (level ground only) or gassing. Gassing is most effective only when all holes are blocked; otherwise, a groggy gopher may emerge from an unblocked hole and you'll have to dispatch him with other means. Water areas around tunnel first to prevent gas from seeping through soil in tunnel sides. Lighted highway flares can work better than gopher gassers.

Poison bait is available, but should be used with care since it's also poison to birds, fish, pets, and people; put it deep in the horizontal main tunnel as shown on page 62 of the *Sunset New Western Garden Book*.

If all else fails, line the bottom and sides of planting holes with light-gauge wire.

Fan-shaped mounds of loose dirt, pushed up from side runs off the main tunnels, distinguish gopher dwellings from mole hills; plugs of earth usually block this critter's exit holes.

MOLES

Notorious pests in good soils throughout the West (especially western Washington, according to our survey), moles have short forelegs tipped outward with large, flattened hands and claws for digging tunnels. Townsend's moles—most common in northwestern California, western Oregon, and Washington—have velvety blue-black fur and a nearly hairless tail and snout.

Insectivores, moles eat earthworms, bugs, and larvae, and only occasionally nibble greens and roots. Irrigation and rain keep them near the soil surface where they do the most damage as they tunnel: heaving plants from the ground, severing tender roots, and disfiguring lawns. Main runways, usually about 6 inches underground, may be used by several moles; feeder offshoots, often capped with volcano-shaped mounds, may be used only once.

Trapping is the most efficient control; the spear-type trap is easiest to set because you don't have to dig into the tunnel. Set scissor-jaw traps carefully into the main runway (probe with a sharp stick to find it); a wily mole will spring, heave out, or go around faultily set traps.

Pouring creosote, lye, tar, or drain-flushing granules into the tunnels may drive moles to more congenial hunting grounds, but these methods can injure plants and contaminate soil. Mole bombs can work if put directly in nests or in the main runways and all holes are blocked.

Whacking a mole with a shovel blade is effective but time-consuming; chances are best at dawn. If you see one scuttling below ground, try the two-shovel method: block the runway in front of him with one shovel blade and dig him out with the other.

Tunneling below the soil's surface, Townsend's mole pushes up ridges of soil that may damage delicate plant roots. It also makes conical mounds of soil above the ground when excavating tunnels.

SQUIRRELS

Tree-hugging fox squirrel (above) has a bushy tail and short ears. Speckled back, narrow tail, and cheek pouches (puffy when filled with nuts) distinguish Beechey ground squirrel (below) from similar-size Western gray squirrel.

Throughout the West, ground squirrels are especially troublesome in gardens that border fields or wild land, and gardeners in inland Southern California ranked them high on the list. The Beechey ground squirrel, illustrated below left, is commonest kind in California, western Oregon, and southwestern Washington; it lives in burrows usually 2½ to 4 feet underground, where it stores food, raises young, and hides when predators (foxes, hawks, or owls) cruise by.

During spring and summer, it scurries around most actively in midmorning or late afternoon, (except in very hot weather) nibbling through tomato patches, digging up bulbs, gnawing roots and bark, sometimes climbing low trees after fruit and nuts.

Controls include trapping with a baited, box-type trap placed outside the burrow, poison grains placed inside the burrow (requires five to six days of continuous feeding to work), and gas bombs placed well back in the burrow (make sure all entry holes are plugged). But check first with your county agent or farm advisor; laws in some areas prohibit catching ground squirrels.

Metal guards around tree trunks can keep ground squirrels out of trees. Protect bulb beds with a cover of fine-mesh chicken wire.

Tree squirrels are common pests around the West, but Southern California gardeners reported most damage from them. Fox squirrel is the commonest tree squirrel there. Introduced from the Eastern United States into parks and campuses in the West, it's usually rusty gray, but sometimes all gray or blackish.

Cute as these furry creatures may be, they can wreak havoc in a garden: biting chunks out of ripening fruit and dropping leftovers to the ground, stripping trees of bark and gnawing the cambium tissue beneath, munching off tender buds in spring. Occasionally, they sneak down from the trees to bury nuts that may sprout into trees in the lawn or in plant containers.

In some areas, tree squirrels are protected and can't be shot, poisoned, or trapped except with a live trap. You may need proof of extensive damage and a permit to kill them. If damage is serious, ask your county agent to recommend a trap (most often a live box trap hung on a tree branch); you may be required to release the squirrel in a park.

Otherwise, learn to live with the pesky creatures. Tie plastic bags or old nylon stockings around ripening fruit. Cover berry patches and wrap tomato plants with fine wire mesh. Protect soil around container plants from misplaced nuts with a layer of fine wire mesh.

ROOF RATS

Roof rats have become entrenched in Southern California. They damage many garden crops including avocados and citrus.

Algerian ivy, an omnipresent ground cover in Southern California, provides a nearly perfect home for rats. It gives them shelter, and the woody stems are a prime food source, as are the snails that hide under the leaves.

If you cut down on roof rats' food and water supply, they will regulate their own numbers naturally. Clear out places where rats hide—dense vegetation or piles of debris—and remove ripened fruit from trees or ground. Remove containers that catch water.

The most effective baits are the anticoagulant types that accumulate in the rat's system; keep a supply available, in a protected spot, at all times. If you use snap traps, try baiting them with walnut kernels or slices of apple tied or wired to the trigger.

Slender-bodied roof rat has pointy nose, large hairless ears, and a long, hairless tail. Snails are his gourmet food.

Pleased but wary fawn (it still has spots) lunches on tender beans in a vegetable garden.

DEER

These gentle creatures invade suburban fringe gardens mostly in western Washington and Oregon and northern California. With their soulful eyes and graceful gait, they may be pleasant to watch, but they can make a garden ragged in no time by chomping off flower heads and nibbling tender leaves. As wild plants dry out, deer spend more time in suburbia looking for food. They develop browsing patterns, visiting tasty gardens regularly—most often in the evening. They are fond of a wide array of flowering plants, especially roses, and will eat foliage or fruit of nearly anything you grow for your table except artichokes and figs. There are other plants that they usually ignore; for a list, see page 125 of the *Sunset New Western Garden Book*.

On level ground, 7-foot woven wire fences usually keep deer out, although some determined deer can jump an 8-foot fence. On sloping ground, a 10- to 11-foot fence may be necessary to guard against deer jumping from above.

If you don't want a fortress around your garden, try covering raised beds with mesh. Another approach is to keep a zealous watchdog always on the premises.

Commercial repellents work if you spray enough to keep new growth covered and replace what rain and watering wash away. Repellents may make sticky, unsightly spots on flowers and foliage, though. Some gardeners repel deer by hanging little cloth bags filled with blood meal among their plants (but it smells bad when wet).

CROWS

The Northwest crow and his slightly larger cousin, the common crow, made the top 10 nuisances in western Oregon and Washington. Crows don't hop the garden, they walk in flocks. After you sow corn, they systematically dig and eat the seeds. Later in the season, they return for fruits and berries.

The best defense against crows is a mesh barrier. Chicken wire folded into a tent shape works best over corn drills; bird netting is better over small fruit trees.

Noisemakers, scarecrows (move them frequently), and strips of foil hung in trees keep crows away for only a short time, so use them just when you really need them.

Crows are protected by treaty in the United States, but an exclusion in some states allows homeowners to kill ones that are injuring crops. Before you go to such an extreme, check with your area game warden or police for any local shooting limitations.

This Northwest crow, on stakeout in the bean patch, warns flock of danger.

GARDEN QUESTIONS & ANSWERS

In a way, gardening is a lifelong pursuit of information. Starting with the day when we buy our first packet of seeds, the questions begin. And they never stop. Layer by layer, we ask and learn our way deeper and deeper into the satisfying and infinitely deep fabric of gardening. That's what the next chapter of this book is about—the questions and problems that gardeners bring to our attention, and the answers that can help them.

Although, for obvious reasons, we cannot include the endless thousands of technical questions which would, in turn, require endless thousands of pages, we can—and do—give answers to more than 400 everyday questions that are most frequently asked of the garden editors of *Sunset Magazine* and *Sunset Books*. Without a book such as this, too often the earnest and important gardening questions would go begging for an answer.

This book and the questions asked and answered in it are meant to serve as a companion to the *Sunset New Western Garden Book.* In a number of cases you'll find the important rudiments of a question's answer given here and, with it, a reference to the page (or perhaps several different pages) of the *Sunset New Western Garden Book* where you can find more details or important related information.

In addition to this chapter's answers to specific questions and problems, many hundreds of additional answers are to be found in other parts of the book: Western climate zones (pages 4, 5), what-to-do-when (pages 6-31), pronunciations (pages 147-148), and gardeners' language (pages 149-153).

Below is a mini-index to the 17 sections which comprise this chapter.

ANNUALS & PERENNIALS

GUIDELINES FOR AVOIDING GENERAL PROBLEMS

Annuals and perennials are the basic flower producers. Annuals complete their life cycle in less than a year. Perennials live longer than two years. (For more particulars, see the first question below.)

The single most important way to keep annuals and perennials problem-free is to place the right plant in the right location. (Heat-loving zinnias can't produce in the shade; cinerarias love the cool shade and won't survive in the sunny spots.) To be sure you avoid problem locations, check the needs of individual plants in the encyclopedia section of the *Sunset New Western Garden Book.*

This chapter will provide you with answers to questions of a general nature, as well as solutions to some specific plant problems you might encounter. But keep in mind that the best way to deal with problems is to prevent them. Here are a few simple guidelines:
- Select healthy plants
- Prepare soil properly before planting
- Plant in the right location at the right time
- Follow a good watering, weeding, and feeding schedule
- Protect from pests and disease
- Mulch to retain water and discourage weeds

What are annuals? Perennials? Biennials?

Question: What is the difference between "annual" and "perennial?" I'm really confused when I read about "perennial grown as an annual." Also, what is an herbaceous perennial? And what does "biennial" mean?
Answer: To set the record straight, here are a few definitions:

Annual—A plant that completes its life cycle within a year and then dies. The life cycle of an annual typically starts when the seed germinates in late winter or early spring. The plant grows and flowers in spring or summer, then dies with the first frosts of fall.

Perennial—Distinguished from an annual by longer life. Wherever climate and garden conditions are suitable, a perennial will live—growing larger and blooming each year—for years. On the other hand, perennials are distinguished from shrubs by the lack of woody plant parts. When you read about an "herbaceous perennial," the term simply means "like an herb"—not woody. Many perennials die down to the ground at the end of the summer growing season, remain dormant and out of sight for the winter, and then grow new stems and leaves at the start of the next growing season in spring.

Perennial grown as an annual—A plant which can probably live for several years but which looks best in the garden when grown for 2 single seasons, then discarded.

Biennial—A small category of plants, neither annual nor perennial, is known as "biennial." These plants behave as though they were lazy annuals. Typically, biennials germinate from seed in spring and devote the first year's growing season to developing. During the second

spring or summer, the following year, they flower, set seed, and die at the end of that growing season.

Achillea in mid-life crisis

Question: For years I've had a large clump of achillea that blooms beautifully every summer. Now I notice that the center of the plant has died out, leaving it doughnut-shaped. Is this caused by disease?
Answer: Disease isn't the cause—your achillea has reached middle age. As the plant ages, the clump grows larger; the center contains the oldest part of the clump, while the newer growth expands around the outside.

When a perennial starts to die out in the center, nature is giving you a sure sign that it's time to divide the plant (fall is the best season). After pruning the plant down to about 6 inches, dig out the entire clump and discard the dead center. Break the outside ring of plants into any number of smaller clumps and replant.

My neighbor's annuals bloom sooner

Problem: The annuals I plant always seem to take longer to bloom than any of my neighbors'. I water them diligently and start fertilizing regularly a week or two after planting.
Solution: You are not getting the food to them quickly enough. Begin feeding immediately after planting in the garden. Dry, granular forms of complete fertilizer are effective, but the liquids are easier to use.

Will annuals reseed themselves?

Problem: I love annuals, but replanting a new flower garden every year is more than I have time for. Are there any annuals that will reseed themselves naturally without any help from me?

Answer: Any annual plant will take care of its own propagation—all it needs from you are proper climatic and cultural conditions. Some annuals, too, reseed freely in less than perfect conditions. Nonhybridized varieties of plants (those closest to the way they were in the wild) tend to reseed much more readily than hybrids.

Any unthirsty annuals?

Question: I've always thought of annuals as being thirsty plants. Here in Tucson, Arizona (Zone 12), the amount of water we're able to use is limited. Are there any annuals that do well with minimum watering?

Answer: Coreopsis, gaillardia, and portulaca all are fairly drought-tolerant. For lists of other unthirsty annuals and other kinds of plants, see pages 148–151, *Sunset New Western Garden Book.*

Are both OK in the same border?

Question: Are there problems with planting annuals and perennials in the same border?

Answer: No rule says that any gardener has to arrange a garden in any specific way. In fact, some of the most attractive flower borders contain not only annuals and perennials, but flowering shrubs, trees, herbs, and even a vegetable or two.

Birds peck at my poppies

Problem: Birds destroyed many of my young Iceland poppies. What can I do to make sure this doesn't happen again?

Solution: Newly set out plants of Iceland poppies should be protected from birds by using individual cones of screening; if the poppies are planted in a row, use a row cover made from the same material (see illustration).

These two won't take mollycoddling!

Question: Can I get the gold California poppy and the blue lupine I see growing so beautifully next to the highway to grow in my yard? Where can I buy plants?

Answer: These wildflowers are generally unavailable as plants, but the seeds are present in most seed racks throughout California. You can get these plants to grow in your garden if you don't baby them with too much water and fertilizer. Remember that where California poppies and lupines grow well, next to highways and on hillsides, conditions are relatively harsh. Neither plant is fussy about soil type and will self-sow, returning year after year. Remember, however, that they don't naturalize easily in meadows or any situation where tall grass can overwhelm them.

Double digging, double trouble?

Question: I have an old book about perennials that was my mother's, and the book practically insists on double-digging as the only way to insure success with perennials. Is this really necessary? It sounds like work to me.

Answer: Double-digging is a rather complex method of cultivating the soil to a depth of 2 feet or more, done in successive stages, that originated in England many years ago. There's no doubt that double-digging is double the work. There's also no doubt that it produces an exceptionally well-prepared bed for perennials. Most gardeners today, however, agree that double-digging may be overdoing it. Adding a liberal layer of organic matter (peat moss, redwood soil conditioner, composted manure, and the like) and tilling it into the soil to a depth of 9 inches, using a rotary tiller or spading fork, will produce a perfectly adequate planting bed for perennial plants.

For cut-flower continuity

Problem: I make floral arrangements for friends and my church so I need to grow an abundance of cut flow-

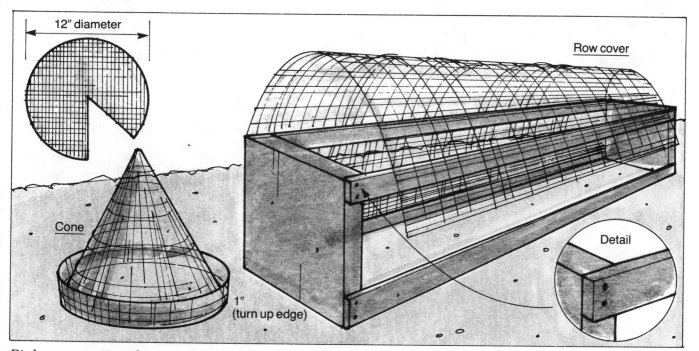

12" diameter

Row cover

Cone

1"
(turn up edge)

Detail

Birds can sometimes be nuisances, eating tender seedlings, transplants, fruits, nuts, and berries. Fine-mesh screen or nylon netting will give protection—cones for individual plants, wood frame for larger areas.

Also see pages 128–142, *Sunset New Western Garden Book*

ers. The trouble is, I have a lot of flowers early in summer and then they taper off to almost none until chrysanthemum time in the fall. How can I plant for better, constant flower production?

Solution: There are literally hundreds of choices for flower color, all four seasons of the year. For listings, and zones, see pages 128-135, *Sunset New Western Garden Book*.

My container combinations are disappointing

Problem: For the past couple of summers, I've tried to plant a variety of annuals together in different-sized containers, but the results have been disappointing. The combined effect has not been as lush and full as the pictures I see in the garden magazines. What am I doing wrong?

Solution: To get that lush, full look, you have to plant more flowers in the container than is generally advised. Use good-sized pots (at least 18 inches in diameter) and put a dozen or more plants in each. Pinch off the tips of the plants after planting to encourage bushiness, use a packaged soil mix to fill the pots, and fertilize every couple of weeks with a complete fertilizer at about half the recommended dosage. Or use a slow-release fertilizer at planting time and follow up with a liquid fertilizer every 3 weeks. Keep soil mix moist, and pick off dead blossoms every day or two.

My rocky slope needs color

Question: There is a hilly, somewhat rocky area in full sun that I see from the kitchen and dining-room windows. I would like to scatter seeds that would give a wildflower look and that would come back each spring without my having to replant. Are wildflower seeds available; will they reseed easily without much care?

Answer: Several seed companies specialize in seeds of native grasses and flowers, and some companies even package special wildflower mixtures for specific climatic regions. Check at your local nursery for more information on the names and addresses of such seed companies. Larger companies also offer less regionalized wildflower packs with seeds that naturalize almost anywhere.

It is important to plant these *early* (fall or winter), and to do at least a minimal amount of soil preparation.

Foxgloves failed me

Question: Why didn't the foxgloves I planted this year bloom?

Answer: How quickly foxgloves bloom depends on the age of the plants, their location, and what time of year they were set out. A strain called Foxy will bloom in 5 months from seed under ideal conditions. Small plants (from flats or 4-inch pots or smaller) set out in the spring will rarely put on much of show that year. Plants in 1-gal-

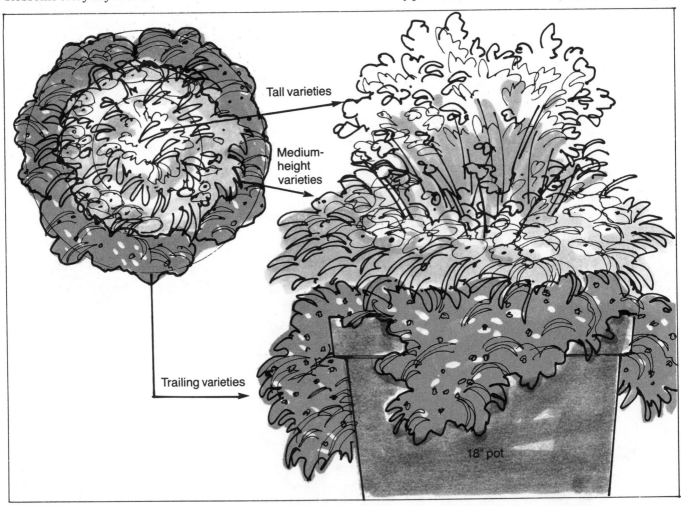

Tall varieties

Medium-height varieties

Trailing varieties

18" pot

Crowd about a dozen annuals into an 18-inch pot for a "living bouquet." Plant tall annuals in the center, circled by medium-height flowers, trailing varieties at the edges.

lon cans or larger are usually mature enough to bloom the same season they are planted. In mild winter climates you can set out small plants in the fall and expect flowers the following spring. Technically, most of the foxgloves in home gardens are biennials. Given the proper conditions, however (a semishaded spot and a humusy soil), foxgloves will self-seed freely and return year after year.

Geraniums in Salt Lake City?

Question: We are being transferred soon to Salt Lake City (Zone 2), and I plan to take geranium slips to plant there. Will the cold winters cause problems?
Answer: All pelargoniums, which include geraniums, are easy to grow and should do well in Zone 2 *if* they are treated as house plants, or grown as outdoor plants only in the summer. Pelargoniums can be grown outdoors year round only in mild climates with comparatively mild winters, such as those near the Pacific Ocean.

Gophers go for gypsophila

Problem: My gypsophila is just too attractive. What snails don't get, gophers do. Help!
Solution: The thick, deep-growing roots of gypsophila (baby's breath) are gourmet food for gophers. The best remedy is to construct wire baskets, similar to those you can make to ward off hungry gophers from lily bulbs. (See illustration below.) Snail bait, either in pellet or granule form, will stop slugs and snails from damaging the above-ground portion of the plant. For more information, see page 46 (gophers) and page 34 (snails).

My hanging baskets won't hold water

Problem: I have trouble watering my hanging wire baskets. The soil doesn't seem to absorb the water.
Solution: Most potting soils have difficulty absorbing water once they have been allowed to dry out; plants with this problem require saturation. Submerge the basket

in a bucket of water for a few minutes. This may not be necessary every time the basket needs watering, but it will help if the plant has gotten too dry to absorb water from a hand-held hose. (See illustration.)

Hanging wire baskets dry out quickly. To saturate, submerge in a bucket of water for a few minutes.

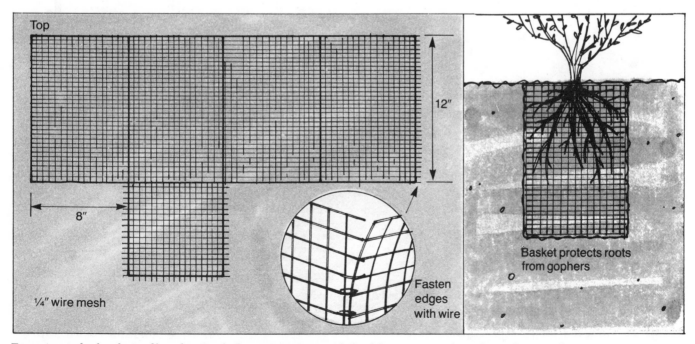

Easy-to-make basket, of hardware cloth, protects gypsophila, lilies, many other plants from gophers.

Horrible hollyhocks: how come?

Problem: I have a terrible problem with rust on hollyhocks. Every year it literally covers the plants and makes them look horrible. Can anything be done about it?

Advice: Rust is one of the more unsightly diseases, and unfortunately hollyhocks are highly susceptible. Methods for controlling rust are discussed on page 42. Because hollyhocks grow rapidly, several applications a week may be necessary to insure that all new leaves acquire protection.

Glum about 'mums, what happened?

Problem: My chrysanthemum plants are enormous. Although I've staked them, I'm afraid they will fall over. Also the number of blooms sure isn't overwhelming. I realize that it's too late this year to do anything about it, but what can I do next year?

Solution: The best way to guarantee more flowers and sturdy, compact plants is to start with new plants. Make tip cuttings from last year's 'mums from May through June. Plant the cuttings in a mixture of half peat moss and half sand. When the cuttings are well rooted (about 3 weeks) plant them in prepared soil. Tip-pinch several times before August 1 to keep plants compact.

However, many gardeners prefer to divide the old clumps, from April into June. Plant young side shoots and throw away the old part of the clump. Pinch back the tips several times before August 1 to produce bushier plants. Starting from divisions is especially recommended for small-flowered, mounding types of 'mums.

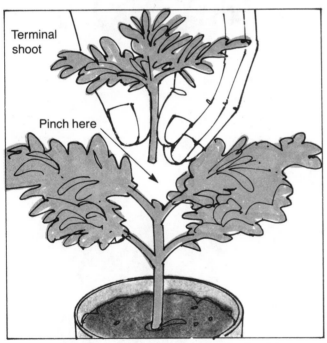

Pinch out the terminal shoot to encourage bushiness.

How can I grow "football" 'mums?

Problem: I want to raise those huge "football" 'mums, but the flowers on my plants are always small and the tall plants fall over. What am I doing that keeps the flowers so little and plants so tall?

Solution: Those big, 8-inch blooms sold in florists' shops and frequently at football games are specially raised for the industry and, at best, are a tricky business for most home gardeners. However, if you follow this procedure, you'll grow 'mums that are, if not immense, certainly *very* big.

First, start with plants of the *large varieties*, such as the big incurves and spider types (available from mail-order firms that specialize in chrysanthemums). From May through June, plant the new cuttings in a mixture of half sand and half peat moss; set out the small plants after they are well rooted, from June into July. Pinch back tips several times, with the last pinch in mid-July.

Remove all but 3 to 5 stems on each plant. Stake the *individual* stems. When the flower buds appear in September, remove all but the center bud in the terminal cluster of buds. (See the illustration.)

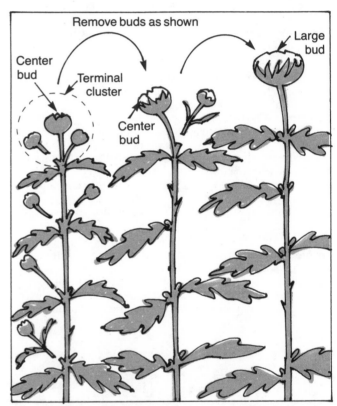

When flower buds appear on chrysanthemums, pinch out all but the center bud in each terminal cluster. Remaining bud will develop into large blossom.

Marigolds "growing out of their socks"

Problem: The marigolds I put in last month are growing "out of their socks." What should I do to make them less gangly and keep them from falling over?

Solution: Pinching (actually, fingertip-pruning) is in order. Almost all annuals benefit from removing the tips of the plants when they are 3 or 4 inches tall. Instead of a single, spindly stem, pinching encourages side branches that produce bushy plants and more flowers.

Mildew's messing my marigolds

Problem: What can I do about mildew on marigolds?

Solution: Marigolds thrive in all regions in locations that are warm, somewhat dry, and with full sun, but mildew prevails in areas that are damp and shaded, so it sounds as if you might have aggravated the problem by planting the marigolds in the wrong location in your garden. Or perhaps you live in an especially foggy, damp area.

If your marigolds seem content where they are despite the mildew, you can keep the plants healthier by maintaining a regular spray progam. Preventive spraying is particularly important, because the longer the mildew becomes established, the harder it is to keep in control. For more information, see page 41.

Mystery of the missing marigolds

Question: I planted a whole flat of small marigolds yesterday. This morning when I got up, there was hardly anything left of them. What ate them so quickly?
Answer: The tender transplants of many annuals, including marigolds, offer tasty treats for slugs and snails in many parts of the West. Immediately after setting out new transplants of any annuals, bait the area with slug and snail killer, just in case. Also, birds often devour seedlings; netting will keep them off.

Will nasturtiums stick around?

Question: I love nasturtiums—the leaves, the flowers, and the seed pods in salads. I would like to plant them in a small vegetable bed I no longer have time to work in. Would nasturtiums stick around for several years after one seeding? Seems to me that I've read that they will naturalize in some conditions.
Answer: Nasturtiums grow easily. They prefer a soil on the sandy side, but will tolerate other types as long as the bed has regular watering in summer and drains well. Nasturtiums naturalize in almost any area with a mild coastal climate and provide an extremely long season of bloom.

Puny peonies—but I tried hard

Problem: I have watered, fed, and nursed along peonies for several years here in Sherman Oaks (Southern California). My results: half grew spindly leaves, the rest gave me nothing at all. But I want to try again. What should I do?
Answer: There are two classes of peonies, herbaceous and tree peonies. Herbaceous peonies die back to the ground each winter; tree peonies are permanent, deciduous shrubs that grow to a height of 6 feet. The herbaceous peony needs a period of winter chilling (temperatures below freezing) to flower well. The tree peony is less dependent on winter chilling to grow and bloom successfully, and is therefore a much better choice for interior Southern California—such as Zone 18 where you live. Both kinds of peony bear similar flowers; the tree peony produces slightly larger blooms. Best to dig out your old peonies and replace with tree peonies. For more information, see Paeonia, page 390, *Sunset New Western Garden Book.*

Do perennials last "forever"?

Question: I'm a new gardener and planted perennials, expecting that I'd never have to replant or replace them—my idea of gardening! Is this concept true?
Answer: In short, your concept is partially true, but some perennials are more long-lived than others. We have seen some, in the Pacific Northwest, that continue to bloom in gardens planted generations ago. Others have a tendency to die out after 3 or 4 years. All perennials will live indefinitely if they are lifted and divided every 2 or 3 years.

Any perennials partial to shade?

Problem: We live in an aged shingled house that looks vaguely English. I would love to plant an old-fashioned perennial border like the ones we saw on a recent trip to England, but the trees in our yard cast so much shade, I don't think perennials would survive. Are there any that will grow in shady places?
Solution: Quite a number of perennials will grow in partial shade. Several, including hosta and Solomon's seal, will even tolerate dense shade. If you expand your list to include annuals and bulbs, you should have no problem in recreating the type of perennial border you saw in England. Consult the list of shade-tolerant annuals, perennials, and bulbs on page 144, *Sunset New Western Garden Book.* Also consider thinning out your trees to admit more light.

Should I prune bloomed-out perennials?

Question: My foxgloves, hybrid lupine, achillea, and delphiniums don't look like much after they bloom. If I prune the old flower stalks down to the base of the plants, will it help the plants to produce a second wave of flowers?
Answer: Pruning the flower stalks of many perennials after they bloom can, indeed, help to produce a second wave of flowers. The second bloom will not be as dramatic, nor the flowers stalks as robust, but you will have more flowers to brighten your garden.

Perennials OK for a sunny balcony?

Question: I have a space problem—only a sunny balcony. Are there any perennials that can be grown in containers in a small, hot location?
Answer: Virtually any perennial plant will tolerate growing in a container as long as you compensate for the limited soil with regular watering and feeding. The lower growing, more compact perennials look more attractive in containers than plants which are tall or rangy in habit. Try Burmese plumbago, basket-of-gold, or pinks.

Which perennials like it wet?

Problem: The only spot I have for a perennial border unfortunately is eternally damp, due to an underground spring. Are there any perennials that will tolerate such wetness?
Solution: Many perennials originate from similar conditions in the wild, so you can create an interesting garden in a damp area. Among the best choices are astilbe, colocasia, beardless iris (most species), mimulus, marsh marigold, rose mallow, and cardinal flower. For a more complete list of perennials that will grow in wet soil, see page 147, *Sunset New Western Garden Book.*

Can I revive my tired petunias?

Problem: We planted two large containers with Cascade petunias. And the blooms really did cascade earlier this summer, but now in July they seem spent and bedraggled. Is there anything I can do to revive them? We live in Medford, Oregon (Zone 7).
Solution: Petunias respond very well to being cut back to about 6 inches and then given a complete fertilizer. Within a few weeks' time, you should have a second blooming from your petunias that will probably last until first frosts. (This does not apply to Southern California and Arizona, where petunias usually are "goners" by about mid-June.)

Problems with pests? See pages 32–48

Overfed phlox needs flushing

Problem: I planted quite a number of annual phlox this spring. I diligently feed, water, and weed them, but the leaves turn white. What is happening?

Solution: Sounds as if you are a little too diligent in your fertilizing. The leaves of annual phlox turn white— sometimes transparent—when the plants are overfed. Hold off on any further feeding, and try flushing the present fertilizer through the soil by watering liberally for a short period.

My purple alyssum came back white

Question: I planted a flat of sweet alyssum, both purple and white, for ground cover. As I expected, it reseeded and totally blanketed the area where it was needed. However, nearly all of this year's seedlings have blooms that are white. What happened?

Answer: Reseeding is a natural process that sometimes provides a surprise or two. The fact that more white-flowered alyssum sprang up the following year indicates some genetic differences between the white and the purple alyssum. Either the white is better adapted to your particular climate, or the white is the more robust of the two alyssum colors. Other than reseeding with purple alyssum to continue the experiment, you can do little to influence the natural selection process.

Seaside suggestions

Problem: Recently we retired and moved to a small place on the Oregon coast near Florence (Zone 5). I would love to have a flower garden, but don't know what will resist the salt air and cool winds here.

Solution: Although the following list is not overly long, it offers more than enough possibilities to help you create a beautiful garden by the sea: California poppies, basket-of-gold, dusty miller, snow-in-summer, tricolor chrysanthemums, marguerites, pampas grass, fleabane, beach asters, English lavender, *Lonas annua*, and lavender cotton. For a wider selection of good seacoast candidates, see pages 157–159, *Sunset New Western Garden Book.*

Save money by saving seeds?

Question: Can I save money by keeping seeds of annuals I like for planting in next year's garden?

Answer: The older they are, the smaller percentage of seeds germinate when planted. Also, many kinds of plants that have come on the market in recent years are sterile or, in the case of F_1 Hybrids, will not come true from random-pollinated seed, and will usually be inferior. Generally you will have better luck spending the small amount to buy fresh new seeds packed for the current growing season.

Any sure-fire ways to start seeds?

Question: I can't believe the prices charged for a single annual plant in a 4-inch container. I know I could save a lot of money by starting my own annuals from seed, but I've never had much luck with these. Are there any sure-fire methods?

Answer: If you are not planning to start great quantities of seedlings, try using small, compressed peat pellets to start your flower garden. These expand when soaked in water. Although starting seeds this way costs a bit more, the seedlings in pellets can be planted directly in the garden. This process eliminates several transplanting steps associated with more traditional methods of starting seeds and yields a higher percentage of plants. (See illustration.)

Suggestions for shady north wall?

Problem: I have a planted strip along the north side of my house. Nothing seems to do well there because it is too shady. Can you suggest something that will look good the year round?

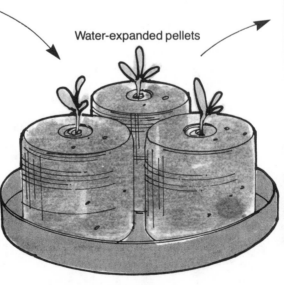

Seed

Peat pellet

Water-expanded pellets

Planted seedling and pellet

Drop seed into small compressed peat pellets; they expand when soaked in water. When they are big enough, seedlings (pellet and all) can be planted directly into the garden.

Solution: Both annuals and perennials take a vacation in winter, either completely dying out or disappearing until spring. If you can stand to have the area bare during the winter, consider planting hostas. They offer an impressive array of leaf patterns and colors, are well-behaved, and thrive in shady areas. Hostas need regular watering in summer, and slugs and snails will have to be guarded against, but otherwise these plants require little care and are relatively pest free. Also see lists on pages 143–145, *Sunset New Western Garden Book*.

What grows well in the smog?

Problem: We are Oregonians about to experience a job transfer to the Los Angeles area. We enjoy gardening, and hope that the smog won't be a big problem. Any suggestions as to what to plant, or not to plant?
Advice: Don't be too concerned; some of the prettiest gardens we've seen are in the Los Angeles area—Pasadena and Claremont are just two of many examples we could mention. Nurseries near your new home will be able to give you good recommendations. For a list of edible and ornamental plants you should *avoid* for sure, see page 160, *Sunset New Western Garden Book*.

They kept keeling over

Problem: The sweet peas I planted in April sprouted and grew to about 10 inches, then keeled over and died. Last summer, my zinnias met the same fate.
Solution: Your sweet peas and zinnias succumbed to a disease known as stem rot or collar rot. It is caused by a fungus that invades the stem of the plant at soil level, preventing the flow of nutrients and water to the upper portion of the plant. Avoid planting seedlings in an area you know to be infested with this fungus. If this word of caution comes too late, treat the soil before planting with a fumigant recommended by your local nursery or garden center.

Where can I find unusual varieties?

Question: Many of the annual varieties mentioned in garden magazines and books are never available in local nurseries. I am especially interested in the new impatiens and the hybrid geraniums, and would like to try growing them from seed. Where can I get these somewhat unusual annuals?
Answer: Your best bet is to order several catalogs from the larger seed companies. Many seed companies advertise in *Sunset* Magazine's fall and winter issues. Most catalogs list and picture some varieties of hard-to-find plants and are fun to browse through.

Can I wipe out weeds organically?

Problem: I have a terrible problem with weeds in my flower bed—they grow more rapidly than the flowers. What can I do that doesn't involve chemical spraying?
Solution: Once weeds become established in a flower bed, they must be physically removed—either by hand or by using a hoe or similar tool. Remove the whole root or as much as possible. Combat the return of the weeds by covering soil with a 1 to 2-inch layer of organic mulch such as redwood soil conditioner, composted fir bark, homemade compost, or comparable material. This layer of mulch dramatically reduces the appearance of annual weeds. (See illustration.) The few perennial weeds that make it through the mulch are much easier to pull than weeds growing in open ground. In addition to weed control, the mulch helps retain soil moisture, keeps the

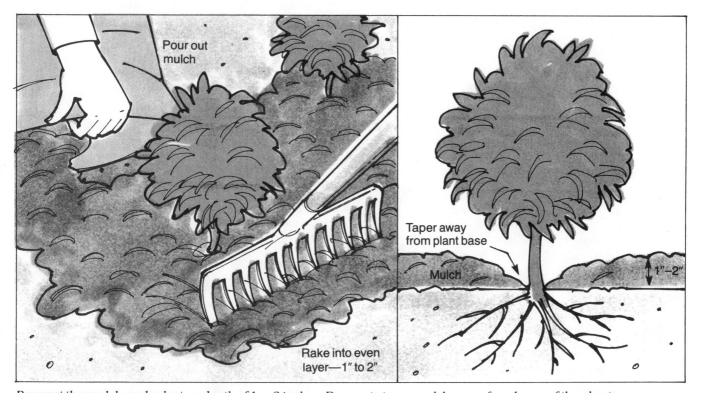

Pour out the mulch and rake to a depth of 1 or 2 inches. Be sure to taper mulch away from bases of the plants.

soil cool to encourage root growth, and has a pronounced effect on improving the over-all quality of the soil.

When to plant a "cottage garden?"

Question: I have recently seen some beautiful photographs of "cottage gardens" featuring a number of perennials. Generally speaking, when is the best time to plant perennials?

Answer: Wherever you live, you can follow a convenient rule-of-thumb for planting perennials. In spring, plant perennials that bloom in summer or autumn. In early autumn, plant perennials that bloom in spring. This is the rule if you are planting perennials that have been dug from established clumps, containers, or bare root. If you have ordered perennials from mail-order nurseries, they will send the plants at the proper planting time for your region.

Did my perennials rot?

Problem: This spring, when I was expecting my perennials to reappear in the garden I was surprised to find that several had, in fact, disappeared. Digging around the areas where they should have been, I noticed quite a bit of decayed matter. Could they have rotted?

Answer: It is a possibility, especially if the plant was not pruned back in the fall. Both for appearance and plant health, you should remove the old stems and dead plant growth just prior to dormancy. Dead leaves that collect at the base of a plant or clump can harbor pests and may provide a source of fungus-disease reinfection the next year. If left in place through winter rain or snow, dead leaves may pack down into a decaying mat that could very well rot the plant.

Perennials from seed?

Question: Are perennials easy to grow from seed? My local nursery doesn't carry many perennial plants, but I recently noticed seeds of a number of my old favorites offered in a catalog.

Answer: Perennials are no more difficult than any other plant to start from seed, but it may take a little longer to produce a plant mature enough to flower. Planted in spring, most won't have any flowers at all until a full year after planting; some may not reach maturity until their second year. Incidentally, be sure to take a good look at nursery seed racks; most stock many perennials as well as annuals.

Do perennials need water when dormant?

Question: Because perennials are still alive during the dormant period do they still need regular watering, the same as during summer?

Answer: Although some perennials will tolerate routine watering during their dormancy, the general rule is to cut back watering by at least half during the resting period.

What plants like sunny window boxes?

Question: The window box outside my apartment faces west and receives quite a bit of sun. Are there flowers especially suited to window boxes?

Answer: Many annuals adapt well to window boxes; since yours faces west, you should favor heat-loving types. Marigolds, dwarf zinnias, creeping zinnias, portulaca, sweet alyssum, and most of the salvia varieties will toler-

ate more heat than others. Plants in window boxes require more attention than plants growing in other kinds of containers. The limited soil in window boxes, as well as difficult growing conditions (usually more wind and reflected sun than in other locations) demand that the gardener compensate with tender loving care, and regular watering and feeding.

How to remove young annuals from cell packs?

Problem: I always seem to have trouble getting annuals out of those little plastic cell-packs. The root ball always shatters as I'm pulling the plants out.

Answer: You can avoid much of the problem by making sure the soil in the cell-pack is moist before you try to remove the plant. Also, instead of pulling the plants out, try turning the cell pack upside-down, with one hand under the cell pack ready to catch the plants as they slide out. You'll experience far less root damage using this method.

Why are her zinnias zestier?

Problem: My neighbor has beautiful luck with zinnias, so I decided to try my hand at them too. I planted them right on the other side of the fence from her garden. They never bloomed very well and the leaves were all covered with a white, powdery film. I felt like a failure—especially when I looked over the fence and saw how well those other zinnias were doing. What could I possibly have done wrong?

Solution: Even the smallest gardens contain a variety of "microclimates" that make a big difference with the success of various plants. In your case, which side of the fence the zinnias were planted on makes all the difference, especially since zinnias need heat and lots of it. Your neighbor's side of the fence probably faces south or west, while yours probably faces north or east. A south or west-facing garden receives maximum sunlight and heat, particularly when the heat is intensified by a neighboring wall or fence, while a northern or eastern exposure is the coolest spot in the garden.

The white, powdery substance you inquire about is mildew, a common problem with zinnias that don't receive enough sun. (See the section on page 41.) Try the zinnias in a warmer, sunnier spot in your garden, and you'll undoubtedly have better luck. As for your fence, see pages 143–145, *Sunset New Western Garden Book*, for a list of shade-tolerant plants.

Baby zinnias zonked out

Question: I started some zinnias from seed in a flat indoors. When the seedlings got their first true leaves, most of them just started falling over and dying. What happened?

Answer: A fungus known as "damping off" attacked your seedlings. You can do several things to address this problem (which, by the way, is common to many kinds of young seedlings, not just zinnias). Buy seeds that have been treated with a fungicide (marked on the seed packet) or dust the seeds with fungicide before planting. Provide good air circulation and ventilation, especially indoors, to keep tops of seedlings dry and standing moisture to a minimum. Use sphagnum moss, vermiculite, perlite, pumice, sand, or sterilized commercial mix to sow seeds or root cuttings. Such materials start the seeds in a disease-free environment. Do *not* use garden soil.

BULBS

GUIDELINES FOR AVOIDING GENERAL PROBLEMS

Compared to other perennials, bulbs are a carefree lot. Even pests and diseases are seldom major problems. Most often, the complaint is, "My bulbs didn't bloom this year." But with proper selection and care throughout the year, they *will* bloom dependably, and many will continue to flower year after year.

It helps to know that a bulb is alive 365 days a year. Just because it has already bloomed and the leaves aren't showy doesn't mean it no longer needs attention. In fact, the most important time for ensuring flowers the following year begins right after the bulb has flowered. Understandably, this is when you are the least interested in the bulb—and problems develop.

Each bulb is a little food package that stores nourishment for the next bloom. The nutrients manufactured in the leaves retreat underground for storage in the bulb until conditions above ground again become favorable for growth and bloom—next year. If the leaves are cut off before the nutrients have gone to the underground bulb, it will have very little nourishment for the following year. Result: few and inferior blooms, if any.

In this chapter, you will most likely find questions and answers that relate to your own bulb problems. (You also can refer to the *Sunset New Western Garden Book* for specific information on use, care, and protection of the individual bulbs.)

To avoid problems generally, be aware of these rules:
- Select healthy bulbs
- Plant at correct depth in good soil
- Plant the right bulb at the right time for your region (see pages 4 and 5)
- Give proper after-bloom care
- Take precautions against pests and diseases

My "red amaryllis" is a "naked lady"

Question: Imagine my surprise when the amaryllis I bought with the expectation that it would have huge crimson flowers at Christmas, bloomed instead in September and turned out to be one of those common pink "naked ladies" you see along every fence in northern California. What should I have ordered to get the flower I expected?

Answer: What you wanted was a hybrid *Hippeastrum*, commonly referred to as the Royal Dutch or giant amaryllis. The flowers of these and "naked ladies" *(Amaryllis belladonna)* are similar enough to cause confusion. And amaryllis is the generally accepted common name for *Hippeastrum* (the real cause of the confusion). For more information see *Amaryllis*, page 177, and *Hippeastrum*, page 324, *Sunset New Western Garden Book*.

OK to use annuals as fillers?

Question: After bulbs have finished blooming, we'd like to plant alyssum and lobelia throughout the area to fill in the gaps. But we're worried that the watering and fertilizing will be too much for the daffodils and they won't bloom next year.

Answer: No need to worry; if the soil has good drainage, the water and fertilizer you apply to the annuals should actually benefit next year's daffodil blossoms. Also, many people plant these *before* bulbs bloom—the hardier alyssum just after the bulbs have been planted.

When is the best time to buy?

Question: When I see gardens full of spring bulbs and go to a nursery for some to plant, they never have any. Same thing happened last summer when I tried to find dahlia bulbs after seeing them in bloom in my neighbor's garden. When is the best time to buy and plant bulbs that bloom in the spring or summer?

Answer: Almost all bulbs are sold in their dormant state, several months before they are due to bloom in the garden. Spring-flowering bulbs are sold in fall; summer-flowering kinds in early spring. Thus, if you want bulb color in your garden, it is necessary to plan ahead.

Is it wrong to buy the "cheapies"?

Question: There is a large area I intend to plant with spring-flowering bulbs. In comparing prices at nurseries, I've noticed a wide range for the same type of bulbs.

(Continued on next page)

To save money, can I buy the cheaper ones and still get good results?

Answer: Bulbs usually are priced according to their size and rarity—the larger or rarer the bulb, the higher the price. Generally, larger bulbs tend to produce larger flowers. For mass planting in a large area, the smaller blooms from smaller bulbs will give you the quantity you are seeking, and at a more affordable price. Look for mixtures of varieties labeled "for naturalizing"; these often are cheaper than named varieties.

My red tulips turned out white!

Problem: I picked out four dozen tulip bulbs last fall that were advertised as red flowered varieties. They bloomed perfectly, but only two of them were red—the rest were white. What happened?

Solution: Unfortunately, bulbs sometimes get rearranged in their bins at the grower's or at the nursery. It's impossible to tell the color of the tulip by looking at the dormant bulb, so mistakes sometimes occur. To be sure of colors you want, it may be best to order bulbs from a mail order source. Or shop for bulbs as soon as the nurseries fill the bins.

Is it a bulb? corm? tuber?

Question: Why is a crocus sometimes called a bulb and sometimes a corm? Are ranunculus bulbs or tubers? How to properly identify these—and everything else I've always called a "bulb"—is confusing.

Answer: Go right on calling them bulbs; it is a useful general name for all of these plants. See the chart on page 64 to help identify which is which when you are buying.

How can I remember the planting location?

Problem: Every year when I cultivate my flower borders, I inadvertently put the shovel through clumps of dormant bulbs. Is there any way of marking these spots in a way that won't be an eyesore?

Solution: Try grouping several medium-sized stones around the perimeter of the clump. Or use a couple of short, sturdy stakes (less than 6 inches high) to mark the spots. Or write bulb names on aluminum tags and attach them to stakes driven in almost to ground level. Surround with low-growing annuals or other plants to camouflage these markers. (See illustration.)

When should I dig up bulbs?

Question: For several years I have dug up bulbs and stored them right after they bloomed. Trouble is, they never seem to bloom worth a darn the second year. Am I digging them up at the wrong time, or what?

Answer: You are digging them up too soon. Tulips, lilies, hyacinths, narcissus, and all the true bulbs rely on their leaves to provide nutrients for bloom the following year. Leaves must be encouraged to grow and stay green as long as possible after the bulb has bloomed, and then be allowed to return nutrients to the bulbs by withering naturally. If you interrupt the foliage-producing stage of the bulb's life cycle, you rob it of food for the next year. The disappointing results are few or no blooms.

Lilies should be dug only to divide them, and immediately replanted with roots intact.

Are there any drought-tolerant bulbs?

Question: I live in Barstow, California, where summers are really hot and we have to be careful of water use. Are there any bulbs that are drought resistant?

Answer: Yes, bearded iris and many of the Pacific Coast native irises (see page 333, *Sunset New Western Garden Book*) would all be considered drought tolerant. These bulbs, along with the perennial red-hot poker (*Kniphofia uvaria*) would provide you with an interesting combination of unusual flowers over a long time.

Any bulbs with evergreen foliage?

Question: I keep my garden very tidy and just hate the mess of bulbs after they flower. Are there any bulbs with tops that don't die down after blooming?

Answer: Daylilies maintain their foliage in any climate. Agapanthus, clivias, and cannas maintain their foliage the year around in most climates. However, agapanthus and clivias won't live in Zones 1–3, and cannas won't keep their leaves in heavy frost.

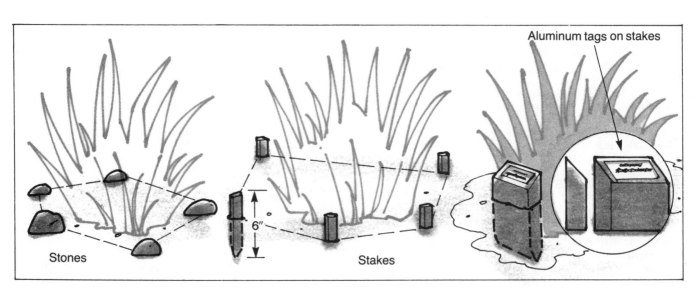

Aluminum tags on stakes

Stones

6"

Stakes

Mark planting bed to prevent the accidental digging up of bulbs during months they are dormant.

Bulbs for a February wedding?

Question: Our daughter is getting married at home next year in early February. She'd like a background of flowering spring bulbs for the ceremony, but this seems too early to expect bulbs to bloom. Can you help us?

Answer: Tulips, hyacinths, narcissus, crocuses, muscari, and *Iris reticulata* can all be "persuaded" to bloom in January or February. Plant the bulbs close together in pots, with their tips just at soil surface. Keep them in a cool, dark place for 8 to 10 weeks. Then bring the potted bulbs into light and warmth for 3 to 4 weeks to bloom. This procedure is called *forcing*. You'll need to start the forcing 11 to 14 weeks prior to the wedding date in February.

I've had bad luck forcing bulbs

Question: Despite repeated attempts to force bulbs, I'm just not getting good results. Mostly I've tried tulips and daffodils for indoor early bloom in January and February. Why are the stems so short and the blooms so irregular in size?

Answer: Successful forcing of bulbs is absolutely dependent on giving them sufficient time in a dark, cool place to develop a healthy root system. (Normal indoor temperatures of 70° are too warm.) If you bring bulbs out to a sunny, warm location prematurely, they try to do too much too soon—they must be gradually conditioned to a warmer, brighter environment.

Can I plant bulbs under shade trees?

Question: Most of my available planting space is under big, shady trees, but I'd love some spring bulbs. Will they grow in these conditions?

Answer: If your trees are deciduous and the ground beneath is not filled with surface roots, you have an ideal growing environment for many of the spring-flowering bulbs. They bloom before new tree leaves develop and shade the planting bed. However, if the trees have needles or are broadleafed evergreens (creating all-year shade), don't expect good blooms from any of the spring bulbs with the exception of lily-of-the-valley.

Where can I find off-beat varieties?

Question: I would like to plant some of the lesser-known bulbs, but the nurseries only seem to carry the same old kinds every year. How can I find a wider selection?

Answer: Late summer and early fall issues of *Sunset* Magazine sometimes include advertisements for mail order catalogs that specialize in bulbs.

How can I keep my bulb bed weed-free?

Question: What can be done to keep a bulb bed free of weeds?

Answer: Hand weed or hoe to clear the bulb area of weeds in the fall before you are ready to plant. Right after planting, use a pre-emergent weed killer. The pre-emergent products prevent weed seeds in the soil from germinating for at least 6 months. There is no damage to the bulbs. Consult your nursery or garden center for specific recommendations for your region.

How can I keep my dahlias from toppling?

Problem: My dahlias frequently topple in the wind. What to do?

Solution: Modern breeding has produced dahlias with blossoms disproportionately large to their supporting plants. If you plant these giants in your garden, put them in an area as free of wind as possible and try one of the staking and tying methods shown in the illustration. Or plant some of the smaller flowered varieties pictured on page 267, *Sunset New Western Garden Book*.

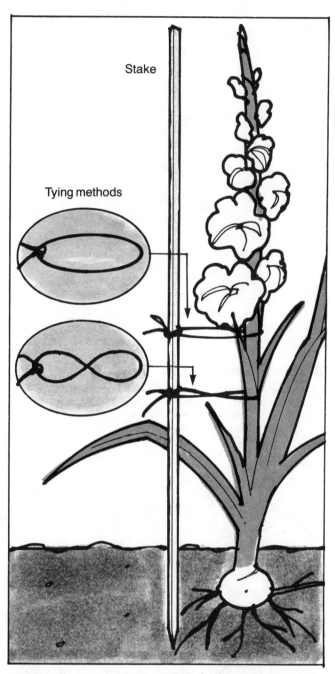

Keep gladiolus, dahlias, or irises from toppling: tie stems in several places by either method shown.

Can I dynamite my daylilies?

Problem: My daylilies have been in for 4 years; it's way past time to divide them. I can't get a spade or shovel through that root mass. Short of dynamite, what can I do?

(Continued on next page)

Solution: The hard soil as well as the root mass may be giving you a problem. Soak the area with a sprinkler for several hours to soften the soil and the roots. Then, if a spade or round-pointed shovel won't get through the mass, use a spading fork. Or use two spading forks, back to back, to pry the plants apart (see illustration).

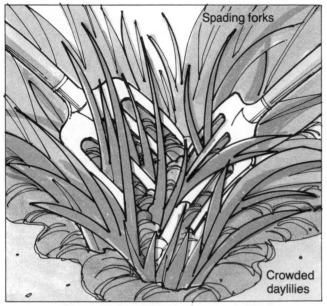

Soak root mass of crowded daylilies to soften soil. Use two spading forks, back to back, to pry plants apart.

Are bulbs fussy about drainage?

Question: The only planting space I have for bulbs is a rather low, poorly drained spot next to the front lawn. Will they rot if I plant them there?

Answer: The majority of bulbs require soil that drains well. However, several of the beardless irises (Siberian, Japanese, and spuria or butterfly irises) perform admirably in low, wet spots in the garden and have both attractive foliage and flowers.

Can I replant my Easter lily?

Question: What can I do with my potted Easter lily now that the blooms are gone? Can I plant it in the garden?

Answer: As soon as the last flower fades, transplant your Easter lily to a sunny or partially shady outdoor spot with good drainage. It may bloom again that fall. After adjusting to outdoor living for a year or two, it will flower in midsummer, its normal blooming time.

My old daffodil leaves look terrible

Problem: Floppy, dried out daffodil foliage looks shabby for many weeks after bloom season. This hurts the garden's appearance when other plants are coming into flower. What can be done with that old foliage?

Solution: When most of the leaves have turned yellow, you can gently fold them over once or twice and secure them in a neat bundle with a rubber band or with one of the old leaves. Once the leaves are completely dry, they can be removed easily from the ground with a slight tug, or by raking the surface. Many gardeners hide the withering foliage of narcissus and other bulbs with a planting of spring annuals such as fairy primroses, calendulas, and poppies.

Any glads for the high desert?

Problem: I have a problem growing gladiolus in the high desert near Albuquerque, New Mexico (Zone 10). Any suggestions?

Solution: Try the gladiolus varieties that reportedly do well in desert regions: 'Black Velvet', 'Green Magic', 'Royal Rose', 'Sunbeam', and two miniatures, 'Twinkle' and 'Wood Violet'. In the high desert section, wait until

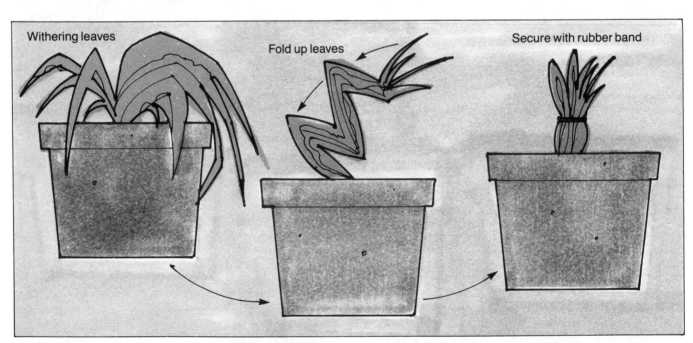

Don't cut off old leaves of bulbs. Fold as shown (or wrap around your hand); secure and bundle with rubber band.

April or May to plant gladiolus corms. In the intermediate desert climates (like that of Tucson) and the low desert areas (like those around Phoenix), glads can be planted as early as January, before the hot weather hits.

Gopher-proofing lilies

Question: How can I protect my lily bulbs from gophers?

Answer: The best protection is afforded by constructing individual 6-inch-square baskets of hardware cloth in which to place the bulbs before you plant them. (Hardware cloth is available at most hardware stores.) The depth that the basket is planted depends on the type of lily. Consult page 350 of *Sunset New Western Garden Book* for planting depths for individual types of lilies.

What will grow under pines?

Problem: Nothing seems to grow under our three pine trees. We would like to keep the area looking natural, but we don't know what will survive there.

Solution: *Cyclamen hederifolium* and most species of trillium are excellent. Also a good choice would be Pacific Coast irises, hybrids of the native species, but hardier, more shapely, and more brightly colored than their wild parents. They are fine choices for under pines or native oaks, or on slopes, or in rock gardens. In mild climate regions, plant rhizomes in the fall, or transplant from nursery containers. Check nurseries that specialize in native plants.

Do all bulbs need dividing?

Question: I have a large clump of bearded irises in my garden that was planted by the former owners. A friend said that they would bloom better if I divided them. What does he mean by "divided"; do all bulbs need to be divided after a few years?

Answer: Bearded irises and other plants with rhizomes (callas, cannas, agapanthus, for example) begin to show signs of crowding every three years or so. Divide the rhizomes in late summer or early fall. Lift out the root mass with a shovel or spading fork, then use a sharp knife to cut off the new rhizomes growing on the outer edge. Discard the rest. Cut the foliage back half way, then replant. See illustration for more details.

Any bulbs that continue to bloom in your garden year after year (naturalize) probably will need to be divided once every 3 to 5 years. Division is necessary when the flowers either diminish in size or in number.

Why did my irises bloom early?

Question: In Mill Valley, northern California, most of my bearded irises bloomed this year in February instead of April. Why was this?

Answer: Early blooming of irises often is caused by an unusually warm, mild winter with considerable rain, and frequently in mild climate regions gardeners will be surprised by blooms in mid-winter. The plants probably are not harmed in any way and should bloom during their normal period next year—providing that the preceding winter is also normal.

Is lily-of-the-valley OK for Sacramento?

Question: I've been warned that lily-of-the-valley is difficult to grow in California. That's hard to believe, because where I came from in Idaho it is considered almost a

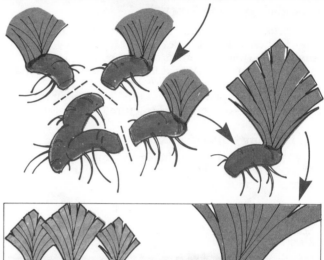

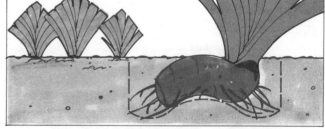

Divide rhizomes of bearded iris (top) when they begin to get crowded (about every 3 years). Best future plants are the rhizomes around clumps' outer edges. Cut foliage back as shown in center illustration, then replant.

weed. I do miss the lovely fragrance. What chances do I have for a big, lush lily-of-the-valley bed in Sacramento?

Answer: Lily-of-the-valley (*Convallaria majalis*) needs cold winters to thrive and bloom well. Sacramento probably will be just cold enough, but don't expect quite the exuberant, weedlike growth you were familiar with in Idaho. Plant the pips close together in clumps (they tend to get lost if you set out only a few) in November or December in a humus-rich soil in filtered sun. Feed when spring growth starts. Also, see *Convallaria majalis*, page 250 of *Sunset New Western Garden Book*.

My lilies have nematodes. Help!

Problem: I'm told my lilies have nematodes (they have deformed leaves, blotches). What should I do?

Advice: Remove the bulbs and destroy them, preferably by burning. Nematodes are soil-borne, microscopic pests that attack roots and keep the plant from utilizing water and food. The only chemical control is soil sterilization before planting—somewhat difficult for home gardeners. If you know that a particular place in your garden is infected with nematodes, avoid planting susceptible plants such as lilies in that spot.

Is oxalis a weed?

Question: My sister gave me an oxalis with a pretty pink flower. I've always considered the yellow-flowered oxalis a weed. Will this one get away in my garden and become a pest?

Answer: Better find out what type of oxalis it is before you plant it in your garden. Runaway *Oxalis corniculata* is the species you want to avoid, but even some of the cultivated kinds can become aggressive pests. For safety's sake, consider growing it as a pot plant.

How deep should bulbs be planted?

Question: I'm never sure how deep to plant each kind of bulb. Is there a general rule?

Answer: A rule of thumb is to plant bulbs 2 to 3 times the bulb's diameter, with the largest planted a little shallower, and the smallest a little deeper.

For depth of planting specific bulbs, consult the chart below. Also, each bulb is pictured "right side up".

Am I raising bulbs or snails?

Problem: Sometimes I think I'm raising snails instead of bulbs. I don't like to use snail bait because I'm afraid my dog will eat it. What can I do?

Solution: Try one of the liquid snail controls. They reportedly are quite effective, and should not attract your dog as the pellets do. Check at your local nurseries. Additionally, you might try discouraging your dog from baited areas with fold-up, foot-high portable fencing. It's inexpensive and inconspicuous; it won't keep out a big dog, but it is a psychological barrier to a little dog. Or put bait inside "traps"—boxes or cans, for example—that offer access to snails but will not attract larger creatures. For more on snails, see page 34.

Can I grow bulbs in heavy soil?

Problem: I'm a new gardener and live in San Mateo, California (Zone 17), where the soil is heavy. The bulbs I planted last year did poorly. Was it the soil?

Solution: Generally, bulbs require a good loam soil to put on their best show. The soil should be porous and drain well, and yet hold enough water for the roots. If you have heavy soil, or clay soil, add organic matter such as peat moss, ground bark, composted manure, or redwood soil conditioner. Put 3 or 4 inches of organic matter on top of soil; dig it in to a depth of 9 to 12 inches.

The list of bulbs that do well in heavy soil without a lot of amendment is woefully short: *Amaryllis belladonna, Scilla peruviana, Zantedeschia aethiopica, Hemerocallis* species.

Are tulips OK for Southern California?

Question: We recently moved to Whittier, California (Zone 23) from the northwest, where we had hundreds of tulips. We'd like to grow them in our new garden, but some people say they are hard to grow here.

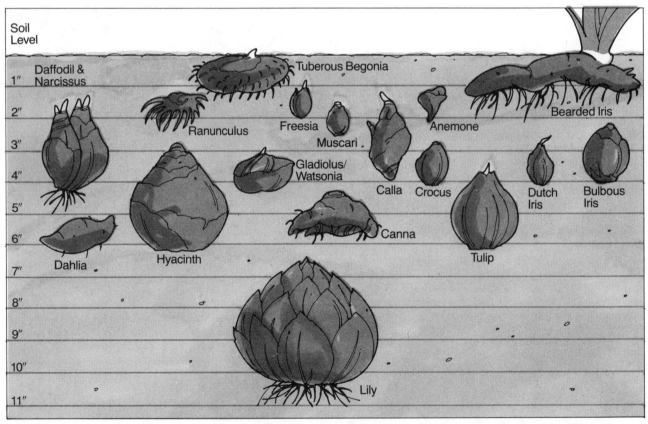

Charted above are recommended planting depths for some of the most popular bulbs. A rule of thumb, for loamy soil, is 2 to 3 times the greatest diameter of the bulb; a little less deeply in heavy soil.

Answer: Tulips will do just fine in southern California, but they won't come back the next year as they will in colder climates. However, many gardeners enjoy them enough to buy and plant new ones each year. Prior to planting, you should refrigerate the bulbs, since tulips need this in order to force the required dormant period they receive naturally when they overwinter in the soil of cold-winter regions. For how to prechill, see below.

Tulips should be planted later in Southern California than in other regions—any time between Thanksgiving and Lincoln's birthday. In Zones 12 and 13, Christmas season is the best time to plant.

Should tulip bulbs be pre-chilled?

Question: I've heard conflicting advice about chilling tulip bulbs prior to planting. Is prechilling the bulbs really necessary? If so, how should I go about it?
Answer: It depends on the region. In Southern California, where winters are very mild, the popular long-stemmed kinds of tulips will give much better performance if you prechill them so they will have the necessary amount of dormancy before starting their springtime growth. This results in the desired stem length for Darwins and Darwin Hybrids, Cottage, Parrots, Triumphs, and Lily-flowering types. In Zones 12 and 13, the desert heat is such that gardeners must prechill tulip bulbs if they are to bloom at all. In cold-winter regions, where they grow most naturally and overwinter in the soil, winter's cold weather provides this dormancy.

To properly prechill tulips, place them in the refrigerator (not in the freezer) for 6–8 weeks. Ideal temperature is about 40° F. They need some air, so don't keep them in plastic bags; mesh sacks are very acceptable, however, Plant the bulbs as soon as you remove them from the refrigerator. Southern California gardeners are strongly advised not to plant until late November (see "Are tulips OK for Southern California?", page 64. In Zones 12 and 13, hyacinths and crocus also benefit from prechilling in warm-winter climates.

We're moving. Can we take our bulbs?

Question: Next fall, a year from now, we will be moving from Seattle to Reno. I would hate to leave my bulb collection behind, especially the cyclamen, daffodils, and tall bearded irises. Will they survive the colder climate? How should I prepare them for the move? What should I do after the move?
Answer: If your cyclamen collection is made up of the so-called florist's cyclamen *(C. persicum)*, best leave them for the enjoyment of the new owners of your home in Seattle—they are unlikely candidates for the cold winters of Reno (Zone 3). If, however, you have the smaller-flowered, hardy cyclamen species, these should transplant beautifully in their new home. Dig up the plants after they have finished flowering, keep them in pots in their old location until you are ready to move.

Daffodils and irises should adjust to the new climate with little problem. Dig the daffodil bulbs after the foliage has completely died down, and store them in a cool, dark place. Keep them in onion sacks or similar containers that provide good air circulation. Plant the bulbs in Reno as soon as the weather cools in the fall.

Dig the iris rhizomes just before you plan to move and plant in their new location as soon as possible.

Luckily, your fall move coincides with an ideal time to dig and divide irises.

Forced hyacinths—how long in the dark?

Question: I put a hyacinth bulb in a "specialty" container a friend gave me, designed for forcing bulbs indoors, and was told to keep it in the dark until it's ready to be brought into the light. How do I know when it's ready?
Answer: Rooting usually takes 10 to 13 weeks. When a good mass of roots has formed and the tips of the bulbs are an inch or two high, move the jars into full light in a cool room. Keep the glasses filled with only enough water to touch the base of the bulbs.

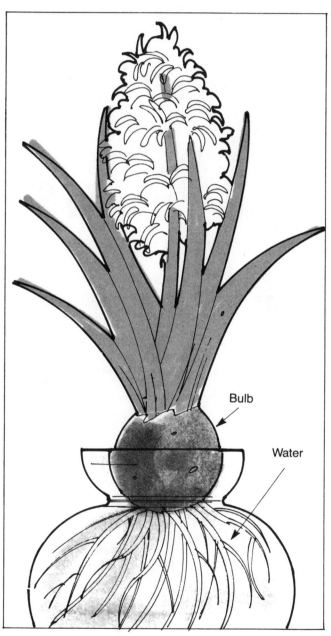

Bulb

Water

Special hyacinth glass is designed so bulb sits on top and only the roots extend below into the water.

VEGETABLES

GUIDELINES FOR AVOIDING GENERAL PROBLEMS

Growing your own vegetables can be one of the most rewarding activities in the garden. It can also be one of the most frustrating. Good vegetable gardeners quickly learn what farmers have always known: you can't always rely on performance of the crop. You can do everything within your power to see through to harvest, but there are variables beyond your control: the weather, seeds that don't sprout, birds that eat rows of seedlings. The most realistic vegetable growers take a certain amount of failure in stride and remain optimistic: "Next year, we'll have better luck."

Problems basic to all vegetables are discussed in this chapter. You'll also find answers to questions about specific plants. For lists that will tell you when-to-plant-what for your zone, consult pages 81–84, *Sunset New Western Garden Book;* and the plant encyclopedia section, pages 161–505, for individual vegetables.

For successful vegetable gardening, observing these guidelines will help you avoid common problems:

- Don't plan a bigger garden than you can manage
- Plant only vegetables you and/or family really like
- Prepare soil properly before planting
- Choose the right vegetable for the season and for your location (see pages 4 and 5)
- Stagger plantings for continuous harvest
- Maintain a good plant-care program—watering, weeding, fertilizing, pest and disease control

How should I pick Brussels sprouts?

Question: I'm growing Brussels sprouts for the first time. How should I harvest them—from the bottom to the top; at random; only those of a certain size?

Answer: Start at the bottom and snap off sprouts. (Leave those that are smaller than 1½ inches in diameter.) Leave small sprouts at top of the plant to mature. When harvesting, remove the lowest leaves below the picked sprouts.

Too many cabbages

Problem: We planted 2 dozen cabbage plants at the same time in early spring, and now there are 2 dozen large heads of cabbage all ready at the same time. What should I do with all this cabbage?

Solution: When your cabbage is ready but you're not, twist the heads gently until you feel the stalks crack, but don't break the heads off. This keeps the cabbage from splitting or flowering. Leave the heads in place until you are ready to harvest. The plants will still be alive, so continue to water them.

We have worms in the cabbage!

Problem: My cabbage and lettuce plants are riddled with holes, and a few days ago I found a fat, green worm on one of the leaves. What is this pest and how can I control it without using chemical sprays?

Solution: Those common white butterflies with black-spotted wings produce cabbage worms, which very likely is what you saw on the leaf. These voracious worms also eat holes in other cole crops and in lettuce. To stop them without chemicals, try using *Bacillus thuringiensis* (BT), sold as Dipel, Thuricide, and Biotrol. Spray wherever you see cabbage worms or their damage. The bacilli cause the worms to die, but will not harm other types of garden insects.

Our carrot seeds never germinate

Problem: Our carrot seeds never seem to germinate even though we seem to be following planting directions explicitly.

Solution: Frequently a crust forms over the top layer of soil, making it impossible for the fine carrot seeds to break through. An easy way to break the crust is to mix radish seeds with the carrots seeds when you sow. Radishes germinate fast and they'll push through the soil in a few days, forging the way for the slower-germinating carrots. In three weeks, the radishes should be ready to harvest. Pull any before that time if they are crowding the young carrots.

How can I grow long carrots?

Question: All my carrots are either stumpy and short, or misshapen. Is there any way to grow long carrots like the ones in the market?

Answer: In addition to selecting the proper long variety and preparing a loose soil, there's a trick that can help produce attractive carrots: sow the seeds shallow, between ¼ and ½ inch deep. Cover them with another ¼ to ½ inch of organic matter and keep the seeds evenly moist until they germinate. When the ferny little plants reach about 1 inch tall—the roots are now slender threads—withhold water until the plants start to wilt. Then resume normal watering until harvest. This practice encourages downward root growth.

Why were my cauliflower heads green?

Question: I raised cauliflower last year for the first time. It tasted okay, but it was a greenish-white rather than snowy-white. Why?

Answer: As the heads of cauliflower begin to form, the outer leaves should be pulled up around the head and secured with a rubber band at the top. This prevents light from reaching the head, resulting in pure white cauliflower that matures in 2 to 4 weeks after tying.

Our celery is bitter and stringy

Problem: Celery is a family favorite, but we can't seem to grow it successfully. It is never very white, and is usually bitter and stringy.

Advice: Although success does not come easily with celery, here's how to improve your chances: Starting with transplants, arrange the plants 6 inches apart in medium to heavy soil. Celery is both a heavy drinker and feeder; heavier soils keep nutrients and water in the root areas where they are most needed. To get crisp, juicy celery, water frequently. Feed with a high-nitrogen fertilizer 30 days after planting, and repeat the feeding a month later.

If you want celery that is especially white, try blanching the plants by keeping light away from the stalks. Cover them with quart milk cartons that have

Blanching celery

If you like your celery to be especially white, blanch by covering with a carton a month before harvesting.

had the tops and bottoms removed; you can also use bottomless 3-pound coffee cans or tarpaper cylinders. Don't cover the leaves, which need the sun. Blanching takes about a month before the celery is ready for harvesting.

My cole crops are dropping leaves

Problem: All of my cole crops—cabbage, cauliflower, broccoli, and Brussels sprouts—are stunted and dropping leaves. I've never had this happen before. Do you know what's causing it?

Advice: The problem is probably caused by a fungus called clubroot. You can make sure by pulling up an afflicted plant and examining the roots: clubroot causes them to develop knotty, lumpy nodes. There's no cure, so pull out and destroy the plants. To save future crops, add a heavy dose of lime to the infected soil. This should inhibit the production of clubroot fungus spores. Plant new cole crops in other areas.

What ails my corn and peppers?

Problem: Although I've been a vegetable gardener in Pendleton, Oregon, for years, my corn and sweet peppers never seem to amount to much.

Solution: Some recent introductions do well in milder climates (Zone 3) east of the Cascades, and seeds are available at nurseries. 'Butterfruit', a supersweet corn, produces 8-inch ears on short stalks, and you can harvest about 72 days after seeds are planted (count on 100 days if you live west of the Cascades). Some growers claim 'Butterfruit' is the best-tasting yellow corn on the market.

'Gypsy' produces dozens of 3- to 4-inch peppers, even in cool weather. The sweet peppers are edible when they are greenish-yellow, but mature to red-orange.

When is corn ripe?

Question: This is our first vegetable garden. I admit to being a little overanxious and picking our first corn before it was ready. How can I tell when corn is ripe?

Answer: When the corn silks turn brown, pop a kernel 2 inches from the top of the ear with your fingernail. If the fluid is watery, wait a few more days; if milky, the corn is just right. If you have waited too long, the fluid will be starchy or gummy.

When you find the perfect ears, be sure you have a pot of water boiling before you pick the corn!

Bitter cukes

Problem: I've had problems growing standard cucumbers here in Tucson, Arizona; they always seem bitter.

Solution: The Armenian cucumber does well in desert gardens and the fruit is not bitter, especially if picked while young. It is a fast-growing variety and an abundant producer. In desert gardens, Armenian cucumber should be watered about 3 times a week; mulch roots, keeping 3-inch layer of compost.

Our cucumbers and squash aren't producing

Problem: Our squash and cucumber plants have lots of flowers, but the blooms drop off before fruit develops.

Advice: Cucumber and squash produce male and female flowers, and both types of flowers must be present to produce a crop. If your plants are young, the problem simply may be that flowers of only one sex have had time to bloom. If so, time will take care of this—the other sex will show up soon.

(Continued on next page)

Problems with pests? See pages 32—48

However, if the plants are mature and unproductive, a lack of bees—primary pollinator of these blooms—may be the problem. Using an artist's paintbrush, you can take over their pollinating chore. Collect the yellow dusty-looking pollen with the brush and dust the female flowers (the ones with the tiny, immature fruit at the base of the bloom). Put pollen on the sticky stigma in the center of each bloom (see illustration).

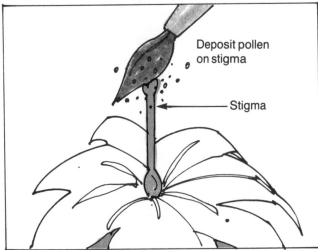

Pollination is a must for squash and cucumbers. Bees take care of this. If bees are scarce, you can do it.

Short-season woes

Question: We live in Provo, Utah, and our growing season is so short that we can only pick a few vegetables before the first frost puts an end to our garden. What can we do?

Answer: Fortunately, plant breeders continue to develop good vegetable varieties for short-season areas. The following is a good starter list: 'Kentucky Wonder' pole beans, 'Tender Crop' or 'Top Crop' bush beans, 'Detroit Red' beets, 'Green Comet' broccoli, 'Copenhagen Market' cabbage, 'Royal Chantenay' carrots, 'Snow King' cauliflower, 'Vates Dwarf' kale, 'Butter King' lettuce, 'Dwarf Grey Sugar' edible pod peas, 'Melody' spinach, 'Table King' acorn squash, 'Waltham' butternut squash, 'Butterbar' yellow summer squash, 'Ambassador' zucchini, and 'Tokyo Cross' turnip.

You can also make simple plastic tent covers, or other structural or mechanical devices, that will give protection against the cold and thereby extend the growing season.

Leeks disappoint

Question: Although my leek plants look good in the garden, the edible white portion is very small. Did I plant the wrong variety?

Answer: Left to themselves, any variety of leek will grow leafy tops and short, thick bottoms shaped like green onions. You can encourage leeks to produce long, well-blanched shafts, like those in the grocery store, by piling dirt around the leeks as they grow. Take care not to mound soil higher than the point at which the leaves separate from the shaft. (See illustration.)

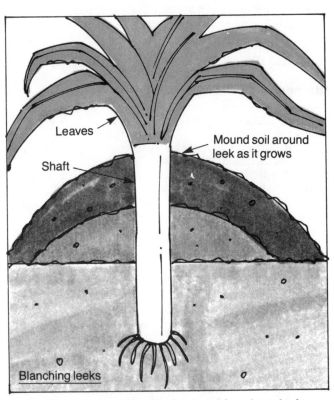

Don't pile soil above the shaft when blanching leeks.

My lettuce gets sunstroke

Problem: I'd like to squeeze in a summer crop of lettuce before it gets too hot, but I live in San Bernardino, California (Zone 18) and I always have trouble with the lettuce getting sunburned.

Solution: The trick is to devise a sun shade for the lettuce. One way is to plant it with corn. Plant the lettuce in the 2-foot space between the corn rows. As the days get warmer, the corn gets taller and shades the lettuce. It matures well before the corn is ready to pick.

Will our lettuce bonanza be wasted?

Question: We have several rows of mature lettuce—a virtual bonanza and certainly more than we can possibly use right away. Is there any way to save it?

Answer: Try harvesting just the outer leaves instead of the whole head, picking enough for one meal from several plants. This method will work with the looseleaf or rosette type lettuce; 'Iceberg' and other crisphead lettuce must be harvested whole.

In the case of romaine, try cutting off heads of a few just above lowest healthy leaf axils; this might result in some later, secondary heads. This won't work during the hottest weather, however.

To avoid the surplus problem next year, plant small amounts every few weeks for a succession of ready lettuce.

How can I keep melons, squash from rotting?

Problem: Some of my cantaloupes and squashes are rotting before they get ripe. They need lots of water, but the young fruit ripening on the trailing vines seems to spoil if it gets wet.

Solution: Here are four ways to give them the water they need without getting the fruit wet:

- Train them up a trellis: This works for some vining vegetables—those with fruit light enough not to break off (cantaloupes, cucumbers, midget watermelons, some squash). The trellis can be vertical or horizontal, as long as it's off the ground.
- Put them on a platform. Cut up pieces of wood large enough to hold the ripening fruit. Set the fruit on top of the wood so it's high and dry.
- Build a basin: If you mound up a ridge of soil around the plants to form a watering basin, you can confine the water near the plant's roots; meanwhile the fruiting part of the plant can sprawl beyond the basin.
- Bury a can: Bury a 1- to 5-gallon can up to its rim and plant around it. Water directly into the can; water drains out holes in bottom into the surrounding soil. This is, essentially, a method of drip irrigation. See the illustration on page 71.

Slip pieces of board under ripening vegetables, melons.

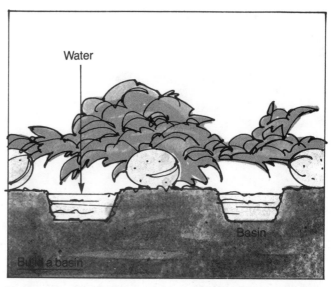

Basin provides roots with water; melons sprawl beyond.

Why did my onions rot in the basement?

Problem: We grew a great crop of onions last year, but lost a good part of the crop to rot while the onions were stored in our basement. How can we avoid this loss next winter?

Solution: All members of the onion family—including garlic, onions, and shallots—need plenty of air circulation during storage to prevent rot. Trim the stems 12 to 16 inches long, and then tie bulbs in bunches of 10 on a length of sturdy twine. When the chain reaches 3 to 4 feet, tie each end to eye screws in the beams under the eaves of your house. Onions will keep for at least 6 months this way.

Train lightweight cucumbers and squash on trellis.

How should I harvest my onions?

Question: My onions are close to maturity; however, I don't know when or how to harvest them. I've read somewhere that the tops need to be pushed over at a certain time. What should I do?

Answer: Onions and garlic keep best if they are properly cured *before* harvest. As the tops begin to yellow, push them over with the back of a rake (see illustration). This action forces the bulbs into their final maturing stage. About 3 weeks after bending the tops, dig up the onions. Lay them on newspapers for 10 days in a dry, shady place. The tops and roots can then be trimmed, and the onions stored for winter-long use.

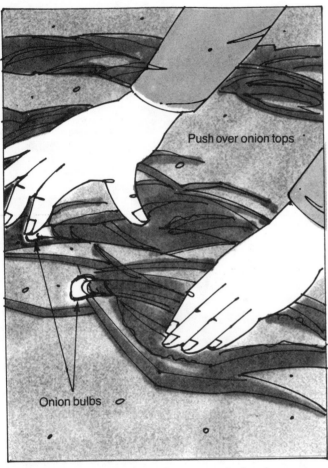

Push over onion tops

Onion bulbs

To help onions mature, push over tops before harvest.

Why are my onion sets bolting?

Question: We live in Southern California, and have tried planting onions from large sets for two years now. The sets planted in spring quickly go to seed before the bulb has matured. Is there any way around this?

Answer: You might try the smallest sets (bulbs), which are less likely to bolt than the larger ones. Or, try starting onions from plants rather than sets. The plants, which look like the green onions you buy at the grocery store, usually are available from well-stocked nurseries in bundles of 50 or more. Gardeners in warm climates like yours report few problems with these onions going to seed prematurely. Planted in April, you should be eating onions from your garden in July.

Our early peas didn't sprout

Problem: We had a few warm, springlike days in early February, so I planted peas, following which the weather turned cold and wet. Only a few seeds ever sprouted.

Solution: Most likely the cold, wet weather caused most of the seeds to rot before they could sprout. Peas will grow but not sprout at lower temperatures, so you can give the plants a head start by sprouting them indoors.

Roll the peas between two damp paper towels and place them in a plastic bag. Check every day or two; as soon as the peas have sprouted, plant them outdoors in the prepared bed. Handle the plants carefully, as the sprouts are brittle and the peas won't grow if the sprouts break off. Plant with the sprouted root down, and cover the seed with an inch of soil.

My late pea crops are flops

Problem: We live in the Pacific northwest, and every year plant a succession of pea crops. The early spring planting is always a success, but the ones later in the season are always a flop. Why?

Solution: The problem you are running into is caused by a virus that affects peas planted late in the season. Until recently, these virus problems limited the pea planting season to early spring. Now a new virus-resistant pea called 'Corvallis' extends the planting season through June for northwest gardeners. 'Corvallis' is a short, dark, freezing type pea. Planting to harvest time is about 65 days.

Peppers, eggplants in coastal gardens

Question: We live near the coast and have never been able to grow satisfactory peppers and eggplants. Do you have some tips?

Answer: Gardeners in cool-summer climates should provide as much warmth as possible for eggplants, peppers, melons, tomatoes, and other heat-lovers. Plant such vegetables near protected, heat-reflecting house walls that face south, or fences where heat is likely to build up. If cool winds from the west and northwest are a problem, erect screens to block them off. Or plant vegetables in 5-gallon nursery cans and move them around to the sunniest spots on your patio or deck.

Peppers—hot or sweet?

Question: I never realized there were so many different kinds of peppers. We'd like to grow the sweet red cherry types, and the long and sweet yellow ones. What varieties can you recommend?

Answer: Not only do the plants look alike, but the peppers of some hot varieties, such as 'Hungarian Hot Wax' and hot cherry pepper look just like their sweet counterparts, the sweet Hungarian yellow pepper and the sweet cherry pepper. The only advice we can give you is to read the labels carefully when purchasing plants in the nursery; otherwise, you will be in for an unwelcome surprise when harvest time rolls around.

How much to plant for two?

Problem: I would like to plant a few vegetables, but I don't want to supply the whole neighborhood—just my wife and myself. How can I know how much of each vegetable I should plant?

Solution: The following chart shows recommended number of feet of row to plant, for some of the most commonly-grown vegetables. Also check individual listings in the encyclopedia section of the *Sunset New Western Garden Book*.

	For fresh eating only	Fresh eating, plus canning, freezing, storing
Beans (bush)	30'	60'
Beans (pole)	15'	30'
Beets	20'	40'
Broccoli	12 plants	20 plants
Cabbage	10 plants	20 plants
Carrots	40'	80'
Lettuce*	10'*	—
Onions	10'	80'
Peas (English)	20'	40'
Peas (Sugar Snap)	20'	40'
Potatoes	20'	100'
Radishes*	3'*	—
Squash (summer)	4 plants each kind	—
Squash (winter)	—	5 hills
Sweet corn	50'	100'
Tomatoes	6 plants	15 plants

*For continuous crops, stagger plantings

OK to plow our old garden under?

Question: I want to plow under my entire vegetable garden when the harvest is over. We don't have room for a compost pile, but it seems to me that all that organic material can become compost right there in the soil. How do I go about this so that everything will decompose properly?

Answer: First, you should have access to a powerful rear-end tiller, especially if you want to till your cornstalks or squash vines. Make several passes with the tiller, sprinkling nitrogen fertilizer on the soil after the first run. (This helps to restore balance, as decomposing plants rob the soil of nitrogen.) All the plant material will decompose naturally by next spring's planting, and will improve the soil structure in the meantime.

Grandpa planted grocery potatoes. Can I?

Problem: My grandfather always planted potatoes in his garden using cut-up sections of grocery-store potatoes. I have followed the same practice, but mine have had a lot of problems with diseases.

Solution: In order to insure a healthy crop, start with potatoes that are certified disease free; these are available at most nurseries and garden centers. While potatoes from the grocery store are good to eat, they are often sprayed with a sprouting inhibitor. Also they may carry ailments harmful to future crops.

Can I grow spinach in the desert?

Question: We live in the desert and never have had any luck growing spinach. What are we doing wrong?

Answer: Spinach is an easy crop to grow in areas with a long, cool growing season. However, in warm climates, spinach quickly goes to seed before it matures. (In low desert climates, grow spinach in winter.) There are three alternates you might want to try growing during the warm season; all are similar in flavor to spinach although not the real McCoy:

Malabar spinach is a fast-growing vine with thick, succulent leaves. Although blander than true spinach, the leaves can be eaten cooked or raw.

New Zealand spinach is a spreading vegetable, considered a weed where it's native. Seed sown in March will produce a crop of tender new leaves in June. It can be cooked or eaten raw.

Tampala spinach is a variety of ornamental amaranth. Leaves are good cooked or raw.

Seeds for these three spinach substitutes are available from racks in nurseries or from seed catalogs.

What is an easy water-saving method?

Question: We live in an area where water is precious. I can't afford to install a sophisticated drip-irrigation system. Is there any simpler method that would give similar results?

Answer: Actually, there are several inexpensive yet effective drip-irrigation systems on the market. However, you can make a simple watering system using empty 2- or 3-pound coffee cans. This method works well with deep-rooted vegetables (squash, cucumbers, melons, corn) that are planted on hills or on level ground in groups. Punch holes in the bottom and sides of the can, or simply remove the bottom. Bury the can in the middle of each hill or group before you sow seeds, as shown in the illustration. Until plants are about a foot high, irrigate by surface watering; then switch to deep soaking by filling the cans with water from the hose. When you want to feed plants, mix fertilizer with water and pour into coffee cans.

In the case of melons, for maximum sweetness it is the standard practice to stop watering the plants three weeks before the anticipated harvest.

Drip irrigation made simple: bury can in middle of each grouping of vegetables before sowing seed.

Also see planting charts, pages 82–84, *Sunset New Western Garden Book*

Which squash for which season?

Question: As a beginning gardener, I'm confused as to when to plant squash. Are winter squash grown in the winter and summer squash in the summer? I would like to have squash all year around.

Answer: Both types of squash are planted in spring, both grow throughout the summer, and both require the same growing conditions. However, you harvest summer squash during the growing season, while winter squash stays on the vine until summer's end. Pick winter squash just before frost, and store for use throughout the winter.

Tomatoes half ripe, cold weather ahead

Problem: Although it is autumn, my tomato vines are still loaded with half-ripe tomatoes. Can I save the plants from the cold weather just ahead?

Solution: To extend the harvest season when fall frosts threaten, cover the plants with a blanket or a sheet of clear plastic at night, as shown in the illustration. Remove blanket or plastic during daytime hours. Also, reduce water to help fruit ripen faster.

Blanket or plastic sheet

Tomato tower with ripening tomatoes

When frost threatens, cover tomatoes with a blanket or sheet of plastic at night; remove it during the day.

How can I grow tomatoes in Puyallup?

Problem: Here in Puyallup, Washington (Zone 4), we have a hard time getting a good tomato crop. If we could get them to ripen faster during our cool, damp summers, we might get some results. Any ideas?

Solution: Growing tomatoes west of the Cascades is not easy; tomatoes need plenty of summer heat and sunshine, both limited commodities in your area. However, you have a good chance of growing healthy tomatoes and having them ready for harvest at the earliest possible date if you plant only those seed varieties that do well in your climate. 'IPB' and 'Pixie Hybrid' are among those tested and recommended.

Additionally, a proven growing technique is to encircle each plant with an old tire to absorb and retain heat, two weeks after setting plants out. If you have plenty of time, you might want to stack on a second tire a month or so later, when plants start to sprawl. (See illustration.)

Although it won't speed up your harvest as much, black plastic mulch is another way to retain warmth from the sun. It will reduce weeds, conserve water around the plants, and reduce rot by keeping fruit from direct contact with the ground.

Encircling each tomato plant with a tire helps to absorb and retain heat to speed up ripening.

Tomatoes vs. cutworms

Question: Every year I lose a lot of tomato transplants to cutworms. Is there any way to deal with them without using a chemical spray?

Answer: Arrange an aluminum-foil sleeve around the main stem of each plant. Make the sleeve from a 4- to 5-inch length of foil, folded into 2 thicknesses. Scratch some soil from around the plant base so that you can slip the sleeve about an inch below ground level. Tie the sleeve to the stem with twine about an inch from the top of the sleeve (don't tie too tightly). Keep foil in place for the entire season. (See illustration.)

Tomato troubles in Tucson

Problem: We live in the desert (Tucson), and the hot summers just never let our tomatoes get very far.

Solution: Tomatoes have poor fruit set when the temperature hovers above 100° F. Choose varieties that will ripen in a short growing season. Plant as early as possible to beat the heat. It's also a good idea to shade plants when temperatures soar (see illustration).

My vegetables bolt before harvest time

Problem: One of the biggest disappointments of my garden here in Palm Springs is that many of my vegetables bolt before I can harvest a crop. I've had the worst problems with cabbage, lettuce, radishes, and broccoli.

Solution: Bolting, the going-to-seed phenomenon, is triggered by warmth, long days, and intense sun. To guarantee a harvestable crop in Palm Springs (Zone 13), plant these vegetables in October so they will mature in late winter instead of spring. This planting time also is best for beets, carrots, cauliflower, celery, onions, and turnips.

Will any vegetables take shade?

Question: I'd like to raise vegetables, but my garden is in shade except for 2 or 3 hours midday. Is there anything I can grow mostly in the shade?

Answer: Yes, most root crops (carrots, beets, radishes, potatoes) grow satisfactorily in areas with a minimum of sun. Lettuce and spinach also do well. If the shade is caused by mature trees close by, root competition will cause trouble.

My zucchinis are dropping off

Problem: I thought zucchini was a super-easy plant to grow. This year I had a problem with the small squashes softening and dropping off before they reached harvest size.

Solution: The most likely cause is overwatering. When squash plants get too much water, they produce huge, lush leaves but meager fruit. A small zucchini on an over-watered vine will often turn yellow, rot, and fall off as it reaches thumb size. Let the plants dry out until leaves begin to droop a little. Within a week or 10 days, the problem should be resolved.

There are brown insects on my zucchini!

Problem: My zucchini plants have not produced any vegetables at all. I have noticed some small brown insects on them. Now the leaves are beginning to wilt badly.

Advice: Could be squash bug. If there are only a few bugs, pick them off the leaves and dispose of them. But the fact that the leaves are wilting means you probably have a sizable infestation; spray with sevin.

Aluminum foil sleeves protect plants from cutworms.

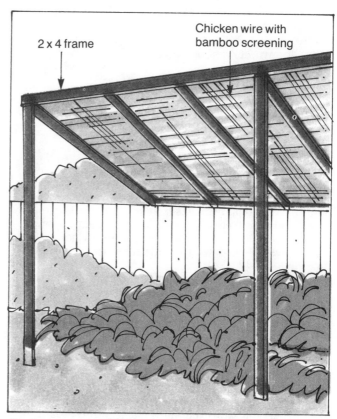

Simple sun screen can be moved into place to protect vegetables from extreme summer heat.

BERRIES & GRAPES

GUIDELINES FOR AVOIDING GENERAL PROBLEMS

Berries and grapes offer an abundant yield in exchange for minimum space and gardening time. Fairly easy to grow, they require little more than general garden maintenance. The biggest problem most gardeners have with these plants is how to prune them.

Each type of berry and grape has its own particular climate requirements. Match your choice to your special climate and you'll be on your way to a successful harvest.

Strawberries grow almost anywhere. Check with your local nursery for recommended varieties. *Blueberries* are at their best in the Pacific Northwest, but do well in other regions too, with special attention. *Raspberries* perform best where summers are cool and there is plenty of water. *Blackberries* (this category includes boysenberry, dewberry, loganberry, ollalieberry, and youngberry)

tolerate warmer climates. *Currants* and *gooseberries* thrive where summers are cool and winters are cold (make sure that they are not illegal plants in your area—they are alternate hosts to white pine blister rust). Not all *grapes* will grow in all climates, but—wherever you live in the West, there are varieties available in local nurseries that will do well for you.

Answers to many of your specific questions about berries and grapes are in this chapter. Also, refer to *Sunset New Western Garden Book*.

Generally, to avoid problems, pay attention to these rules:

- Select varieties suited to your area
- Improve soil as needed
- Plant berries at correct time; observe proper planting procedures and later care
- Prune annually

Blackberry blackout

Problem: Each year we put in a good sized vegetable garden to give us a variety of crops through the year. Last year, we decided to grow blackberries as well, so we bought a dozen plants and set them out in the good soil at one end of the vegetable plot. To put it mildly, they were a failure. At first the canes would grow vigorously; then leaves yellowed, wilted, and canes died. What could have happened?

Solution: No doubt you thought you were planting blackberries in good soil. But the probability is that you have grown one of the solanaceous plants (tomatoes, peppers, eggplant, potatoes) in the same soil within two years. These plants can carry the verticillium wilt disease, which will stunt or kill blackberries (also raspberries). Try again, starting with new plants in fresh soil.

Berried alive

Problem: We love blackberries and used to make several annual berrypicking excursions along country roads in our area where plants grow wild. But when we got our own garden, we decided to grow our own plants—so we

dug up a few starts from a roadside and set them out in some well-prepared soil. Now, try as we might, we can't keep the plants under control. They're sending out thumb-sized canes to 10 feet and more, and they're armed with enough thorns to terrify a shark. What should we do?

Answer: You brought into your garden the variety 'Himalaya', a rampant plant that knows no boundaries nor inhibition, and for the reasons you mentioned, is not usually sold. You should dig out your sharp-toothed foe and replace it with nursery plants of one of the good named varieties (you'd probably appreciate one of the thornless kinds). These are vigorous and productive but far less aggressive than 'Himalaya'. One virtue Himalaya does have is a long bearing season. When your garden plants are finished fruiting, you can resume your country road excursions for late-season berries.

Trim those trailing canes?

Question: We recently moved to the West Coast from Connecticut, and I was surprised at the "trailing blackberries" out here. Back home, the blackberries grow on upright, short canes. Should the trailing canes be pruned?

Answer: The first year, let the canes go unpruned, as trailing blackberries bear fruit only on canes that are 2 years old. At the start of growth in the second year, tie canes to a trellis. Either cut off the tops of the canes at 5 feet or weave the long canes onto the trellis (see illustration). Remove those that are weak, dead, or diseased. After harvest, cut to the ground all the canes that bore berries. Next year, tie to the trellis the new canes that grow during the summer.

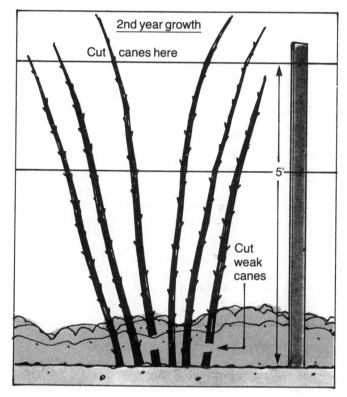

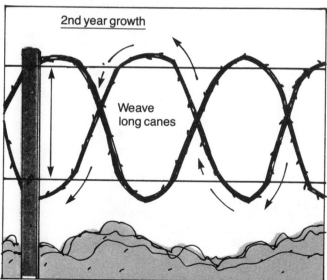

At start of blackberries' second-year growth, either cut off tops of canes at 5 feet or weave long canes into a trellis. Do not prune blackberries during the first year.

Our blueberries have the blues

Problem: We live in Caldwell, Idaho, and although I know the climate should be conducive to growing high-bush blueberries, we never seem to have much luck with them.

Solution: Your location (Zone 3) should indeed be satisfactory for blueberries. They prosper where winters are cold and summers are not too hot and dry. (They are at their best in Zones 4–6, and 17.)

Perhaps you haven't taken into account one of their most important requirements. Blueberries need a very acid soil (pH between 3.5 and 4.5), rich in organic matter. To increase soil acidity, mix one pound of soil sulfur per 100 square feet of sandy soil; or 3 to 4 pounds per 100 square feet of loam. Most soils will benefit from the yearly addition of generous amounts of peat moss, composted pine needles, or similar acidic organic material.

Gooseberries OK in hot climates?

Problem: Two years ago, we planted gooseberries along a sunny fence and they have been disappointing—very few berries. Is it our hot climate? (Modesto, California).

Solution: Generally, gooseberries prefer a cool climate (they are best in higher elevations of Zones 1–6, 17). The sunny spot where you have them is too hot. In warm areas like Modesto (Zone 14), gooseberries should be planted against a *north* wall or a similarly shaded location. Also provide them with a fertile, well-drained, sandy loam or clay loam.

My grapes died. Did I drown them?

Question: I understood that grapes need plenty of water when the fruit is developing, so last summer I watered them every other day—and they died! Why?

Answer: Maybe you killed them with kindness. The symptoms of drought and overwatering are often the same, because both conditions kill the roots of the plant. When the roots die, the plant cannot absorb any water; the leaves wither. The unwitting gardener mistakes this for drought and waters even more. Grapes are deep rooted, and once established, usually perform admirably with one or two deep soakings during summer.

Why fewer and fewer grapes?

Problem: Our old arbor is completely covered with a 'Perlette' grape vine. Over the past couple of years it seems to be producing fewer and fewer grapes. What might be the trouble?

Solution: In all probability, your problem is a result of lack of pruning. A vigorous pruning each winter keeps grape vines attractive with sturdy new canes and good fruiting and ripening. How to prune depends on the variety of grape. One of the methods is called spur pruning and the other long-cane pruning.

Spur pruning is used on most European grape varieties except for 'Thompson Seedless'; use it, for example, for 'Cardinal', 'Muscat', 'Perlette', 'Red Malaga', 'Ribier', 'Tokay', and the California wine varieties.

Long-cane pruning is the method for 'Thompson Seedless' and for most American grapes such as 'Concord', 'Delaware', 'Niagara', and 'Pierce'. These kinds don't produce much fruit when cut back to short spurs. They bear most of their fruit from buds farther out on the canes (the part that's cut off when branches are spur pruned).

Since your grape is a 'Perlette', spur pruning is called

for. With your first cuts, take out all dead, weak, or thin canes. Then, as an intermediate step, cut back all canes to five buds. Cut back all older unwanted arms even with the trunk. Don't leave stubs—they don't heal and they tend to have unwanted sprouts.

Choose the strongest 1-year-old, 5-bud spurs located at 1½ to 2-foot intervals (you can recognize 1-year-old canes by their smooth, rather than fibrous, texture). Cut them back again, leaving two or three buds on each. Leave about ¼ inch of wood above the endmost bud. Cut back even with the trunk all 5-bud spurs that you don't want to keep.

Techniques for pruning grapes are illustrated on page 314, *Sunset New Western Garden Book.*

What makes my grapes shrivel?

Problem: Many of my grapes start to shrivel as soon as they begin to ripen. What's wrong?
Solution: Could be mites. Dust with sulfur or spray with a wettable sulfur. Early next spring, spray with lime sulfur before the leaves open. Be sure to follow label directions exactly.

Lush vine, so-so grapes

Problem: We live in Mountain View, California, and have a 7-year-old 'Thompson Seedless' grape growing on an arbor. The vine itself is very healthy and lush, but the grapes have been consistently small and the flavor disappointing.
Advice: To develop their full size and flavor, 'Thompson Seedless' need plenty of summer heat—more than your Zone 15 location can offer. Considering the age of the vine, this might be a good time to take it out and replace it with 'Perlette'. Although somewhat less sweet, it has a very good flavor and requires less heat than the 'Thompson Seedless' to develop well.

Our 'Thompson Seedless' grape has mildew

Problem: Every year we run into trouble with mildew on our 'Thompson Seedless' grape vine. This year it seems worse than usual. Is there anything that can be done to prevent it from occurring?
Solution: Mildew can be a major problem with 'Thompson Seedless' and other European grapes (most American varieties are immune). To control, dust vines with one of the chemical controls suggested on page 41. Start when shoots are 6 inches long, repeat when they are 12 to 15 inches, then every 2 weeks until harvest. Vines growing near lawns may need additional dusting.

Can any grape make wine?

Question: We have a large enough lot to plant a small family vineyard, but we aren't sure what type of grapes to plant. Can any grape be made into wine?
Answer: In the most general sense, yes—any grape will produce wine, but some varieties are much better for wine production than others. Two basic classes are: European (*Vitis vinifera*)—tight skins, winelike flavor, generally high heat requirements, cold tolerance to about 5° F.; and American (*V. labrusca*)—slipskin, Concord-type flavor, moderate summer heat requirements, cold tolerance well below 0° F.

European varieties are the favored grapes for wine production. For the best success, be sure to consult with your nursery or county extension agent for recommended grape varieties in your area.

What, exactly, is an Olallieberry?

Question: My neighbor just planted Olallieberries in his garden. I've tasted Olallieberries before, and although they are good, they taste just like old-fashioned blackberries to me. Are they just a type of blackberry or are they a completely different berry?
Answer: Olallieberries are simply a named blackberry variety. Technically, they should be referred to as 'Olallie' blackberries. The same holds true for 'Boysen', 'Logan', and 'Young' berries.

My raspberry cuttings were duds

Problem: I made several dozen cuttings from a friend's raspberry vines, but only six or seven survived.
Solution: You probably took cuttings from canes that had borne berries that season. Canes die back after fruiting, and consequently cannot be used for propagation. Make 4- to 6-inch cuttings from fruitless canes; strip off the bottom leaves and plant in moist rooting medium.

What are "ever-bearing" raspberries?

Question: What is the difference between an ever-bearing raspberry and other varieties?
Answer: Standard varieties of raspberries bear their fruit in summer. One group of raspberries, known as the fall- or ever-bearing kinds, has a pattern of growth and fruit bearing that differs from the usual. These plants bear a crop of fruit in the autumn of the first year of their growth. The fruit is borne on the upper third of the new canes. The summer of the second year, these canes bear a second crop of fruit on the lower part of the cane. As new canes grow from the ground, this process is repeated year after year.

Remove first-year strawberry blossoms?

Question: I've heard that you should remove all blooms that form on strawberry plants the first year you put them out. Is this true? It seems extreme.
Answer: The practice of removing the blossoms during the first year ensures that ample nourishment will strengthen mother plants, fostering the early production of runners. Early runners of the first year will bear the best fruit the following year. If you have planted an everbearing variety you need only remove the blossoms until plants are well established, which usually is midsummer.

Strawberries in 'Vegas?

Question: Strawberries don't seem to like my Las Vegas, Nevada garden, but I still want to try to raise them. Are there kinds that do okay in the desert?
Answer: Your main problem may be the desert soil. Strawberries are hard to grow in the desert or other areas where soil and water salinity are high. Try planting them in a strawberry barrel or other large container. Use a good potting soil and a variety, such as 'Fresno', that will tolerate some salinity acquired through watering.

I'd like more flavor in strawberries

Question: When I recently moved here from Europe, I planted strawberries and was delighted when I saw the beautiful, large berries. But I was disappointed when I tasted them. Is there something I should have done to grow berries with more flavor?

Answer: You probably are used to the intensely flavorful little *fraises des bois* grown throughout Europe. American varieties are larger with a much milder flavor. Although some nurseries handle bare-root *fraises des bois* plants, your best bet is to order them from one of the large seed suppliers. They are very reliable about shipping bare-root plants early in spring.

"Lopsided" results for strawberry barrel

Problem: I have a large strawberry barrel planted with 24 plants in all pockets of the barrel. One side has lots of berries, but the other side has only a few and those do not ripen well.

Solution: Strawberries definitely do their best in full sun. For good flavor and red color, sun is the most important element. If you rotate the barrel a quarter turn every few days, you should notice soon that the plants are growing uniformly and evenly, producing ripe, red berries. (See illustration.)

Give strawberry barrel a quarter-turn every few days.

Snow snuffs out our strawberries

Question: We live in Estes Park, Colorado, and have had problems keeping strawberry plants alive during our cold winters. After the snow melts, my poor plants all appear to have been pushed out of the ground. Can I prevent this?

Answer: Mulching strawberries to prevent winter damage is vital in cold areas. Alternating periods of freezing and thawing can cause the ground to heave, uprooting the plants. In late November, when temperatures have dropped to freezing several times, loosely cover the

plants completely with an organic mulch such as straw.

As the new growth starts the following spring, brush the straw into the alleys between rows (be sure to clear mulch off the leaves). The mulch will help keep the fruit clean and hold down weeds. You can heap mulch over plants again whenever a late frost threatens; just remember to clear it away again the next day.

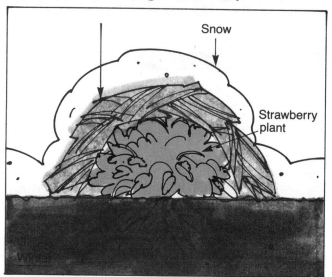

Cover strawberries with straw to protect them from snow.

Rake straw into "alleys" between rows to prevent weeds.

Why did my strawberries rot?

Question: I bought two dozen bare root strawberry plants a few weeks ago and planted them in my garden. Half of them are doing OK, but the others rotted. What went wrong?

Answer: When you plant strawberries, you need to pay special attention to the depth that you place them in the soil. If you plant them too high, the roots will dry out and wither. If you plant them too deep, the plants will rot, as you found out. For the best results, the crowns should be right at soil level. When you purchase bare-root strawberries, keep the roots moist until you are ready to plant. Before planting, trim the roots with a pair of scissors, to about 4 inches.

Know your climate zone—see pages 4 & 5

GUIDELINES FOR AVOIDING GENERAL PROBLEMS

Herbs are *botanically* nonexistent. By common agreement, they are called herbs—the name covering a wide variety of plants primarily useful for cooking, scents, and remedies. Herbs may be annuals, perennials, biennials, grasses, vegetables, shrubs, or even weeds.

The herbs discussed in this chapter are mainly culinary varieties. They may be set out in kitchen gardens; used as ground covers, borders, hedges, in rock gardens, or in containers; raised indoors or out. Their common denominator is hardiness—they are relatively pest and problem-free, and have no special water and feeding requirements. Most do well in a sunny location in well-drained soil.

Don't be deceived by the small size of some nursery plants. The perennial herbs, especially, form large, long-lived plants that will give plenty of leaves to dry or freeze for out-of-season use.

The biggest problem may be timing—having fresh dill when the cucumbers are ready for pickling, for instance. See the listings of herbs on pages 321 and 322, *Sunset New Western Garden Book;* then look up individual plants in the encyclopedia section, pages 161–505.

Generally, remember these tips:
- Plant in the proper location; if combining several kinds of herbs (as most gardeners do), be sure you are not grouping shade plants and sun lovers in the same place
- Prepare the soil well and provide good drainage
- Water regularly (deep soaking in most cases), and fertilize once or twice a year

Must herbs be dried before using?

Question: Do I have to dry my herbs before using them? I just don't have time.

Answer: It's not even essential to chop them up. You can cut and use whole sprigs from the garden, wash them, and let them simmer or soak with foods, then use in soup, gravy or soup stock, or soak in marinades. Remove before serving as you would a bay leaf. Or snip leaves into tiny pieces with kitchen scissors or a knife. With most herbs you can use approximately twice the volume of fresh, undried herb as you would if it were dried.

Which herbs with what foods?

Question: I recently planted several kinds of herbs, and am looking forward to using them in my everyday cooking as much as possible. How can I find out which foods to use them with?

Answer: The *Sunset* book, *Easy Basics for Good Cooking,* includes a chart which gives ideas for 21 kinds of herbs and spices. Also, special publications are sometimes available in gourmet stores and some bookstores. Some cooks don't always follow the rules, preferring to rely on their noses, their taste buds, and their experiences dining out with friends, in restaurants, or even traveling. Ethnic restaurants often present combinations (the Armenian use of mint in green salads, or with yogurt and meat) you won't find elsewhere. Some combinations are so universal they deserve mention here: basil or tarragon with tomatoes, mint with lamb, cilantro with Mexican or Chinese, or Indian mixtures, dill with fish.

I only have room for a few

Question: I would like to have some herbs to use in cooking, but only have growing space for a few. Which ones do you recommend?

Suggestion: The answer depends a great deal on both your cooking and gardening habits. One approach would be to start with the herbs that lose most when dried, and therefore are least satisfactory to buy: basil, cilantro, dill, tarragon, parsley, chives, also mint if you use it frequently. Lemon thyme is another good choice, because it is almost never sold.

Can herbs cope with clay?

Question: The first herb garden I planted in our adobe soil in Redwood City, California, did not grow well. Now I'm planning another garden and want to avoid problems with the hard soil this time. What should I do?

Answer: If you only plan to grow a modest number of herbs, consider planting in containers or a raised bed.

But if you prefer to grow them in your adobe-soil garden, make sure of good drainage. Most herbs, even moisture-loving mints, like well-drained soil and many won't grow at all if roots are constantly wet. For good drainage, dig and turn the soil to a depth of about 12 inches; break up the clods. Incorporate 6 inches or more of organic matter (peat moss, leaf mold, sawdust, compost) to improve soil texture. (See Organic soil amendments, page 33, *Sunset New Western Garden Book.*)

Hungry for basil—when can I pluck?

Question: My basil plants are about 6 inches high and look fairly healthy. Would I be damaging the plants if I began using a few leaves?

Answer: A few leaves of most culinary herbs—including basil, oregano, tarragon, thyme, and rosemary—can be picked while the plants are small. As they grow, cutting the tips actually encourages bushy growth and side-branching. (See illustration.)

Cut tips for kitchen use

Cutting tips of basil and most culinary herbs when you need them for cooking encourages bushy growth. Even very young plants won't miss a few leaves.

The perils of potted parsley

Problem: The only outdoor garden space I have is a sunny balcony. I've grown basil and oregano in pots, but don't have success with parsley.

Advice: Parsley, like dill, has taproots too long for growing in small to medium-sized pots. The container must be at least 16 inches deep to accommodate the full-grown root. But most herbs do well in containers if they are large enough and the plants are put in good soil and given the proper sun and water.

Several herbs planted in one large container work well in a limited space. You might try a large pot of Italian herbs and another of salad herbs for kitchen use.

OK to spray insect pests?

Problem: My herb plants get chewed from time to time, like any plants, but I'm hesitant to spray them since eventually they'll be used at the dinner table. How about this?

Solution: Chemical sprays and dusts for pest control are not recommended for kitchen herbs, but a weak solution of yellow naphtha soap and water applied as a spray should control any infestations. Most small insect pests, such as aphids, can be knocked off with a strong stream of water from the hose. Always wash herbs well before eating them.

Shrub for a garden potpourri?

Question: There is a warm blank wall in my herb garden that I'd like to soften with a tall shrub. But I want something that will fit in with my other fragrance herbs—lavender, sweet woodruff, bee balm, lemon verbena—and several scented geraniums.

Answer: One of the best treats you can give yourself and your fragrance herb garden is to plant one of the old roses (including wild or species roses and their hybrids). Among the best of the vigorous, hardy shrubs are cabbage rose *(Rosa centifolia)* with big, pink, very fragrant bloom; damask rose *(R. damascena)* with clusters of sweet-scented, double, pink flowers; and musk rose *(R. moschata)* whose blooms range from red through pink to yellow and white, and are heavily scented. All grow to around 6 feet. For specific varieties, see Old Roses, page 454 of the *Sunset New Western Garden Book.*

Tasteless tarragon: what went wrong?

Question: I planted tarragon seed this spring with hopes of using it for cooking, and especially for flavoring vinegar. But it just doesn't taste like tarragon. What went wrong?

Answer: You probably planted Russian tarragon, not the favored variety for culinary use. You want French tarragon, also called true tarragon. This does not produce usable seeds and plants must be started from divisions or cuttings. At your nursery, buy rooted cuttings specifically marked "French tarragon" or "culinary tarragon". Or ask for names of local herb growers that start tarragon from cuttings. Started cuttings usually come in 2-inch pots and are quite small, but grow rapidly once planted in the garden. For more information, see *Artemesia dracunculus*, page 189, *Sunset New Western Garden Book.*

I'd like something unusual

Question: I have all the basic herbs. Can you recommend something a little different, and suggest ways to use them in the kitchen?

Suggestions: Try sweet woodruff, a lovely, delicate green spreader for shade. Its leaves add an elusive cinnamon-vanilla flavor to fruit punches and salads. Let sprigs soak in liquid for several hours; remove them before serving. Two other herbs that can be used in the same way are pineapple sage and lemon verbena.

FRUIT TREES

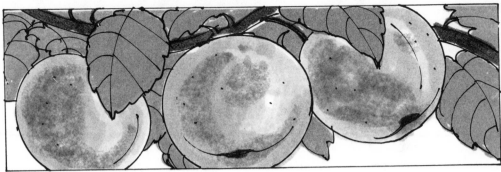

GUIDELINES FOR AVOIDING GENERAL PROBLEMS

Fruit trees are notable for their list of afflictions and problems. To grow top quality fruit demands some type of organized spray schedule. The pests and diseases that attack fruit trees do so with great regularity, and unless you don't mind a few worms in your apples, or losing the majority of your cherry crop to the birds, some protective measures must be taken.

It is very important to give careful thought to variety selection. Many varieties of apples, peaches, and pears, to cite just one example, need a requisite number of hours below 45° F. in order to set a respectable crop. If you live in a mild winter area, you would want to think twice about taking a chance with one of these varieties.

Yearly pruning is another demand of fruit trees. Unlike ornamental trees and shrubs that need pruning primarily for cosmetic reasons, fruit trees need proper pruning in order to produce a good crop. And not all fruit trees are pruned in the same manner. Before you go into the family orchard with a pair of pruning shears, check the individual fruit tree listings in *Sunset New Western Garden Book* for advice.

To sum up briefly, you will grow better fruit with minimum fuss if you follow this advice:
- Make variety selection with care, matching the tree's needs with your climate
- Set up a spray schedule, and follow it
- Prune correctly and at the proper time

My apples have black spots

Problem: There are rough black spots on my 'Gravenstein' apples this year.
Solution: The spots probably result from scab or black spot fungus. To make sure that the condition does not recur next year, treat with a dormant spray of lime sulfur just before the flower buds open. When the blossoms show pink, and again when three-quarters of the petals have fallen, spray with wettable sulfur.

Our apples and cherries are stingy

Problem: We moved to El Monte, California (Zone 20) about two years ago. Last year the trees in our garden produced all the fruit we could use. But this spring they are stingy—just a handful of cherries appeared, and now in late fall, only a few apples.
Solution: Winters in Southern California can sometimes be quite warm, depriving cherries, apples, and some other deciduous fruit trees of the cold period required to produce fruit. In late fall, you can try a method of shocking the trees into blooming heavily next spring and setting fruit: Don't water them at all during the winter. The theory is that the tree is forced into dormancy, so it works hard to produce a large crop of seed-bearing fruit to perpetuate itself.

In addition to shocking your trees, feed them with a time-release fertilizer next spring, just after the new growth starts.

Which apples are best for cider?

Question: We live in good apple-growing country, and have enough room to grow a small family orchard. We particularly would like to grow apples for making into cider. Are there any apple varieties that are particularly recommended for this purpose?
Answer: Too sweet an apple, such as 'Golden Delicious', will produce cider that ferments too quickly. The less sweet 'Grimes Golden' and 'Macoun' are good for a light cider. For sharper flavor, 'Red Winesap', 'Tydeman's Red', and 'Spartan' are good choices. For a good all-around cider choice, 'Gravenstein' is hard to beat.

Apple maggot messed up our fruit

Problem: Last fall, my apples looked great on the outside, but were riddled with brown tunnels on the inside. I live near Portland, Oregon, and am afraid that my ruined crop may have been caused by apple maggot fly. What should I do?
Solution: You are right to be concerned. Larvae of the apple maggot fly, which looks like a striped housefly, are persistent destroyers. The fly lays its eggs first in early apples, then in later apples as the season passes. The maggot that does the damage is white, legless, and about ¼ inch long.

To control the situation next season, spray in mid-July with diazinon, and continue spraying every 2 weeks until September 1.

Why suckers after pruning?

Question: After a really heavy dormant pruning, my apple trees produced a lot of new sprouts from where the major cuts were made. Why this reaction?

Answer: Sometimes apple trees (and pear trees) react to heavy pruning by overgrowth. To help control it, a growth-regulating hormone called naphthalene acetic acid can be painted or sprayed on the pruning cuts. Also recommended is to do selective pruning in midsummer, which will mean less pruning in the dormant season later on.

Apple tree for a small garden?

Question: I would love to have an apple tree, both for its fruits and for shade. The problem, though, is that my yard is a bit small for apple trees as I remember them from orchards in my childhood. Dwarf trees would provide the fruit, but not the shade. Is there possibly some way I could prune a full-sized apple variety to achieve my desire?

Answer: The sort of apple you want already exists: there are spur-type apples—mutations of some popular varieties—that grow to about ⅔ the size of a standard tree. If your nursery doesn't have the variety you want in a spur-type plant, you may be satisfied with a regular variety grafted on a semi-dwarfing rootstock. These trees will mature at a size smaller than the standard size but larger than those on dwarfing rootstock.

Must organic apples be wormy?

Question: I'm an organic gardener, and recently bought a place with several mature apple trees. Virtually every apple we pick has a worm in it. I'd like to get good apples next year without using chemical controls. Possible?

Answer: Sounds like codling moths, which are notoriously difficult to control. *Bacillus thuringiensis*, a nonchemical microbial insecticide, can be an effective organic control, with proper timing being the key to success. (For more information about control of codling moths, see pages 56 and 57, *Sunset New Western Garden Book*.)

My apricots have freckles

Problem: Spots like freckles, and also some cracks, are damaging all my apricots before they are fully ripe. Is there anything I can do this year or next to prevent this?

Solution: It's too late this year to cure your apricots of "freckle," a disease caused by a fungus. But next spring, spray with a copper fungicide such as zineb when the flowers first show color; spray again when the petals drop. Carefully read and follow all label directions.

Gummy apricot trees

Problem: For several years, our apricot trees have been blighted with gummy, sticky black splits. Can this be prevented?

Solution: Bacterial canker probably is the cause. It can be controlled with a copper spray when the blossoms first show color, and in autumn when the leaves are dropping.

When bees went, so did avocados

Question: My avocado tree no longer produces any avocados. I've noticed that the bees are gone, too. Do the two go together?

Answer: Yes, bees are the pollinating agents for avocados and these useful insects suffer from the widespread use of certain pesticides. Sometimes, though, certain varieties of avocado just pick a bad time of year to bloom, such as when the weather is cold and wet. Even though bees may be present then, they don't work actively during that kind of weather.

My first avocado: 90% pit!

Question: I thought I was a winner finally when the avocado I planted from a pit seven years ago bore fruit this summer. But when I cut open the first avocado, it was about 90% pit. So were the others. What caused this?

Answer: Some seedlings give poor fruit. Sometimes the grower is lucky, and the avocados are excellent. But as likely as not, they will be stringy and all pit—inferior to those in the market. If you really want a tree for fruit, better plant another one. Ask at your local nursery for the name of a variety especially adapted to your area. (For more information on avocados, see page 193, *Sunset New Western Garden Book*.)

Yes, we have no bananas

Problem: In the garden of our new house in El Cajon, Southern California, is a dwarf banana (*Musa acuminata* 'Dwarf Cavendish', we were told last year when we bought the house). But—yes, we have no bananas. Seems to me that El Cajon (Zone 23) should be hot enough. Could it be the soil?

Solution: El Cajon is hot enough; so are Zones 21–24. The soil could definitely be part of the problem. Banana plants prefer a rich soil with lots of organic matter, routine watering, regular applications of fertilizer. Also, if you want to make sure of a banana crop, remove all but one or two of the suckers. This permits the plant's energy to concentrate on producing one or two mature, fruiting stalks, rather than a large clump of banana plants with foliage only.

Will bare-root trees keep for awhile?

Question: This weekend we purchased several bare-root fruit trees, along with a number of other plants. We got everything planted—except for the fruit trees. Is it necessary to get them in the ground right away, or will they keep for awhile?

Answer: It is very important to not let the roots dry out. The easiest thing to do is to "heel them in" as follows: lay each tree on its side, dig a shallow hole for the root system, and cover the roots with moist sawdust or peat moss, or even damp soil. It's also a good idea to cover the sawdust or other protective material with a tarp or piece of plastic to reduce evaporation. If the heeled-in trees are in a cool, shaded location they should be fine for a week or two, perhaps longer—but don't let them leaf out too much or take root.

Our bare-root apricot is scraggly

Question: We planted a bare-root apricot last January. This April, the tree has grown long, weak branches. My grandfather had an orchard, and I know those scraggly branches don't look like his trees. What did we do wrong?

Answer: It's what you *didn't* do that resulted in the problem. The illustration shows how the tree should have been pruned at planting time. To establish a good basic framework, you have to grit your teeth and cut back your brand-new tree probably more than seems right to you at the time. Had you pruned it in January, the result in April would have been a smaller tree, but with sturdier, more heavily foliaged branches—the beginnings of a well-shaped tree.

Next time you plant a bare-root fruit tree, prune off the top so the tree stands around 3 to 4 feet high. Then select 2 or 3 side branches that are spaced spirally around the trunk. Cut off the remaining branches, and prune back the ones you've kept by one-third to one-half.

There is nothing you can do now in April, but in late fall or winter prune your apricot tree as described for cutting back at planting time.

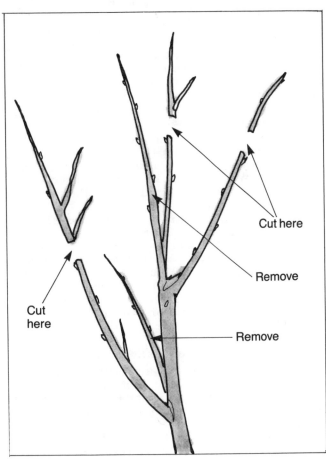

Arrows show where pruning cuts should be made on a bare-root tree, after planting, to avoid spindly growth.

Can citrus cope with caliche?

Question: We live in Tucson, Arizona, and our garden soil is the typical native caliche. Is there any way we can have success with dwarf citrus trees in this awful hardpan soil?

Answer: Yes, if you're willing to do some work. Take a look at the illustration and these steps:

Planting: First, dig through the caliche layers with pick and shovel (or rent special steel tools, or an electric or pneumatic jackhammer, depending on how tough and deep the caliche is). Dig holes 8 by 8 feet wide and 5 feet deep, haul away caliche, and dig a 4–6-inch drainage chimney down to a gravelly layer. Refill the holes with good soil and plant trees—generally in March and April.

(Also see Shallow soil, page 34, *Sunset New Western Garden Book.*)

Watering basins: Dig basin at least out to the tree's dripline, but keep water away from the trunk.

Irrigation: Water deeply when needed. A soil-sampling tube can help to determine how fast the soil is drying. (See illustration, page 129.) Water established trees by slow overnight irrigation when the soil is dry 6 inches down.

Feeding: Nitrogen-rich fertilizer is best for Arizona soils. Mature trees can be fed four times a year (February, April, June, and August) to give a total of 2 pounds nitrogen per 100 square feet of root area.

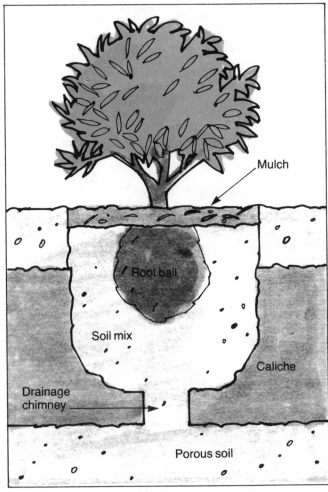

Drainage chimney, bored through the layer of caliche, allows excess water to escape into porous soil beneath.

Best time to plant fruit trees?

Question: When is the best time to plant fruit trees?
Answer: Any time during the dormant season. Nurseries usually carry a good supply of bare-root trees in late winter and very early spring. Fruit trees are not only less expensive at this time, but the selection is also at its best. If you live in an area with significant winter rains, the condition of your soil will be a major consideration as to when you plant. The soil should have dried out enough so you can work easily with a shovel. But, by all

means, plant bare-root trees *before* new growth starts to push out on them.

Who gets cherries—we or the birds?

Problem: Every year, we have a race with the birds to see who's going to get the cherry crop from our two trees. Is there any simple solution to this problem? We don't want to hurt the birds.

Solution: The most effective preventative is light netting (sold as "bird netting") placed over the tree and gathered at base. This should be done well ahead of the ripening season. Another often-overlooked method is to use black cotton thread. Simply tie one end to a low branch, then play catch with the unwinding spool back and forth across the tree. The job is finished—usually a spool or two later—when there's a random network of thread over the tree, with 4 to 6 inches between the threads. Unlike netting, the thread isn't rigid and evenly spaced, so it's hard for the birds to see the openings. Rather than risk getting their wings tangled in threads, they'll usually go somewhere else for cherries. Be sure to use cotton thread, since it will disintegrate and not interfere with pruning later.

To ward off hungry birds, encase fruit tree in netting.

No cherries for 8 years. Why?

Question: We have an 8-year-old sweet cherry tree that forms flowers every spring but never has any cherries afterward. Is it some special kind?

Answer: No, the tree just needs a companion. Most sweet cherry varieties need another tree close by to mutually pollinate and produce crops. (Sour cherries, on the other hand, are self-pollinating.) But not all sweet cherry varieties will pollinate each other. If you decide to plant a companion cherry tree, see the correct varieties on page 236, *Sunset New Western Garden Book.*

Some sweet cherry varieties need pollination from another variety in order to produce a crop.

What distance should we leave between trees?

Question: Can you tell me how far to space standard (non-dwarf) fruit trees? We are in the process of planning a family orchard with about 16 trees, and I can't seem to find the information on how far apart they should be planted.

Answer: Apples need the most space and are usually spaced on 30-foot centers. Peaches, pears, and plums require less space, and should be on 20-foot centers.

What about dwarfs and semi-dwarfs?

Question: We live on a small lot and would like to plant a few fruit trees. I've been told that I should consider planting dwarf varieties, given our limited space. At the nursery, both dwarf and semi-dwarf trees are offered. What's the difference?

Answer: The dwarf trees will be smaller (usually around 6 feet) when mature than the semi-dwarf. It is hard to be more specific regarding eventual sizes without knowing what kind of fruit tree you prefer and the types of dwarfing rootstock available. For example, five different dwarfing rootstocks are commonly used to reduce the growth of standard apple varieties from 30 to

Problems with pests? See pages 32—48

70 percent. If the exact size of the mature tree is important, ask at your nursery or garden center to see whether they can find out what rootstock was used on the trees.

What is a genetic dwarf?

Question: I keep seeing advertisements for genetic dwarf fruit trees—especially peaches. What are genetic dwarfs?

Answer: The majority of dwarf fruit trees are standard varieties grafted on a dwarfing rootstock. With genetic dwarfs, the opposite is true: the above-ground portion of the tree is a naturally occurring dwarf which, in turn, is grafted onto a standard rootstock. These trees are generally very small, rarely over 3 feet, and quite productive.

Can an old fig foster figlets?

Question: We have an old fig tree. No one seems to know what variety it is, but everyone who tastes the fruit wants to plant the same kind of tree. Is there any way I can propagate new plants from my old tree?

Answer: In January, cut off pieces of healthy twigs with a sharp knife, making a diagonal cut (as shown in the illustration), and leave the terminal bud in place. After taking a slice of bark off the lower end of the cutting, dip the cutting into rooting hormone, and bury it halfway in sandy soil. Place the cuttings in a coldframe or next to a south-facing wall for the winter. By June, the cutting should have a few sprouts and some roots, and be ready to transplant. (For detailed information about propagating plants from cuttings, see pages 38 and 39, *Sunset New Western Garden Book*.)

Help for fruit-laden trees

Question: How can I keep the heavily laden branches of my peach trees from breaking?

Answer: The most immediate method is to prop branches on stakes. But the difficulty with this is that the stakes interfere with working under the tree. A better way is to tie a long 4-by-4 post upright to the trunk of the tree. At the top of the post, tie ropes down to the fruit-burdened branches; this gently supports them. Don't pull up on the branches—tie just firmly enough to take the weight of the fruit. (See illustration.)

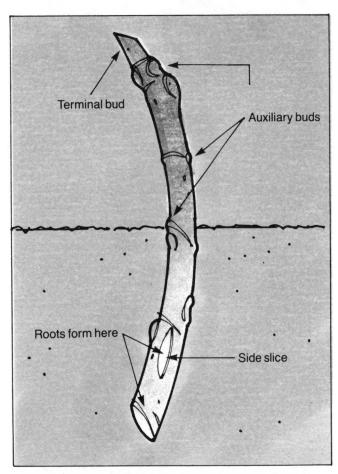

Fig cutting started in sandy soil in January should have a few sprouts and be ready to transplant in June.

Ropes, tied near the top of a long 4-by-4 post, prevent the fruit-laden branches from sagging.

My mandarin is lopsided

Problem: Although I rotate my tubbed mandarin orange regularly, the foliage is very sparse on one side. The leaves are yellow and droopy.

Advice: If you rotate the container regularly, the problem probably has little to do with the amount of sun it receives. When one side of a citrus has the symptoms you describe, it is usually caused by root rot. Check to see that water drains through the container thoroughly; make sure that the drainage holes are not clogged. Containers should be filled with a soil mix that drains thoroughly and evenly.

Some of my nectarines won't ripen

Problem: Few nectarines develop toward the middle section of my young trees, and what there is never ripens fully. What's the cause?

Solution: Because of the rapid growth of new fruit trees, dense upright branches sometimes leave the interior of the tree in deep shade. Lack of light discourages fruiting. One way to let in the sun is to use simple notched stakes for spreading the young branches and promoting a slower, wider-angled growth. (See illustration.)

Notched stake spreads branches of young fruit tree and allows sunlight into center to speed ripening of fruit.

Our nut trees have oak root fungus

Problem: Oak root fungus has done in most of our nut trees, but our two pecans seem to be okay. Is it just a matter of time before they, too, die? We'd really like to have nut-producing trees. What do you suggest? We live in Tulare, California (Zone 8).

Answer: Luckily, pecans *(Carya illinoensis)* are resistant to oak root fungus. Big, fast-growing trees, pecans usually start to bear nuts in four to seven years. (See *Carya illinoensis,* page 223 of the *Sunset New Western Garden Book,* which also has a list—on page 156—of trees that are resistant to oak root fungus.) Also, turn to page 42 of this book for a special section on this fungus infection, which for various reasons is more of a problem in California than elsewhere in the West.

Why won't young orange tree produce?

Question: We have had our orange tree two years, and have had no fruit since the oranges that were on it when we bought it. Why is it failing to bear fruit? We live in Bakersfield, California (Zone 8).

Answer: The branches of container-grown citrus nurseries mature early because the restricted root space dwarfs the plant. Once it is removed from the nursery container and transplanted into the garden, a larger root system develops, and the leafy portion responds by sending out new shoots. When those new shoots mature, you will start having fruit again. Be patient.

Our grapefruits were "lemons"

Problem: Although our grapefruit tree bloomed profusely, what little grapefruit that appeared soon shriveled and fell.

Advice: One possible cause of this problem is a scab fungus, which attacks the plant just after blossoming. Toward the end of the blossoming period next year, spray the tree with fungicide such as Bordeaux mixture or a lime-sulfur combination. Read and follow all label directions.

The trunk of my lemon is rotting

Problem: All along the bottom of the trunk of my lemon tree, the bark is splayed out and the wood beneath looks rotten.

Solution: Sounds like a fungus called collar rot—a particular problem when the citrus is planted too low and moisture collects near the bud union. Once the condition exists, the best procedure is to remove all the rotted wood with a sharp instrument, and then to spray the area with a copper spray (such as Bordeaux mixture). Seal the wound with an application of pruning paint.

My fruit trees have small crops

Problem: I have a small garden in Santa Monica, California (Zone 24) with one peach tree and one apricot tree that I ordered from an out-of-state mail-order nursery. They are several years old and, although they bloom well, have had very small crops.

Advice: Many deciduous fruit trees, including peach and apricot, need several hundred hours of winter temperature below 45°F. (7°C.) to produce a satisfactory crop. Santa Monica's winters are too mild for many standard fruit varieties. If you need replacements for your existing trees, purchase them at a local nursery or garden center familiar with varieties adapted to your climate. Or consider an Oriental or Asiatic pear tree. Although their fruit can't compare to the European varieties for eating fresh, the firm texture makes them good for cooking or for combining with other fruits in salads.

What to do when? See pages 6–31

Why are my fruits so small?

Problem: I inherited several plum, peach, and apricot trees with the purchase of our home two years ago. The trees seem healthy (and last year I was extra careful to water), but all the fruit is small. It tastes okay but is definitely undersized. How can I get larger fruit?
Solution: One way to get large fruit from your trees is to thin out the excess. It also keeps branches from breaking. The time to do it is when the fruits are ½ to ¾ inch in diameter; at that stage, they come off easily.

Thin plums and apricots until they are 4 to 6 inches apart. Space peaches 8 to 12 inches apart; early peaches especially need thinning or they'll be undersized. (See illustration).

For biggest plums, apricots, or peaches, thin as shown.

Our oranges look sooty

Problem: We have noticed black sooty areas on our oranges. It wipes off easily, but we would like to get rid of it.
Solution: Your orange tree probably is infected with some type of scale insect. Look for small white shell-like infestations stuck to the branches of the tree. The scale insects exude a sticky substance called "honeydew" that attracts ants and provides a home for the sooty fungus you described. Aphids and other sucking insects also produce honeydew. Rather than treating the sooty fungus, you should get rid of the cause—the scale insects. Spray the tree in winter with an oil-base dormant spray. But, until the tree goes dormant, wash it (and the fruit) with the hose frequently. (Also, see Scale, page 36.)

Sour lemons, yes, but sour *oranges*?

Problem: I live in San Mateo County, in the San Francisco Bay Area, and although our orange trees are healthy and have a lot of fruit, the oranges are always sour.
Advice: Although oranges make beautiful ornamental trees in San Mateo County and in other areas on or near the northern California coast, there simply isn't enough heat during the ripening period for most varieties to produce a sweet-tasting orange. However, 'Valencia' and the navel varieties will produce reasonably sweet oranges in many parts of coastal California.

Why do our peach leaves curl?

Problem: Every year, the new leaves on our peach tree become blistered and distorted, curl up and become reddish in color, then wither and drop. Is there something to prevent this?
Solution: The disease is called "peach leaf curl" and it also affects nectarines and almonds. It can be controlled by spraying the entire tree with lime sulfur or Bordeaux mixture. Treat the tree after all the leaves drop in the fall, and again just before buds open in the spring.

Organic control for peach leaf curl?

Problem: I'm a devout organic gardener, but have yet to find an organic cure for peach leaf curl. Every year the trees are severely affected. Is there anything I can do?
Advice: There is one method—yet to be proven scientifically—that began in Europe generations ago. There, farmers observed that where garlic grows wild, peach trees are remarkably free of the disease. At the same time that you plant any peach or nectarine tree, plant garlic to cover an 8-foot circle around its trunk. Chives or shallots might also be used. The plants are not for harvesting, but to grow as permanent companions.

When you hoe around the tree to loosen soil or to get rid of weeds, chop lightly into the companion plants also to help assure their good growth.

Non-organic gardeners (and organic gardeners except for the most devout) spray the entire tree with Bordeaux mixture. See "Why do our peach leaves curl?" immediately above.

Pears droopy and "scorched"—overnight

Problem: Overnight, branches on my two pear trees suddenly wilted; they look as if they have been scorched.
Advice: Unfortunately, that is fireblight, one of the most damaging pear tree diseases. The recommended treatment is to spray with streptomycin, but when you do it is all-important. For a complete discussion of fireblight, see page 43.

What a letdown: mealy pears

Problem: Our 'Comice' pear tree produced its first crop this year. We picked the pears when they turned yellow, but the flavor wasn't very good and the texture was mealy. I thought 'Comice' was an excellent variety.
Solution: 'Comice' pears are excellent, but all pears should be picked when they are green, and allowed to ripen in a cool, dark place. Tree-ripened pears do not have the quality of those ripened indoors.

Our pecans are pathetic

Problem: We have a large pecan tree in our garden in Sacramento, California. The nuts have never been satisfactory—they are pathetically small and don't fill out the shell.

Explanation: Although Sacramento (Zone 14) offers enough warm weather to be considered good pecan territory in general, some varieties need even more intense heat over a long period of time. (The hot summers of Zones 9, 12–14, 18–20 are excellent.) Insufficient heat results in the kind of inferior nuts you described. You probably cannot count on ever getting a desirable crop from the tree. Contact your county extension agent for varieties that do well in your area. Some varieties need pollenizers; see page 223, *Sunset New Western Garden Book.*

Pecan trees twiggy, leaves sickly

Problem: We live in Arizona, which supposedly is a great area for pecan trees. This year our 5-year-old trees have odd-looking clumps of twigs on the ends of the branches, and the leaves look kind of a sickly yellow-green.

Solution: Pecans suffer from one serious problem in Arizona soils: a zinc deficiency. January is the month to correct this for established trees. The best cure—and preventative—is to feed trees yearly with zinc sulfate, given through the soil or by leaf sprays. For soil applications, give trees 1 pound of zinc sulfate per inch of trunk diameter. You can either bore 12 to 15 auger holes 15 to 20 inches deep, inside the tree's dripline, or dig a flat-bottomed 3-inch-deep trench at the line. Spread the proper amount of zinc sulfate, and water it in.

To spray trees, use a solution of 1 teaspoon zinc sulfate per gallon of water. First spray trees when leaf buds start to open in February, and then repeat sprayings twice at 10- to 14-day intervals. Wet foliage thoroughly each time.

Is there a "pucker-proof" persimmon?

Question: Is there such a thing as a persimmon that doesn't pucker the mouth?

Answer: None will if dead ripe. One variety, 'Fuyu', is non-astringent even when it is underripe. 'Fuyu' is firm-fleshed, about like an apple, and a little smaller than a baseball. For more information, see page 402, *Sunset New Western Garden Book.*

Should pruning cuts be sealed?

Question: It's pruning time again, and I am just as confused by what I read as I was last year. Should I not seal over the cuts after pruning my fruit trees?

Answer: There is still much debate about sealing over the cuts, and most experts even seem to feel that nature can heal the wounds best. On the side of using sealing compounds, however, is the fact that naphthalene acetic acid (NAA) will inhibit the growth of water sprouts next summer.

Our tree trunks are sunburned?

Problem: We live in southern California and planted a small "family orchard" last spring. This fall, we noticed that many of the trunks were cracked and appeared to be burned.

Solution: Until a young fruit tree develops thick enough bark to protect its trunk, the tree is susceptible to many hazards, particularly sunburn, if you live in hot-summer areas. Protect the trunk by painting it with white-wash or white latex paint; by wrapping it loosely with gauze bandage; or by placing a cylinder of heavy paper around the trunk.

Winter sun scald—what to do?

Problem: The bark of several of our apple and cherry trees has been afflicted with winter sun scald (or so we're told). Can you tell us what causes this and how to prevent it? We live east of the Cascades in Spokane, Washington (Zone 2).

Solution: Winter sun scald is a serious problem in your area. In January and February, days are often bright and clear, and the warmth of the sun on the southwest side of the tree trunk begins to activate growth cells. Then, when the sun goes down, temperature plummets, and the cold ruptures those cells and dries them out. Apple, cherry, and smooth-barked shade trees are particularly susceptible.

There are two good ways to protect the trees. One is to wrap them in strips of burlap and secure with twine. Or you can place a wide board several inches away from the tree on the southwest side, which will cast a shadow on the trunk (see illustration for details). In March or April, when the weather is milder, you can remove the sun screen.

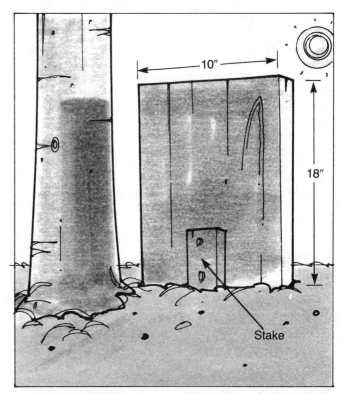

For winter sun protection, wide board (nailed to stake and driven into ground) casts a shadow on the trunk.

Isn't thinning wasteful?

Question: We have a 10-year-old 'Red Delicious' apple that has set quite a crop this year. I've heard that it is a good idea to thin the crop when the fruits are small. This seems like a waste to me. Is it really necessary?

Answer: Thinning a large crop is a good idea because you will harvest bigger and better fruit. The best time to thin is just after the tree naturally drops some of its young fruit. As a general rule, thin so that fruits are 6 to 8 inches apart or 2 to each fruit spur.

ORNAMENTAL TREES

GUIDELINES FOR AVOIDING GENERAL PROBLEMS

The biggest problems with ornamental and shade trees usually have more to do with the owners than the trees. The first trouble often comes with the choice of the tree; the second, with overzealous pruning practices—and the two problems are usually related.

In this highly mobile and transitory society, most gardeners want a tree that looks like a tree in a hurry. The simple fact is that fast-growing trees present far more problems than moderate or slow-growing trees. Many fast-growing trees are marked by invasive root systems, weak branch structures, the tendency to outgrow their allotted space, and short life span. And because they grow so fast, owners of fast-growing trees tend to over prune them, further compounding the problem.

The best tree buyer is one who looks to the future. Even though *you* may not intend to live in the same house for the next 20 years, think about the subsequent owners, or what it would be like to move into a new house whose garden was graced with a sensitive selection of beautiful problem-free trees.

Check the various tree selection charts in the Plant Selection Guide, pages 97–160, *Sunset New Western Garden Book,* for suggestions as to "which tree is best for what."

To avoid tree problems generally, consider these points:

- Don't buy fast-growing trees *just* because they are fast
- Don't prune unnecessarily, or too dramatically
- Know what the ultimate height and spread of a tree is before you plant it
- Choose trees well-adapted to your climate
- Stake trees properly after planting to avoid wind damage
- Maintain a good fertilizing and irrigating schedule

Are aphids inevitable?

Question: We live in Salem, Oregon (Zone 6), and have long admired the beautiful birch trees we see in our neighborhood. We'd like to plant several in our own yard, but the people we have talked to say they have a messy problem with aphids. Are they worth the trouble?

Answer: Although many commercial sprays help dispose of aphids, it is best to begin with aphid-resistant birches. The little-known Monarch birch *(Betula maximowicziana),* seems to offer little attraction for these pests. Official studies have not been done on this, but growers of the Monarch in the Northwest claim that this birch has remained pest free, while other nearby varieties are afflicted with aphids. Ask your nursery people if they will order the Monarch for you.

Dread drought: is there a defense?

Question: Ever since the historic drought that plagued California several years ago, I have lived in fear that another severe dry spell might ruin our prized trees. Is there anything we can do in advance of summer to protect our trees?

Answer: In years when the preceding winter's rainfall was normal-to-heavy, there's no need to take special measures. But if early winter rains were sparse, deep watering each February and March will help. Plants that start the growing season with wet soil at their roots, particularly at the deepest roots, stand a much better chance of surviving stress during the hot, dry summer days. Dig or drill holes at 2-foot intervals and at least a foot deep (18 to 24 inches is better), near each tree's drip line. Then run water slowly into each hole. How long you let water run will depend on your particular soil conditions—ideally until soil samples show that the root zone is saturated.

Dutch elm disease: what are signs?

Question: We live on a street lined with beautiful, 60-year-old elm trees. I've heard so much about the terrible Dutch elm disease; I'd hate for anything to happen to our trees. What signs should I watch out for?

Answer: Dutch elm disease starts at the top of the trees, with yellowing leaves and drooping branches. If the afflicted tree is destroyed early on, the spread of the disease to other elms will be less likely. This serious disease, spread by the elm bark beetle, is relatively new to the West. If you have a "suspect" tree, call your county agricultural agent.

Any cold-tolerant eucalyptus?

Question: We live on a ranch west of the Cascades in Washington (Zone 4), and would love to plant some of the eucalyptus that we saw on a recent trip to California. We've been told that they are very sensitive to cold weather. Are there any that would tolerate our climate?

Answer: Yes, both the cider gum *(Eucalyptus gunnii)* and the snow gum *(E. niphophila)* have survived hard freezes in western Oregon and Washington since 1960. For details on these trees, see page 289 and page 291, *Sunset New Western Garden Book.* A hard freeze can defoliate a eucalyptus, but don't be quick to cut it down; it's very likely to resprout.

When can we transplant evergreens?

Question: We're redesigning a garden that has several nice evergreen trees, but in the wrong place. Rather than just cutting down the trees, we'd like to transplant them to another part of the garden. Is any one time better than another to ensure success?

Answer: Yes. The best time to transplant evergreens in the low-elevation West is in November. Conifers (as well as hardy, broadleafed, evergreen shrubs and trees) can be lifted and transplanted with a minimum of shock while the weather is cool. Dig the trees, leaving balls of earth around the roots, and wrap with burlap to keep the soil in place. Be sure the soil is moist before digging. See detailed directions for transplanting trees on pages 47–48, *Sunset New Western Garden Book.* (The time to transplant deciduous trees is in December or January, after they drop their leaves and become dormant.)

Any "ocean-going" evergreens?

Question: We have a home in northern California near the ocean, and the often-windy salt air climate has made it difficult for us to get young trees started. We'd like to plant a row of relatively small evergreen trees next to our driveway. What do you suggest?

Answer: Try the New Zealand Christmas tree *(Metrosideros excelsus).* Salty winds and ocean spray won't bother this tree; it grows to about 30 feet, and has red blossoms from May to July. For further information, see page 374 of the *Sunset New Western Garden Book.*

How can we hide surface roots?

Question: We have a very large, old ornamental fig tree in our back yard. The roots grow along the surface of the soil and are quite big and extensive. The tree is planted in a conspicuous spot, and I'd love to disguise those roots. Is there any way to do it?

Answer: Consider planting Kaffir lily *(Clivia miniata)* or agapanthus among the roots. Fall is a good time to plant these drought-resistant, tuberous rooted perennials. Both clivias and agapanthus grow and bloom in the shade of large-rooted figs, and provide color in the spring and summer. To plant them, dig into the soil between roots or fill gaps with planting mix. Place plants in the natural containers formed by the fig roots, and water well. In a year's time, you will barely be able to see the roots.

Did pruning stunt my firs?

Question: A couple of years ago, I wanted to plant some annuals under my young fir trees, so I cut off the bottom branches to make room for the flower border. Since then, the firs have hardly grown at all. Did the pruning cause this?

Answer: Probably. For fast growth (or even healthy growth) from firs, it is best to leave the lower branches alone. Pruning reduces the fir's ability to develop new roots, and slows the trunk diameter growth. Also, without the shading branches the bark can be scalded by the sun.

Our honey locust is in trouble

Problem: The leaves on our 8-year-old honey locust *(Gleditsia triacanthos)* are rolled, and the tree has started dropping podlike galls. What in the world is wrong with it? We live in Bakersfield, California.

Comments: The problem is caused by the honey locust pod gall midge, an insect that apparently hitchhiked here on trees from the east. So far, no effective controls exist for the midge. University of California entomologists simply recommend that honey locust should not be planted in California. The insect does not attack the black locust *(Robinia pseudoacacia).*

Mulberry expiring in desert heat

Problem: Our 12-year-old mulberry looks like it doesn't have the will to live or the decency to die. We live in Albuquerque, New Mexico (Zone 10), and the tree is planted in our lawn. We can't find any insects on the tree. What could be the problem?

Advice: In the desert, warm temperatures, combined with heavy watering and fertilizing, will hasten the maturity of mulberry trees. These can live about 40 years under optimum conditions, but most desert climates do not have long enough winters to allow the mulberry to rest. Gardeners aggravate the problem by watering and fertilizing lawns, which force nearby trees to grow through the winter. Also, the common practice of pruning each year further weakens the tree. You would do well to remove the ailing mulberry and replace it with a better choice. For trees that do well in Zone 10, see page 149, *Sunset New Western Garden Book.*

How should I prune fruitless mulberry?

Question: My neighbor and I both planted several fruitless mulberry trees across our front yards several years ago. He says they should be severely pruned this January to give them a better shape. Is this the right thing to do?

Answer: Pruning the tree back to stubs (pollarding) is a common mistake. It weakens the tree and makes it more susceptible to disease. Pollarding also causes thick masses of foliage to sprout from each cut; such foliage is subject to wind damage. To maintain the natural beauty and health of the tree, remove only dead wood, crossed branches, or parallel branches too close together. You can head back branches that are too long and droopy; cut back to the juncture with another branch.

What grows under live oaks?

Problem: We live in Altadena, California, and have a large, very beautiful live oak in our back yard. We would like to have a nice shade garden under it, but haven't had much luck with our plantings.

Solution: There are many plants that not only will grow, but *thrive* under an oak tree. Some good choices for permanent plantings are: rhododendrons and azaleas, ferns, clivia, nandina, fuchsias, hydrangeas, and camellias. There also are many other plants to consider, including ajuga, hosta, crested iris, and begonias, to name just a few. For more information, check the list of shade-tolerant plants, pages 143–145, *Sunset New Western Garden Book.*

When to prune our live oak?

Question: We live in southern California, on a lot with many live oak trees. The trees are quite old and would benefit from a good pruning. Should they be pruned in winter, like our other trees?

Answer: Recent evidence suggests that the best time to prune live oaks is during the summer, when an oak's internal process slows down and there is little growth. Trees pruned during winter or spring are susceptible to the fungus called witches'-broom, resulting in wispy, dense growth at the tips of the branches. Make all pruning cuts as close as possible to the branches. Avoid leaving stubs—they may never heal over, and can be an entryway to moisture that may eventually cause rot problems in the trunk.

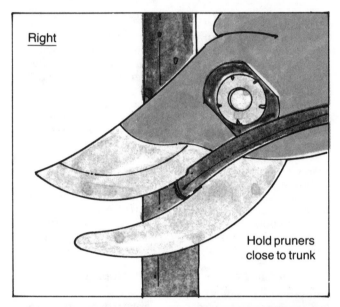

Right

Hold pruners close to trunk

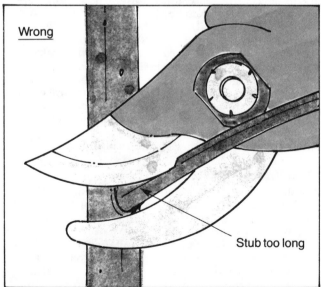

Wrong

Stub too long

Cut off limbs close to trunk; do not leave long stubs.

Oh, those messy olives!

Problem: Our olive trees are attractive, but I'm tired of cleaning up the fruit that drops all over the lawn and driveway.

Solution: One control method is to harvest the olives before many have dropped. Another is to spray the tree with a fruit hormone when blossoms appear. Spray again 10 days later.

You can avoid the problem altogether if you can locate a fruitless olive tree to plant in your new garden. 'Swan Hill' is said to be almost 100 percent fruitless.

Can I tote my palm to San Diego?

Question: We are moving from our home in Long Beach, California, and I want to dig up my 15-foot kentia palm and transplant it in San Diego. Is this advisable or would the problems be overwhelming?

Answer: It's tricky, but possible. Take it in steps: 1) Remove all dead leaves and tie the living fronds together to protect the crown. 2) As you dig, take as many roots as you can (if possible, the root ball should be twice the diameter of the trunk). Wrap the root ball in plastic or burlap; keep the tree out of the sun until it is replanted. 3) Prepare a planting hole 2 feet wider than the root ball, and 8 inches deeper. Work a complete fertilizer into the soil at the bottom of the hole; cover with 6 inches of soil and water thoroughly. 4) Before planting, let the hose drip on the root ball until it's well soaked. Place the palm in the hole, backfill half way, and water well. Then finish filling the hole and water again. It would be a wise idea to support your palm with guy wires for several months.

What ails my Aleppo?

Problem: Several of the Aleppo pines here in our Phoenix garden (Zone 13) have a problem: Some branches suddenly dry up, changing from grayish-green to completely brown. Several have completely died back.

Advice: Aleppo pine blight is worse in some years than in others. An unseasonably warm autumn seems to encourage the blight. Obviously you can do little about the weather conditions that cause this noninfectious problem, but too-frequent and too-shallow watering do encourage Aleppo pine blight. For local controls, discuss the problem with your nurseryman. (Also, see *Pinus halepensis,* page 412, *Sunset New Western Garden Book.*)

Pine problems in San Diego

Problem: We live in San Diego, and have several large Monterey pines on our property. Almost overnight the tips of the branches have turned brown and there are clumps of dead needles on all the trees. What's happening?

Advice: The tiny Nantucket pine tip moth is a particular threat to Monterey pines, Aleppo pines, Ponderosa pines, and Calabrian pines in the San Diego area. Unfortunately, there are no lasting controls at this time. But you can make a stand against it: In December, prune off at least 6 inches of affected tip growth and bury it 2 feet deep in the ground. That only takes care of this winter's larvae; the tree will probably become reinfested in the spring. The only promising controls are still in the research stage; check regularly with your nursery, garden center, or local county extension agent for any progress. In the meantime, try to protect your healthy trees with adequate deep watering and feeding.

How to water a patio tree

Problem: I'm concerned about our most important shade tree, an Australian willow, planted by the previous owners of our home. A concrete patio divided by 2 x 4s covers most of its root area. Although the tree is drought tolerant, it still needs *some* water, I think. We live in Wickenburg, Arizona (Zone 12).

Solution: One solution that might work for you is to use a deep root feeder—a metal tube 2 feet long with hose connector. To get it through the patio, drill holes in the crisscrossed wooden screeds. At watering time, insert the rod in the holes one at a time. If the rod won't pierce the dry soil beneath, turn on the water and let the device drill its way down.

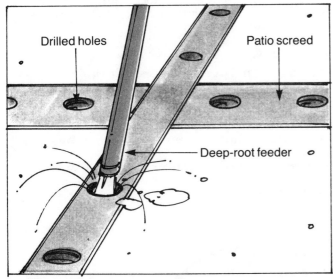

Nearby tree is watered with deep-root feeder inserted into holes that have been drilled in patio wood screed.

Pruning a living Christmas tree

Question: We bought a 5-foot living Douglas fir tree last year to use as a Christmas tree. This spring I've noticed quite a bit of new growth. I was wondering how and when to prune so that it will go on looking like a Christmas tree.

Answer: Christmas trees should be shaped in spring. Shear the tree as you would a hedge. New growth will cover ragged branch ends quickly, and if you shear once again in August, your tree should be in close to perfect shape by Christmas.

Pruner, spare that shade tree!

Problem: Put a pair of pruning shears or a saw in my husband's hands, and he goes crazy. This fall I'm going to try and head him off at the pass before he overdoes it. I'm particularly worried about several deciduous shade trees in our yard that have finally gotten large enough to cast some shade.

Solution: Tell him to give careful thought to any deciduous shade-tree pruning he does, except for the removal of weak or diseased branches. Severe annual pruning can devastate the natural form of shade trees, weaken scaffold limbs, and create an extensive network of bare

stubs in winter and shapeless crossing limbs in summer. If you need to open up a tree to allow passage of wind or let in more light, remove excessive or crossing *interior* limbs from the point of origin. To reduce a tree's height, prune back the primary upright branches to side branches; this encourages spreading, rather than taller growth. (Also, see Pruning, pages 68–71, *Sunset New Western Garden Book.*)

I expected TALL redwoods!

Problem: Five years ago, I planted a group of coast redwood seedlings on our hillside property near Eureka, California, and they have hardly grown at all. There is a lot of wind; has that caused the problem?

Solution: Not entirely. Any healthy coast redwood (*Sequoia sempervirens*) will put on about 4 feet of growth a year, so you have a problem in addition to wind. Chances are the planting holes were not prepared properly, dooming the tiny redwoods from the beginning. It would be best to remove the trees and start with new ones. For correct preparation of planting holes and soil, see *S. sempervirens*, page 406, *Sunset New Western Garden Book.* Additionally, build a screen from stakes and bur-

Shear tubbed Christmas tree in spring, again in August. New growth covers cut branch ends quickly.

lap on the windward side of the new trees to protect them and to increase humidity. Screens can be removed once the trees have become established.

Needed: a high hedge in a hurry!

Problem: We recently moved and would like to screen our house from an unsightly view; unfortunately, however, the view is at eye level. We don't want to wait for a hedge to get tall, and local ordinances prevent us from placing a fence there because of a neighboring driveway. Is there any other solution?

Solution: Planting evergreen trees close together may be the best way to create a garden screen in a hurry. Arranged in this fashion, the screen is sometimes called an "aerial hedge." Young trees in 5- or 15-gallon cans provide immediate eye-level foliage, and they fit into narrow space along walkways and fences better than most leafy-to-the-ground shubs. Several low-growing trees can be planted 6 to 8 feet apart without being too crowded.

Strong wind, rocky slope

Problem: The strong winds that blow down the rocky hill into my garden in Lakeport, California (Zone 7), make it almost impossible to grow anything. Any suggestions?

Solution: How about an evergreen windbreak? Trees planted in a line, particularly evergreens, provide excellent wind protection. If possible, plant two or three "layers" of windbreaks. Many species of eucalyptus are especially good choices for rocky hillsides where growing conditions are poor. For a list of evergreen trees that make good windbreaks, see page 108, *Sunset New Western Garden Book.*

How to prune Rocky Mountain juniper?

Question: I live in Grand Junction, Colorado (Zone 2). How and when do I prune a Rocky Mountain juniper to accent its natural shape and character?

Answer: To preserve the natural shape of Rocky Mountain juniper *(Juniperus scopulorum)*, first remove dead branches and limbs that are shaded out and dying. Next, remove any crossing branches. Finally, to balance the tree's appearance, cut out a few healthy limbs (not more than 10 percent of the total pruning job). September— before the first snow fall—is the best time to prune.

Incidentally, shearing junipers into unnatural geometric shapes can cause branches to break when snow builds up and can't slide off easily.

Elm roots wrecked our sidewalk

Question: The large elm we used to have in front of our house finally had to be cut down. In addition to being diseased, the roots of the tree had cracked and buckled the surrounding sidewalk. We have since had new sections of the sidewalk replaced, and are about to plant a new tree. How can we be sure the same thing won't happen again?

Answer: Although some trees are worse than others, those planted in the narrow strip between the sidewalk and the street generally cause damage to sidewalks. It

Plant 6 to 8 feet apart

Trees planted close together form "aerial hedge" which keeps foliage at eye level while blocking out view.

happens this way: Roots grow outward in all directions, but usually stop under the street because of compaction and lack of moisture. On the other side of the tree, however, roots explore under the sidewalk to the lawn beyond, then expand when they encounter food and water. As the roots expand, they push up and crack the sidewalk. See the illustration below for two ways to prevent this problem.

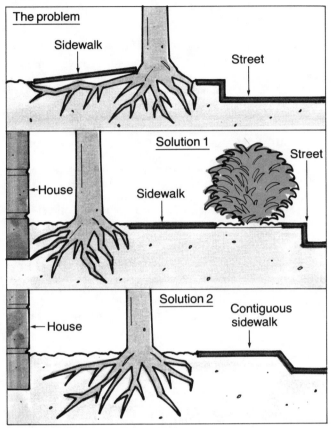

Your sidewalk won't be cracked or tipped in the future if you plant tree between sidewalk and house.

Suffering blue spruce—why?

Problem: Something is happening to my Colorado blue spruce. The top portion is dying out, but the rest of the tree seems fine.
Solution: The problem, most likely, is an infestation of aphids. In spring, check the new growth for these insects and spray with diazinon. Carefully read and follow all label directions. For light infestations, you can just blast the tree with a strong jet of water from the hose. Do it several times, at one-week intervals.

Sycamore problems in Tucson

Question: This summer, we planted four sycamores from 5-gallon cans in our garden here in Tucson, Arizona. Shortly after we planted the trees, the tips of almost all the leaves turned brown, and now they seem to have stopped growing. What's wrong?
Answer: Sycamore trees planted in the summer's heat and wind tend to languish and suffer the tip burn you mentioned. (Sycamores do best when planted in the fall,

after the weather starts to cool.) Because they are slow to recover from drought, be sure to water these trees attentively during the period of little rain.

Salty breeze, tough on trees

Problem: We have a small weekend place on the beach, and have had a terrible time getting young trees started.
Solution: Easy-to-make devices for wind-and-salt protection, such as the one in the illustration, can help. Use three 2-by-2-inch redwood stakes and 73 percent plastic shade cloth on two sides. The stakes should be 3 feet higher than the trees. The plastic forms a wedge that helps divert onshore winds and catches some salt droplets before they get on the foliage. The tree can be tied to all three stakes with plastic tape. This allows the tree to move in the wind and develop a stronger trunk than if the tree were rigidly tied to a single stake.

Be sure the trees you select are adapted to beachfront gardens (see page 157, *Sunset New Western Garden Book*).

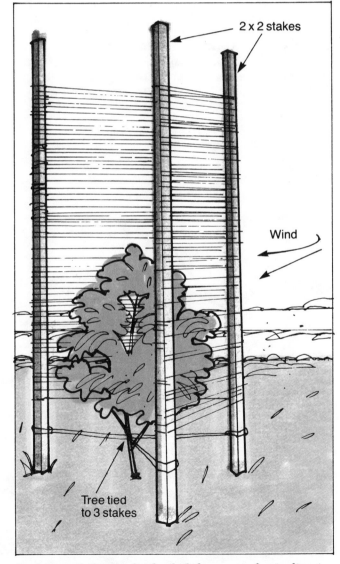

Stakes and plastic shade cloth form a wedge to divert ocean breezes from young beachside trees.

Problems with pests? See pages 32—48

Why didn't flowering trees bloom?

Question: Our flowering peach and cherry trees, which normally are the talk of the neighborhood in spring, had very few blossoms this year. Is it a sign of age or disease?

Answer: Probably neither. More than likely it was the effect of a mild winter. If winter months are unseasonably warm, flower and fruit bud development on many deciduous trees and shrubs may be impaired. Hope for a colder winter next year.

How should we stake young trees?

Question: Two of the trees we planted last fall blew over in a big storm we had this winter. The trunk of one of them actually broke in half. I told my husband when we planted them that I didn't think the stakes were big enough. What's the best way to stake young trees?

Answer: On each side of the tree, pound a 2-by-2-inch stake into the ground to a point below the root ball. Place the stakes so that a crossbar brace will be perpendicular to the prevailing wind, then nail the crossbar in place. You can support the trunk in two ways, both of which permit some movement. The first does less damage to the bark and allows the trunk to expand under the ties. (See illustration.)

Flowering trees for the cold country?

Question: Whenever we make a springtime visit to Portland, Oregon, we marvel at all of the beautiful flowering trees. What spring flowering trees do you recommend for us in Bend, Oregon, where our winters are a lot colder?

Answer: Here are three very different flowering trees that will bloom just as attractively under the harsher conditions of your garden in Bend (Zone 1): Eastern redbud (*Cercis canadensis*) will reach 30 feet; its black branches are filled with delicate rosy pink blooms before the leaves begin to emerge. Goldenchain tree (*Laburnum anagyroides*) grows to only 25 feet; in later April long, drooping clusters of yellow flowers will hang from its branches. Common horsechestnut (*Aesculus hippocastanum*) can grow to 60 feet, with foot-tall plumes of ivory-covered blossoms with pink markings. Don't overlook the familiar flowering hawthorns (*Crataegus*) and crabapples (*Malus*).

Our sycamores are nearly leafless

Problem: We have two huge and well-loved sycamores around our home in Anaheim, California, that are almost defoliated. What is causing this and is there anything I can do about it?

Solution: Your sycamores are most likely suffering from sycamore anthracnose, or blight, a fungus that infects southern California's native sycamore, *Platanus racemosa*. The fungus dwells in small twigs and branches; infected leaves turn brown near veins, then fall off. It's hard to control completely, but midwinter (January and February) pruning can help. First, try to prune off as much infected growth as possible (look for dead twigs and cankers on small branches). Spores that spread the fungus come from fungus already living in this growth.

Next, prune to open up the tree—to make it less dense so it can dry out quickly after rain. The fungus needs water to grow and spread; the drier the branches and leaves, the less chance it has.

In spring, give the tree a good feeding to encourage healthy new growth.

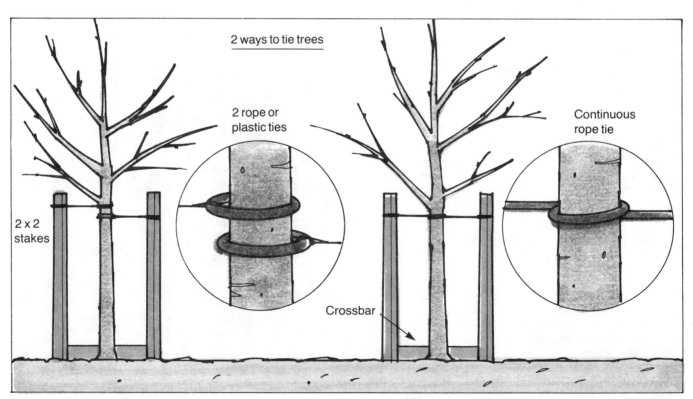

Trees can be secured with separate ties from each stake (left) or with one continuous rope tie (right).

Can I stake without damaging roots?

Question: I have a tree several years old that is not as upright as it should be and needs bracing. How can I stake it without damaging the roots?

Answer: Drive a 2-by-2 wooden stake into the ground at a 45° angle so that it crosses the trunk diagonally on the upwind side. Secure the tree to the stake with interlocking plastic chain looped in a figure 8 around the stake and the trunk, as shown below. (The plastic chain is sold in hardware stores; you could also use plastic tree tie or twine.) Secure the tree to the stake about two-thirds up the trunk. Remove the stake after one year.

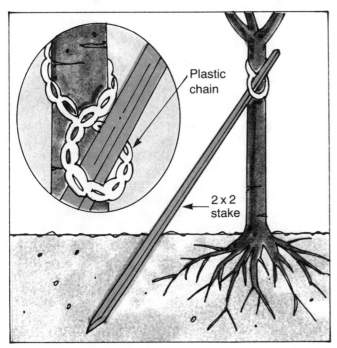

Plastic chain

2 x 2 stake

Stake angled at 45° is easy to drive, misses tree roots.

Will summer watering kill a young oak?

Question: Is there an oak tree I can plant here in Altadena, California (Zone 21) that can tolerate the summer watering that goes along with some lawn and ground cover plantings?

Answer: Many California gardeners mistakenly believe that all native oaks are sensitive to normal garden watering. While this may be the case with old, drought-conditioned trees, it's not really true of young, nursery-grown trees or volunteer seedlings in your garden.

Actually, young native oaks (especially *Quercus agrifolia, Q. lobata,* and *C. wislizenii*) adapt readily to most situations. Nursery-grown trees are raised on a regular watering (and fertilizing) regime; you needn't worry about planting them in lawns or among watered shrubs and ground covers. They'll grow quickly, too, often 2 to 4 feet a year.

What ails our tulip tree?

Problem: We have a 6-year old tulip tree (*Liriodendron tulipifera*) that was growing quite well until just this summer. The leaves turned prematurely yellow, and now there's this black sooty sticky substance on many of the leaves. When I park the car under it I've noticed a lot of sticky spots all over the hood and windshield. What's causing this?

Advice: The problem could be scale or aphids. Both suck vital plant juices from leaves and stems, causing leaves to turn yellow, and both excrete honeydew—the substance you noticed on your car. The honeydew is, in turn, host for an affliction known as sooty mold.

The best method of tackling the problem is to deal with the scale or aphids—the cause of the problem—rather than just dealing with the symptomatic sooty mold. During the winter months, scale insects can be controlled by spraying the bare tree with a dormant oil spray, which smothers the pest. In spring, both scale and aphids can be controlled with a systemic insecticide. If you prefer not to use chemical controls, aphids will succumb to a strong stream of water from a hose to knock them off; or spray with a soap-and-water solution.

For more information, see pages 34 (aphids) and 36 (scale).

Can my small garden take a southern magnolia?

Question: I'm well aware of the drawbacks of the southern magnolia, with its falling leaves and petals all summer, but it's one of those plants I simply must have. That fragrance just carries me away! Anyway, the problem is that I don't think I have the room—our garden is fairly small. Is there any way that I can keep it from growing to its full size?

Answer: One of the best ways to grow the southern magnolia, especially where space is a problem or the climate is a little too severe, is to espalier it against a sunny wall. You can keep it pruned to within 18 inches of the wall or fence and let it grow as tall as you like. And you should get plenty of fragrance—the flowers seem to really pop out with the reflected warmth of the wall.

What's a good desert windbreak?

Question: We live in north Phoenix, Arizona (Zone 13) and would like a tree well-adapted to the rigors of desert life, to use as a windbreak. Any suggestions?

Answer: The narrow-leafed gimlet (*Eucalyptus spathulata*) is a short, round, multistemmed eucalyptus that doesn't look much like its relatives. It has willowy gray-green leaves and smooth reddish-brown bark. Mature trees range anywhere from 6 to 20 feet tall. With its dense, bushy foliage, the narrow-leafed gimlet naturally makes a good choice for screening and wind-barrier plantings. It tolerates poor soil and considerable drought once established, but will grow better with regular deep watering.

Desert wind damage—what to do?

Problem: We live in Pasadena, California, and have an older garden with many mature trees. Every year the Santa Ana winds blow off the desert and break several limbs off our trees. Is there anything we can do to minimize the possibilities of damage?

Solution: September is a good time to take precautionary measures. Before the destructive winds arrive, thin the dense foliage canopy that has developed after the long, vigorous growing season. The object of thinning is to permit winds to pass through the branches. Carob, eucalyptus, evergreen elms, pepper, pines, and any other trees with large heads and dense foliage benefit from thinning.

ROSES

GUIDELINES FOR AVOIDING GENERAL PROBLEMS

Throughout gardening history, roses have been perhaps the most loved and revered of all flowers. Their color, form, and fragrance—as well as their willingness to bloom over a long season—make them a gardener's treasure.

For all that they give, roses need something in return; that is, conscientious care. Basically, to produce the most abundant blooms and the healthiest growth, roses require proper planting and generous watering and fertilizing during their growing season, and yearly pruning. In this chapter are answers and solutions to everyday questions and problems about proper rose culture. For more information, see pages 450–455, *Sunset New Western Garden Book.*

Roses that are growing in healthy conditions are far less susceptible to attack from insects and diseases than plants that are just struggling along. A program which incorporates the following basic advice will help you to avoid most potential problems:

- Select varieties favored for your region
- Plant in a sunny location (less than 6 hours of sunlight in very hot regions, more in foggy coastal areas)
- Use plenty of organic matter to improve soil
- Be sure your roses have good drainage
- Location should be free of competing roots of other plants
- Water and fertilize regularly
- Keep a constant lookout for pests and diseases; never let them get a head start
- Do a major pruning of all roses once a year, during dormant season

Should I buy bare-root or in cans?

Question: I'm a newcomer to gardening. I would like to know the advantages and disadvantages of planting roses bare root as opposed to buying them in cans from the nursery.

Answer: Both offer advantages. When you go the bare-root route, plants are less expensive, there is better variety selection, and the plant will have a longer season in which to get established.

However, roses in nursery cans offer one important advantage—you can see the roses in bloom and know what you are getting. With bare-root plants, you need to be familiar with what you are buying, or trust the pictures attached to the plants (generally these are reliable, although they may have become water spotted and stained in the nursery).

How should I plant bare-root roses?

Problem: I received a wonderful Christmas present of six bare-root hybrid tea roses. I want to make sure that they grow and bloom well, but haven't the faintest idea of how to plant them in the garden.

Advice: Before planting, they should be soaked in a bucket of water to help restore moisture they may have lost during storage. Submerge the entire plant, or at least cover roots and the bud union (where the canes emerge). Soak several hours or overnight.

Then follow steps shown in the illustrations. Dig a hole large enough to hold rose roots without bending them; mix in soil amendments. Mound a cone of soil in the center.

Place the plant on top of the cone, draping the roots over it and down toward the bottom of the hole. Fill in with soil around the roots, firming it as you go with your hands or a stick. Thoroughly water, making sure the bush doesn't settle below the established level.

Mound up moist soil over the bud union and the lower part of the canes. Keep the mound moist until new growth begins, then carefully remove it.

Can I beat problems to the punch?

Problem: I just don't seem to get the hang of growing healthy roses; insects and diseases give me trouble no matter what. What can I do to get the jump on these problems before they occur?

Solution: Giving the rose garden a thorough cleanup in winter will go a long way in helping to prevent problems. Old leaves and debris can harbor overwintering fungus spores and insect eggs. As you prune, strip any leaves still clinging to the branches. Then rake up prunings and fallen leaves from the ground, and dump the whole lot in the garbage. Don't compost rose prunings—they may harbor diseases and their thorns may not decompose.

A dormant spray of oil and lime sulfur provides further preventive medicine. Apply only to plants that are still dormant (do not apply if new leaf buds have started to swell), following label directions for use in dormant season. Drench the ground around plants as well as all twigs and stems. Avoid spraying near house walls, since the solution can stain.

How should I cut roses for bouquets?

Question: I have a neighbor, an old-timer, who says there is a right way and a wrong way to cut roses for indoor bouquets. Something about cutting just above a leaf with 5 leaflets. Ever heard of this?

Answer: Yes, indeed. This old rule of thumb still works. Cut roses just above a leaf with 5 leaflets (leaves closer to the flower will have fewer leaflets), preferably one that is facing away from the interior of the plant so that future growth will grow outward rather than crossing over the interior of the plant. For long-lasting cut roses, pick flowers in early morning or late afternoon, re-cut the stems under water, and then plunge them into water up to the bases of the blooms. Leave all foliage on the stems:

it absorbs water, too. Keep the blooms in a cool place overnight (if afternoon-picked) or for several hours (if picked in the morning), then arrange the flowers.

Can I grow roses in containers?

Question: We have a very small garden that was completely landscaped when we bought the home. I'd love to have a few rose bushes, but I don't want to upset the existing landscape, which looks pretty good. What I was wondering was if roses could be grown successfully in containers? We have a good sized deck that would accommodate four or five of them very nicely.

Answer: Yes, roses will grow very well in containers if you follow a few guidelines. A 14-inch square wooden box is about the smallest size container you would want to choose for polyanthas and the smaller floribundas. For hybrid teas and the more robust varieties of floribunda, a box 20 inches square is ideal, and 16 inches an absolute minimum. For any container, a 16-inch depth is minimum.

The soil in the container is of utmost importance. In most cases it is best to buy a packaged soil mix at the

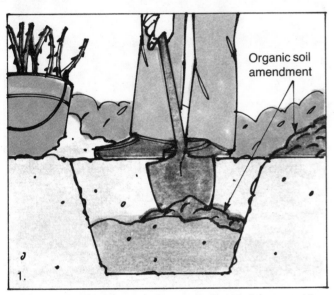

1. *Planting hole must be big enough to hold rose without crowding roots. Mix in soil amendments.*

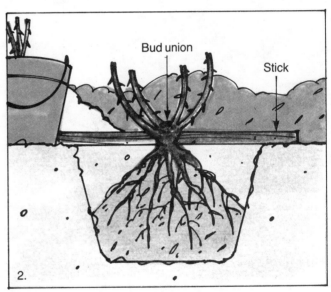

2. *Spread roots over cone of soil. Stick across hole helps you determine position of bud union.*

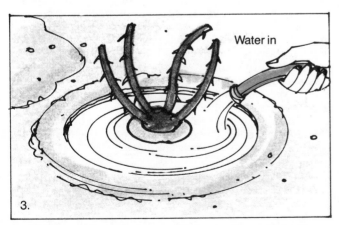

3. *Firm in soil around roots. Water in thoroughly. Do not allow plant to settle below the established level.*

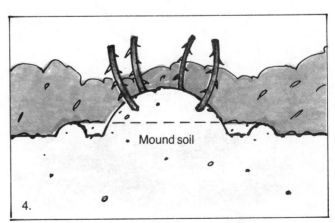

4. *Keep moist soil mounded over bud union and lower part of canes until new growth starts; then remove it.*

What to do when? See pages 6—31

nursery or garden center unless your garden soil is a top-quality, porous loam.

Watering and fertilizing must receive special attention. Keep soil moist, but not soggy; never let it dry out to the point that the plant droops. Fertilize regularly during the growing season with a complete liquid fertilizer. Because roses are heavy feeders, you can feed them as often as once every two weeks.

How to revitalize old climbers?

Problem: We moved into an old house with a garden that has been neglected for some time. There are several beautiful climbing roses on a fence, but they are totally overgrown. When and how should I prune these roses to restore them?

Solution: The best time to prune your climbing roses is in winter, or early spring, before new growth has started. (See illustrations.) Do *not* prune them if freezing

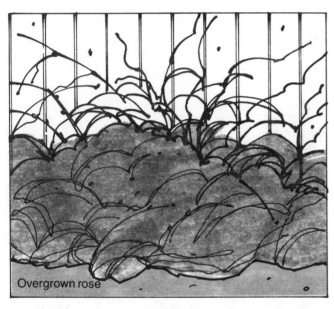

Overgrown rose

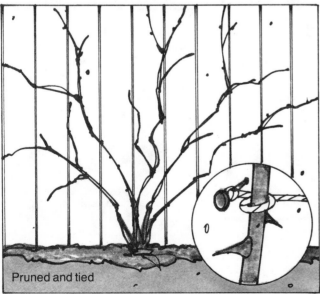

Pruned and tied

Pruning can restore good looks of old, overgrown climbing roses. Cut off dead, broken, and crossing branches. Tie healthy canes loosely for support and direction.

weather is still expected. Begin by lining up your tools—pruning shears, saw, loppers, and gloves—and do some serious cutting. Remove any canes that shoot out at right angles to the supporting wall or fence. Then remove canes that are dead, broken, or badly scarred, and any that cross.

The remaining canes should be healthy, arching, and well spaced. Tie them down loosely to give the canes support and direction: the more horizontal you can get them, the more lateral shoots the canes are likely to produce (laterals are the side shoots that do the flowering).

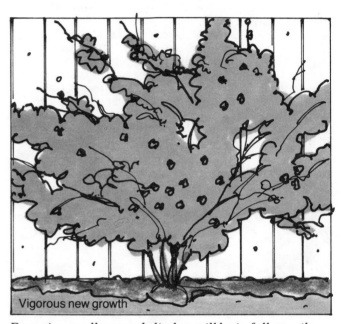

Vigorous new growth

By spring, well-pruned climber will be in full growth.

Any disease-resistant kinds?

Question: I love roses and would like to grow a few. But I've heard they are subject to many diseases and need to be sprayed frequently in order to have healthy plants and good bloom. Are there any disease-resistant varieties?

Answer: Three foliage diseases can bother roses: mildew, rust, and black spot. Here in the West, only mildew and rust are likely to be persistent problems; black spot thrives where summer rainfall is normal and humidity remains high (and you do need to combat it with spray—it can defoliate a plant). Actually, there are quite a few modern roses that have high resistance to mildew and rust. Choose from these widely available varieties.

Hybrid Teas and Grandifloras: 'Honor' (white), 'Miss All-American Beauty' (dark pink), 'National Trust' (red), 'New Day' (yellow), 'Pink Favorite' (pink), 'Prominent' (orange), 'Typhoo Tea' (red and white).

Floribundas: 'French Lace' (ivory), 'Iceberg' (white), 'Marina' (orange), 'Razzle-Dazzle' (red and white), 'Redgold' (red, orange, yellow), 'Sunflare' (yellow), 'Trumpeter' (orange-red), 'Viva' (red).

Climbers: 'America' (coral), 'High Noon' (yellow), 'Tempo' (red).

Wanted: fragrance like Grandma's roses

Question: I'm looking for several roses to plant in my garden, but I don't want just any variety. What I'm really looking for are the ones that smell the way a rose is *supposed* to smell—like the ones I remember from my Grandmother's garden. Any suggestion?

Answer: Yes, the following readily-available varieties, all of which grow well anywhere in the West, were among the top-rated roses for fragrance in a poll taken of 187 rose experts.

Hybrid teas: 'Mr. Lincoln' (red), 'Chrysler Imperial' (red), 'Fragrant Cloud' (orange), 'Tropicana' (orange), 'Perfume Delight' (pink), 'Honor' (white), 'Kings' Ransom' (yellow), 'Double Delight' (multi-color).

Floribunda: 'Angel Face' (lavender).

For more blooms in hot climates

Problem: We live in Los Banos, California (Zone 8), and have several rose bushes. The summers are quite hot here, and the roses never seem to bloom much after the first flush of blossoms in spring. Is there anything we can do to encourage more flowers?

Solution: Gardeners in Zone 8 and other hot summer areas are familiar with the slowdown of roses during the worst heat; the plants actually go semidormant during this period. To promote a second wave of blossoms after this semidormancy, keep roots thoroughly moist all during September and into November. Early in September, apply a complete fertilizer. Remove faded flowers and seed pods regularly.

Can we grow roses in the shade?

Question: Are there any roses that will grow in the shade? Our yard receives very little direct sunlight, but I'd still like to have some roses for cutting. Any chance?

Answer: No rose will bloom in the darkest corner of a shady garden but there are quite a few that will grow in both light and medium shade, even in cool coastal areas of the West. You should bear in mind, though, that any rose fares best with some direct sun during some part of the day. The list below contains roses with a good to excellent record of performance in light shade, as reported by a number of Western rose experts. Roses that accept medium shade are marked with an asterisk (*).

Fungus diseases, a problem even with roses grown in the sun, can be a particular problem in the shade.

Hybrid teas: 'Brandy', 'Chicago Peace', 'Electron', 'Elizabeth Harkness'*, 'Fantastique', 'First Prize', 'Honey Favorite', 'Just Joey', 'Irish Gold', 'Miss All-American Beauty'*, 'Mon Cheri', 'Peace', 'Peter Frankenfeld'*, 'Pink Favorite', 'Precious Platinum', 'Princess Margaret of England', 'Red Planet', 'Rose Gaujard', 'Rosy Cheeks', 'Silver Jubilee', 'Typhoon'.

Floribundas: 'Anna Wheatcroft', 'Bambi', 'Chanelle'*, 'City of Belfast', 'Courvoisier', 'Dream Waltz', 'Eye Paint', 'French Lace', 'Gay Princess'*, 'Goldilocks', 'Iceberg', 'Redgold', 'Rose of Tralee', 'Winifred Coulter'.

Polyantha: 'Margo Koster'.

Grandifloras: 'Olé', 'Prominent', 'Shreveport'.

Problems—in Portland, yet!

Problem: Here we are in Portland—one of the rose capitals of the world—and our roses are constantly in trouble. We continually have to battle mildew, rust, and black spot on our flowers. I know that the wet summers here in Zone 6 contribute to these conditions. Are there any steps I can take to keep these problems at bay?

Solution: Some basic planting and maintenance practices should help:

- *Plant resistant varieties.* Rust- and mildew-resistant plants have been developed; your nurseryman can advise you on the right ones for Zone 6.
- *Choose location carefully.* Plant bushes in your driest, sunniest areas, and keep them uncrowded by other plants.
- *Prune effectively.* Prune to open up the centers of bushes so air can circulate.
- *Use fungicides.* Early treatment with the right fungicides helps enormously in checking diseases. Look for mildew on new leaves and buds. Rust tends to come later (most commonly along the foggy coast). Black spot generally appears as dark ¼- to ½-inch spots on mature foliage in late spring and summer. Funginex controls all three of these problems, and the solution doesn't leave a visible deposit. You can also combine this fungicide with malathion, orthene, or other insecticides as needed. For detailed information on these diseases, see the chapter beginning on page 32.

My neighbor's blooms are bigger

Question: My neighbor and I have many of the same varieties of hybrid tea roses. The blossoms I see over the fence are always bigger than those I grow. What can I do to uphold the family honor?

Answer: Assuming that you and your neighbor are both giving your roses the proper feeding and general care, here's a suggestion: For the showiest hybrid tea rose blooms, pinch or snip out the small side buds. This permits the central bud to develop into a larger, more attractive flower.

Pruning is a mystery

Problem: It's rose pruning time again, and although I read a lot about it and study the diagrams, it seems to be a problem. Do you have any suggestions?

Advice: In January and February, rose pruning time, nurseries in most areas give demonstrations of proper procedures on all types of rose. These experts will answer questions and also warn you about making the *wrong* cuts. Most demonstrations are free. (Also, even though you've done some reading on the subject, you will find concise information on pruning all types of roses on page 452, *Sunset New Western Garden Book*.)

What are those strange-looking branches?

Problem: What are all these strange-looking canes growing from the base of my rose bushes? Should they be removed?

Solution: Those are almost certainly suckers, and unless you recognize and remove them, you may get an unwelcome surprise later on when they bear flowers different from (and less desirable than) those on the rest of the plant. Sucker canes usually have different foliage size and shape, and thorns of a different size. A rapidly climbing cane that so far has been flowerless is almost certainly a sucker.

Since most roses are grafted onto rootstock, you essentially have two plants: the sturdy root plant below and the flower-bearing one above. If the rootstock manages to sprout above ground, it will eventually produce the "surprise" flowers. To avoid this, remove any shoots (suckers) that appear below the graft union (you'll see this as a slight bulge in the trunk just above the roots), since these sap the strength of the plant.

AZALEAS & RHODODENDRONS

GUIDELINES FOR AVOIDING GENERAL PROBLEMS

Rhododendrons and azaleas comprise one of the largest and most important groups of flowering plants in the West. Technically, all azaleas are rhododendrons, but most gardeners know azaleas as a separate group of plants with smaller flowers and a shorter, more compact growth habit. While there are exceptions—rhododendrons that are smaller than azaleas, azaleas that tower over rhododendrons—it is more important for the home gardener to concentrate on finding the best plant for the best location. The *Sunset New Western Garden Book,* pages 442 to 447, describes various kinds of commonly sold rhododendrons and azaleas, and suggests the best varieties for your region.

Rhododendrons and azaleas have a reputation for being somewhat finicky. But satisfy their basic needs, and these plants can be virtually problem-free. An important prerequisite for good growth is loose, porous, moist (but well-drained) soil, with a high content of organic matter and high acid (*p*H 4.5–6.0). Shelter them from wind and excessive sun, and provide a cool, humid atmosphere. Water frequently, but not so heavily that plants' roots are in soggy soil for long periods of time. Fertilize properly, keep an eye out for pests and diseases—and you will be rewarded with a spectacular flower display each year.

Here, then, is a brief summary of things to remember:

- Choose the right species for your garden and region
- Plant where the light is good, but where there is protection from extremes of wind and sun
- Provide soil that is well-drained, moisture retentive, acid, and rich
- Plant with top of root ball slightly above soil level, and make sure drifting soil doesn't cover it later on
- Water frequently but not too heavily
- Fertilize, and control pests

Azalea leaves are turning yellow

Problem: We have a mound covered with low-growing, white-flowered azaleas. They were beautiful in the spring, but now, 2 months later, the leaves are all beginning to turn yellow between the veins. Some leaves are dropping.

Solution: Some yellowing and falling of leaves is natural with all evergreen plants. If the yellow leaves are the oldest (the ones farthest down on the stems), and the new growth is healthy and green, don't worry. But if leaves range from sickly yellow-green to yellow, with green markings along veins and ribs, your plant has chlorosis. This ailment is an iron deficiency (corresponding to anemia in people). Apply a chelated iron product, available at nurseries and garden centers, as a foliar (leaf) spray; the condition should improve within 2 or 3 weeks. (Also, see Chlorosis, page 34, *Sunset New Western Garden Book.*)

How much winter watering?

Question: It's December, and I've stopped watering my azaleas because we have had a little rain and quite a lot of fog (I live in Long Beach, California). But the leaves seem somewhat limp. Do I have to water azaleas all winter?

Answer: Since azaleas are shallow-rooted, they cannot draw on reservoirs of water deep within the soil; they can feel the effects of drought even with some rainfall. If rain has been light, you probably should water your azaleas every two weeks throughout the winter, to make sure that they get the moisture they need. Don't depend on fog as a substitute for water. Fog just doesn't carry a sufficient amount of moisture. A 1- to 2-inch layer of organic mulch will also help keep the roots moist.

I have good soil—why peat moss?

Question: I am a new gardener and live in Bakersfield, California. Yesterday, when I bought some azaleas, I was advised to add 50 percent peat moss to the garden soil. My garden soil is supposed to be very good. Is it really necessary to add peat moss?

Answer: Azaleas require an acid soil, and peat moss is an acid-soil additive. More than any other garden plant, azaleas also need air in the root zone; at the same time, they must have a constant moisture supply, which can be a problem in hot, dry areas such as Bakersfield (Zone 8). More simply, azaleas need a soil that drains rapidly, and at the same time retains moisture. The only way to achieve such a condition is to add plenty of organic matter—no matter how good your native soil is. Peat moss, with its exceptional moisture-retention capability and open-pore structure, is an ideal choice for this. (For more information on growing and caring for azaleas, see page 442, *Sunset New Western Garden Book*.)

My azaleas have gone gangly

Question: My azaleas have long, gangly stems with leaves only at the ends. What should I do?

Answer: Azaleas respond well to pruning right after they finish flowering. Clip back leggy stems to force new, more compact growth. Remove awkward crossing branches and old weak stems.

When to fertilize azaleas?

Question: I just planted three new azaleas and gave them a shot of fertilizer. My mother-in-law said that I should have waited until after they had finished blooming. Who is right—and why?

Answer: You're both right—or wrong—depending on what type of fertilizer you are talking about. The three major plant nutrients are nitrogen, phosphorus, and potassium (sometimes called "potash"); labels always list these ingredients.

Since azaleas start new growth right after blooming, they then need *nitrogen*—the nutrient that speeds leafy growth and promotes a rich, green foliage. In mild climates, after blooming, apply ammonium phosphate, a fertilizer high in nitrogen. If plants don't respond with new growth after three weeks, repeat the procedure.

A month after the first feeding with ammonium phosphate, start monthly applications of a fertilizer high in equal amounts of *phosphorus* and *potassium*; such products are labeled 0-10-10, or the like. (For explanation of labels, see Fertilizing your garden, page 52, *Sunset New Western Garden Book*.) The time for the last application is late November.

With both fertilizers, allow 1 tablespoon for each foot of plant height, scattered beneath the plants and watered in thoroughly.

In areas with severe winters, *nitrogen* should only be applied up to mid-June; growth stimulated after the normal first flush may be injured by cold. When cold season ends each year, you can resume feedings with *phosphorus* and *potassium* until the end of summer.

How can I get "sheets of blooms"?

Question: I had envisioned the 20 Kurume 'Snow' azaleas in a special display area to grow and fill into one big sheet of white spring blooms in a couple of years. Well, it hasn't happened. They are growing more upright than horizontal, and the problem is obviously in pruning. How and when do I prune them to promote the flowing sheet of blooms I admire in Japanese gardens?

Answer: Undertake any pruning or trimming right after plants have flowered. New growth formed after such pruning will likely bear flower buds for the next year's bloom. For a compact plant rather than one that's open and irregular, cut back some of the thicker limbs to a foot or less; the cut branches will put forth strong new shoots to fill in the plant. Then, the next year, after the plants have flowered, you can start shaping the group of azaleas into a "flowing sheet" by cutting back the tips of the new growth with a pair of hedge shears.

Why are my azaleas losing color?

Problem: I have a 20-year-old azalea 'Temperance' that has bloomed gloriously every spring. This year, just as the buds opened, the petals started to lose color—they became almost transparent. Then they became slimy, turned brown, and were a long time in falling off. What can I do to prevent this next year?

Advice: The problem with your old 'Temperance' is known as azalea petal blight. You can reduce the risk from this serious fungus disease next year by drenching the soil with terraclor solution (available at nurseries and garden centers) just before bloom time. To be sure of control, spray the flowers twice a week with the fungicide thiram or zineb.

Soil is collecting around my azaleas

Problem: I'm going to plant a couple of azaleas this weekend. In the past I've had trouble with soil washing in around the crown of my plants, and I'd like to correct this problem when I plant my new azaleas.

Solution: Build redwood collars for your new azaleas to keep the soil away from the crowns and also to create a water basin around them. Place an 18-inch-square collar of 1 by 4's around the planting hole and work it down so it is only an inch above the ground. Then plant a 1-gallon azalea in the hole and backfill with straight peat moss. (See illustration.) As the azaleas grow, their foliage hides the wood collars.

1 x 4 x 18 inch redwood

Redwood collar of 1 by 4's is 18 inches square, keeps soil from being washed in around azalea's crown.

Same food for camellias, rhododendrons?

Question: Are rhododendrons, azaleas, and camellias related? I ask because I have some of all three, and would like to fertilize them with one kind of plant food instead of three separate kinds.

Answer: Technically, rhododendrons and azaleas are all rhododendrons, but the camellia is quite unrelated, belonging to the tea family. As different as the two plant groups are in many ways, they are alike in where you grow them (part shade), when they bloom (late fall to late spring), and what you feed them (acid plant food).

My old rhodies are sprawling all over

Problem: The old rhodies in our garden are really out of shape, sprawling all over, with branches that have long spaces without leaves. How do I go about getting them to look presentable—and also bloom?

Answer: Rangy, overgrown old rhodies may need heavy pruning to get them back into shape, but it is essential to restore them in stages. Very heavy pruning all at once results in a loss of flowers for a year or two, and the risk of losing the whole plant. Prune the rhododendrons while they are blooming, if you want cut flowers; otherwise, prune just after flowering. Proceed this way:

Cut individual limbs back to a side branch, leaf whorl, or ring of dormant leaf buds (marked by tiny nubbins on the bark where leaves once grew). If there are scraggly or overgrown branches, cut back to near the base, but no more than one branch in three. Dormant buds grow within a month on smaller limbs, or within 10 weeks on tall main trunks.

Some growers have found that an application of fertilizer containing only nitrogen and phosphorus (such as 16-20-0) at the time of pruning stimulates new growth on a heavily pruned rhododendron that is reluctant to send out shoots from old, bare wood.

OK to plant beneath rhododendrons?

Problem: For summer color, I would like to plant trailing lobelia under my rhododendron. Now I'm told that I shouldn't dig into all that ground under the shrub. What harm can it possibly do?

Answer: Rhododendrons are shallow-rooted plants—most of their feeder roots (those that take in vital nutrients and moisture) are in the top few inches of soil. Harm the feeder roots, and the upper portion of the plant will quickly show damage. That's why it's best to keep soil under rhododendrons free of other plantings.

Can I dig up wild ones?

Question: I live in Washington, and know of a wonderful place in the wilds to dig up a few rhododendrons to transplant into my garden. Is this okay?

Answer: In western Washington and Oregon, you can collect wild rhododendrons if you have access to private land where plants grow, or if you get a permit to collect them in a national forest. Permits are available from local ranger stations. (Coast rhododendrons *cannot* be collected in the California wilderness.)

February through April is the best time to dig wild rhododendrons in western Washington and Oregon. Soil is moist and temperatures are cool. Plants are dormant at that time, but their roots are ready to surge into spring growth. By transplanting early, you can avoid losing the flower buds.

The trick to transplanting successfully is in getting as much of the root as possible. You won't have to dig as deep as most other plants, since rhododendrons have broad, shallow root systems. Plants less than 3 feet high take best to the move. Get them home and into the ground quickly; then keep them watered, if nature doesn't. In summer, a heavy mulch around the plants helps keep roots moist.

Why so bloom-shy?

Question: A year ago I planted four rhododendrons in acid soil and good light, and they bloomed profusely. I removed the faded flowers, fertilized, and watered according to directions from the nursery. This spring there were only two blooms on one plant. What is wrong?

Answer: Since it sounds like you did everything else right, perhaps you removed the faded flowers incorrectly. You are right to remove them (a procedure called "deadheading") to prevent seed formation, but your timing has to be right. The small, new growth buds are immediately beneath the flower trusses (see illustration). Damage to the growth buds could influence the amount of bloom on your rhododendrons the following year. Plants pruned late in the year, when the plump flower buds have already formed, will also limit the number of spring blossoms. Unless they've been long neglected, rhododendrons look very presentable with little or no pruning.

A second possibility: You indicated that your plants gave a fine performance last year. Although heavy bloom

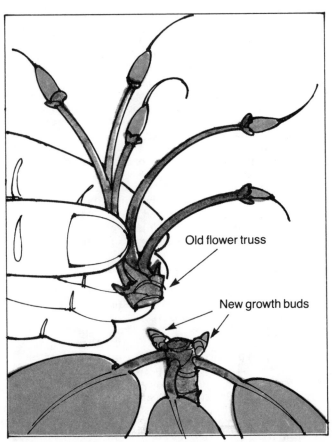

Old flower truss

New growth buds

Be careful not to disturb the young growth buds below faded blooms when you remove the old flower trusses.

one year tends to interfere with the next year's bloom and growth, if you removed faded flowers correctly it would seem to rule this out as the cause. So a more likely explanation is that the blooms you had last year had been set on the plants while in nursery cans, and that since then they have been putting on new growth at the expense of flower buds.

Still another possibility: Because rhododendrons are usually field-grown commercially under fairly bright conditions—open fields in the Pacific Northwest, or in fog belts—they may never bloom as profusely if their permanent home turns out to be in too-heavy shade.

Climate just right, soil all wrong

Problem: I live in San Bruno, California (Zone 17), and I know that rhododendrons can thrive in our foggy climate. My problem is soil: in my garden it is a sticky clay that stays wet for weeks. Just the thought of adding vast quantities of organic matter exhausts me. Is there any less backbreaking way to accommodate these plants?

Solution: Rhododendrons are shallow rooted: their dense root systems need coolness, moisture, and air, but little depth. Because of this, they are just right for planting in raised beds of specially prepared soil mixture as explained on page 442, *Sunset New Western Garden Book.* These beds can be on top of your existing soil and need be no more than two feet deep. Just make sure you provide drainage holes at the base of such a bed—about one 1-inch hole for every two feet of bed length—so water can escape from the root zone.

Rhododendrons in Southern California?

Question: We just moved from Seattle (Zone 4) to Pasadena, California (Zone 21). Our Northwest garden grew rhododendrons like weeds, but we've heard they are next to impossible in Southern California. Are there any species or varieties we could plant and expect to be proud of in time?

Answer: You *can* surprise the friends back home with California-raised rhododendrons that will look like they grew up in Seattle. But you have to pay close attention to cultural needs and selection of adaptable varieties. Southern California soils and water are likely to be neutral to alkaline, the soils low in organic matter—and rhododendrons need acid conditions and plenty of organic matter in their root zone. You'll need to prepare soil thoroughly and feed plants regularly with acid fertilizer to insure success.

It is important to choose varieties that are able to grow easily in less-than-ideal conditions of low humidity and summer heat. The old "ironclad" hybrids and many Dutch and English hybrids will do it; see specific recommendations on page 443 of Sunset's *New Western Garden Book.* Also, you can grow outdoors the flashy Malesian species and hybrids from southeast Asia that are strictly greenhouse subjects in a Seattle winter.

What gives leaves the winter droops?

Question: Why do the rhododendron leaves look so droopy during the winter? With all the rain, I expect them to look better.

Answer: Last year's leaves naturally droop a little or roll up like cigars when temperatures get low. The tendency is greater in some varieties than others. The plant begins to look perky again in spring with blossom buds and new leaves. (See illustration.)

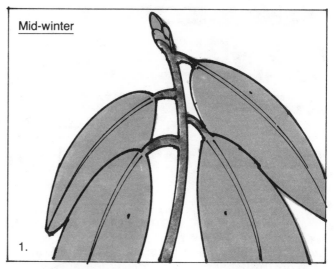
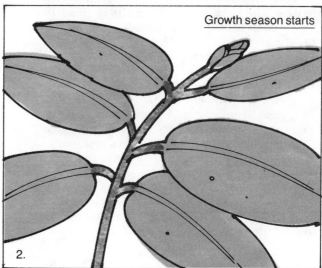
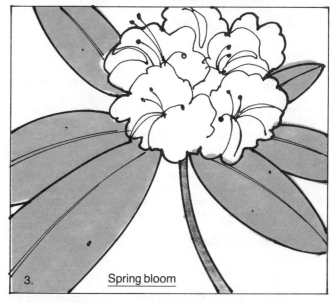

1. *Rhododendron leaves droop naturally a little in midwinter.* **2.** *and* **3.** *In early spring, the plants perk up again and produce new leaves and blossoms. Most varieties bloom in May, but some are earlier.*

CAMELLIAS

Even if camellias never flowered, most would rank high on any list of recommended landscape shrubs. The fact that they send forth beautiful blossoms in months when garden color is at a low ebb (during late fall and through winter for many varieties), makes camellias especially valuable. With minimal pruning, these glossy-leafed shrubs are attractive all year.

Camellia growers are lucky that so lovely a plant is so little bothered by pests and diseases. Most camellia failures can be traced to neglect, which suggests that the camellia's number one problem is the gardener! This is not to say that camellias are never victims of pests and diseases—it is simply that their problems will be few, with proper care.

These basic rules will help you to keep any future problems to a minimum:

- Plant during dormant season, which—unlike many plants—is when they are in bloom
- Choose a location in part shade, protected from weather extremes
- Plant in soil that is well-drained, fortified with organic matter, and slightly on the acid side.
- Plant so that trunk base is *above* soil line, never permit soil to wash over and cover the base
- Water to ensure that soil is constantly moist but never soggy
- Fertilize after bloom period, and not too heavily
- To discourage disease problems, don't let fallen flowers and leaves accumulate beneath plants

How big, over the years?

Question: I've been thinking of filling a vacant spot in my none-too-enormous garden with a camellia. I know they get bushy, but *how* bushy, how high, and how fast? I love camellias, but I don't want this thing to get way out of hand.

Answer: *Camellia japonica* grows initially like a small shrub, then becomes a large shrub, and finally (many years later) can become a small tree. Some varieties grow faster and bigger than others. In Pasadena and Sacramento, some dowager camellias of this type are 31 feet high. *C. reticulata* grows more treelike and in great age as high as 50 feet. Most varieties of *C. sasanqua* grow like open bushes but some can be grown as ground covers or vines.

What's this? Chickenpox?

Problem: My camellia leaves have turned dull brown, with dozens of tiny spots, and the lovely bushes look like they have chickenpox.

Solution: Removing the spider mites that probably are causing the problem should restore your bushes to all their beauty. These microscopic pests are warm-weather creatures. Deal with light infestations by hosing down the leaves with a strong spray of water, especially on the

leaves' undersides. Heavy, established populations of spider mites require attention with an insecticide. Systemic insecticides are effective, particularly those that include kelthane. Also see page 35.

When and how should I fertilize?

Question: When and how should I fertilize my camellia to promote the showiest possible bloom season next year?

Answer: You don't say how old your camellia is. If it has just been planted in your garden, hold off fertilizing for the first year. In the second and third years, apply fertilizer at only half the rate recommended on the package for older plants. You'll get good results from one of the commercial fertilizers referred to as "for acid-loving plants." Package directions tell you how much to apply, according to the size of your bush. Apply the first dosage at the start of bloom season, followed by another just before the onset of new growth. Or, if you prefer, you can apply cottonseed meal, a slow-acting organic fertilizer, just at the onset of bloom and thereafter at 1-month intervals.

Be sure the soil is moist when you apply either fertilizer, and water well right afterwards. If you have any doubt on the amount, too little is safer than too much.

Leaves yellowed, then "burned"

Problem: I have several large camellias in containers that I have grown in our Riverside, California garden successfully for a number of years. Recently the leaves started to yellow, so I treated them with an application of chelated iron. The yellowness went away, but now I notice that the leaves look like they have been burned on the edges.

Solution: In parts of California and the Southwest, water may contain various salts that in time will harm camellias (and other plants), resulting in the burned appearance you mentioned. These salts accumulate in the soil over a period of time, and the only method of treatment is to leach the salts from the soil. Do this by thoroughly flooding the container for 5 to 15 minutes depending on the size of the container. Leaching every 6 months, just before the onset of new growth and again 6 months later, should be sufficient. (See illustration.)

Genetic idiosyncrasies

Question: Why do some camellias hang on to their flowers after they have turned brown, while others neatly shed their old blossoms?

Answer: It's genetic, like blue eyes and brown eyes... depends on the variety.

My mulch repels water

Problem: Last spring, I mulched our camellia bed with a thick layer of peat moss, which I understood to be good for the plants. This summer, however, the peat moss is so dry that no matter how much water I apply, it just seems to run off the top. I'm afraid the plants are going to suffer soon.

Advice: Peat moss is usually dry when you buy it; whenever using some of it as a mulch, knead water into it with your hands. Or, to moisten the entire bag's contents, open the bag partially and stick a hose inside. Let the water run into it very slowly, until the peat has been saturated.

As long as you water consistently, the peat moss will serve as a mulch. But if you let it dry out completely, it can be blown away by the wind and any that does remain will actually repel water. To prevent this, buy a wetting agent at your nursery, mix according to package directions, and pour it over the mulch from a sprinkling can. This will help the water get through the peat. Be alert and make sure that the mulch is then kept consistently moist.

Although peat moss is an excellent mulch, preferred by some gardeners, there are other easier-to-use mulches (such as ground bark) that are effective and sometimes cheaper.

What's causing scabs on leaves?

Problem: There are very strange, corklike scabs on the camellia leaves in our yard. We just moved into this house, and never had camellias before, so I don't know what's wrong.

Explanation: Corky scabs on the undersides of leaves are a sure sign of leaf scurf. The former owner of your house probably overwatered the camellias, or watered them irregularly. The roots absorbed more water than the leaves could transpire, so blisters developed on the leaves and eventually scabbed over. Follow a regular watering program, and the problem should not recur.

Allow water from hose to run through soil in container to thoroughly leach out (flush) harmful salt deposits.

Flush with running water

When is best planting time?

Question: I have a perfect spot to plant several camellias. When is the best time to plant them?

Answer: Camellias, like other shrubs, are best planted and transplanted when dormant, with roots, leaves, and stems inactive. But keep in mind that unlike most other shrubs, camellias are in bloom during their dormant period. This offers a pleasant advantage—you can shop for camellias at a time when you can actually see what the blossoms look like.

Tell me about petal blight

Problem: Tell me about the much-talked-about camellia petal blight. My plants look OK now, but how would I know if they caught this disease? What is it, and what does it look like?

Solution: Camellia petal blight can, indeed, be serious. While sun or wind may brown the edges of healthy blos-

Also see pages 216—219, *Sunset New Western Garden Book*

soms, if flowers rapidly turn an ugly brown, suspect the disease. As you pick up fallen, brown blossoms, run your finger over their centers; if you feel (and then see) hard black masses about the size of rice grains, petal blight has struck the plant. The remedy against spread is to pick up and burn all infected blooms, whether on the plant or the ground (urge your neighbors to do the same). Remove mulch away from your property, and replace with new. The best precaution against petal blight is to spray the ground under plants with PCNB several weeks before flowers open. Benomyl prevents infestation if present on blossoms when spores alight.

Do camellias need pruning?

Problem: My camellia is pretty as a picture—but too big and rangy. If fact, it's beginning to outgrow its site. Is it safe to prune a camellia and, if so, when's the best time of year?
Solution: Unlike rose bushes and many other flowering shrubs, camellias don't require pruning to stay healthy and to produce the most flowers. But, in some cases—especially in overly shady locations—they can get a little open and lanky instead of compact and even. The best time to prune is right after flowering or during summer or early fall. For maximum bushiness, remove terminal growth bud to stimulate growth from dormant buds at bases of leaves along stem. Or cut out last year's growth just above the annual growth scar; 3 to 4 branches will start below cut. On a much overgrown bush, you can cut the plant way back. Though the result may at first resemble a pruned rose bush you can expect it to put forth plenty of new growth. After the first year, trim out the new unwanted or unnecessary shoots, removing, for example, those that would only grow up to obscure a window again. After any camellia is more than one year old, you can thin out unwanted shoots at any time of year.

Leaves falling, branches dying

Problem: The leaves are falling off the 2-foot high camellia that I have planted in a large wooden container. Some of the branches have died, too. What is wrong?
Solution: Although some leaf fall is natural, the dying-back of entire branches is a sure sign that the plant is in trouble. Check to make sure that water drains out of your container freely. Standing water can cause root rot, which can destroy whole branches. Too frequent, heavy applications of fertilizer can cause similar symptoms. Also, be sure water is penetrating the soil mass—not running down the sides of it and out the drainage holes, leaving the root ball dry.

Many flowers, but they're small

Problem: Every year my camellias have lots of blooms, but they are very small.
Advice: Most camellias will produce more than one flower at each budding point, and some varieties may have three to six in a cluster. For the latter, the result is plenty of color, but smaller flowers. Despite the variety, you can encourage larger (though fewer) blooms by disbudding the flowers regularly. But be sure to distinguish between the plump, oval flower buds and the long, slender growth buds in the same cluster. To remove a flower bud, grasp it firmly and gently twist it off; use care not to *pull* it, or you may remove the growth bud as well.

Leave one or two flower buds at the end of each branch; and moving back on the stem, leave one flower bud every 3 to 4 inches. Spare flower buds of different sizes, as the smaller ones will mature later and prolong the bloom season.

Move camellias to a cold climate?

Problem: We have been transferred to Bend, Oregon, and I want to dig up and take along the four camellias I recently planted (we now live in Eureka, California). Will they stand the change of climate and soil?
Advice: Bend, Oregon (Zone 1), is not camellia country, but if they are properly planted in containers you can control the soil, water, and nutrient factors. The containers also will help control such environmental problems as sun, wind, and frost, to increase your chance of success. In cold-winter areas such as Bend, camellias must be protected—on an unheated but sunny porch, for example. During the summer, the containers can be moved outdoors into partial shade.

(See illustration for proper method of planting camellias in containers.)

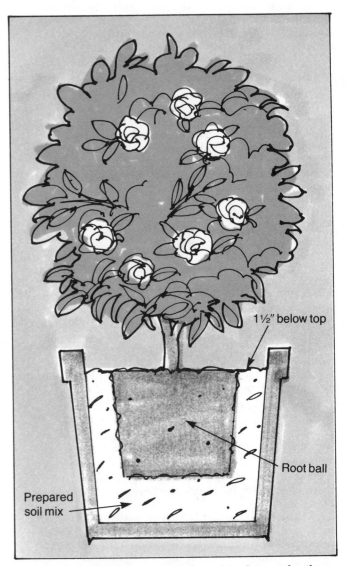

Inside of container is no more than 4 inches wider than the plant's root ball and 1 1/2 times as deep; top of root ball is 1 1/2 inches below the container top.

FUCHSIAS

GUIDELINES FOR AVOIDING GENERAL PROBLEMS

Fuchsias are special plants with some special requirements—the most important of which are a cool, humid climate; good light, but with protection from scorching sun and drying winds; and plenty of moisture. If all that sounds suspiciously like the coastal climate of much of California and the Northwest, you're right. Gardeners outside these regions have to work a little harder to have success with fuchsias, but it can be done.

These beautiful shrubs require soil that is porous, yet water-retentive enough so that roots don't entirely dry out; use soil mix with plenty of organic matter. Provide good drainage and water frequently, especially plants in hanging baskets or other containers. Fertilize regularly.

Fuchsias have some special pruning requirements, too, as illustrated on page 108. Pruning and pinching are regular duties for the avid fuchsia-grower, and result in the most attractive plants and the most profuse blooms.

Primary enemies of fuchsias are whiteflies, aphids, and mites, all of which are easiest to control when infestations are first noticed (see the pests section, pages 32–48, for recommended controls).

For more information on varieties and care, see Fuchsia, pages 304–305, *Sunset New Western Garden Book*.

In summary, here are primary points to keep in mind for growing healthy, problem-free fuchsias:

- Plant in fast-draining soil with plenty of organic material
- Place in cool spots in the garden that are protected from frosts and heavy winds
- Water frequently and thoroughly
- For maximum bloom, fertilize lightly but frequently
- Control insect pests
- Prune each spring

Can fuchsias take the heat?

Question: We recently moved from a foggy coastal town where fuchsias grew like weeds. Now that we're here in Napa, California (Zone 14), I was wondering if we can still grow fuchsias successfully. It gets pretty hot here in the summer.

Answer: One basic guideline is that fuchsias with huge, fully double flowers, and those with white or pastel pink blooms, are generally the most heat-sensitive—reliable only near the coast. The kinds most tolerant of inland heat usually have single or small double flowers in red or orange shades.

Which varieties for baskets?

Question: I went to the nursery recently to look over their selection of fuchsias. Each little container had a tag with the name of the fuchsia, and whether it was a trailing, upright, or semi-upright variety. I know you can make almost any fuchsia into a trailing variety with enough prodding and pinching, but I don't want to go to all that work. What I really want are several good, naturally trailing varieties to use in hanging baskets on my patio.

Answer: The following are some of the highest-ranked hanging-basket fuchsias, especially good for beginning fuchsia gardeners: 'Marinka', 'Swingtime', 'Pink Galore', 'Pink Marshmallow', 'Cascade', 'Tinker Bell', 'Red Spider', 'Wood Violet', 'Icicle', and 'Lisa'. For further details on growing fuchsias, see page 304, *Sunset New Western Garden Book*.

My fuchsias are looking sickly

Problem: My fuchsias seemed to be in good condition until very recently. Now the leaves don't have any luster and the surfaces have tiny pits.

Advice: They probably are infested with mites. These common pests are pictured on page 35, and methods of control are discussed. Misting your fuchsias during summer heat will help to discourage reinfestation.

Sudden wilting in the heat

Problem: Although I water them once each day, my fuchsias are given to sudden wilting during hot weather. Could the problem be something other than water?

Solution: The once-a-day watering is not sufficient in hot spells. Place a mulch around your plants; increase the amount of water; mist the plants daily to improve moisture.

Good cuttings, poor plants

Problem: I don't have much luck with fuchsias in Camarillo, California (Zone 23), although a neighbor has beauties. Mine come from cuttings of his, so I know the problem doesn't lie with the variety. I've followed his suggestions to a "T" for planting, watering, and feeding, and I'm growing them in pots, as he does.

Advice: Maybe your plants are getting too much sun, particularly in the afternoon. If they are in pots, move them to a shady, cool spot in your garden. Fuchsias do best in Zones 4–6, 15–17, 22–24—especially where the fog rolls in on summer afternoons. For more details on fuchsia care, see page 304, *Sunset New Western Garden Book*.

Many leaves, few flowers

Problem: My fuchsias have put on lots of new growth with many leaves. But there haven't been many blossoms this summer.

Solution: Your fuchsias probably are not getting a complete diet. Nitrogen is essential for foliage growth and good green color, but phosphorus is necessary also in adequate amounts. Use a complete fertilizer

on your fuchsias, feed them once monthly during the growing season, and the problem should be eliminated.

How much to prune?

Question: Last summer we planted some new fuchsias in containers and I'm happy to report that we had great success with them. We live in good fuchsia country (Pt. Arena, California, Zone 17), but now it is March and I'm wondering what to do to repeat our success. Also, we have inherited an older fuchsia that has been neglected. Should they be pruned and, if so, how much?

Answer: March is the time to give fuchsias their annual heavy pruning in mild-winter areas, such as Zone 17. (In cold-winter areas, wait until danger of frost is past.) Fuchsias take to what may seem extreme pruning, but this is the best way to produce a lush, full plant with an abundance of flowers (see illustration).

- *Young fuchsias.* Fuchsias bloom only on new wood—the current season's growth of branches. All you want to leave after pruning is a basic structural framework for the new branches. If this procedure is followed during a plant's youth, you will prune in approximately the same places annually.

- *Older fuchsias.* If you are working on a big, old fuchsia that hasn't been pruned properly in

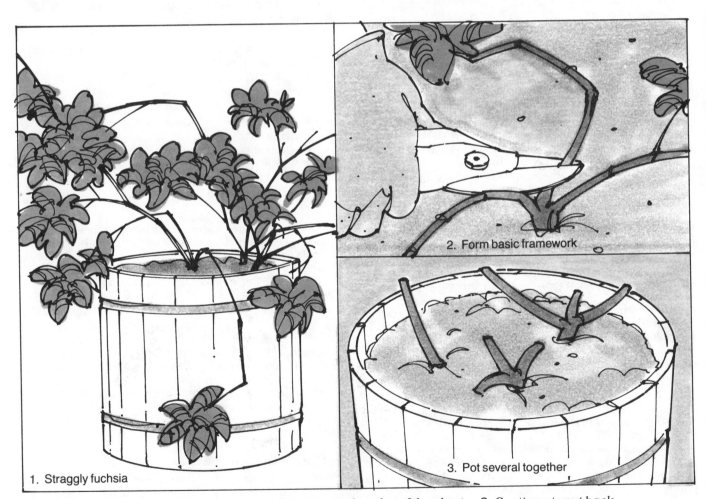

1. Straggly fuchsia

2. Form basic framework

3. Pot several together

1. *Straggly fuchsia should be pruned back all the way to the edge of the planter.* **2.** *Continue to cut back old stems to develop a basic framework for next year's branches and blooms.* **3.** *After pruning, several fuchsias can be potted together for a spectacular flower show next season.*

years, it is best not to cut back too far into old wood. The plant may not have enough dormant buds under the bark to produce new growth. In this case, just remove most of last year's growth.

Is low pruning necessary for taller kinds?

Question: We live near the ocean in Southern California, and the most eye-catching plants in our garden are fuchsias—the taller, upright kinds. They are our most bountiful flowering shrubs. But we wonder about pruning them. We have always cut them back heavily each winter so that no more than two eyes of the last year's growth are left on each stem. But they grow so vigorously that perhaps we are just wasting time and effort by cutting them back so low.

Answer: You certainly don't *have* to cut back upright fuchsias that severely, but there are good reasons for doing it. They are vigorous plants, as you know, and will grow strongly after heavy pruning—so no harm is done by pruning low. Most growers do this so that leafy new growth will cover the woody plant skeleton quickly and completely. Frequent pinching of resultant growth will promote much branching so the plant will be a compact mass of leaves and flowers.

It is perfectly acceptable to do only a light pruning if you don't mind seeing plants' bare bases and some of the limb structure. The more lightly pruned specimens will grow taller and more open, but still would be pinched frequently during the growing season (same as with hard-pruned plants) to encourage density and blossoms.

Best environment for fuchsias?

Question: We are easterners planning to move to California. During previous visits to the San Francisco Bay Area, we have been impressed by the many kinds and varieties of fuchsias—we never saw them back home. We plan to grow a lot of them in our new home. What kind of environment do they prefer?

Answer: You didn't mention *where* you plan to live in California. Fuchsias grow best in cool summer temperatures, modified sunlight, and with much moisture in the atmosphere and soil. If you will be living near the coast where fog rolls in on summer afternoons, anyplace in your garden will supply these conditions. If your new home is to be in an inland area where summers are warm, windy, dry, or sunny, seek or create a favorable exposure that is protected from wind and afternoon sun. Morning sun or all-day dappled shade is fine—in short, a place where you, yourself, are comfortable on hot summer days.

Cold climate problems

Question: I brought back a fuchsia from California last summer and planted it outside. We've had one light frost already (we live near Great Falls, Montana), and I noticed the tips of the plant were frostbitten. What should I do to keep it alive during the cold winter?

Answer: Fuchsias are too tender to over winter in cold climates, but many gardeners in cold regions love fuchsias and grow them anyway. It does require some special measures, as follows: Dig up the fuchsia and plant it in a container. Place it in a cool room or cellar, and water it lightly through the winter. Prune back the plant in March and move it gradually to warmer, lighter conditions, increasing the water. Plant the fuchsia outside in the spring, when all danger of frost is past. Each year, when frosts begin, repeat the entire procedure.

They didn't like the move

Question: When we painted our house, I moved the fuchsias in containers to another shady location. Soon after, they started to drop a few leaves. Why did this happen?

Answer: Fuchsias like to stay put during their blooming season. So it's natural for them to drop a few leaves if they are moved around. If the location is similar to the old one, they'll adapt before long.

Small flower clusters, at tips only

Problem: My fuchsias seem to grow nothing more than a few straggly branches with small clusters of flowers right at the tips.

Solution: Your fuchsias need a good pinching to get them started. After the annual late February or March pruning (see "How much to prune?", page 108), watch the new shoots as they emerge.

When each new green branch has developed four sets of leaves, use your thumbnail and forefinger (or small shears) to pinch off the growing tip with its newest set of leaves. The remaining shoot will branch. When those two new shoots develop their own four sets of leaves, pinch them in the same manner; they will then branch into four. Continue this pinching until about mid-May. Flowers will appear by late June. All you will sacrifice will be a few early flowers; and full plants covered with blooms from midsummer on will be your reward.

Those little white flies

Problem: Generally, I've had good luck with fuchsias. This summer, however, the leaves are turning yellow and dropping, despite a regular feeding and watering program. I've noticed that there are hundreds (thousands?) of very tiny white flies on the undersides of the leaves. Could they be the problem?

Solution: Not could be—they *are!* Your fuchsias are infested with whiteflies, which can be really pesky. For information on whiteflies, see page 35.

What about winter frosts?

Question: We really admire fuchsias but live in an area that gets frequent frosts in winter. We would like to plant some fuchsias in a corner of our back yard that is only semi-protected. Is it worth trying?

Answer: Where frosts are light, fuchsias lose their leaves and sometimes tender growth is killed. Where frosts are heavy, most plants die back to hard wood, sometimes to the roots. The best plan is to protect outdoor fuchsias by mounding 5 to 6 inches of sawdust over roots in case of a hard frost. Otherwise, just expect a little frost damage each year.

Is my husband water-happy?

Question: My husband, who is a real fuchsia hobbyist, waters his hanging basket fuchsias nearly every day during the summer. They look great, but I can't see why any plants would need that much water. I've told him he's water-happy. Am I right?

Answer: Afraid not. It's almost impossible to give thriving fuchsias in well-drained containers too much water during the warm summer months.

Problems with pests? See pages 32—48

LANDSCAPE SHRUBS & HEDGES

GUIDELINES FOR AVOIDING GENERAL PROBLEMS

Shrubs comprise the backbone of most landscape plantings. Because they are so widely used, mistakes (which, in turn, lead to problems) are frequently made.

The most common mistake is planting the wrong plant in the wrong spot. For a shrub, or any other plant, to thrive, the gardener must know what the plant's likes and dislikes are. For example, that means not planting shade-loving ferns in the sun; making sure that azaleas, camellias, and rhododendrons (among others) are planted in an acid soil; making sure that a prized daphne plant receives the excellent drainage that it requires.

Be sure you don't overplant. With the exception of a few notoriously slow-growing plants, shrubs are often surprising in their rate of growth. Don't waste time, money, and effort by planting too many shrubs in any given space.

Hedges are merely a collection of shrubs (usually of all the same variety) planted together for a special effect—namely a living wall or fence. Most require regular pruning to keep their neat appearance and vitality. And if a flower bed is to make its appearance directly in front of a hedge, some kind of a subterranean barrier will be necessary to keep a multitude of roots from making planting all but impossible.

Here is a brief summary of primary points:
- When you go to the nursery or garden center, know what the conditions are like in your garden, and buy only those plants whose requirements match those conditions
- Don't overplant
- As is true with all kinds of plants, keep a watchful eye out for the first sign of any pest or disease attack. Small infestations are always easier to control than larger ones

The Plant Selection Guide, pages 97–160 of the *Sunset New Western Garden Book*, will give you many ideas as to which landscape shrubs and hedges will do the job you have in mind.

The bamboo is taking over!

Problem: Bamboo planted by the previous owners of our house is literally taking over our backyard. Originally planted near the rear fence, it stayed in place for a number of years. About two years ago, sprouts began to pop up 35 to 40 feet into the yard, and they are now appearing all over the place. I'd like to get rid of it entirely. How do I do it?

Solution: The many kinds of running bamboo spread rapidly by underground stems (rhizomes), but these do not readily grow into dry, hard soil. Perhaps you increased water and food rations two years ago. If you want to get rid of bamboo entirely, the best way is to dig out the main mass of tangled rhizomes with mattock and spade, then eliminate the long-ranging rhizomes and the stems they give rise to. If the soil is thoroughly wet, you can sometimes tear rhizomes out of the ground back to the parent clump; you may rip up sod, but it can be trodden back into place.

You can starve bamboo out by removing shoots as soon as they appear, or at any rate before they reach 2 feet in height. Deprived of its food-making foliage, the rhizome mass will eventually run out of stored nourishment and die. The process is a slow one; you will have to cut off many stems over a long period.

You can also use glyphosate applied on the leaves to kill wandering sprouts. Either spray it on the foliage or, if desirable plants are nearby, paint it on with care. Again, it will be necessary to repeat this process.

If you wish to keep the original planting by the fence, isolate it by an 18-inch deep barrier of poured concrete or galvanized sheet metal. An alternative: separate it from your garden by a foot-deep trench. Rhizomes that grow into the trench can be cut off with pruning shears or loppers. Or consider replacing a running bamboo with a clumping kind that won't leave its post. For a list of these, see pages 195-197, *Sunset New Western Garden Book*.

Can golden bamboo roots be contained?

Problem: Although I'm well aware that golden bamboo can invade an entire garden, I want to plant several as a privacy screen on the street side of a front patio. Do you know of anything that will keep them from spreading so fast?

Advice: Several old half wine-barrel planters should keep golden bamboo *(Phyllostachys aurea)* in its place. Provided with rich topsoil, all bamboo needs for thriving is regular watering three or four times a week (daily in hot weather). Apply manure once a year. In 4 or 5 years, the barrels will be crowded and the bamboo should be repotted. (Also see *Phyllostachys aurea*, page 196, *Sunset New Western Garden Book*.)

Golden bamboo planted in half barrels provides streetside privacy. Repot in 4 or 5 years.

Heavenly bamboo with measles

Question: One of our heavenly bamboo plants has acquired red spots all over its leaves. My son says it looks like it has measles. Is the plant sick? It seems okay otherwise.

Answer: Your heavenly bamboo *(Nandina domestica)* does have a fairly common, but not too serious disease—cucumber mosaic virus. In fact, some gardeners favor the spots and actually seek plants with the disease, finding it attractive. The virus seems to stunt nandina's growth slightly, but doesn't hurt the plants otherwise. There is no cure for cucumber mosaic virus, but that's not a cause for alarm, just for caution.

Warning: Since winged aphids can transmit the virus, locate your vegetable garden a distance away (around the corner of a house, for instance) from infected plants. Cucumber mosaic can severely stunt the growth of celery, cucumber, spinach, squash, and tomatoes.

Bees love our old, rangy hedge

Problem: Our daughter is allergic to bee stings, and unfortunately our big, old rangy hedge has lots of flowers that attract the bees.

Advice: It sounds like your hedge is a privet of some sort, and you are not keeping it closely clipped. Heavy and regular pruning would eliminate most of the flowers—and give the bees nothing to buzz around for.

Brick wall cover-up

Problem: We have a 10-foot brick wall in our backyard in Merced, California (Zone 8) that catches the afternoon sun. I know the bricks add to the heat—it makes me feel hot just looking at the wall. To complicate the matter, there's less than 2 feet of planting space in front of the wall, hardly enough room for a few uninspired marigolds. What I really want is a green, leafy wall. Is that impossible?

Suggestion: What you need is an evergreen shrub with soft, pliable stems that can be trained to grow flat. Several plants might work, but one of your best bets is *Cocculus laurifolius* (even it might not do it if wall is *too* hot). Cocculus is an evergreen shrub or small tree (to about 25 feet high). You can grow it in sun or dense shade, and it thrives in almost any kind of soil in Zones 8, 9, and 12–24. Though this shrub is often a bit slow growing when first planted, it speeds up once the root system is well established.

(See Cocculus, page 248, *Sunset New Western Garden Book*.)

What's colorful for Northwest winters?

Question: I'm bored with winter landscapes of imposing evergreens and naked deciduous trees. What can I plant here in Hood River, Oregon (Zone 3), that will contribute some color to this dreary season?

Answer: You can plant shrubs that bloom; *Jasminum nudiflorum* is a good candidate, although it's deciduous. Yellow, half-inch flowers appear in January and bloom on into March. Later, glossy green leaves unfold. Give this jasmine rich garden soil, a sunny location, and keep it pinched back to avoid rangy growth. It's an especially good plant to cascade over a wall or down a bank. This jasmine adapts best to cooler climates, but grows well in Zones 3–21. (See *Jasminum nudiflorum*, page 335, *Sunset New Western Garden Book*.)

Another possibility is Cornelian cherry *(Cornus mas)*, one of the earliest dogwoods to bloom. This open, twiggy shrub (which can be trained as a small, 15 to 20-foot tree) has clusters of yellow flowers that appear on its bare branches in February and often stay through March. Later in the spring, the glossy oval leaves begin to emerge, and will become 2 to 4 inches long. In autumn, the foliage turns yellow, sometimes red, and clusters of bright scarlet fruits (edible but acid) decorate the tree from September until the birds devour them. Plant the shrub near a window or walkway where it can be seen. (See *Cornus mas*, page 253, *Sunset New Western Garden Book*.)

Gardener, spare that creosote bush!

Question: Our new home in Globe, Arizona (Zone 10), has a *very* natural landscape. It is mostly rock, with a few weedy-looking shrubs I've been told are creosote bushes. They don't look like much and I'm thinking that I should pull them out. Would they ever amount to much?

Answer: Think twice before you yank out the creosote bushes *(Larrea tridentata)*. They may not look like much growing bare and straggly, but while they endure neglect, they really thrive on care. If you water them every two weeks, feed occasionally, and prune as you wish, they will leaf out and bloom. The flushes of small yellow blooms followed by fuzzy white seed clusters will continue all year.

(Also see *Larrea tridentata*, page 344, *Sunset New Western Garden Book*.)

Why is my daphne dying?

Problem: My daphne was lovely for years and bloomed as usual late this last winter. Suddenly it just started to die back. I'm saddened to think of losing it. What could be wrong?

Advice: Unfortunately, winter daphne *(Daphne odora)* is quite unpredictable. Its roots are delicate and require a porous, fast-draining soil that allows plenty of air to circulate. If things go a little awry, one of several water mold diseases can take over. At that point there is really nothing you can do to reverse the situation. Remove the daphne and plant a new one.

(Also see Daphne, pages 267–268, *Sunset New Western Garden Book*.)

Is redtwig dogwood a nuisance?

Question: I love the red stems of the native redtwig dogwood, but a friend warned me against planting it. Such an attractive plant couldn't be that much of a nuisance, could it?

Answer: Redtwig dogwood *(Cornus stolonifera)*, for all its beauty, has been known to get out of bounds and spread quickly by means of invasive roots. The trick is to slice off those roots with a spade, and clip off any ground-touching branches before they root.

However, this dogwood will serve you well if you have a medium or large garden. Plant it in a moist area that you'd like to cover quickly. Or plant it along a property line to grow into a handsome deciduous screen. In February, the dense, smooth red twigs make a good show. Clusters of white flowers follow in late spring. Fruit appears in summer; and in fall, the leaves turn red and drop.

(Also see *Cornus stolonifera*, page 254, *Sunset New Western Garden Book*.)

How should I trim my English laurel?

Problem: We moved into a house with a mature hedge of English laurel. I've tried trimming it with my electric hedge trimmers, but they don't seem to be doing a very good job.

Solution: Large-leafed hedge plants such as English laurel should not be pruned with electric shears; power trimmers leave unsightly cut and chewed leaves in their wake. Large-leafed hedges should be cut back selectively with hand pruning shears. Remove errant branches one by one, rather than trying to give the entire hedge surface a haircut. (See Hedge Shears, page 93, *Sunset New Western Garden Book*.)

Alternative for English laurel?

Question: I want to plant a row of tall shrubs—and I don't want English laurel. I've been through that before. What is a good alternative here in Eugene, Oregon (Zone 6)?

Answer: When you want medium- to large-size shrubs for an evergreen screen, the obvious temptation is to plant English laurel. But as one horticulturist said of its fast-growing ways, "Planting English laurel on your property line is an act of aggression against your neighbor."

Laurustinus *(Viburnum tinus)* is an excellent alternative. It grows well in Zones 4–10 and 12–23. This well-mannered, broadleaf evergreen with handsome foliage and shape bears profuse white flowers from November through May. Blue-black berries follow in summer. Birds are attracted to both the fruit and the shelter it offers.

In the fall, plant laurustinus in full sun for best flowering, or in part shade if you don't mind fewer flowers. Water well until fall rains take over.

(Also see *Viburnum tinus*, page 497, *Sunset New Western Garden Book*.)

Forsythia for my small garden?

Problem: Seattle (Zone 5), is our new home. I loved gardening in Southern California, but honestly, the beauty and diversity of springtime here in the Northwest is incomparable. I'd like to have at least one plant of that magnificent forsythia I've seen here, but am afraid it will outgrow my limited space. Suggestions?

Solution: Throughout Zones 2–11, 14–16, 18, and 19, golden-flowered forsythia is the biggest and brightest herald of spring. Its color and its early blooming attract attention, but it has other virtues—hardiness to cold, tolerance of city life and city air, adaptability to most soils and moisture levels, and heavy bloom.

Another feature is its pliability under pruning shears. If there isn't enough room at the base for the mature plant's normal spread of 6 to 10 feet, you can simply thin out lower growth and let your forsythia spread out overhead.

Prune while the plant is in bloom, using cut branches for arrangements. If a cold spring delays bloom, cut a few branches anyway; they will bloom inside the house if placed in water.

(Also see *Forsythia*, pages 301–302, *Sunset New Western Garden Book*.)

Hedge height in a hurry?

Problem: We live in an older house in Berkeley, California (Zone 16), that fronts onto a rather busy street. We recently added a deck off the front of our house, and now need something that will produce a tall hedge or screen in a hurry. The deck is about 3 feet off the ground, so we need something that will screen at least 4 or 5 feet above that level. Any suggestions?

Advice: Eucalyptus solves a number of landscaping problems in mild winter regions such as Zone 16. You might try using the silver dollar gum *(Eucalyptus polyanthemos)* planted in a straight line, like a hedge, about 5 feet apart. They are very fast growing and will already have much of the height you require. With regular pruning, they will develop bushy, dense tops.

Wanted: a low, formal hedge

Question: We want a low (not much over 18 inches) evergreen hedge to grow between our lawn and a pathway. We've seen small hedges like this in Europe and in some formal gardens in public parks, but don't know what to look for at the nursery.

Answer: Several plants would do, but one of the best—and probably the one you've seen most often—is a dwarf form of boxwood *(Buxus* species). Generally planted from 1-gallon cans, the dwarf boxwoods make a very fine, low-growing, formal-looking hedge. The closer plants are placed together, the faster they will fill in for a dense appearance. (For more information on the various choices of dwarf boxwoods, see pages 210–211, *Sunset New Western Garden Book*.)

What's a good low hedge for Phoenix?

Problem: I'm still landscaping my new Phoenix (Zone 13) home—I've only been at it for a year! I'd like your suggestion for a low hedge. I need one to separate the patio and vegetable garden area. It has full sun.

Advice: Feathery cassia (*Cassia artemisioides*) is useful as an accent plant in desert landscapes, and it works as a low hedge (space plants 3 to 4 feet apart). In spring, plants are covered with a profusion of ¾-inch sulfur-yellow blossoms that exude a faint honey scent.

Its finely cut leaves and pale, silvery-gray color give feathery cassia a deceptively delicate look. Don't be fooled—this plant does nicely with the hot, dry conditions of low and intermediate desert areas. The dense, 4- to 5-foot shrub stands up to heat and wind, and does well with minimum watering once it's established. It prefers fast-draining soil and infrequent but deep watering.

(Also see Cassia, page 224, *Sunset New Western Garden Book*.)

We'd like a curvy hedge

Question: We want to plant a curving hedge to border one side of our front garden. Are there special problems in laying out and planting a curved hedge?

Answer: Not really. If you use the following for digging your planting trench, putting in a curved hedge is about as easy as putting in a straight hedge: Arrange a hose in the curve you want, and keep it in place with stakes. Cut along the hose with a spade to make one side of the trench, move the hose and stakes 18 inches, and cut another curved line. Dig the trench. Arrange your plants 1 foot apart for a 1-foot-high hedge, or 3 feet apart for taller hedges. (See illustration.)

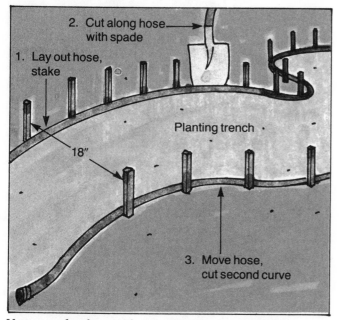

Use a garden hose to lay out line for curved hedge.

Hedge needs healthier haircut

Question: My tall privet hedge just looks awful—big bunches of leaves at the top, gaps in the middle, and skinny branches at the bottom. I was told that I haven't been pruning it right, that the proper way was to make it wider at the bottom. Why in the world would that help?

Answer: You were given good advice. Hedges should be sheared so that the sides slope in somewhat at the top. In a hedge that flares out at the top, the top gets most of the sunlight, and the deprived lower leaves and branches become straggly. (See illustration.)

To allow lower branches to get enough light to develop, shear hedges so sides slope in a little at the top.

Any ideas for a "no-shear" hedge?

Question: The word "hedges" scares me. I had a hedge once before, and what it really meant was endless shearing and too much weekend work. Are there any no-shear hedges? I live in Palm Springs (Zone 13).

Answer: Look for the dwarf varieties of such old favorites as oleander, pittosporum, pyracantha, and nandina.

Full-size oleanders can reach gigantic proportions, but the dwarf varieties usually can be kept to a modest 3 or 4 feet with minimum trimming. Try 'Petite Pink' or 'Petite Salmon'. Both form attractive mounds of medium-green leaves. They are as drought tolerant as full-sized oleanders, but more sensitive to frost.

Pittosporum tobira 'Wheeler's Dwarf', an attractive mini-version of full-size pittosporum, adds an elegant tailored look to a garden. This plant has shiny, leathery leaves, 2 to 5 inches long, on a dense, slow-growing bush that does not exceed 3 to 4 feet in height.

Dwarf pyracanthas grow less than 3 feet high. They're attractive as accent shrubs or low borders. Varieties that do well in desert climates include 'Red Elf', 'Tiny Tim', and *P. augustifolia* 'Gnome'.

Dwarf nandinas have an almost ferny look, while

Pronunciation problems? See pages 147 & 148

retaining the scarlet, orange, and yellow leaf colors of full-size nandinas. The better-known petite nandinas include 'Compacta' (4 to 5 feet tall), 'Harbour Dwarf' (1½ to 2 feet tall), and 'Nana' (1 foot tall).

Tall hedges make good neighbors

Question: Our house in Santa Clara, California, has no privacy from our neighbors. As a matter of fact, my kitchen window looks directly into theirs. It's not that we don't get along, it's just that I'd like a little privacy. Can you suggest a fast growing evergreen shrub we can plant in our sideyard to screen the view and still allow us to walk through the sideyard?

Answer: Try either *Pittosporum eugenioides* or *P. tenuifolium*. Both are great problem-solvers in exactly the situation you describe, and do well in your climate zone (15), as well as in many other California zones. They're evergreen, fast-growing, and can be easily trimmed up from the bottom to allow walking space. Both have unique and interesting leaf patterns and grow easily in a variety of situations. Check to be sure your sideyard is not so narrow that it will be too shady for pittosporum.

How can I keep hedge roots at bay?

Problem: I plan to plant a privet hedge next to the sidewalk, and then put in a flower bed between my front lawn and the hedge. I know that hedge roots can be invasive. Is there any way to prevent the roots from entering the flower bed?

Solution: Dig a trench about 10 inches wide and 18 inches deep between the hedge and the flower border. Install a rootproof barrier in the trench, using specially treated lumber, sheet metal, or fiberglas panels. Fill with soil. The barrier should keep roots from reentering the border. This solution also works well when planting a new hedge, to prevent the problem in the first place. (See illustration.)

How often should hedges be sheared?

Question: I'm afraid I'll damage my hedge by shearing it too often. Is there a general rule for when and how much to prune?

Answer: Fast-growing hedges, such as privet, require at least three shearings a season. Slower growers, such as boxwood, need only one cutting a year. Either type should be pruned when the tops grow about 3 inches.

Can hibiscus make a hedge?

Question: During my Hawaii vacation this year (first time ever!), I found hibiscus flowers spellbinding. Now I learn that these plants thrive here in Irvine, California (Zone 22). Would these wonderful shrubs work as a hedge?

Answer: Chinese, or tropical hibiscus *(H. rosa-sinensis)*, of which there are numerous colorful varieties, can make an excellent evergreen hedge or screen in Zones 9, 12, 13, 15, 16, and 19–24. The foliage is glossy and handsome. It blooms best when cut back hard, so the fact that you must prune to keep it in bounds as a hedge

Pruning hibiscus hedge one side a year ensures enough (on one side) for privacy all the time.

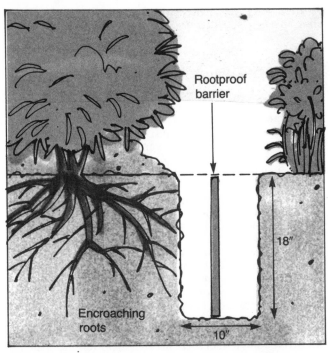

Rootproof barrier

18"

10"

Encroaching roots

Install barrier (sheet metal, fiberglas, treated lumber) near shrubs or hedge to keep roots out of flower bed.

actually encourages flowers. In Irvine's mild climate, you'll see some flowers almost every month of the year. Prune the hedge one side at a time, after it is established, every other year. This encourages enough leaves on one side for privacy all the time. (See illustration.)

(See *H. rosa-sinensis*, page 324, *Sunset New Western Garden Book*.)

Which holly for the holidays?

Question: I know that there are many, many kinds of holly. Which ones will grow well here in Burbank, California (Zone 20), and produce branches with berries for Christmas decoration?

Answer: December is a good month to shop for and plant holly. Here are some kinds that grow well in Burbank and throughout Southern California: American holly *(Ilex opaca)*, Chinese holly *(I. cornuta* and varieties), English holly *(I. aquifolium* and varieties), Wilson holly *(I. altaclarensis* 'Wilsonii'), and *I. aquipernyi*. Also try *I. meserveae, I.* 'Nellie Stevens', *I. pernyi, I.* 'San Jose Hybrid', and *I. vomitoria*.

Plants are male or female, and female plants may or may not yield berries without pollination (males never will). (See Ilex, pages 329–330, *Sunset New Western Garden Book*.)

Brown edges on hydrangea blossoms

Problem: The blue blossoms on my hydrangeas are edged with brown.

Solution: Although they are easy to grow nearly everywhere in the West, hydrangeas do demand heavy watering. Probably, during a heat spell, your hydrangeas dried out, causing burning at the edges of the petals. In addition to heavy watering, give them some protection from the sun during the hottest months.

Lackluster lilacs in Southern California

Problem: My lilacs are very important to me. They are my link to my roots in Maine. Lilacs in Maine are a gorgeous, unforgettable sight, but here in Compton, California (Zone 22), they just don't thrive. How can I help them?

Solution: Zone 22 and most of Southern California don't get cold enough for lilacs to go into complete dormancy, so blooms often come too early and are frequently small and scattered.

To get lilacs to go dormant and stay that way so they build strength for a showy bloom, stop watering them completely in September. *Don't water again until January.* Then, if the soil isn't already soaked from rains, resume watering once a week or as often as necessary. Don't worry about the lilacs dying from drought during the fall—roots of big, old lilacs are deep enough to sustain the plant for the rest of the dry season. *(But don't try this method on shrubs less than 5 years old.)*

Pep up plants by feeding them when you see buds forming.

I thought all magnolias were trees!?

Question: A neighbor here in Palo Alto, California (Zone 15) has an incredibly beautiful shrub in full flower right now (February). Flowers are pure white and leaves don't show yet. She says it is a magnolia, but I thought all magnolias were trees. Do you know?

Answer: We figure that your neighbor is right. It is a magnolia—specifically the star magnolia *(Magnolia*

stellata). The bloom, in February or early March, is like a cloud of 6-inch white stars. Its size is not great and its growth slow. In fact, the plants are not likely to exceed 6 feet tall and wide in 10 years.

Star magnolia looks like a broad, twiggy dome with leaves smaller than those of the larger magnolias. It is an excellent plant for borders and entryways. Although frosts nip the flowers in Zones 1-7, it is quite hardy.

(See *Magnolia stellata*, page 364, *Sunset New Western Garden Book*.)

Mahonias OK for Southern California?

Question: When I relandscape this fall, I'm going to use Western native shrubs primarily. My question regards the mahonias: considering these are primarily Northwest natives, would you recommend them here in Southern California?

Advice: There is one mahonia or another for every region in the West. In Southern California, you might try a hybrid California native, *Mahonia* 'Golden Abundance', that isn't as fussy as some. It has deep yellow 6-inch flower clusters in spring, followed by small, dark purple, grapelike berries which birds relish. Like other mahonias, this one has prickly hollylike leaves. 'Golden Abundance' grows up to 8 feet, with an upright form. It's erect enough to make a good hedge if plants are set 4 feet apart.

Fall is the best time to plant this mahonia. Make sure it gets full sun. You can give it regular garden watering for the rest of its life, or just water it infrequently the first year or two, then let it fend for itself. It's drought resistant, like most native California plants.

(For more information, see Mahonia, page 366, *Sunset New Western Garden Book*.)

Are Natal plums edible?

Question: I was surprised to see bright red fruit follow the pretty blossoms on my Natal plum. I had planted it for a flowering shrub, so the fruit is a bonus—is it edible?

Answer: The little 1- to 2-inch fruits are not only ornamental, but edible. Their sweetness varies from shrub to shrub; in general, they make good sauce, tasting somewhat like a sweet cranberry. You can also eat them fresh, although they are a bit tart for some tastes.

Which poppies look like fried eggs?

Question: Several years ago, I took an early July trip to Mendocino County on the northern California coast. The hillsides and vacant lots were covered with amazing shrubs that seemed to be blooming huge fried eggs. A local resident said that it was some kind of poppy. I'm finally ready to plant the hillside on my Oroville, California (Zone 7), property and I'd like to try that "fried egg poppy". Can you identify it for me? Would it grow in Oroville?

Answer: Those huge "fried eggs" bloom on the Matilija poppy *(Romneya coulteri)*. The flowers, white paperlike petals surrounding a large golden center, often reach 9 inches across. It's a Southern California and Mexican native that wandered north and flourishes on many hillsides in the early summer. It is an excellent soil binder, and does best in full sun. Your Oroville location would seem ideal. (For further information on care, see *Romneya coulteri*, page 450, *Sunset New Western Garden Book*.)

Privacy and heat protection needed

Question: Our new Wickenburg, Arizona (Zone 12) home needs some planting—not only to buffer the heat, but also for privacy. I'm sure it's a big question, but what are some hedge options?

Answer: You can enjoy a lush hedge in your desert garden if you choose plants carefully. For a tall privacy hedge (say 8 to 15 feet), good choices include 'Double Red' pomegranate, oleander, four-wing saltbush, and the columnar junipers.

Middle-size hedges with a clipped height up to 8 feet include Arizona rosewood, silverberry, xylosma, glossy privet, hop bush, true myrtle, pyracantha, Texas ranger, and *Euonymus japonica*.

March and October are the best times to plant. Choose young shrubs and prune them back halfway to induce low branching. Once established, the hedge should be sheared regularly to encourage dense growth.

Why such ratty-looking privet?

Problem: We bought bare-root privet plants for a hedge at the side of our house this winter. I thought we did everything right, but now, at the end of summer, the plants are kind of ratty looking, uneven, and have bare trunks at the bottom. Did we do something wrong?

Solution: Sounds as if you forgot to prune the privets right after planting. Bare-root privet plants should be cut back by one-half to two-thirds at planting time to ensure a bushy, full hedge. You should go ahead and do this dramatic pruning in the late fall or early spring, ideally before new growth starts. Most gardeners find it hard to prune this heavily, but it's the only way to get a hedge started right.

Pyracantha's berries scanty

Problem: I have a carefully manicured pyracantha hedge that screens off the back part of my garden. My only complaint is that it has very few berries.

Solution: The more you prune, the fewer berries you will see on your pyracantha hedge. Pyracanthas flower and produce berries only on the last year's growth. Gardeners usually prune pyracanthas during the winter, when the berries are used for decoration. But it sounds as if, in keeping your hedge "manicured", you are constantly nipping away at the growing tips. Ease off a bit, and leave some of last year's growth to produce berries. (Also see Pyracantha, page 435, *Sunset New Western Garden Book*.)

My pyracanthas have fungus problems

Problem: I live in Half Moon Bay on the northern California coast and I've had real problems with fungus on pyracanthas. Any ideas?

Suggestion: Gardeners in foggy coastal areas might be interested in two recent introductions, 'Teton' and 'Navaho', since they are reported to be resistant to the fungus disease, scab, which is rare except in areas with foggy summers. (Leaves and berries infected with this disease develop dark, scablike areas before withering and dropping.)

Both varieties are also resistant to the more common fireblight, which causes sudden "scorching" of foliage.

'Teton', which can reach 12 feet high, is notable for its upright growth. Since branches tend to grow upward instead of spreading, this variety is a particularly good choice where you want a narrow hedge or screen. The blooms are white and the berries are orange-yellow.

'Navaho' is low growing and usually stays shorter than 3 feet. Its mounding form provides an attractive low hedge or foundation planting. In spring, the plant is blanketed with white flowers, and the fruit matures to orange-red in fall.

Is raphiolepis a good background screen?

Question: I need a background screen of something tough for our garden in Chico, California (Zone 8), and would like to use raphiolepis. How tall will it get?

Answer: Depends on how tall you want it. There are over a dozen kinds of raphiolepis to choose from. Here are two examples, one of which might be the plant for you.

'Majestic Beauty' is a big, bold raphiolepis, growing to about 15 feet. Leaves are about 4 inches long, and the clusters of light pink flowers can measure 10 inches across. (You can use it as a large background shrub or train it to become a small free-standing tree.)

On the other end of the scale is *R. indica* 'Ballerina', the lowest-growing raphiolepis available. It seldom gets taller than 2 feet and stays compact—no wider than 4 feet. Flowers are a deep rosy-pink, and in the winter leaves tend to take on a wine-red color. It makes an attractive low hedge or knee-high ground cover.

(See *Raphiolepis*, page 440, *Sunset New Western Garden Book*.)

How can I block out an eyesore?

Problem: I'm looking for a shrub that will block the view of a ramshackle-looking building nearby that is really an eyesore. The shrub has to be medium sized because available space couldn't handle a full-sized tree. Also, if I'm not being too exacting, I'd like a plant with cool-looking, green leaves that can tolerate the blistering summers here in Barstow, California (Zone 11).

Solution: In the right kind of soil (not too salty), Carolina laurel cherry *(Prunus caroliniana)* is a splendid shrub or tree for hot-summer regions. It stands up well to heat and wind, and, once established, endures considerable drought.

Carolina laurel cherry, which normally grows 20 feet tall as a shrub, should fit your space. An upright shrub, it has multiple branches from the ground up, excellent for blocking unsightly views.

Between February and April, there are small white flowers, followed by black, inedible fruits. Because the falling fruits are messy, plant away from paved areas or prune trees back. (For more information, see *Prunus caroliniana*, page 429, *Sunset New Western Garden Book*.)

"It" thrives in a vacant lot

Question: I recently noticed an incredible flowering shrub in a vacant lot in Mountain View, California (Zone 15). It was about 6 feet high, and covered with white poppylike flowers and narrow leaves. Growing as it was on a vacant lot, the shrub obviously requires no gardener's encouragement. So it's perfect for a no-maintenance yard. Any idea what it is?

Answer: Probably the shrub you noticed is a California native, *Carpenteria californica*, or bush anemone. Carpenteria doesn't demand much water, and unlike many natives looks good when it's out of bloom. Fall is the best time to plant this and other San Francisco Bay Area natives. Give it light shade for best results. Check occasionally for aphids; if they should become a problem, spray as new leaves develop.

(See *Carpenteria californica*, page 222, *Sunset New Western Garden Book*.)

Is there a shrub for heavy, wet soil?

Problem: We have a serious problem with heavy soil that drains very poorly. Often puddles of water stand for a time. What sort of shrub can you suggest that can withstand these bad conditions?

Advice: Wet soil also indicates poor soil aeration. Consider a rose-gold pussy willow *(Salix gracilistyla)*. It not only can tolerate both of these negative conditions, it also produces lovely, furry gray catkins in spring. Rose-gold pussy willow grows well in all zones. (For a list of other plants that grow in wet soil, see page 147, *Sunset New Western Garden Book*.)

Can I transplant a big, old shrub?

Problem: Can I transplant a mature broadleafed shrub, specifically an aucuba, without killing it? If so, how and when?

Solution: It's a real chore, but certainly possible. Springtime is the prime time to move older, established plants, especially broadleafed evergreens. Wait until the ground is warm and dry enough to dig, and the plant is just coming out of dormancy. (The end of March in the Northwest; 4 to 8 weeks earlier in Southern California.) Later transplanting would interrupt active growth.

Two people can successfully handle a huge old plant. First, tie up the shrub's branches. Then dig a circular trench around the trunk, following the shrub's dripline. As you dig down, gradually dig in and under to shape a large root ball.

Trench exposes root ball

Before transplanting a large shrub, tie up branches out of the way. Dig a wide trench to expose root ball.

When the root ball seems to be standing on a pedestal, rock the plant back and forth, slicing at the bottom of the pedestal with the shovel until the last few roots come free.

With the plant dug free, pull it from the hole, roll it onto an old canvas tarpaulin. Then drag the aucuba to its new site, where a new hole has been prepared. (See illustration.)

Use tarpaulin as sled

Rock shrub back and forth to dislodge. Roll it onto heavy tarpaulin and drag it to the new planting site.

Which shrub for dry summers?

Question: I'm new in Southern California and miss the abundant water of the Northwest. Is there such a thing as a flowering shrub that requires no water through the summer months?

Answer: It may sound impossible, but there's a handsome garden shrub with abundant lavender flowers and aromatic foliage which thrives on neglect. It is woolly blue curls *(Trichostema lanatum)*, a California native that grows 3 to 5 feet tall and actually should not be given any summer water *after it's established.* (You can see *Trichostema* in bloom from mid-July through autumn at Rancho Santa Ana Botanic Garden in Claremont.) Buy and plant nursery stock in spring or plant seeds in the ground.

(For more information, see *Trichostema lanatum*, page 488, *Sunset New Western Garden Book*.)

What's a good evergreen for Ogden?

Question: Can you recommend an ornamental, native, evergreen shrub for my area, Ogden, Utah (Zone 2)? Something that will look good all year.

Answer: Look for *Arctostaphylos patula* 'Temple Square' in Ogden nurseries. This Rocky Mountain na-

Problems with pests? See pages 32-48

tive manzanita keeps its 2-inch-long oval leaves through the winter (they turn yellow-green). In summer, the leaves turn back to a deep, glossy green; clusters of pink flowers cover the plant in May and June. Manzanita 'Temple Square' eventually grows into a rounded 3- to 6-foot shrub. The attractive, smooth bark ranges from gray to brown or red; branches are prized for use in flower arrangements.

Heavy snow broke off branches

Problem: Last winter we had lots of snow and lost some branches on several mature shrubs due to the weight of the snow. Is there any way to prevent this?

Solution: Don't go out in the midst of a blizzard, but as soon as possible after a snow, brush the snow off the branches. For tall shrubs or trees, use a pole to shake the branches. (See illustration.)

Knock snow from branches to prevent breakage.

First aid for Texas root rot

Problem: Several of the mature shrubs around the border of our lawn suddenly wilted, and the foliage dried out. What could have caused the problem so quickly? We live in Clovis, New Mexico (Zone 10).

Solution: The symptoms are typical of Texas root rot, a widespread fungus disease in semiarid areas of the Southwest and Southern California. The rot attacks roots of plants that have been watered regularly. If you act promptly, the treatment suggested here may save your shrubs and also help protect other nearby plants. (See illustration.)

1. Loosen the soil around the affected shrub out to the dripline.

2. Cover the soil surface with 2 inches of well-composted manure.

3. On top of the manure, scatter equal amounts of ammonium *sulfate* and soil sulfur, each at the rate of

1 pound to 10 square feet. Water in immediately (see below); the resulting solution kills the fungus without injuring the roots and also stimulates root growth. (Be sure not to use ammonium *nitrate*—it actually encourages the growth of fungus.)

4. Soak the treated area to a depth of 3 feet by flooding in a basin, or allow sprinklers to run until water has penetrated to 3 feet.

5. Cut back wilted branches to the main trunk to prevent loss of water through transpiration.

(For more information, see page 66, *Sunset New Western Garden Book.*)

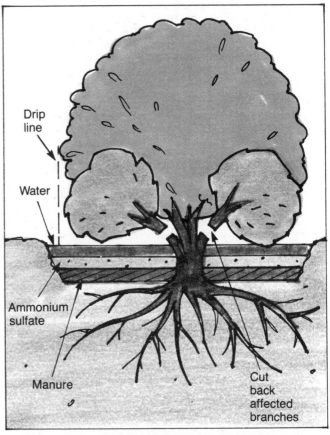

Drip line

Water

Ammonium sulfate

Manure

Cut back affected branches

Texas root rot treatment kills fungus without injuring shrub (or tree) roots; stimulates fast new growth.

What's tough and fast with multiple trunks?

Problem: There is a spot in my garden that needs a single unusual shrub. I'd like one that can be pruned to show multiple trunks, and that will grow with minimum fuss and bother.

Solution: Italian buckthorn *(Rhamnus alaternus)* has a lot going for it. Not only can it be easily trained as a multistemmed 12- to 20-foot shrub, but it also grows quickly, survives drought and wind. You can grow it if you live nearly anywhere west of the Sierra. (Zones 4 to 24 are recommended.) It likes full sun, but also does well in part shade. Leaves are shiny and dense, so it makes an attractive solid background too. (For more information, see *Rhamnus alaternus*, pages 441–442, *Sunset New Western Garden Book.*)

Topiary boxwood in two years?

Question: There is a small boxwood growing in our yard. We'll be transferred in another two years. Is there enough time for me to train and prune it into one of those "smooth gumdrop" shrubs?

Answer: Probably not. Topiary—the pruning technique that produces stylized shapes—is an exacting, time-consuming process. And in two years, you would have to leave it. Why not buy a young boxwood now and plant it in a container? Begin pruning and training the plant to shape. Then when you move, you can take your handiwork with you and continue to shape and train it in its new environment.

Is it topiary or espalier?

Question: I have a pyracantha that I thought was espaliered, but my son-in-law insists that it is topiary style. How do these techniques differ?

Answer: See the illustrations for the differences between these two types of ornamental pruning and training. Espaliering usually needs some formal structure for support. Topiary is a style of pruning plants into imaginative shapes.

We'd like some winter greenery

Problem: It's November and here in Corvallis, Oregon (Zone 6), there's hardly a green leaf to be seen in our garden. For some reason, the previous owners went too heavy with deciduous trees and shrubs. What are some interesting looking evergreens we can add and substitute?

Solution: Camellias, mountain laurel, butcher's broom (*Ruscus*), rhododendrons, and evergreen azaleas all are good bets. Or, try the following for leaves and form: aucuba, Japanese aralia, mahonia, sarcococca, skimmia, and *Viburnum davidii*. All are shade tolerant.

Planted in November beneath deciduous trees, these evergreens will benefit from the extra light that comes through leafless branches during winter. And they will still do well in summer, when longer daylight compensates for overhead foliage. (See individual plant listings in the encyclopedia section, *Sunset New Western Garden Book*.)

How can I tell witch hazel?

Question: A neighbor has a shrub that looks very similar to the common witch hazel, except its flowers are red. I inquired at the nursery, but I wasn't sure what I was asking for. Can you solve the mystery? I live in Portland, Oregon (Zone 6).

Answer: Most gardeners west of the Cascades like you are familiar with Chinese witch hazel (*Hamamelis mollis*), with its bright yellow, sweetly fragrant flowers in January. But there is also a red-flowering witch hazel, *Hamamelis intermedia* 'Diane'. This red form is a bit more arching than *H. mollis*. Its leaves are large and roundish—bright green in summer, brilliant orange in autumn. If you decide to plant one, place it where you can see it from indoors, or wherever you'll pass it regularly to get the most enjoyment out of its bloom. When you plant it, enrich the planting hole with generous amounts of peat moss. Keep it well watered. (For more information, see *Hamamelis*, page 317, *Sunset New Western Garden Book*.)

Espalier— supported against wall

Many shrubs, such as pyracantha and cotoneaster, can be espaliered (symmetrically pruned and trained) on a wood fence or masonry wall.

Topiary— free-standing

Topiary, imaginatively shaped, takes years of pruning. Best plants for topiary have buds and branches close to one another; every cut is close to a growing point.

VINES

GUIDELINES FOR AVOIDING GENERAL PROBLEMS

Because of their unique growth habits, vines perform specific functions in the garden. Often they are problem solvers, used to mask or soften structures such as walls, roofs, or fences; sometimes they serve as decorative sun, wind, or view screens. Vines that flower—and many of them do—bring beauty and fragrance to unexpected places.

Two major problems beset gardeners with vines. First, a significant number of vines are what can only be described as "rampant growers." What starts out as a couple of innocent-looking 1-gallon can plants, within a few seasons, becomes a maintenance nightmare, growing and covering far more than was originally intended. Knowledgeable, regular pruning of such vines is an absolute necessity. Secondly, many vines have tenacious growth and support habits, and can cause damage to wooden houses and other structures.

Choose your vines carefully, and you can avoid both of the above problems. If, on the other hand, quick and total coverage is what you are after, make sure that the supporting structure can hold the weight of the vine as it grows bigger and heavier. Once a structure is vine covered, it is difficult to make any necessary repairs without drastically pruning the vine itself.

(For more information, see pages 120–123, *Sunset New Western Garden Book.*)

Here is a brief summary of procedures that will help you to grow healthy, handsome, and relatively trouble-free vines:

- Select the right vine for your situation
- Provide a sturdy support
- Train, prune, and tie
- Fertilize and water according to the individual vine's needs (see encyclopedia section, pages 161–505, *Sunset New Western Garden Book.*)
- Never let pests get a running start

Frost protection for bougainvilleas

Problem: We bought a 5-gallon bougainvillea this spring, and planted it in a large wooden tub. We placed the tub against the south wall of the house, where it gets considerable sunlight and warmth, and the vine really took off. We live outside the normal growing range for bougainvilleas, and would hate to see it die from winter cold. Is there anything we can do to protect it through the cold winter?

Solution: Really reliable only in Zones 22–24, but satisfactory in Zones 12, 13, 15–17, 19, 21, bougainvilleas can be kept warm with a protective wood frame covered with clear plastic (see illustration.) The frame is made from 1 by 2s nailed together, with metal corner brackets to increase sturdiness. Wrap heavy-gauge clear plastic (sold in rolls at hardware or variety stores) around the frame and secure with thumbtacks or staples. To keep cold air from seeping underneath the frame, tack a rectangular cloth to the bottom, and another cloth to the top to prevent warm air from escaping. When the first frost is predicted, put the protective cover into action. You can secure it to the wall with two right-angle brackets at the bottom and top. Small-headed nails that pro-

trude from the eaves and the wooden planter hook onto the brackets. Keep the cover in place all winter, until all danger of cold weather has passed.

Our clematis is running wild!

Problem: We planted several evergreen clematis about 4 years ago, and now they are "running wild" along the eaves of our house. The plants produce a splendid display of flowers every spring, but they really need to be pruned. I don't want to prune them incorrectly, though, and would hate to do it at the wrong time and limit the flowers for next year. Any advice?

Advice: When evergreen clematis *(Clematis armandii)* drops its last white star-shaped flower in early May, that is the time to prune. This will ensure next year's cascading flower show.

Clematis is a fast grower, as you have noticed, and will develop a tangled mass of stems and dead wood if you don't prune heavily. Using sharp shears, cut out any weak, spindly stems, those going in the wrong direction, and any that cross good vines. Bruised or damaged wood should be cut out as well. Tie the remaining stems to their supports with stretchy plastic ties. As the new growth begins, pinch each branch occasionally just beyond a pair of buds to make the plant more compact and vigorous. If two shoots are growing from the same spot, pinch both. (Also, see *Clematis armandii*, page 246, *Sunset New Western Garden Book*.)

We want to cover a fence—fast

Problem: We have a fence that we wish to cover as rapidly as possible with permanent vines. What do you suggest?

Solution: There are a number of good vine possibilities to consider for your fence, some faster-growing than others. (See pages 120 to 123, *Sunset New Western Garden Book*.)

Even the fastest of permanent vines can take two or more seasons to grow fence-top high. A good solution: plant an annual vine to do the job during the permanent vines' scrawny years. Morning glories are a good choice, as is scarlet runner bean which is not only handsome and colorful, but provides an edible bonus. Any pole bean will work the same way, as will squash, gourds, or cucumbers.

It is important not to plant the annual vines so close to the struggling young permanent vines that they compete for space, sunshine and soil nutrients. About 3 to 5 feet away is usually a safe distance.

Wood frame

Plastic

To protect a vine, staple heavy plastic to a simple wood frame; fasten to wall with right-angle brackets.

Needed: Colorful vine for a screen

Problem: A latticework screen helps to shut off the messy part of our garden, but we'd like to hide the unsightly section even more by planting some sort of vine. Can you suggest a screen that would keep its leaves, and maybe have nice spring flowers, too?

Solution: Honeysuckle (*Lonicera japonica* 'Halliana') would be a winner. It's a very vigorous grower, with fragrant flowers in spring and summer. Semideciduous in cold climates, this vine probably will need severe pruning once a year to keep it within bounds. (See page 356, *Sunset New Western Garden Book*.)

Ivy: home-sweet-home for rats?

Question: I was about to plant our front slope with large-leafed Algerian ivy, when a neighbor cautioned me that it was a favorite home for rats. Is this true?

Answer: Afraid so. In fact, a study performed by a Southern California health department concluded that the number of roof rats living in a community is directly related to its amount of broad-leafed ivy. Algerian ivy is broad-leafed and rampant, which makes it a perfect nesting place for garden-dwelling rats. It also provides them safe runways from one place to another, and it attracts plenty of snails—a favorite rat food. If you haven't already planted Algerian ivy, choose another ground cover. If you already have Algerian ivy, keep it within bounds. Thin it out regularly and keep it from climbing over fences, trees, and house walls.

Will ivy wreck shingles?

Question: We have an older wood-shingled house, and would love to plant Boston ivy in front to further its rustic cottage effect. Is Boston ivy as invasive as regular ivy? Will it damage the sides of the house?

Answer: Yes, Boston ivy (*Parthenocissus tricuspidata*) and its relative Virginia creeper (*P. quinquefolia*) are vigorous growers that cling with small tendrils like suction cups. These plants are invasive, and can really wreak havoc if and when they have to be pulled away from a wall. Any vine that clings by suction cups or tendrils should be avoided on shingled walls. To achieve a similar cottage effect, train a climbing rose or star jasmine on a trellis or other support.

Our ivy is burning up

Problem: We have a ground cover of Algerian ivy in our parking strip, and every summer the leaves burn and look terrible. We live in Pasadena, California (Zone 21), and the summers are pretty hot.

Solution: If the ivy is in need of water, the sun and intense heat can brown the plants almost before you know it's happened. To keep ivy from burning, make sure that it is irrigated regularly and doesn't dry out completely between waterings. If your ivy burns in patches, cut off the scorched leaves and begin a regular watering program. New leaves should fill the gaps in about a month. When the weather service forecasts a hot spell or Santa Ana winds, water everything in the morning before the heat hits.

Climbing rose mystery

Problem: We have an old-fashioned arbor over the gate in our front yard. We planted a climbing 'Blaze' rose next to the arbor and trained the canes both horizontally along the adjoining fence and vertically up the side of the arbor. After about four years, the part of the rose that grows on the fence puts on a spectacular show, but there are never any flowers on the arbor. It's a mystery to me— it's all part of the same plant. What would cause this?

Advice: Left to its steady vertical growth, a long climbing cane will continue to build new tissues to increase only its upward growth. This is a situation known as *apical dominance:* the topmost growth continues at the expense of any lateral growth. When a long, upright cane is arched over or bent down to a horizontal position, however, the apex of growth is thwarted so that many eyes along the cane will begin to grow, each one growing upward. It is these laterals off the main canes and long branches that give you flowers. This natural phenomenon is why the vertical branches did not have any flowers while the horizontal ones did.

If you want flowers on the vertical surface of the arbor, let the vertical canes grow to about 10 feet long. Then, lean them out at an angle from the plant's base on both sides of the plant. Tie canes horizontally and space them 18 to 24 inches apart, paralleling one above the other. Arch the end of each cane downward and tie it in place. Flowering shoots will come from all along the canes.

Needed: a quick screen

Problem: We're renting a house for a short time in Grass Valley, California (Zone 7), but want to plant something on a wire fence that will quickly screen a view we don't like. Is there anything we can plant that would do the job in a hurry, and not take a lot of care?

Advice: Try old-fashioned morning glories—they love the hot summers of Zone 7. Planted from seed in the early spring, they will give a cover by summer and bloom continuously throughout summer and fall. Sow seeds in place in full sun, when all danger of frost is past. For dependable seed germination, notch the seed coat with a knife or file; or soak the seeds in warm water for 2 hours. Plant morning glories in a soil that is not too rich; do not fertilize. Water moderately. If frosts are not severe (or in areas where they are nonexistent), some varieties may survive to provide color the following summer.

Flowering vine for a tiny garden?

Problem: The postage-stamp-sized garden in my rented condominium is all lawn—it goes right up to the fence on three sides. The owner has said that I can plant some vines on the fence. I'd like something that has flowers I can use for cutting. What do you suggest?

Advice: If your small garden has enough sun, climbing roses would give you a quantity of flowers for bouquets, as well as year-round green foliage. Remember that climbing roses require the same general care as other roses. Pruning is especially important. For a list of colors and varieties, see Climbing Roses, page 454, *Sunset New Western Garden Book.*

How to choose the right vine?

Question: I've always liked the way vines look on houses, fences, and arbors, but I don't see many around anymore. I've decided to change the trend in my own garden. Are there any general rules to choosing vines?

Answer: Here are a few guidelines. First, though, realize that many vines are rapid growers and need regular attention if they are to be kept within bounds; and, secondly, some vines can be quite invasive, and can actually damage architectural structures.

Unsightly walls, fences, or stumps call for covering with fairly heavy, preferably evergreen vines. If you appreciate winter sunlight, those chosen to train over an arbor, pergola, or porch might be heavily foliaged in summer, deciduous in winter. Vines of light character, such as hybrid clematis and star jasmine, which do not obliterate architectural features, are more appropriate on small structures or in small gardens.

Vines for a shaded fence

Question: One far corner of our garden in Mill Valley, California (Zone 15) is in dense shade all day—in fact, all year. I know that the choice must be very limited, but are there any shade-tolerant vines we could grow along the fence to soften its bare look?

Answer: In Zones 1–17, winter creeper (*Euonymus fortunei radicans*) is one of the best evergreen vines for shade (or sun). Its branches, covered with dark, rich leaves, trail and climb to 20 feet or more. Climbing hydrangea (*Hydrangea anomala*) is a good deciduous choice. The plant climbs high and clings by aerial rootlets; it has 4-inch, heart-shaped, deciduous leaves. Older plants have short, stiff branches with clusters of white flowers. Climbing hydrangea does well in Zones 1–21.

Fast-growing vine for a car port?

Problem: We live in Wickenburg, Arizona (Zone 12), and have a car port with open sides. My husband has put up a 2-inch mesh wire screen on three sides, and now I want to plant some fast-growing vines on it to keep the sun from hitting the cars. What would grow well, and fast, in our area?

Advice: Star jasmine is a fast-growing vine in hot weather areas, provided that it receives enough water and regular fertilizer. The plant will produce a formal-looking screen with small, pointed, glossy leaves, and a multitude of white, star-shaped flowers that are very fragrant. See *Trachelospermum,* page 487, *Sunset New Western Garden Book,* for more information.

How should we prune our wisteria?

Question: We live in an older neighborhood and have always admired the beauty of wisteria. We recently built a trellis over our back porch, planted two wisteria vines, and are now wondering what the proper training method is. We'd like the vines to cover the trellis as quickly as possible.

Answer: First, decide how many main trunks you want; remove the rest.

For the first two or three years, don't worry about flowers. Just direct the vine's growth up and over the support. If you want a particular branch of new growth to become part of the vine's permanent network of branches, cut it back, leaving a short spur with three or four nodes. A new branch will take off from near the cut, and flowers will form on the short spurs. You may have to do this cutting and nipping as often as every three weeks or so during the growing season.

In later years, the following program will usually suffice: In late spring remove dead flower stems. In June and again in August cut back new growth, leaving three or four nodes, and remove dead wood. Repeat the process in late fall after the leaves have dropped.

LAWNS

GUIDELINES FOR AVOIDING GENERAL PROBLEMS

Garden experts are asked more questions about lawns than any other plantings. To explain this, nurserymen stress two things: 1) Lawns *do* have problems, lots of them; and 2) It is important to most home gardeners that their lawns look at least as good as their neighbors' lawns!

It's best to get the jump on lawn problems even before the grass is planted. Start with the thorough and deep preparation of the soil; then choose the right type of grass for your climate; and water, fertilize, weed, and mow on a regular basis.

In arid climates, sprinkler systems are a real boon to lawn owners. A well-designed system in good working order will solve many of the problems associated with summer lawn care.

Above all, a lawn that is kept actively growing and healthy is resistant to invasions from weeds, and to damage from insect pests and disease.

It can't be overemphasized that a well-fed, well-watered lawn will give you few problems over the long term.

For detailed information, see Lawns, pages 85–88, *Sunset New Western Garden Book.* In general, be aware of these basic tips that can help you avoid future lawn problems.

- Choose a lawn variety for your climate, and your needs
- Decide whether you should use seeds, sod, sprigs, stolons, or plugs
- Prepare soil properly before planting or sodding
- Maintain a program of good watering, fertilizing, pest and disease control
- Mow regularly during growing season
- Rake debris and leaves
- Dethatch when necessary

Will Bermuda activate allergies?

Question: I went to a lot of trouble, not to mention expense, to have a Bermuda grass lawn because I'd heard that it would not contribute to my wife's allergy problems. Now I am alarmed to see the hybrid grass beginning to bloom, and my wife is afraid of possible pollen.

Answer: Allergy sufferers may be alarmed to see their so-called "pollen-free" hybrid Bermuda lawns start to produce flower stalks in the spring. There is no need for concern; hybrid Bermuda grasses are capable of blooming, but their flowers cannot produce pollen or viable seed. And regular mowing will nip off most flower stalks before they become prominent.

Our Bermuda has dead spots

Problem: We didn't pay much attention to the small dead spots that were appearing in our Bermuda grass, but then the damage spread to large areas. I think that the culprits are small orange butterflies that are all over our lawn during the day. Could this be the case? If so, what are they?

Advice: Orange, brown, and yellow butterflies on the lawn are usually fiery skippers; they especially are attracted to Bermuda grass. The damage caused by their

worms forms isolated, round dead spots, 1–2 inches in diameter, which eventually join together so that large areas of the lawn are dead. (Small brownish yellow worms may be inside and underneath the dead patches.) Sometimes white cottony masses show in the lawn. If so, it's a good thing—these cottonlike masses are the cocoons of a parasite that preys on the larvae of the skipper and should eliminate the problem. If these cocoons are *not* apparent in your lawn, then apply diazinon in spray or granules.

Is common Bermuda a weed?

Question: Is common Bermuda grass (or "devil grass") just a weed, or can it make a decent lawn?

Answer: It can make a reasonably good lawn if you understand its needs and are willing to tolerate its liabilities. See page 43, pests section, Bermuda grass.

Best care for Bermuda?

Question: How do I care for a common Bermuda grass lawn so it will look its best?

Answer: *Fertilize.* Use a high-nitrogen fertilizer (ammonium sulfate, for example) every month to 6 weeks;

begin in February to early March (whenever grass starts to green up) and continue until November.

Water regularly. Give the lawn a weekly deep watering.

Mow regularly. Mow weekly with a power mower set at ¾-inch.

Edge the lawn—each time you mow.

Dethatch lawn each year. In October or November, rough up the stolons with a thatching rake, then mow closely to remove them.

Bermuda or bluegrass for Southern Cal?

Question: Is Bermuda grass better than bluegrass for a lawn in Southern California?

Answer: Yes. Bermuda grass requires much less watering than bluegrass, rye, or fescue. That in itself makes it ideal for Southern California and Arizona. In addition, it is tough, taking plenty of foot traffic (such as home football games) without damage. It is virtually free of pests and diseases. It grows well where summers are hot, dry. It crowds out (or renders inconspicuous) the common lawn weeds.

With all the points in its favor, Bermuda does have a dark side: it continually pops up in garden beds. For ways to control, see page 43.

Can I get rid of Bermuda with chemicals?

Question: If I decide I don't want a Bermuda grass lawn, is there a sure way to get rid of it without laboriously digging it up?

Answer: Yes, use glyphosate according to directions. This herbicide is absorbed by the plant and is translocated throughout the stem and root systems, killing the entire plant—or lawn in this case. *Use with extreme caution:* careless spraying can just as easily damage or kill nearby desirable plants.

Is there a way to lick "Bermuda brown?"

Question: Can I do anything to offset common Bermuda's winter brown color?

Answer: Yes, you can overseed the lawn with an annual winter grass that will grow during the winter months and mask the Bermuda's brown. First, do the annual dethatching in mid-October, then sow winter grass seed immediately afterward (annual ryegrass, red fescue, even perennial ryegrass are common choices). Continue regular watering and mowing.

Are the hybrid Bermudas better?

Question: I hear much about "hybrid Bermuda grasses." In what ways are they better than common Bermuda?

Answer: Characteristics of the hybrid Bermuda grasses vary somewhat, so choice will depend on your area's climate. In general they score higher than common Bermuda on these points: they are finer-textured, a bit more dense, and turn a more attractive winter tan in foresty regions; they produce no seed heads; they are much less invasive.

Can clippings be useful in the garden?

Question: I've never really known what to do with grass clippings—let them stay on the lawn, throw them in the compost bin, or toss them around the garden. What's your opinion?

Answer: You can let *short* clippings stay on the lawn; they serve as a natural mulch and return some nutrients to the soil. If you rake up your grass clippings or use a grass catcher, don't just let them accumulate in a pile—they're likely to become a breeding place for flies. The most efficient ways to use grass clippings are to put them in a compost pile, or use them in very thin layers as a mulch for flower beds.

The *only* place to put clippings from common Bermuda grass is in the garbage can.

Can compacted soil be aerated?

Problem: We had an expert come take a look at our lawn, and were told that many of our problems were the result of compacted soil. We got an aerating tool at the nursery to help relieve the problem, but our soil is so compacted that we couldn't get the tool to go into the dirt more than about an inch. No wonder the grass is having a hard time growing! Is there anything we can do to make the tool work better?

Solution: Let water come to the rescue. Water the area slowly up to its capacity the day before you begin work. Aerate the area to whatever depth you can, then run a sprinkler at low pressure until the soil is watered to capacity again. After the soil has dried enough so that it is no longer sticky, repeat the aeration. The first pass with the aerator should have opened the ground so that the water can soften the soil.

Push aerator's sharp-tipped tubes into ground with foot.

How can I identify crabgrass?

Question: Are all those hairy, flat clumps of weeds in my lawn real crabgrass? How can I identify it?

Answer: Several hairy, flat weeds turn up in lawns—here is how to distinguish hairy crabgrass (*Digitaria sanguinalis*): Small seedlings with 2 to 4 leaves that form large, flat, stem-rooting, weedy clumps in summer. Mature, pale-green blades grow 2-5 inches long and ⅓ inch wide, with undersides covered with coarse, tiny hairs. Fingerlike flower spikelets arise from 2-6-inch-high narrow stems (see illustration below and on page 44). Flowers seed heavily, so immediate eradication of the weed is required to prevent infestation the following year. (Seeds germinate as early as February in mild-winter areas, and through summer.) To control, hand-pull or use a specified crabgrass control.

Smooth crabgrass *(Digitaria ischaemum)* resembles hairy crabgrass, but grows smaller and obviously isn't hairy.

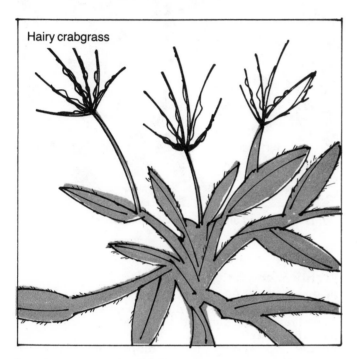
Hairy crabgrass

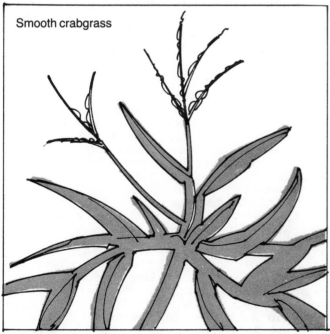
Smooth crabgrass

Try to eliminate crabgrass when the seedlings first show up in the lawn; later it is more difficult to control.

Crabgrass killer didn't work!

Problem: I have something in my lawn that I thought was crabgrass, but the product I bought at the garden center, labeled specifically for crabgrass, didn't do a thing. Did I misdiagnose the problem, or is the product at fault?

Advice: Since crabgrass products are generally effective, we can conclude that you don't have crabgrass. Although it is king of the grassy weeds, gardeners everywhere often mistake other weeds for crabgrass. This frequently results in the use of crabgrass-killing chemicals on weeds that won't be fazed by them. To identify your weed, take a sample weed to your nursery.

Can you diagnose our dowdy dichondra?

Problem: Seems like every summer we have brown patches in our dichondra lawn. I'd like to do something to prevent them from spoiling the look of our yard this year. Any idea what may be causing it?

Advice: Brown patches in dichondra lawns signal any of several problems. Begin by checking to see if the cause is a lack of water or fertilizer—two of the most common reasons for browning.

Poke a brown patch with a screwdriver. If it doesn't sink easily into the ground, the ground is too dry. Inspect your sprinklers to make sure they're doing a good job: turn them on and watch for irregular spray patterns. Flush out clogged heads, and trim back any growth that may be blocking the spray.

Lack of nutrients will fade dichondra color, and cause thin, patchy growth. Dichondra is a hungry lawn and needs feeding monthly, or every two months when you use a slow-release fertilizer.

If watering and feeding seem alright, check for insects. Two kinds of pests get more active as summer progresses: flea beetles and cutworms. Early treatment prevents more serious problems later.

To find out which culprit is doing the damage, apply the handkerchief test: lay a white cloth—or the flat of your hand—where brown and green areas meet. Little black dots jumping around will be tiny adult flea beetles. These beetles strip dichondra leaves of moisture, so affected areas may be crisp, like corn flakes. Apply dursban or diazinon according to package directions, treating also the bordering green areas where insects may migrate. Until weather cools in the fall, monthly applications may be necessary to control new generations of beetles developing in the soil.

If the culprits are cutworms, you'll find brown spots the size of a quarter or fifty-cent piece. Leaf tops are munched off, with stalks left bare. For identification and control, see page 37.

Don't tread on me (when frozen)!

Question: We had an unusual cold spell in Fresno, California (Zone 8), and woke up to see our dichondra lawn covered with frost one morning. I walked across the lawn to get the morning paper; the next day, long after the frost had gone, my footprints were still visible on the dichondra. What happened?

Answer: People—or even big dogs—can cause injury to dichondra by walking on it when it is frozen. Black footprints, indicating dead foliage, appear within hours. The prints gradually lighten, but remain visible until new growth fills in the dead area.

Problems with pests? See pages 32-48

I pulled up a wet doormat!

Problem: When a couple of dead patches appeared in our lawn, I decided to investigate a little more closely. I started poking and pulling, and to my surprise the whole dead area came up like a wet doormat. What could cause such a thing?

Solution: Probably white grubs. You may even find some grubs underneath the grass—U-shaped, grayish-white worms (see illustration) shaped much like fat shrimp. If you are not squeamish, you can hand-pick the worms and know that you've dealt with them in the most direct way. Then replace the mat of brown grass. It may replenish itself from the roots in a few weeks.

For chemical control, use diazinon or dursban for white grubs. After applying the chemical treatments, water the lawn heavily. This helps leach the chemicals into the ground where the larvae eat.

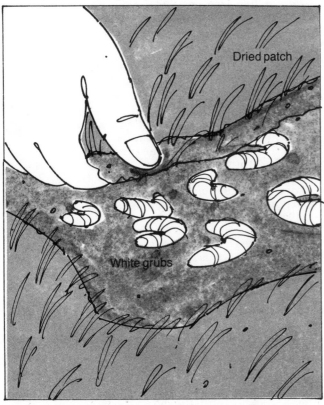

Dried patch

White grubs

If dried, brown lawn area pulls up like a doormat, it is probably due to an infestation of white grubs.

Big gray driveway spoils our front yard

Problem: In my opinion, there are few things that ruin the looks of a lovely front yard as much as a big, gray expanse of driveway. We've put men on the moon—surely there is some solution for my problem.

Solution: It's not quite in the same rank as space technology, but there is a solution. It's okay to drive on a lawn planted in among sturdy paving blocks. An area paved with these blocks not only looks better than solid concrete, it is also cooler; such an area doesn't reflect heat. Also, the blocks permit water to soak into the soil instead of running off down the gutter. The car's weight falls mostly on raised parts of each block. Between the

raised parts, you can plant lawn grass (or any low-growing ground cover). A tall grass, such as 'Alta' fescue or perennial rye, would grow well. See the illustration.

Turf block for driveway

Car is supported on paving blocks with lawn pockets.

Fertilizer confusion

Problem: Every time I go to the nursery to buy some lawn fertilizer I wind up buying a different product because I really don't know what I'm looking for. Do you have any advice?

Advice: Whatever the product, the package label should contain three numbers, such as 26-3-3, or 6-4-2 (these numbers are not necessarily recommended). The first number is the most important; it refers to the percentage of *nitrogen* present. The second number refers to *phosphorus,* the third to *potassium.* If one of the numbers is zero, that element isn't included.

Nitrogen stimulates leaf growth and helps grass maintain a rich green color. Less important to lawns than to other plants, phosphorus promotes sturdy cell structure and healthy root growth, and aids in flower and fruit production. Potassium helps normal plant functions and development. When you buy a fertilizer specifically formulated for grass, these three elements should be in proper balance.

(Also see Fertilizing your garden, page 52, *Sunset New Western Garden Book.*)

Did I goof with the fertilizer spreader?

Problem: I just fertilized my new sod lawn, following the directions to the letter. The garden center loaned me a drop-type spreader. Now my lawn is striped in bands of green and yellow. I think there was something wrong with the spreader—or did I goof?

Solution: If lawns were single organisms rather than thousands of individual plants, feeding them would be easy. But they aren't, so you must be very careful when you fertilize. Every plant your fertilizer spreader misses will stay light green or yellow. Every one it hits will become dark green. And every one it hits too much will turn brown. Since most people fertilize in strips with wheeled spreaders, it's all too easy to create a striped lawn.

Here's how to get an evenly green lawn: Before you feed your grass, make two or three short practice passes over your garage floor to check the width your spreader covers in one swipe (be sure no holes are clogged). Position the spreader so that the next row of fertilizer will line up with, but not overlap, the previous one. Observe how much wheel overlap it takes to get this perfect coverage. Then, when you feed the lawn, overlap by just that much. Usually, you can see the wheel tracks of the preceding run. (See illustration.)

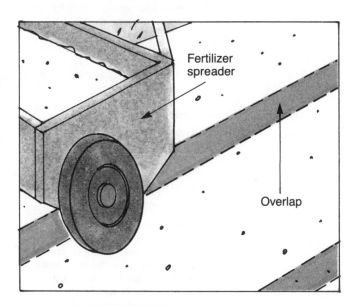

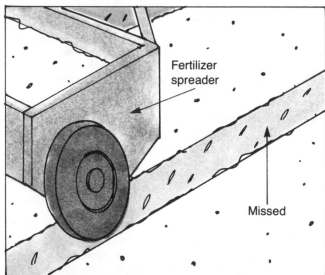

Set spreader wheel just inside previous track to avoid stripes caused by over- or under-fertilizing.

Can I just toss on the fertilizer?

Question: We recently moved from a big house to a townhouse. Our new lawn isn't very large, and I was wondering if I could spread the fertilizer by hand, rather than going to the trouble of renting a spreader?

Answer: You can apply any type of solid fertilizer by hand. In fact, it's safest with organic fertilizers since there's less danger of grass burn. Handcast the fertilizer across the lawn in one direction, applying at full strength. Then repeat at right angles, using only half as much fertilizer in certain spots; rake the area lightly to spread it more evenly.

Walking slowly, handcast fertilizer over the lawn in parallel strips; repeat at right angles.

How frequently to fertilize?

Question: Is there any general rule that applies to fertilizing lawns? I'm never really sure when I should make an application.

Answer: One good rule of thumb for timing fertilizer applications on lawn grasses is to feed when their rate of growth slows down and the deep green color fades to a yellowish shade. Other gardeners may prefer to fertilize by the calendar, once a month during the growing season—spring through fall. If you use a combination weed and feed product, proper timing is critical for success. Be sure to carefully read the timing instructions on the package.

Something's chewing our grass

Problem: We have just noticed that there are dead spots in our lawn. They are about 2 inches in diameter. When we looked closely at them, we could see that something had been chewing on the leaves. Do you know what causes this?

Solution: The pest is probably cutworms. They chew off grass leaves right on down into the roots, which results in dead spots about 1 to 2 inches in diameter. To identify and control this pest, see page 37.

Grass seedlings uprooted

Problem: We just planted a new lawn, and were surprised to see that many of the new grass seedlings had been uprooted—by some insect, we suppose. We also noticed that many of the blades of grass had been severed from their roots. What's causing the problem?

Solution: The problem is probably being caused by mole crickets. These tiny creatures freeload in moist, light soils of newly seeded lawns. Burrowing into the ground, using their shovel-like front legs, they destroy seedlings as they excavate. To control mole crickets, spray with diazinon.

Why is our lawn "blotchy"?

Problem: Our lawn has certain areas that always are pale, dull-looking—almost a pattern in some places. Does it have a fatal fungus or infestation of insidious insects?

Solution: When the same parts of a lawn always appear less healthy, look to lack of water as the cause—even though you water regularly. The culprit is likely to be water *distribution*. Any sprinkler's output will vary in a definite pattern over the area it covers, with the least amount falling toward the perimeter of its coverage. If your sprinkler settings do not overlap far enough, the same parts of your lawn will get less water every time you apply it, particularly if you have a sprinkler system or set the sprinklers in precisely the same locations each time you water.

To check a sprinkler's water-distribution pattern, place equal-sized containers (such as coffee cans) at varying distances in a straight line from the sprinkler head. Turn on the water for an hour, then measure the level of water that has collected in each container; this will show you the amount of water the sprinkler delivers at various distances from the head. From this information you can calculate how far the coverage of one sprinkler should overlap that of another in order to give nearly equal amounts of water to all parts of the lawn. (For more information on watering and sprinklers, see pages 48–51, *Sunset New Western Garden Book*.)

Our lawn had "instant brownout"

Problem: We live in Walnut Creek, California (Zone 14). Large sections of our lawn turned brown almost overnight this month (June), and it seemed so healthy this spring. Is this some kind of disease? What do we do?

Solution: Sounds as if you have a lawn that is all or mostly all annual bluegrass *(Poa annua)* that is going through a yearly change from green to brown. This happens in May or June (or in April during a warm or dry spring). You can identify this weed by the white speckled seedhead clusters growing close to the ground. On the first really hot day, *Poa annua* can die and change into straw almost instantly. To repair scorched area, rough up the surface with a rake or renovator. Fertilize and sow lawn seed; keep seed bed moist. Repeat fertilizing every 6–8 weeks. In mid-August, apply a weed control containing betasan or dacthal to prevent *Poa annua* seeds from sprouting when rains return in the fall.

Our lawn has brown patches

Problem: We have a fairly new lawn that *was* a nice, even expanse of green. Now, in August, there are irregularly shaped brown patches scattered about. What is causing this?

Solution: Most lawns, no matter what their age, are susceptible to attack by armyworms or sod webworms. These worms feed on grass crowns and bases of blades.

In warmer climates they can destroy whole lawns. To control these invading insects, treat with diazinon or dursban, either in spray or granule form.

Lawn order

Question: Neither my husband nor myself have the time (or inclination) to keep our lawn in tip-top shape. Since it does represent a considerable investment, we feel obliged to maintain it the right way. Do you know of any good lawn maintenance services that don't charge an arm and a leg?

Answer: If you can't give your lawn the TLC it requires, consider signing up for a lawn-care service. There are several national companies with branch locations, and similar local services are available in many communities. Most companies make about six visits a year to fertilize, thatch, aerate, control pests and weeds, and renovate lawns. They don't water or mow, and charges are based on lawn sizes and conditions. A preliminary visit should establish the maintenance agreement and costs. Find such services in the yellow pages under Gardening, Pest Control, Sod, or Maintenance.

Is it wrong to mow wet grass?

Question: I keep trying to convince our daughter not to mow the lawn so early while it's still wet from dew. She said she likes to get her chores done early, but I said that it's not good for the lawn. When she asked why not, I didn't really know what to tell her. So I'll ask you—why not?

Answer: Consider yourself lucky to have such a diligent daughter—but tell her this: it's really best not to mow wet grass, and not just because it might wake up the neighbors. It will mash under the mower wheels, stick to the cutting blades, or just lie down under the mower and spring back later. If your daughter must mow it that early, she should get rid of some surface moisture by brushing the grass with a piece of burlap or a tree branch. (Side benefit: it will put her on a later schedule!)

Another answer: It is the practice of thousands of professional gardeners—who must mow at all hours of the day—to use a front-throwing power reel mower. These machines do not mash the wet grass so cutting blades can't get to it. Cut grass goes directly into the basket at the front of the mower.

Lower the mower blades?

Question: My young son, who does the lawn mowing for our household, thinks we should lower the lawn mower blades so they will cut the grass shorter, hence making the job of cutting it less frequent. I thought it prudent to write to you before doing the deed. What do you think?

Answer: It's not a good idea to cut off more than ⅓ of the total grass blade surface—removing more can cause shock because food production will be curtailed. If your son wants to cut lower once in a while, don't worry about it—but he should avoid making a habit of very close cutting. During the growing season, mow at least weekly.

How much nitrogen is necessary?

Problem: I recently read in the gardening section of our local newspaper that the University of California Agricultural Extension recommends applying 1 pound of actual nitrogen per 1,000 square feet of lawn once a month during periods of active growth. How do I figure out how much "actual nitrogen" I'm applying?

Solution: To find out how many pounds of nitrogen your bag of fertilizer contains, check the first number (the nitrogen symbol) on the three-number formula; it gives the percentage of the actual amount of nitrogen your bag contains. If you have a 25-pound bag of 10-5-0 fertilizer, the nitrogen content is 10 percent of 25 pounds, or 2½ pounds of actual nitrogen. (Also see Nitrogen, page 52, *Sunset New Western Garden Book*.)

Which is best, St. Augustine or Bermuda?

Question: We just bought a new home near San Diego, and are considering putting in St. Augustine grass. Do you recommend it over Bermuda grass?

Answer: Both are excellent subtropical grasses, so we are not going to recommend one over the other. St. Augustine, which has dark green blades on coarse, wiry stems, is relatively pest-free, fairly salt-tolerant, and endures shade better than Bermuda. Like Bermuda, it goes dormant and turns brown in winter. (For information on Bermuda, see pages 123, 124.)

Seed keeps washing off our slope

Problem: The grass seed we planted in our small, sloping front yard just washed away in the first heavy rainfall. All we have left are a few patches of grass.

Solution: On slopes, don't plant lawn seed, plant *sod*. While sod is more expensive than seeds as an initial investment, it provides an instant weed-free lawn that will stay in place in your sloping front yard. In the long run, you should save not only headaches but dollars. Consult your local nursery about purchase and installation.

Too much tree shade

Problem: As our shade trees have gotten larger, so have the problems with our lawn. It's very hard to keep the grass growing well under the trees. Any suggestions?

Advice: Grass is basically a sun plant. In nature you find it in fields, not under trees. However, the problem you have is one common to most home gardeners, who like to have the best of both worlds—trees *and* grass. Following are some things you can do to help the situation:

1. Thin out branches of the shade trees to allow grass more light.

2. Fertilize grass growing under trees about three times a year to replace the nutrients taken by the trees.

3. Some trees are moisture-robbers, so give the grass around the trees more water than the rest of the lawn.

4. Cut grass higher under trees, too, to allow more leaf surface for photosynthesis (absorbing sunlight).

Perhaps, rather than following the program described above, you might prefer to remove the lawn completely and replace it with a shade-tolerant ground cover; or with gravel, ground bark, decking, or other inert materials that will allow air and water to get through to the tree roots.

How can I keep edges trimmed?

Problem: Our landscape features a "dry creek" of smooth stones edged by a lawn. Our problem is how to keep that edge trimmed so that the grass doesn't obscure the rocks.

Solution: Instead of tedious hand trimming, try one of the easy-to-use nylon string trimmer-weeders. Powered by household current, battery, or gasoline engine, the fast-moving nylon string tidily nips off grass or weeds. These trimmers are superb for *any* kind of hard-to-reach areas where mowers and ordinary edgers just can't get to the grass.

How long between drinks?

Question: I have a simple question: How can I tell when to water my lawn? We're a little tight on water where we live, and I'd like not to waste it.

Answer: You can judge when a lawn needs water by its appearance. Grass shows its need for water first by loss of resilience. When you walk across it, the grass doesn't spring back. Next, the color changes from fresh green and takes on a dull, blue-green overcast. The grass tops turn brown and die. Once you can "sense" this timing, *try to water just before the loss of resilience*. Don't let your lawn get to the brown stage; it will take considerable time for it to recover.

For a more scientific approach, you can use a soil probe (see illustration). Take a sample core of at least 5 or 10 inches. If the sample is dry below the first 3 inches, you need to water longer.

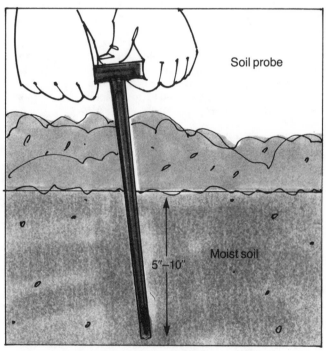

Soil probe

5"–10"

Moist soil

Take a sample of moist soil with a sharp probe.

Is hand-watering acceptable?

Question: I'm retired and recently discovered the joys of gardening. One of the things I enjoy doing the most is watering the lawn, which I do by hand. Recently, my neighbor told me that it's nearly impossible to water a lawn properly by hand. The lawn looks all right to me.

Answer: As long as your lawn doesn't appear to be suffering, you must be doing a good job. You might as well continue hand-watering—especially if you enjoy it. Lawns *can* be kept green with daily light sprinklings, but this practice produces shallow root systems and necessitates continued daily light waterings during the growing season. The difference is that when you water deeply, grass roots will extend deeper into the soil. You will have to apply more water with each sprinkling to moisten the lower soil layers—but you can water less frequently, since the soil will lose moisture more slowly.

We're watering the sidewalks!

Problem: We live in an area with fairly heavy clay soil. Every time we turn on the sprinkler system to water our lawn, the water almost immediately starts running across the sidewalk and into the street.

Solution: There are several ways to deal with this problem. You can help the lawn with an aerator that removes plugs of soil. (Spiking soil isn't recommended, because the spikes are likely to compact the soil around the holes they drive.) You can slow down your sprinkler so the soil can absorb the water, or select a sprinkler that emits water more slowly. Another good solution is to run sprinklers at full rate until runoff starts, shut them off for a half-hour while some water sinks in, and then repeat the process.

Best time to water?

Question: My husband and I seem to have a running disagreement concerning the best time to water a lawn. Will you settle it once and for all? When is the best time to water a lawn?

Answer: The best time to water is whenever there's no wind and when water pressure is high. Typically, this is during the night or in the first hours of the morning. Most lawns that are sprinkled automatically (time clock) get their water between midnight and 6 A.M.

Weed categories important on labels

Question: I keep coming across the words "broad-leafed weeds" on the labels of various weed-killing products I'm considering for getting rid of my lawn weeds. What's the difference between broad-leafed weeds and any others? Aren't all weeds just weeds?

Answer: Weeds are classified into two groups: broad-leafed weeds and grassy weeds. The weed section on pages 43–45 identifies some common weeds.

The term "broad-leafed weeds" describes all weeds that are not grass-like. Many of these broad-leafed weeds, such as chickweed and spotted spurge, have leaves only the size of large freckles.

Any grass that destroys the even texture and uniform color of a lawn is considered a "grassy weed." The list is long. Some of the most common grassy weeds are annual bluegrass, Bermuda grass, crabgrass, dallisgrass, quackgrass, and rye grass.

Weed killer burns or insect damage?

Problem: About a week after my husband applied weed killer on our lawn, we noticed some rather odd dead spots—like stripes. I say it had something to do with the weed killer, and he says he thinks it's insect or disease damage.

Advice: If spots appear in your lawn after chemicals have been applied, check whether the shape of the spots bears any relationship to the course you traveled with the dispenser or spreader. Spots that appear as streaks, squares, or half moons are probably chemical burns. Water the areas heavily to leach the excess chemicals into the ground, and the lawn will eventually recover.

What to do about quackgrass?

Problem: How can I get rid of quackgrass in my lawn? I live in Chehalis, Washington (Zone 4).

Solution: Quackgrass has long been a problem in Zones 4–7 of the Pacific Northwest. The best chemical control is an application of glyphosate (sold as Roundup or Kleanup) per label directions. Another good control, without using chemicals, is to mow the grass frequently to about 1¼″ high (¾″ in bent grass lawns). The roots soon run out of the reserves needed to replace top growth, and as a result quackgrass will die out.

Grass grows right up to the tree trunk

Problem: I have a tree in the middle of my lawn and would like to get rid of the grass that grows right up to the base. How can I do this?

Solution: A simple way to kill the grass is to install a collar of black plastic around the base of the tree to keep light from the grass. Keep it in place with stones or bricks for at least a month (see illustration).

Place black plastic collar around tree to kill grass.

Will any one weed killer get 'em all?

Question: I have an assortment of weeds in my lawn. I'm not sure what type of weeds they are. Can you recommend a chemical weed killer that will knock them all out?

Answer: No single weed killer will kill all weeds, unless you want to use a soil fumigant—which will not only kill your weeds but your lawn along with it!

Any weed killer you use on your lawn should have the chemical name, the specific weeds it will kill, and the types of grass you can apply it to listed on the label. Therefore, it's a good idea to know exactly what weeds are growing in your lawn before you use *any* chemical product. Several of the most prevalent weeds are shown on pages 43–45. There are so many different kinds, however, that a good bet is to pull some and show them to a knowledgeable person at your local nursery.

GROUND COVERS

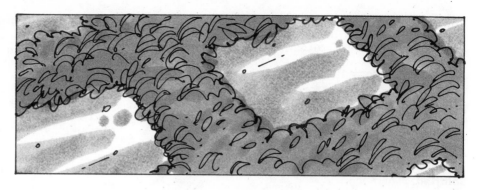

GUIDELINES FOR AVOIDING GENERAL PROBLEMS

Ground covers could probably be called "the problem solvers of the landscape world." They are used when the gardener is tired of maintaining a lawn; needs plants to cover a hillside and control erosion, or act as a fire retardant; or is looking for a "little something" to fill in around stepping stones on a shady walk. For all these situations, there is a ground cover to meet the particular need.

Varied in appearance, ground covers offer a wide range of colors and textures which may combine in attractive patterns. Many have vivid flowers. They also vary in height—from velvety carpets to impenetrable covers a foot or two high. See the lists on pages 112–114, *Sunset New Western Garden Book*, then check the plants that interest you in the Plant Encyclopedia section, pages 161–505.

Although generally considered low-maintenance plants, it takes awhile for an area planted in

ground cover to actually become low-maintenance. The first few seasons after planting, the small plants need to be well watered, fertilized, and protected from weed and pest invasions. Once established, maintenance usually is limited to an occasional feeding and irrigation, and a yearly mowing or pruning.

Generally, ground covers don't have problems, they solve problems. But they have to be healthy to do it; observe these basics:

- Select the right ground cover for the right situation
- Plant them properly, in good soil
- Space young plants the proper distance apart
- Keep area free of weeds; apply mulch
- Water, spray, fertilize, and mow or prune according to individual plant needs

Suggestions for unsightly site?

Question: We have an area that receives no foot traffic, no water, and very little attention in general. We can, however, see it from our deck. Is there a ground cover you'd recommend that would make the area look a little more attractive? We live in Grass Valley, California (Zone 7).

Answer: Try one of the many varieties of *Ceanothus*. As a California native, their water requirements are almost nil. They bloom, usually in March or April, in an array of blue shades, depending on the variety. There are more than 30 varieties available, ranging in size from 6 inches to 20 feet tall. Several make excellent ground covers. (See *Ceanothus*, page 226, *Sunset New Western Garden Book*.)

Is there a cover that also climbs?

Question: We just moved into a new condominium, and there is a rough masonry wall (part of the garage) that faces the front patio. There is a weedy bed in front of the wall, and the whole thing looks kind of bleak. Is there anything attractive we can plant that would cover the bed and climb the masonry wall without support?

Answer: Consider *Euonymus fortunei* (often sold as *E. radicans*). It's actually an evergreen that thinks it's a ground cover or climber, and serves both purposes. This versatile plant either trails or climbs by rootlets. It will cover the bed, and cling on its own to climb the rough surface of the masonry wall you described. Euonymus grows best in a rich, loose, quick-draining soil. A light spring feeding with an evergreen plant food will encourage strong new growth. It grows happily in either sun or shade.

(For more information on *Euonymus fortunei*, see page 294, *Sunset New Western Garden Book*.)

"Comb" across the bald spot

Problem: I followed all the rules for proper spacing, as well as feeding and watering, but the horizontal ceanothus plants I put in as a ground cover have big, bald patches of ground showing. The plants are healthy and vigorous.

Solution: Rearrange new growth to point toward the bald spot; anchor the new growth in place with a piece of wire bent like a big hairpin. Pinch out ends of long and leggy tips to start them branching out. Vining or trailing plants other than ceanothus can also be coaxed this way: lantana, star jasmine, honeysuckle, ivy, ivy geranium, verbena, and prostrate manzanita. (See illustration.)

Cover bare spots with branches of trailing ground covers secured by 12-inch lengths of wire, bent like hairpins. Pinch plant tips to encourage branching.

Bent wire pins

It's the berries

Question: I'm looking for an unusual ground cover plant, preferably something with seasonal flower color or berries. The area I want to plant is fairly out-of-the-way, doesn't receive much attention, but is in full view of our dining room window. Any suggestions?

Answer: You might try one of the low-growing forms of cotoneaster. They are easy-to-grow plants that thrive on neglect, with inconspicuous flowers followed by a multitude of orange or red berries. Although they won't tolerate any foot traffic, they are perfect for the type of location you describe. Most grow 1-3 feet tall, and form a large, rather loose mat of arching branches. Look for the following kinds at your nursery or garden center: *Cotoneaster adpressus, C. conspicuus* 'Decorus', *C. dammeri, C. horizontalis, C. microphyllus,* or *C. salicifolius* 'Herbstfeuer'. (For more information on cotoneaster, see page 255, *Sunset New Western Garden Book*.)

Fire-retardant ground covers

Question: We live in an area that is, unfortunately, frequented by brush fires. We are just getting started on landscaping and wonder whether or not there are any ground covers that might act as a deterrent to fire.

Answer: Although no plant will act as a complete deterrent to fire, there are a number of ground covers that will certainly resist burning far better than most and thereby may slow a fire's progress.

Many of the low-growing Aloes (most notably *Aloe aristata, A. brevifolia, A. ciliaris,* and *A. distans*) perform well as fire retardant ground covers, with the added bonus of unusual flowers. They are actually succulent members of the lily family—easy to grow in well-drained soil, but not frost-hardy.

Several of the silver-foliaged artemisias (*Artemisia absinthium, A. caucasica, A. schmidtiana,* and *A. stellerana*) would also be good choices. Plants should be kept on the dry side and planted in full sun.

Three varieties of the common saltbush (*Atriplex canescens, A. lentiformis breweri,* and *A. semibaccata*) are well adapted to both seaside and alkaline desert conditions. In addition to being fire resistant and drought tolerant, these plants are good for erosion control.

The bush morning glory (*Convolvulus cneorum*), grows rapidly to 2 to 4 feet with an equal spread and has flowers similar to the morning glory vine. It likes full sun and a light, fast-draining soil. Avoid overwatering.

The many different types of ice plant are fast-growing, drought-tolerant choices. All need full sun, take most soils; won't take walking on. They give a showy splash of flower color.

For more fire-retardant ground cover choices, see the list on page 160, *Sunset New Western Garden Book*. It also lists some plants other than ground covers that you might wish to consider.

Ground cover on a low budget?

Question: We're trying to fill in a large area with a ground cover, but we've just about reached the end of our budget for buying more flats at the nursery. Is there any way I can propagate my own ground cover?

Answer: Many ground covers—Indian mock strawberry, epimedium, and fragaria, to name just three—can be grown from cuttings taken from established plants, usually in mid to late spring. Simply cut off a branch tip with at least three sets of leaves, insert the cut end several inches into prepared soil (don't bury any of the foliage), firm the soil around it, and water well. Roots should develop along the buried stem in a few weeks. Or you can place the cuttings in a flat filled with sand or a similar rooting material. When these cuttings have formed a root system, remove them from the flat, and arrange them individually in prepared soil.

Tips for Tucson: what to plant

Question: We just moved to Tucson, Arizona (Zone 12), and would like to plant a ground cover in our front yard. Can you tell me the best time of year to plant, and offer a few good suggestions adapted for the area?

Answer: Fall is the best time to plant hardy ground covers in mild-winter desert areas. Plants will make good root growth in the next few months, and will be established by spring—well equipped to survive the heat of summer.

Some excellent choices for sunny areas are low-growing pyracanthas, Mexican primrose, creeping rosemary, germander, and Lady Banks' rose. For shady spots, you might try *Ajuga reptans*, English ivy, star jasmine, *Vinca major*, or mondo grass.

(For more detailed information on each plant, consult the encyclopedia section, *Sunset New Western Garden Book*.)

How much will one flat cover?

Problem: We have an area in our front yard where we want to plant ground cover, but I have no idea how many flats to buy, or even how many plants are in a flat. Is there any convenient way to tell?

Solution: In the nursery, flats of plants may come in three or four different sizes. Often the label will tell you how far apart to plant them; otherwise ask one of the nursery clerks or check the spacing recommended for the plant you select in the *Sunset New Western Garden Book*.

Before you go to the nursery, though, measure the area to be planted. Sketch it out on paper, noting the dimensions and the total number of square feet. When you go to buy plants, take your diagram and the chart below. If you know from the plant label the number of inches to leave between plants, the chart below can help you to determine how much coverage to expect from flats, pony packs, etc.

Inches between plants	48 plants per flat	64 plants per flat	72 plants per flat	100 plants per flat
4"	5 sq. ft.	7 sq. ft.	8 sq. ft.	11 sq. ft.
6"	12 sq. ft.	16 sq. ft.	18 sq. ft.	25 sq. ft.
8"	21 sq. ft.	28 sq. ft.	32 sq. ft.	44 sq. ft.
10"	33 sq. ft.	45 sq. ft.	50 sq. ft.	70 sq. ft.
12"	48 sq. ft.	64 sq. ft.	72 sq. ft.	100 sq. ft.
15"	75 sq. ft.	100 sq. ft.	112 sq. ft.	156 sq. ft.
18"	108 sq. ft.	144 sq. ft.	162 sq. ft.	225 sq. ft.
24"	192 sq. ft.	256 sq. ft.	288 sq. ft.	400 sq. ft.

Standard or solid flats usually contain 100 plants per flat or 64 per flat
Pony packs contain 6 plants per pack, 12 packs per flat: 72 total
Cell packs contain 6 plants per pack, 8 packs per flat: 48 total

How to break it out of a flat?

Question: If the ground cover moss purchased at the nursery has filled the entire flat, how in the world do you plant it? Do you break it into pieces? If so, how big should the pieces be?

Answer: If you buy carpeting plants, such as Irish or Scotch moss, chamomile, or ajuga, in flats, turn the flat over to remove the plants in one large piece. With a sharp knife, cut the contents like a sheetcake into 1½-inch squares in a grid pattern. Spacing in the garden will depend on the type of ground cover, and how fast you want it to fill in. The closer you arrange the plants, the faster they will cover the area.

What works to stop erosion?

Problem: We live in Barstow, California (Zone 11), and need a quick-growing ground cover to prevent erosion on a steep bank. Is there any plant that grows especially well in our climate? Our soil is somewhat alkaline and we don't have much water for irrigation.

Solution: A good bet would be Australian saltbush (*Atriplex semibaccata*) 'Corto'. Grown from seed, it has proven a useful ground cover for erosion control in home gardens. It's fire-resistant, and tolerant of drought and alkaline soil. Growth is low (8 to 10 inches) but wide (up to 6 feet). It prefers a light to medium-textured soil. The established plants will naturalize in areas with 10 or more inches of rain a year. Although the plants are short-lived, they will re-establish themselves rapidly from seed. (See *Atriplex semibaccata*, page 193, *Sunset New Western Garden Book*.)

Junipers turned sickly gray

Problem: Recently our 6-year-old planting of tam junipers (*Juniperus sabina 'Tamariscifolia'*) has started to turn a sickly gray. I've also noticed that there are fine webs covering some of the affected plants. Do you know what the problem could be?

Solution: The symptoms you describe are the telltale signs of spider mites. For illustration and ways to control, see page 35.

For Elko, something tough

Question: We're looking for a ground cover that doesn't need much water, but still looks good. We live in Elko, Nevada (Zone 1), so whatever we plant has to be pretty tough to survive the conditions up here.

Answer: Indian mock strawberry is a drought-tolerant ground cover that performs well in high-elevation gardens. As its name implies, the plant's foliage, fruit, and flowers resemble those of edible strawberries—but the strawberries are sour-tasting, except to birds. Plant in full sun or shade, and space plants 12 to 18 inches apart; runners will fill in quickly. Once plants are established, water sparingly or they may invade the rest of your garden. Remove runners that grow where they aren't wanted.

No longer neat: what can I do?

Question: What can be done with a ground cover that has lost its neat appearance and become rather rank? I'm certainly not going to go in there and shear by hand.

Answer: A lawn mower, set 6 inches or higher, is a good fast way to renew many ground covers. The best time of year is just prior to when the plant normally sends out new growth—which means spring for most plants. If your lawn mower doesn't go up high enough for this (or if you don't even own a lawn mower), check with your local rental yard for mowers especially for this purpose. Some of the more powerful nylon string trimmer-weeders (or those outfitted with metal blades) will also do a good job of trimming large and small areas of ground covers.

A no-mow, walk-on

Problem: Is there anything we can plant in our parking strip that doesn't take as much maintenance as a lawn? We'd have to be able to walk on it to get back and forth to our car. We live in Denver, Colorado (Zone 2).

Solution: In place of grass, arrange two rows of native flagstone running parallel to the sidewalk. Between the rows, plant two kinds of thyme. Woolly thyme becomes a carpet of pale purple flowers in June and July. Lemon thyme's bright green foliage contrasts nicely with the grayish woolly thyme.

Color to spark up my parking strip?

Question: I have a parking strip that needs something colorful. So many ground covers seem to be primarily green. Any color suggestions?

Answer: *Verbena peruviana*, an attractive, fast-growing ground cover, takes care of itself and provides spring-to-fall color. Several kinds of verbena are sold as bedding plants for seasonal color; they're all tender perennials that most gardeners plant as annuals. But if you live where winter temperatures stay above 15° F., *Verbena peruviana* probably will be a permanent planting in your garden. Peruvian verbena hybrids come in a range of bright colors—crimson, red, raspberry, rose, salmon, pure white purple, and blue. (For details on growth and care, see *Verbena*, page 494, *Sunset New Western Garden Book*.)

Periwinkle nemesis: our Irish setter

Problem: We have a sloped area where we are trying to establish some small periwinkle plants. But our large Irish setter continually curls up for a snooze in the new planting bed. Is there anything we can do to discourage him?

Solution: Try creating planting pockets with a staggered pattern of bricks, as shown in the illustration. In addition to taking some of the fun out of your dog's naps, the bricks trap water on the sloping ground. They also help to insulate roots and keep them moist during hot summers. When the periwinkle is full grown, it will cover the bricks.

(For more on dwarf periwinkle, see *Vinca minor*, page 497, *Sunset New Western Garden Book*.)

Alternating pattern of bricks and plants discourages lounging dogs. Pockets retain water for plants.

Any ground cover of hedge height?

Question: Are there any low-growing shrubs that would act as both a ground cover and a hedge? We have a rather formal walk leading to our front door, and need something on either side to deter people from straying off the path. The planting space is about 2 feet wide on each side.

Answer: Consider *Pittosporum tobira* 'Wheeler's Dwarf'. It grows much, much smaller (rarely to 3 feet) than its relative, *P. tobira*, and never needs pruning to keep a tight, rounded shape. Foliage is a dark glossy green. That and its dense, well-filled form give the plant a polished, formal look. Because 'Wheeler's Dwarf' grows so low and wide (the spread is double the height), it works as a ground cover, border, or very small hedge. (For more details, see *Pittosporum*, page 416, *Sunset New Western Garden Book*.)

Anything carefree by the sea?

Problem: We have a vacation place at Stinson Beach, California (Zone 17). We aren't there regularly, but would like to cover a good size area in front of the cottage with a ground cover to block blowing sand from the walks and driveway. Is there any ground cover that can stand seaside conditions and very little care (including water)?

Solution: Try a relatively recent introduction, *Artemisia californica* 'Canyon Gray'. Botanists from the Santa Barbara Botanic Garden discovered it on the Channel Islands. Naturally ground-hugging, 'Canyon Gray' forms a broad, compact mat (about 6 inches high) of finely cut foliage. Coastal weather naturally suits the plant, and it grows well in heavy or light soil. Like its rugged relatives, this particular artemisia withstands drought nicely. You can improve the plant's garden manners by cutting it back occasionally to keep it looking fresh and reasonably dense.

Shade lover for steep slope?

Question: The window over my kitchen sink looks directly onto a bare, steep bank. Large trees on the bank completely shade the area, but the soil is rich, moist, and humusy. I'd like to look out to some lush, green, woodland scene. Are there any ground covers that would do well in this situation and not need a lot of attention? We live in Eugene, Oregon (Zone 6).

Answer: It's hard to beat native ground covers when you're trying to fill in shady, moist places, but some imports do well, too. Some of the most attractive garden scenes can be created by combining several ground covers with differing leaf textures.

For impact, try the bold, heavily veined leaves of *Hosta sieboldiana*, a Japanese native. It thrives during summer, but dies back to the ground with the first frost. If you grow this hosta, you must bait for slugs; they love its leaves.

Redwood sorrel, with its cloverlike leaves, contrasts nicely with hosta. It is native to the West's coastal forests, but won't make it through the winter east of the Cascades. For a little spring color, add a few plants of the native bleeding heart, with its delicate pink-and-white flowers and finely cut, fernlike foliage.

Any special tricks for slope planting?

Problem: Are there any special tricks to planting ground covers on a slope? We're getting ready to tackle a large scale planting, and I'd like to know before I start.

Solution: There are several ways to approach planting on a slope. Vining or spreading covers can be planted flush with the slope, if it isn't too steep, then trained to grow either up or down. (Use bent wire shaped like big hairpins or like wickets to hold vines or upright branches in place.) You can terrace the entire slope with retaining walls. Or you can create an individual terrace for each plant. (See illustration.) The individual terrace

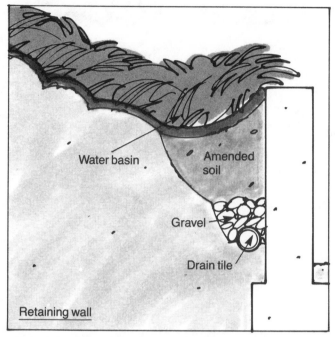

Retaining wall

Retaining walls create space for a planting area with amended soil; gravel and drain tile provide drainage.

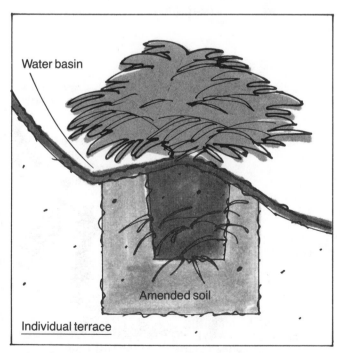

Individual terrace

Individual terracing allows the addition of soil amendments and provides a watering basin for each plant.

method permits you to improve the soil in the planting hole if your ground cover selection needs special soil. This method also creates a watering basin for each plant, helping to prevent excessive runoff.

Stepping stones look bare

Question: Our house has a small, enclosed, fairly shady patio. We used different-sized concrete stepping stones for the flooring, and left about 2 inches between each one. Our plan was just to fill the empty spaces with sand or gravel, but it looks a little bare and uninviting. Is there any fine-textured, well-behaved ground cover that we could plant between the stones to soften the look a little?

Answer: Try baby's tears *(Soleirolia soleirolii).* It does very well in shaded areas, is fine-textured, and grows slowly enough to need little trimming. The plant's only requirements are regular watering during the summer, probably every other day, and feeding three times a year with a mild fertilizer (such as liquid fish emulsion) mixed one-quarter strength. (Also see *Soleirolia soleirolii,* page 470, *Sunset New Western Garden Book.)*

Checklist for spring bloomers

Question: We are getting ready to plant a bank in ground covers, and I don't know the first thing about them. All I know is that I want something that blooms, preferably in spring, and complements my trees and shrubs. Can you provide me with a list so that I can see what these plants look like when I go to the nursery?

Answer: Here is a list of spring-blooming ground covers; number refers to page in *Sunset New Western Garden Book* where each can be checked. (Be sure to check your zone number to help determine which ground cover will grow best in your area.)

Arctotheca	187	Ice plant	329
Armeria	188	*Jasminum*	305
Bergenia	201	*Osteospermum*	388
Ceanothus	227	Phlox	405
Cistus	242	*Phyla*	406
Coreopsis	251	*Potentilla*	425
Cornus	252	*Ranunculus*	439
Fragaria	302	*Rosa*	450
Galium	306	*Rosmarinus*	455
Gazania	307	*Sedum*	464
Helianthemum	320	*Thymus*	484
Hemerocallis	321	*Veronica*	495
Iberis	329	*Vinca*	497

Cool ideas for northside shade?

Question: We have a fairly small area next to our front walkway in which we would like to plant some ground cover. The area is on the north side of the house, has several lacy Japanese maples, and is shaded by mature trees across the walls. The place has a cool, dappled creekside feel to it, and we'd like something to complement that feeling.

Answer: Try planting dwarf periwinkle *(Vinca minor).* Its leaves are smaller than the standard periwinkle *(Vinca major),* and the overall look is more compact and refined. Dwarf periwinkle needs shade to look its best, and regular waterings. It should fit right in with the creekside feeling you are trying to achieve. (See *Vinca,* page 497, *Sunset New Western Garden Book.)*

Problems with pests? See pages 32–48

HOUSE PLANTS

GUIDELINES FOR AVOIDING GENERAL PROBLEMS

Whether you have a wide variety of small indoor plants or just a couple of large specimens, house plants can make a dramatic difference in the way an interior looks. The number and diversity of house plants available has increased substantially over the years, helping to make them more and more popular.

Like outdoor plants, house plants have their problems. First of all, many homes are too hot and dry to favor healthy, active growth. Ways to increase humidity and keep plants from getting too warm are tops on the list for avoiding trouble. Next in importance would be to know the watering needs of your individual plants, rather than join ranks with those millions of people who use a "for-one-for-all" approach, which can only result in some plants being underwatered and others overwatered. Also, remember that plants living in containers need regular applications of fertilizer during the growing season to remain healthy.

Don't be lulled by a sense of false security about pests and diseases because the plants are indoors. Always keep a sharp eye out for insect or disease problems, which are much easier to control in the early stages than when the infestation becomes extensive.

To keep house plants generally problem-free, follow these rules:

- Be sure the plant you choose is in the right location in the room—proper light, humidity, freedom from drafts
- Plant in good soil and repot when necessary
- Pinch and prune to control plant and keep it in shape
- Routinely inspect for insects and disease; spray or otherwise control
- Fertilize and water according to type of house plant (see individual listings in the encyclopedia section of the *Sunset New Western Garden Book*)

How much light for an African violet?

Question: I just bought several beautiful African violets. The clerk at the nursery told me that the more light I could give it, the more it would bloom. Does this mean I should put it in direct sunlight?

Answer: No! The term "bright light" refers to the type of light that is found in the interior portions of a sunny room, or light reflected from light-colored walls. African violets need this kind of exposure throughout the daylight hours. A north-facing exposure provides bright light with no direct sun.

Leaves have brown tips and edges

Problem: The leaves of my anthurium have brown tips and edges. Seems like this happens to many of my house plants, and the condition frequently gets much worse. What am I doing wrong?

Advice: That is a complicated question, because so many conditions cause this problem. Possible causes include overwatering or underwatering, too much sun or heat through a window, too much fertilizer, water too high in salt concentration, not enough humidity, or lo-

cation in a draft. Any one of these situations, or a combination, may result in browned tips or margins. The only way to solve this mystery is to study the plant's situation, and try to locate the cause by checking the above list. Determine which you think might be the most probable cause, and then remedy it. (For help, check House plants, page 80, *Sunset New Western Garden Book*.) If you aren't successful with the first remedy, check out the list again. Sometimes, patient experimentation such as this is the only possible way to solve house plant problems.

Scruffy and sprawling: why?

Problem: I have an arrowhead plant *(Syngonium podophyllum)* that was compact and attractive when I first brought it home. I put it in a basket on a bathroom shelf. Now, after a couple of months, the plant is all over the place and looks unsightly.

Advice: Leggy growth is caused by insufficient light. Bring your arrowhead plant out of the bathroom to a cheerier location with more light; pinch back the leggy stems.

Any house plants like it dusky?

Problem: I want some house plants for a dark corner of the living room. How dark is too dark?

Advice: Test for enough growing light by passing your hand between the light source and the plant. If you can see a shadow, the chances are that you can keep a plant alive, even though it may not grow a great deal. (See illustration.) Try cast iron plant *(Aspidistra)*, Moses-in-the-cradle *(Rhoeo spathacea)*, or snake plant *(Sansevieria)*. (For detailed growing information on these plants, see pages 191, 447, and 459, *Sunset New Western Garden Book.*)

Plant has enough light to survive if your hand creates a shadow when passed between light source and plant.

What are those white furry things?

Question: When I finally got around to giving a close inspection to a sick-looking grape ivy, I noticed little white furry creatures clustered on the leaf stems. What are they?

Answer: They are mealybugs—sucking insects that cause stunted growth and frequently are fatal to many house plants. You can remove them by daubing them with a cotton swab dipped in alcohol, working them off with water from a hose or a spray mister, or using a chemical spray. Mealybugs are pictured and discussed on page 38.

Fern drip will ruin my floors!

Problem: Ferns in hanging pots are my favorite house plants, but I have to put down pans to catch the drip or it will ruin the floors.

Suggestion: Slip each fern pot into a second pot, one that is solid-bottomed and will catch the drips when you water the hanging plants. The second pot should be emptied every two or three waterings. The slip-on pots made of plastic are lightest in weight.

Tarzan would love my living room

Question: I have a vine-type philodendron that is growing all over the room. Is there anything I can do to "hold back the jungle"?

Answer: Count it a blessing that your philodendron is growing so well. Other than that, keep cutting off the tips. Stick them back in the pot with the original plant; or, if you prefer, you can root them first in a glass of water. By pinching the stems and rooting the cuttings, you will get a bushier plant that will not grow out of bounds.

A tale of two philodendrons

Problem: I have two philodendrons—one in my living room, and one in the dining room. The one in the dining room is doing great, and the one in the living room is failing miserably. The living room receives quite a bit less light than the dining room. Could that be the problem? If so, I'm in trouble—the philodendron in the living room is in a pot too big to move.

Advice: It definitely sounds as if the problem is a lack of light. Since the plant cannot be moved, try compensating with artificial light especially made for plant growth, available at nurseries and garden centers. You might also try leaving the curtains or drapes open during the day if you don't already, to let maximum light into the room.

Poinsettia pointers

Problem: Each year, I receive at least one poinsettia at Christmas time. Each year, I am determined to make them bloom again the next winter, but no luck. Just floppy branches and a few dismal reddish leaves.

Solution: You have discovered what many other gardeners also know: those potted gift poinsettias are difficult to bring into bloom again. However, the following directions will increase your chances of success:

When leaves fall in late winter or early spring, cut stems back to two buds and reduce watering to a bare minimum—just enough to keep the stems plump and healthy. Store potted plants in a cool spot indoors until late spring. When frosts are past, set pots in sun outdoors, fertilize and expect new growth. If you think plants are too big for the pot, this is a good time to repot, using a good quality house plant soil mix. Pinch the new growth to encourage bushiness.

Bring the plant back indoors in autumn, as soon as the weather begins to turn cold at night. Starting in October, the plants will require *14 hours of total darkness* nightly to insure blossoms for Christmas. Best bet is to move them into a closet every night, and bring into the light in the morning for a maximum of 10 hours. Repeat procedure for 10 weeks, and you should have poinsettia blossoms by Christmas.

Planting in a pot without a hole

Question: I have a very attractive plant container that was given to me by a friend. I want to plant an indoor palm in it, but the container doesn't have a drainage hole. I really don't want to drill a hole in the container because it is rather valuable and the neck is too narrow to accept a secondary planting pot. Is there any way to use this container for a house plant?

Answer: Putting a house plant in a container without a drainage hole is far from ideal, but it can be done. Place a layer of small rocks or pebbles in the bottom of the container. This layer should take up about one-quarter of the total container volume. The drainage layer allows water to seep through the soil and retains it until the moisture can be utilized by the plant or until it evaporates. Spread a thin layer of charcoal bits directly over the drainage layer. Charcoal keeps the soil "sweet" by absorbing any noxious by-products created in decaying matter in the soil. Put the planting soil on top of this layer and plant as usual. Monitor your waterings carefully, being careful not to consistently overwater.

Can I mix my own potting soil?

Question: I've had great luck with the commercially prepared potting soils but I've got so many indoor plants now, I was wondering whether or not I could make my own potting soil and save a little money?

Answer: You certainly can—here's how: Blend equal amount of coarse sand (be sure to buy washed sand; the salt in unwashed sea sand may damage tender plants), garden loam or good garden topsoil, and peat moss, leaf mold, or fir bark. To each 2 quarts of this mix, add ½ cup each charcoal and perlite. These ingredients are usually available at most nurseries, garden centers, or indoor plant stores. Don't skip anything in the recipe, as each ingredient is important to the final mix.

Any potting mix that you make yourself which contains soil from the garden must be sterilized to remove harmful pests, weed seeds, or diseases. Follow these steps to sterilize your soil: 1) Mix all the ingredients thoroughly. 2) Dampen the mix slightly with water; then spread—no more than 4 inches deep—in shallow oven-proof pans. 3) Place the filled pans in 180° oven and bake for at least 2 hours. This is a smelly but important process; fortunately, the odor doesn't last long.

It won't spin any "spiders"

Question: My spider plant doesn't have any "spiders" on it. What am I doing wrong?

Answer: Maybe it's too young. When the plant is old enough to bloom, it will produce bloom stalks, which in turn will produce runners at the ends—the familiar spider-shaped plants. Or, it could be that your plant is failing to "spider" because it is not receiving enough light. These plants are very easy to grow, given enough light and sufficient time to dry out somewhat between waterings.

Wandering Jew isn't wandering

Problem: My wandering Jew produced long runners that use to hang almost to the floor. Now the stems seem to be rotting at the base, and whole runners are falling off. I have had it in the same hanging pot for about a year.

Advice: Several conditions may be contributing to the problem. The plant may not be receiving enough light—a common occurrence with plants hanging near the ceiling. You may be watering it too often, or there may not be adequate drainage in the container. Or perhaps the soil is too heavy: house plants need a lightweight, porous soil mix that allows water to drain quickly. Try repotting your wandering Jew in a new hanging container with adequate drainage holes, and use a good quality house plant soil mix. You can take new cuttings from the healthy ends of damaged runners, and simply stick them in the soil. Keep the soil slightly moist, and they will root and start growing in no time at all.

Webbed leaves, sick plants

Question: Several of my house plants look rather sick. On close inspection, I noticed a fine webbing on the leaves. Could spiders be the cause of this decline?

Answer: Not spiders, but spider mites—a common house plant pest. Spider mites are very small, and can only be detected in clusters, or by the webbing you noticed. Isolate infested plants immediately; spider mites spread like wildfire. Wash off the pests with water from a hose, or with a soapy (not detergent) solution. Regular misting also helps to control mites. For more information, see page 35.

Does softened water kill plants?

Question: I've been told that watering my house plants with softened water can kill them. Can that be?

Answer: Yes. Water that is chemically treated in a home water-softener that uses salt for ion exchange is fine for laundry and other household uses, but *not* for plants. The high concentration of salts in softened water causes leaf burn and dieback; repeated use can kill most plants. To avoid this problem, use water from faucets that bypass the water softener (such as those in your garden). Or better yet, collect rain water to use on potted plants; it's the purest of all.

It is possible to find commercially-sold mechanical processes for de-ionizing water, but it should be remembered that the resultant "pure" water will lack not only salt but possibly some other properties which actually benefit plants.

Water stains on wood floors

Problem: My house plants are very important to me, but I've yet to find a way to keep them from making marks on tables. Even with a saucer, the drainage water still manages to leave a mark. Any suggestions?

Solution: Many indoor gardeners protect surfaces by creating a "buffer zone" between drip saucers and the furniture (or floor) that they sit on. This buffer zone forms an air space in which any absorbed moisture or moisture caused by condensation can be dissipated. Coasters, mats, blocks of wood, metal or wooden plant holders, or any means of raising the plant container and saucer off furniture or carpet surfaces, can serve as a buffer zone.

Weeping fig wants comforting

Problem: I have a 5-foot-tall weeping fig (*Ficus benjamina*) that was given to me. It started dropping leaves right away, and has never stopped. Now the tree is almost bare—a terrible sight. I have tried very hard to take good care of it, and wonder what am I doing wrong?

Active: Weeping figs do not like to be moved. Additionally, they dislike overwatering, dark growing conditions, drafts, and placement near heat registers. Unless the new location is similar to the conditions of its former home, weeping fig will almost always lose most of its leaves. The concerned new owner might think that it needs more water, and so proceed to kill the plant by overwatering. If you don't fall into that trap, the fig may gradually adapt to its new environment and grow a new set of leaves. It may take quite some time to do this. Give it good normal care, and try not to worry.

MISCELLANEOUS

There are many garden questions and problems that do not fit neatly into the chapters of this book. Finding the right tool for a difficult job, trapping earwigs, or hanging up a hose out of the way are among the miscellaneous problems that—although minor—can make a significant difference in the garden.

Garden tools can become a problem if you don't have the ones you need, can't find where you last put them, or are rusted and dull when you do finally locate them. For this reason, it's a very good idea to keep all of your garden tools in one place, out of the elements, and well sharpened to make the job easier.

Many gardeners have found a garden diary to be an indispensible aid. A separate calendar or daybook works well, filled with information perti-

nent to your own garden. Dates certain vegetables were planted as well as the first harvest dates, the first appearance of mildew on roses (so you can apply a preventive spray next year), or the date that you last fertilized the container and house plants—keeping a record of this kind of information can make gardening a less haphazard, more organized activity. (To have a try at this, see the "gardener's notepads" throughout the seasonal activities chapter, pages 6–31.)

As you read through the following miscellaneous questions and problems, we hope you'll find a few tips that will make your gardening more trouble-free. We have also included in this chapter a few plants that did not seem to fit naturally into other chapters. Where else, for example, could tumbleweeds go?

Special tools for bonsai?

Problem: Since I retired and moved to the mountains I've started to raise bonsai—evergreens, mostly. I really need some precision cutters for working on these little trees. Are there special tools available?

Advice: There are many highly specialized tools made especially for working on bonsai plant material. They range from moderately expensive precision cutters to simple, elementary chopsticks (for delicate digging around roots). Ask your local nursery to locate for you some garden specialty catalogs and the addresses of bonsai societies. Both of these sources could give you names of shops where tools can be ordered.

Are some bugs insecticide-resistant?

Question: Some of the insecticides I've used for years don't seem to be as effective as they once were. Is it possible that some bugs are becoming resistant to them?

Answer: The answer is basically yes—some insecticides can lose their effectiveness as the insects become more resistant to the active chemical ingredient in the product. Within each new generation of insects, there are a few that will be naturally resistant to the chemicals commonly used to control them. There is intense pressure in the process of natural selection to favor these individuals. Frequently there are several generations of insects born each year, so the number of resistant insects can multiply with considerable speed.

Compost is smelly

Problem: According to my experience, composting is much better in theory than in practice. The two raw materials I have the most of—kitchen scraps and grass clippings—are becoming smelly piles that draw flies. Help me before I give up.

Solution: Grass clippings and kitchen scraps, if added to compost piles in big lumps, can soon congeal into airless, stinking masses. Add such materials in very thin layers alternately with soil or coarse material, such as tree prunings or stalky plants. (Or, put the kitchen scraps through a grinder with the coarser materials.)

Lightly water often enough to keep compost moist but never soggy. Locating the pile under a tree or other shade lets it dry out more slowly and decompose better. (Also see Compost, page 35, *Sunset New Western Garden Book*.)

Transplanting cactus

Problem: My little cactus plants grow imperceptibly, but grow they do. I'm sure some should be transplanted into larger containers, but I don't know how to avoid the spines.

Solution: Two techniques will help you do the job easily and painlessly: For small plants, kitchen tongs or rubber-tipped crucible tongs give a firm but gentle grip as you move spiny cactus from pot to pot. Use tongs only on cactus that are smaller than fist-size.

For larger cactus, fold a newspaper lengthwise three times and wrap the strip around the cactus. Hold it firmly in place and lift the cactus. (See illustration.)

May is the best time to transplant most cactus—the growth is just beginning.

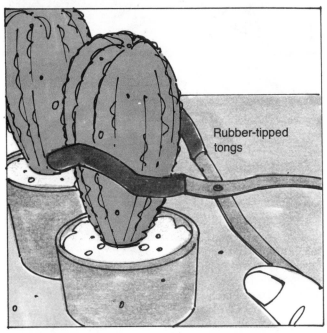

To aid in transplanting, hold small cactus with tongs.

Rubber-tipped tongs

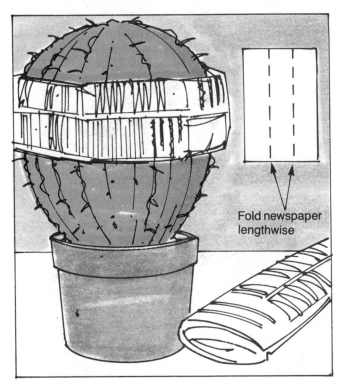

Fold newspaper lengthwise

Make a thick pad of folded newspaper to hold cactus.

Cats and dogs in new seed beds

Problem: Cats and dogs keep messing up my new seed beds. How can I prevent this?

Solution: There is nothing like a freshly tilled and planted seed bed to attract cats and dogs. One simple way of keeping them out is with chicken wire—not around, but *on* the garden beds. Buy just enough to cover newly planted parts of the garden, crumple it up and partially straighten it out. Lay it on the beds. Since the crumpling won't allow the wire to lie flat, cats and small dogs won't walk over it, perhaps because they are afraid of tangling their feet. After the seed crops are up and young plants are plentiful and sturdy enough not to be damaged by pets, you can remove the wire to be used another time.

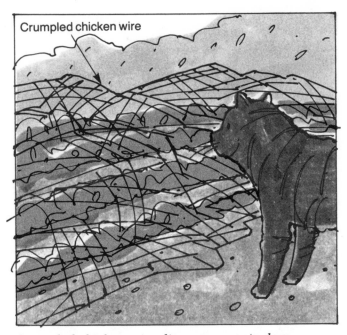

Crumpled chicken wire

Crumpled chicken wire discourages cats, dogs.

What's eating holes in my fern?

Problem: The lower leaves (fronds, I think) of my fern now have several unsightly holes. Are these holes natural or should I look for bugs?

Solution: Look for bugs. Sowbugs and pillbugs are creatures that favor the naturally decaying shields (lower fronds) of many kinds of ferns. These little bugs eat through and make the holes you see.

To stop them from defacing the fern, sprinkle a bit of sowbug bait over the top of the plant every week or so.

For additional information on sowbugs and pillbugs, see page 37.

Trap those earwigs

Problem: Our entire garden seems to be crawling with earwigs. A friend in the country lets her chickens help keep the earwig population down. But the only way I like chickens is fried! So what can I do, short of poison sprays, to get rid of earwigs?

Advice: Here are a couple of suggestions: Rolled-up newspapers make effective temporary traps. Set them out in the garden at night; pick them up and destroy the earwigs in the morning.

Or, you can rig up something more permanent,

such as a trap made from old garden hose. For each trap, bundle together three 6- to 10-inch lengths of hose with plastic garden ties. Place traps between rows of vegetables and at the base of shrubs. Next morning, empty them by knocking the earwigs into a bucket of water.

For more information, see page 36.

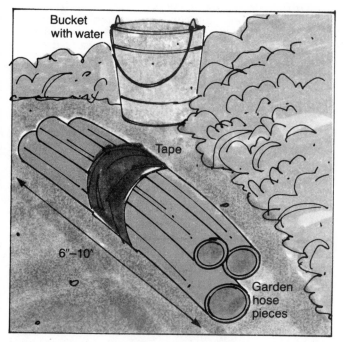

Put out traps for earwigs at night; next morning, knock the trapped pests into a bucket of water.

Do fertilizers and insecticides mix?

Question: Garden chemicals mystify me. Can I mix a pest spray with a fertilizer and save a step when I spray? How do you know what will mix with another product?

Answer: Never mix any product with another, unless it is actually recommended on the label. Leave the mixing of chemicals to chemists. It is actually *illegal* to use any chemical product in any way that is not recommended on the label. For the best results, and for safety, always read and follow all label directions.

Longer lasting Christmas holly

Question: I've made a habit of sending my sister in Minnesota some holly branches for her Christmas decorating. (She was awestruck by the vivid-green winter landscape here in Albany, Oregon, when she visited some years back.) The problem is time, as usual. Considering delivery time to Minnesota, my sister has a week with fresh branches at best. Is there any way to prolong the life of cut holly?

Answer: In our experience, cut holly branches last 10 days until leaves begin to drop. But there is a hormone treatment that doubles their useful life.

The product, naphthaleneacetic acid (NAA), is available at most nurseries and garden centers. You mix the chemical into water (a bucket or bathtub works well) and totally immerse the cut holly branches for a few seconds. Air-dry the holly for home use, or wrap it still moist in

waxed paper for mailing. (Make sure your shipping container has a few ¼-inch holes for ventilation.)

I keep tripping over the hose

Problem: One of these days I'm going to break my leg tripping over the garden hose. I never seem to have any place to put it.

Solution: This wooden hose hanger fits well into the garden scene, and should keep you on your feet. It also makes a good storage place for the hose when it is temporarily out of use in winter.

The hanger is made from scrap wood, or a 6-foot length of 4 by 8 and four short pieces of 2 by 4. Nail two 8-inch lengths of the 2 by 4 horizontally across the 4 by 8, about a foot from the end. Then nail the other 2 by 4's parallel to the post to keep the hose in place. (See illustration.) Finally, creosote the bottom 2 feet of the post and sink it into a post hole.

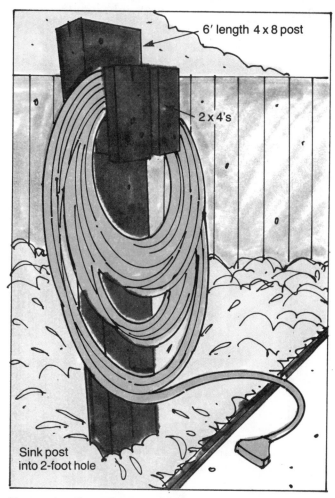

Hanger made with post and 2 X 4's is a simple yet effective way to keep garden hose in place.

What to do with kiwis?

Problem: I had a few kiwi plants given to me and I don't know what to do with them. I live in Santa Maria, California (Zone 15) and assume that they will grow here.

Pronunciation problems? See pages 147 & 148

Advice: Unless you plan to go into the kiwi fruit business, a "few" plants may be too many. The common kiwi vine *(Actinidia chinensis)* grows vigorously in Zone 15 (also in Zones 4–9, 14–24) and often reaches a towering 30 feet, with enormous leaves and sturdy, fuzzy stems. Give them plenty of room, and a support to grow on. To get the delicious fruit, you must keep at least two plants, a male and a female. Your local nursery can help you identify your plants when they bloom. (Also see *Actinidia chinensis*, page 169, *Sunset New Western Garden Book.)*

How to get mud off shoes?

Question: Is there some sort of handy gadget we can install that would help us scrape the mud off our shoes after we've worked in the garden?

Answer: This is a question asked at one time or another by nearly every gardener. Here is a mudscraper that is easy to make. It consists of two scrub brushes. Anchor each brush against a short 2-by-4 that's firmly fixed to a base. For scrapers, use two 4-inch corner braces fastened to the base below the brushes. (See illustration.)

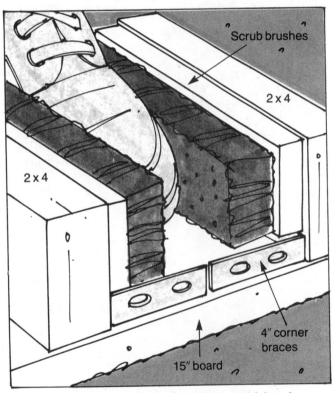

Scrub brushes

2 x 4

2 x 4

4" corner braces

15" board

Scrape boot over metal braces between scrub brushes.

What to do with dead palm fronds?

Question: I want to remove dead palm fronds from my Washingtonia palm, as I feel that they look unattractive. But I wonder if they protect the trunk, and if I should leave the dead fronds to fall naturally?

Advice: Dead palm fronds don't benefit the trunk. Some gardeners feel that dried leaves add character to

a palm tree, but most prefer to trim off the old foliage. Pruning has several advantages: it reveals more of the trunk, reduces fire hazard, and prevents litter drop as the old leaves dry and partially shred.

Many palm leaves are killed by winter frosts. You can prune off most of the damaged leaves, but leave the cluster of foliage near the top to protect new growth.

With a pruning saw, make a clean cut at the base of each damaged frond; take care not to gouge the trunk. For tough, old, dried-out stalks, you may resort to an ax. (For young citrus trees, there's no friend like an old frond—tie them around the trees' trunks for frost protection in winter.)

What can I plant in fall?

Question: Back in Billings, Montana (Zone 1), we never planted a thing in fall. But here in Anaheim, California (Zone 23), it's all turned around for me. There's more garden action now in fall than spring. My question is this: Can I plant all shrubs and trees now, or should some wait until spring? I am eager to plant some citrus trees.

Answer: Fall is an ideal time in Zone 23 to transplant most evergreen shrubs and California native plants. The soil is still warm, allowing time for some root growth. Then the winter rains and cool temperatures will help to establish the plant, giving it a fast start come spring. But wait until spring to plant your citrus—also tender plants such as gardenias and hibiscus.

Can't keep track of all my plants

Problem: I just can't keep track of all my plants—I keep forgetting what they are, and also when I planted them.

Solution: Plant tags are great reminders; they cost about 2 to 12 cents apiece. The metal tags last indefinitely on shrubs, but the plastic and wood labels are adequate for vegetable rows and annuals. Use a marking pen with waterproof ink to write the name, date of planting, where the plant came from, and special care required. Then attach the tag to a branch about a foot from the ground.

For large plants or large groupings of one kind of plant, you can drive in redwood stakes with the names and planting dates painted on them.

Which landscape "pro" is which?

Problem: Here we are with a new house and a bare yard all set for landscaping. We don't know where to start. Should we talk with a landscape architect, a landscape designer, a landscape contractor? Or are they all the same?

Advice: No, they are not all the same, although they all work in the same general field. A landscape architect heads the list in the degree of education and experience, and has had training in both the structural and esthetic aspects of designing landscapes. (In some states, the title is carefully restricted to licensed professionals.) A landscape contractor installs landscapes, and is rarely involved in the design process or plant selection. In some states it is necessary for a person calling him or herself a "landscape contractor" to be both licensed and bonded. A landscape designer is the least regulated of all the terms, and can be used by anyone who is self-considered to be proficient in garden design.

What's that short-handled shovel?

Question: I noticed a different kind of shovel at the garden center recently. It had a very long, narrow blade and short handle. I'm kind of a nut for having the proper tool for each job. Tell me, what kind of jobs is this shovel for?

Answer: This special spade is used for transplanting and trenching, accomplishing both jobs with greater efficiency than an ordinary shovel or spade. As you noticed, the tool's hallmark is a narrow, extra-long blade (averaging 5 by 15 inches). The digging end is usually tapered. It digs several inches deeper than a conventional short-handled spade, and holds about the same amount of soil. (See illustration.)

Short handle

Long blade

Transplanting spade

Long blade of transplanting spade digs deeper than most shovels, gets the most rootball with least work.

Drown snail sorrows in beer?

Question: I keep hearing this idea of leaving stale beer for slugs and snails to drown in as an effective, "organic" control. I tried it once and did catch several slugs. What's your experience?

Answer: Although many people still recommend this method, a *Sunset* test some years ago found beer no more effective than pans of water. For better results, take a flashlight to find slugs and snails while they're out at night, and do away with them. Use a stick; or, if you're

squeamish, drop them in a pail of 10 percent liquid bleach—90 percent water. (Also see page 34.)

How much soil amendment will I need?

Problem: Last summer our garden soil dried into a hard mass like concrete that discouraged even the weeds. This fall I want to mix in manure or some other soil amendment, but I have no idea how much I should order. Is there any kind of rule-of-thumb I can use?

Solution: First, determine the square footage of your planting bed. The chart will tell you the amount of soil amendment needed to cover the area to the depth you want. (Three inches of amendment turned into the first 8 or 9 inches of soil is a good rule-of-thumb. An inch is all right for mulching.) The quantities given allow for some settling.

(Also see Soil amendments, page 33, *Sunset New Western Garden Book*.)

Area in square feet	Sacks needed to cover to a depth of:			Cubic yards needed to cover to a depth of:		
	1″	2″	3″	1″	2″	3″
25	1	2	3			
50	2	4	6			
100	4	8	12			
200	8	16	24	⅔	1⅓	2
300	12	24	36	1	2	3
400				1⅓	2⅔	4
500				1⅔	3⅓	5
600				2	4	6
700				2⅓	4⅔	7
800				2⅔	5⅓	8
900				3	6	9
1,000				3⅓	6⅔	10

- One sack equals 2 cubic feet (this is the size of many prepackaged soil conditioners sold in nurseries).
- One cubic yard equals 27 cubic feet (most suppliers call it simply a "yard").
- For coverage of 4 inches or more, just multiply the figure in the 1-inch column by the depth you need.

Try this with sevin spray

Problem: Several of our ornamental shrubs were plagued by insect pests this summer. Sevin was the recommended spray, but it didn't seem to do much good. We followed the label directions carefully. Is it possible to get a "bum" bottle? We live in Sparks, Nevada (near Reno).

Suggestion: In certain areas such as yours (Zone 3) where the water is naturally alkaline (above 7.0 on the pH scale) there may be a problem using the liquid form of sevin. It seems that the alkaline water breaks down the chemical, rendering it ineffective. Try this: Add 2 to 3 tablespoons of vinegar per gallon of water; this will lower the alkalinity, in effect "buffering" the water, and this should allow the chemical sevin to do its job.

Trees and shrubs from seed?

Question: I've got some hilly property in Napa Valley, California (Zone 14) that I hope to build on in a few years. It's pretty barren, and I'd like to get some shrubs or trees started. The problem is that I want to avoid the expense and maintenance of planting nursery stock from containers. A friend suggested *seeds* of trees and shrubs. How do I go about this?

Solution: Here's a technique developed by the University of California several years ago to plant trees and shrubs from seed. It is especially useful for property like yours that has a large unirrigated area where conventional nursery-grown plants would be too expensive and too difficult to maintain.

Dig a hole about 4 inches deep and about 1 inch wide. Put a pinch of slow-release fertilizer in the bottom of the hole and fill it to within ½ inch of the top.

In each hole, plant 5 to 20 seeds (depending on what you're planting) at the recommended depth.

Make a cylindrical collar by cutting the bottom out of a pint cottage cheese container; or cut the top and bottom out of a half-gallon milk carton, then cut in half for two collars.

Sink each collar halfway into the ground so it surrounds the planting hole. This collar helps protect the seeds from creatures, helps contain water without encouraging weeds, and helps shade the seed so it germinates quickly. Covering the cylinder with hardware cloth will also protect the seed from birds and rodents.

For a list of shrubs and trees that are easy to start this way, contact your nearest county cooperative extension office.

How to water a deep garden bed?

Problem: I need a bright idea. The planting beds in my garden are deep, and it is a problem watering the plants adequately. I can use a sprinkler, but too much water is wasted and goes where I don't want it to go. I've tried using a hose with an extension watering wand; this is okay, but dragging the hose around through the garden bed is a hassle and the hose keeps hitting the plants.

Solution: A long-nose watering can permits you to reach distant roots without stepping into garden beds (or onto trailing branches), and without wasting water or getting it on leaves susceptible to mildew. To extend the spout of a galvanized watering can, fasten a length of plastic pipe in place with a hose clamp, sold at auto parts stores. (See illustration.)

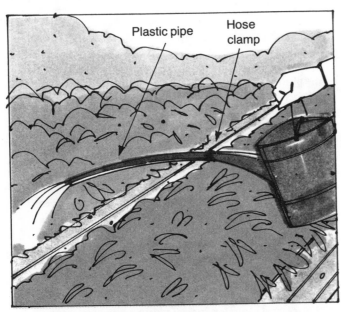

Plastic pipe can extend the spout of a watering can.

How can we foil the squirrels?

Problem: Help! We have a large deck overlooking a wooded area. We garden primarily in containers, but the squirrels from the neighboring trees are driving us crazy. They have dug up and discarded some of our choicest potted plants to make a burial site for a lousy acorn or walnut. Is there any way to stop them from doing this?

Solution: Try this proven method: pieces of hardware cloth cut to fit the pot, and then slit from edge to center to go around the plant base, will keep squirrels (and equally industrious blue jays) from digging in your potted plants. For more about squirrels, see page 47.

Seed showing has been miserable

Problem: For three years in a row we have tried to start a variety of flowers and vegetables from seed. Granted, our soil is not the best—in fact, it's fairly heavy clay—but we're attentive with water and fertilizer. Each year the showing has been miserable. Is there any way to increase the chances of getting seeds to germinate in our heavy soil?

Solution: A seedling's most critical period occurs right at germination when it thrusts up through the soil and into the light. If the soil has a high clay content, it is likely to bake so hard that the seedling just can't make it.

One of the best ways to help the sprouts along is to cover the seed with sand rather than soil. The sand won't bake hard, and the seedlings pop up quickly and evenly. Two fringe benefits are: 1) the newly sown rows are highly visible (if you use light-colored sand), and 2) weed pulling is easier in the sand-covered rows.

Plagued by crown rot

Problem: Recently we seem to be plagued by crown rot. We've lost two trees and several shrubs this year alone. Are we doing something wrong?

Solution: You may not be doing something wrong, but you may not be doing everything you could to prevent it. Crown rot attacks plants at the base of their trunks, on the large roots, or (most typically) at the crown—the point where trunks and roots meet. The symptoms are an unhealthy paleness followed by withering, wilting, or collapse of the plant, branch by branch, or all at once.

Here are three suggestions to help prevent this damaging disease: 1) Plant high. Set the plant on a broad, low mound—broad enough and low enough to keep soil from washing away. Plant so the top root is just below soil surface. 2) Keep base of the trunk dry. If soil is exceptionally heavy, put a collar of coarse sand around the trunk. Water the root ball of a container plant or balled and burlapped plant only until roots get into surrounding soil, then enlarge the watering basin and reduce frequency of irrigation. 3) Assure good drainage. Test the planting hole for good drainage before setting the plant in place. Don't add soil near an established plant or allow soil to wash over crown.

What if a plant is pot bound?

Question: Almost everything I've ever read says to avoid plants at the nursery that have become pot bound. Recently I've seen, at our local nursery, several kinds of shrubs I would like to have for our garden. However, there are coiled roots coming out of the bottom of the rusted can. Should I take a chance and buy them, or forget it?

Answer: The problem with plants with a tight, entangled root system is that even when you take them out of the can and plant them, they can continue to grow in the same orbit, encircling inner roots. This seriously reduces the roots' capacity to take in nutrients and to anchor the tree or shrub in the soil. There are, however, some steps you can take to remedy the situation.

To help roots grow out from the old root ball into the ground, cut off excess roots at the bottom of the root mass and loosen the roots encircling the root ball (see illustration). If the root encirclement is extreme, score the root ball in two or three places, from top to bottom. Remove or cut only the outer roots; don't cut deeply enough to break up the soil ball.

Once you've removed or cut tangled roots around the outside of the root ball, set the tree in a hole bigger than the root ball and fill in around it with soil. Tamp soil beneath and around the root ball firmly enough so that watering won't cause it to settle significantly. The top of the root ball should stay at or slightly above ground level. Make a watering basin by raising a dike around the dripline of the plant, not by putting the plant in a basin below ground level.

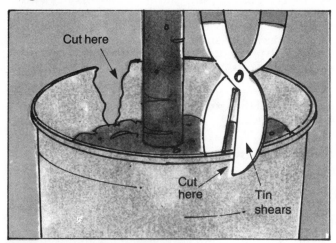

Cut can to facilitate removing tree. Long roots encircling rootball must be loosened before tree is planted.

Why is organic matter so important?

Question: I hear a lot about "organic matter"—that a soil needs it to grow plants well. What I don't know is *why* organic matter is so important.

Answer: Organic matter is a general term for the decaying remains of once-living material. This includes plant parts, animal manures, and even such animal remains as bone meal and blood meal. Added to soil, organic matter (especially plant remains and animal manures) improves the texture by fitting between soil particles and groups of particles. This "opens up" a dense clay soil and actually "fills in" spaces between particles of a sandy soil. The organic matter continues to decompose while in the soil, and as it does it also releases small quantities of nutrients. Its overall importance, then, is providing a better environment for plant roots. For more information, refer to "Organic soil amendments" on page 33, *Sunset New Western Garden Book.*

Is there any age limit for seeds?

Question: I've heard that many seeds are less likely to germinate as they get older. How can I be sure the seeds I buy out of the rack at my garden center are fresh?

Answer: Somewhere on the packet, usually on the flap, it should say for what season the seeds were packed. Almost all large seed companies completely replace all of the seeds in racks on a yearly basis.

Flower seed mixture was a flop

Question: I planted a small bed with a special mixture of flower seeds. Although I followed the instructions on the seed packet, only three seedlings came up. What could have happened?

Advice: Two common problem areas may have influenced the poor showing: 1) The soil may have been too heavy for the seeds to properly germinate, or it may have crusted over in between waterings. Either condition can be avoided by incorporating plenty of organic matter into the soil before planting and by keeping the seed bed evenly moist during the germination period. 2) Snails, cutworms, and birds could have eaten the tender shoots right after the seeds germinated. Always bait the area with the proper control when you seed it, and make a second application a few days later. The only way to discourage birds is to cover the area with bird netting while the plants are small and tempting (see page 51).

Soil lingo has me confused

Question: I need clarification of terms used to describe soil. *Clay* and *sand* are reasonably clear to me, but I've also run across "adobe," "gumbo," "loam," "silt," combination terms like "clay loam," and reference to "heavy soil." What do these different terms mean—and what are their implications?

Answer: In describing soils, soil scientists use certain words to indicate size of particles that compose the soils. *Clay* soils contain the smallest particles, and these are characteristically flattened so that they fit closely together. *Sandy* soils are made up of the largest particles, and these are rounded so that a sandy soil does not compact as a clay soil does. *Silt* refers to particle size larger than clay but smaller than sand.

The more tightly soil particles fit together, the more difficulty water and air have penetrating the soil. This is the reason water "puddles" so quickly on a clay soil. On the other hand, once clay soil absorbs water, the water is retained longer than in other soil types. The properties of sand are just the opposite: water penetrates easily but is more quickly lost.

The other words you mentioned are gardeners' terms. Both "adobe" and "gumbo" are regional words that describe clay soil, and "heavy soil" also is another clay synonym (as "light soil" is for sand). "Loam" is the word gardeners use to indicate an "ideal" garden soil—one that contains a mixture of particle sizes, from clay through sand, plus organic matter. These soils retain moisture without remaining waterlogged. "Clay loam" and "sandy loam" indicate soils that are inclined to one or the other end of the particle-size scale.

Did our trees die in the truck?

Question: We were out-of-town when we came upon a great sale at a nursery. We put two large birch trees in the back of our truck, laid them down, and drove home. I told my husband that we should have wrapped them up in something, but we didn't have anything available at the time. Anyway, we got them in the ground, and now, 2 weeks later, most of the leaves have turned brown. Are the trees dying, or did the unprotected trip in the truck damage the leaves? It was plenty hot the day we bought them.

Answer: The combination of warm temperatures and 55 mile an hour winds whipping the foliage can quickly desiccate the leaves of any plant. The trees will probably remain damaged for the rest of this growing season but will recover with the new growth of next spring. Anytime you take a foliage plant in leaf in an open car or truck, it should be carefully wrapped with a tarp or blanket. When in doubt, it's always best to have the nursery deliver your plants in an enclosed truck.

Stop tumbleweeds before they tumble

Problem: Before moving here to Minden, Nevada (Zone 3), I never took tumbleweeds seriously. They were just in movies and songs, I thought. Now I'm here, and so are the tumbleweeds, and they sure are a nuisance.

Solution: Necessary as they are to cowboy movies and the romantic notion of the West, tumbleweeds—whether tumbling or growing in place—are not welcome in a garden.

In winter apply the pre-emergent herbicide, trifluralin, to destroy the seeds as they sprout in the spring. Follow label instructions exactly. Be very careful to avoid applying the herbicide to areas where you want to raise plants from seed in the spring—the pre-emergent would also destroy desirable seeds as they sprout.

Tubbed annuals never took off

Problem: Earlier this year I purchased four large half-barrels to use as planters. I wanted an impressive display of annuals to bring some color to my front patio, but the plants never really took off. Even though I watered the plants every evening, they looked wilted and droopy by the time I returned home from work the next day.

Advice: Sounds like the plants aren't getting enough water (although obviously you are trying). Often this is caused by the pot or box being filled with too much soil. Depending on the size of the container, you should leave anywhere from 1 to 3 inches of space between the top of the soil and the top of the container. Fill this space completely with water once or twice each time you water. The plant has not been thoroughly watered until water drains through the bottom of the container.

Can pulp pots go right into the ground?

Question: We recently moved to a new house. Before we left our old house, we potted up all of our prized plants in those inexpensive pulp pots. We'd like to replant these plants in our new garden, but are a little leery about disturbing the roots all over again. Is it possible to put our plants, pulp containers and all, right in the ground? Will they eventually decompose?

Answer: The answer to both questions is yes. Here's how to do it: 1) Knock several holes all around the sides of the pulp pots with a hammer, pick, stout trowel, or weeding knife. These holes will speed the roots out into the surrounding soil and hasten the breakdown of the pot. 2) Set plants into planting hole, making sure soil level in the pot is even with the surrounding soil (or a little higher, to allow for settling). Fill in with soil that has been improved by peat moss, ground bark, or other coarse organic additive. 3) Water thoroughly. For the rest of the first season you can use the elevated rim of the pot as a watering basin. (Note: you should do this only with plants in large pulp pots. Annuals or other small plants in 2 or 3-inch pulp pots should have the top edges of the pots torn away at planting time or, in the case of tomatoes (which prefer deep planting), buried entirely. Rims on small pots can act as wicks which suck up moisture and evaporate it to the air, causing roots to dry out dangerously. 4) When winter rains begin, tear away the exposed rim. In the second year pull up a water basin with a hoe as you would for any plant.

How can I move the "big guys"?

Question: Every year we struggle to get two very large white standard azaleas into the dining room for Easter dinner. It's been a real tradition around our house, but it's going to be an *ex*-tradition—unless you can recommend some way to make the job easier.

Answer: A hand truck is the best way to move heavy containers; use a piece of rope to hold the container against the truck frame. If you don't have a hand truck, you can rent one—but you should own one if you have much occasion to move heavy objects around.

Another good way to move a heavy container plant across a fairly smooth surface is to rock it onto a skid. A big burlap square works well on tiles or smooth wooden decks. On rougher areas try a large cardboard box, broken down to lie flat. Fold over one edge of the cardboard to give a good grip for both hands, then tug away. Use boards as ramps if you have to change levels.

A wheelbarrow is useful but risky because of its top-heaviness, and the risk is multiplied by a top-heavy load such as a big container plant. Get a friend to steady the plant if you move it in a wheelbarrow.

When and how to plant trees?

Question: We recently moved into a new house in Redwood City, California, and would like to start landscaping the yard. We never gardened before, and would like to know when and how we should go about planting some trees and shrubs.

Answer: In low elevations of California and Oregon, fall is generally the best time to plant permanent landscape plants from containers. This gives the plants a chance to become established over the winter and early spring, before being subjected to the rigors of the growing season and the hot summer months.

PRONUNCIATION GUIDE

The English language is rich in vowel sounds but poor in letters to express them. It is also inconsistent in the way it represents sounds. To explain what we have in mind, we have included a chart to serve as a pronunciation key.

Our spelling	represents the sound	as in the word
a	a	hat, hand
ay	a	baby
ah	a	hall
ai	a	air
e	e	met, bed
ee	e	we
i	i	tin
ye	i	wine
o	o	hot
oe	o	romance
u	u	must, bur
oo	u	rumor
ew	u	human
uh	a,e,i,o,u	comma, consider, sinister, vapor, minus

A Abelia—uh-BEE-lee-uh
Abutilon—uh-BEW-tuh-lon
Acacia—uh-KAY-shuh
Acer—AY-sir
Achillea—ak-il-LEE-uh
Achimenes—uh-KIM-muh-neez
Aconitum—ak-oe-NYE-tuhm
Actinidia—AK-ti-NID-ee-uh
Adiantum—ad-ee-AN-tuhm
Aesculus—ES-keew-luhs
Agapanthus—ag-uh-PAN-thuhs
Agave—ah-GAH-vay
Ageratum—ah-JER-ah-tum (usually pronounced ad-juh-RAY-tuhm)
Ailanthus—uh-LAN-thuhs
Ajuga—uh-JEW-guh
Alstroemeria—al-struh-MEE-ree-uh
Amaryllis—am-uh-RIL-is
Anemone—uh-NEM-uh-nee
Anthurium—an-THU-ree-uhm

Aquilegia—ak-wuh-LEE-jee-uh
Arabis—AIR-uh-bis
Aralia—uh-RAY-lee-uh
Arctostaphylos—ark-toe-STAF-i-luhs
Arctotheca—ark-toe-THEE-kuh
Artemisia—AHR-tuh-MEE-zee-uh
Aspidistra—as-puh-DIS-truh
Astilbe—as-STIL-bee
Atriplex—AT-rip-lex

B Babiana—bab-ee-ANE-uh
Baccharis—BAK-uh-ris
Bauhinia—bo-HIN-ee-uh
Berberis—BUR-buh-ris
Bergenia—bur-GEN-ee-uh
Betula—BET-ewe-luh
Bougainvillea—boo-guhn-VIL-ee-uh
Buddleia—BUD-lee-uh

C Caladium—kuh-LAY-dee-uhm
Calceolaria—kal-see-oe-LAIR-ee-uh
Calendula—kuh-LEN-dew-luh
Callistemon—ka-lis-STEE-muhn
Callistephus—ka-LIS-tee-fuhs
Calochortus—kal-oh-COR-tuhs
Campanula—kam-PAN-ewe-luh
Carpenteria—CAHR-pen-TEER-ee-a
Cattleya—KAT-lee-uh
Ceanothus—see-uh-NO-thuhs
Celosia—see-LOW-she-uh
Centaurea—sen-tah-REE-uh
Ceratonia—sair-uh-TONE-ee-uh
Ceratostigma—sair-uh-toe-STIG-muh
Cercidium—sair-CID-ee-uhm
Cercis—SIR-suhs
Chamaecyparis—kam-uh-SIP-uh-ris
Cheiranthus—keye-RAN-thuhs
Chionanthus—kye-oe-NAN-thuhs
Chlorophytum—klor-oe-FYE-tum
Choisya—SHOY-zee-uh
Cimicifuga—sim-uh-SIF-ewe-guh
Clematis—KLEM-uh-tis
Cleome—KLEE-oe-mee

Clivia—KLYE-vee-uh
Cocculus—COC-ew-lus
Colchicum—KAHL-chik-uhm
Colocasia—kahl-oe-KAY-zee-uh
Convallaria—con-va-LAIR-ee-uh
Convolvulus—kon-VOL-vew-luhs
Coreopsis—kor-ee-OP-suhs
Cotinus—koe-TEYE-nuhs
Cotoneaster—koe-toe-nee-AS-tuhr
Crataegus—kruh-TEE-guhs
Crocosmia—kroe-KOZ-mee-uh
Cuphea—KEW-fee-uh
Cymbidium—sim-BID-ee-uhm
Cynoglossum—sin-oh-GLOS-uhm

D Daboecia—dab-EE-shee-uh
Daphne—DAFF-nee
Davallia—duh-VAL-ee-uh
Deutzia—DOOT-zee-uh or DOYT-zee-uh
Dieffenbachia—deef-uhn-BAK-ee-uh
Dizygotheca—diz-uh-GOTH-ik-uh or diz-uh-goe-THEE-kah
Dracaena—druh-SEE-nuh
Dryopteris—drye-OP-ter-uhs
Duchesnea—dew-KEZ-nee-uh

E Echeveria—ek-uh-VAIR-ee-uh
Echinacea—ek-uh-NAY-see-uh
Echinops—EK-uh-nops
Echium—EK-ee-uhm
Elaeagnus—el-ee-AG-nuhs
Epidendrum—ep-uh-DEN-druhm
Epiphyllum—ep-uh-FIL-uhm
Equisetum—ek-wah-SEE-tuhm
Eremurus—er-uh-MEWR-uhs
Erica—ee-RYE-kuh (Correct, but universally pronounced AIR-ik-uh.)
Erigeron—ee-RIJ-uh-ron
Erythrina—air-i-THRYE-nuh
Eschscholzia—eh-SCHOELT-see-uh
Eucalyptus—ewe-kuh-LIP-tuhs
Euonymus—ew-ON-uh-mas
Exacum—EK-suh-kuhm

Exochorda—ek-so-KOR-duh

F *Fatshedera*—fats-HED-uh-ruh
Feijoa—fay-HOE-uh
Ficus—FYEE-kuhs
Forsythia—for-SITH-ee-uh
Fragaria—fra-GAIR-ee-uh
Fraxinus—FRAK-suh-nuhs
Fuchsia—FEW-shee-uh

G *Gaillardia*—gay-LAHR-dee-uh
Gazania—guh-ZAY-nee-uh
Genista—jen-NIS-tuh
Gentiana—jen-shee-AY-nah
Gerbera—GUR-bur-uh
Geum—JEE-uhm
Gleditsia—gluh-DIT-see-uh
Gomphrena—gom-FREE-nuh
Grevillea—gruh-VIL-ee-uh
Gypsophila—jip-SOF-uh-luh

H *Hamamelis*—ham-uh-MEE-luhs
Hebe—HEE-bee
Hedera—HED-uh-reh
Helianthemum—hee-lee-AN-thuh-muhm
Helianthus—hee-lee-AN-thuhs
Heliopsis—hee-lee-OP-suhs
Heliotropium—hee-lee-oe-TROE-pee-uhm
Hemerocallis—hem-uh-roe-KAL-uhs
Heteromeles—het-uh-roe-MEE-leez
Heuchera—HEWE-kuh-ruh
Hibiscus—hye-BIS-kuhs
Hippeastrum—hip-ee-AS-truhm
Hosta—HAHST-uh
Hydrangea—heye-DRAIN-jee-uh
Hymenocallis—hye-muh-noe-KAL-uhs
Hypericum—hye-PEER-ik-uhm

I *Iberis*—eye-BEE-ruhs
Ilex—EYE-lex
Impatiens—im-PAY-shuns
Ipomoea—ip-oe-MEE-uh
Iresine—ir-uh-SIGH-nee

J *Jacaranda*—jak-uh-RAN-duh
Jasminum—JAZ-muh-nuhm
Juniperus—joo-NIP-uh-ruhs

K *Kalanchoe*—kal-an-KO-ee
Kniphofia—nip-HOE-fee-uh
Kochia—KO-kee-uh
Koelreuteria—kell-rew-TEE-ree-uh
Kolkwitzia—koel-KWIT-zee-uh

L *Lagerstroemia*—lay-gur-STREE-mee-uh
Lampranthus—lam-PRAN-thuhs
Lathyrus—LATH-uh-ruhs
Leptospermum—lep-toe-SPUR-muhm
Leucothoe—lew-KOTH-oe-ee

Liatris—lie-AT-ruhs
Liriodendron—lear-ee-oe-DEN-druhn
Liriope—leer-EYE-oh-pee
Lobelia—loe-BEE-lee-uh
Lonicera—lo-NIS-uh-ruh
Lychnis—LIK-nis
Lysimachia—lye-suh-MAY-ke-uh

M *Malus*—MAY-lus
Mandevilla—man-duh-VIL-uh
Matricaria—mat-ri-KAIR-ee-uh
Matthiola—ma-thee-OE-luh
Maytenus—MAY-te-nuhs
Melaleuca—mel-uh-LOO-kuh
Metrosideros—MET-roe-SID-uh-ruhs
Mimulus—MIM-ewe-luhs
Musa—MEW-zuh
Myosotis—mye-oh-SO-tuhs
Myrica—mi-RYE-kuh

N *Nandina*—nan-DEE-nuh
Narcissus—nahr-SIS-uhs
Nerine—nuh-RYE-nee
Nerium—NEE-ree-uhm
Nicotiana—ni-koe-shee-AY-nuh
Nierembergia—nee-rem-BURG-ee-uh
Nyssa—NIS-uh

O *Olea*—O-lee-uh
Osmanthus—oz-MAN-thuhs
Osteospermum—os-tee-oe-SPUR-muhm
Oxalis—OK-sal-uhs
Oxydendrum—OK-see-DEN-druhm

P *Pachysandra*—pak-ee-SAN-druh
Papaver—puh-PAY-vur
Parthenocissus—PAHR-thuh-noe-SIS-uhs
Pelargonium—pel-ahr-GOE-nee-uhm
Pennisetum—pen-uh-SEE-tuhm
Penstemon—PEN-stuh-muhn
Peperomia—pep-uh-ROE-mee-uh
Philadelphus—fil-uh-DEL-fuhs
Photinia—foe-TIN-ee-uh
Phyla—FIE-luh
Phyllostachys—FIL-oe-STACK-ees
Physalis—FEYE-suh-luhs
Picea—peye-SEE-uh
Pieris—pee-AIR-uhs
Pinus—PIE-nuhs
Pittosporum—pit-TOS-poe-ruhm, pit-toe-SPOER-uhm
Platanus—PLAT-uh-nuhs
Platycladus—plat-i-CLAD-uhs
Podocarpus—poe-doe-KAR-puhs
Polianthes—pol-ee-AN-thez
Polygonatum—pol-ee-GON-uh-tuhm
Portulaca—por-tew-LAK-a

Potentilla—poe-ten-TIL-uh
Primula—PRIM-ew-luh
Protea—PROE-tee-uh or proe-TEE-uh
Pseudotsuga—soo-doe-TSOO-guh
Puschkinia—push-KIN-ee-uh
Pyrostegia—pye-roe-STEE-jee-uh
Pyrus—PYE-ruhs

Q *Quercus*—KWER-kuhs

R *Ranunculus*—ra-NUN-kew-luhs
Raphiolepis—raf-ee-OL-uh-pis, or raf-ee-o-LEP-uhs
Rhoeo—REE-oe
Romneya—ROM-nee-uh
Rosmarinus—ros-muh-RYE-nuhs
Rudbeckia—rud-BECK-ee-uh

S *Sagina*—sa-JYE-nuh
Salpiglossis—sal-pi-GLOS-sis
Sanvitalia—san-vi-TALE-ee-uh
Scabiosa—skay-bee-OH-suh
Schefflera—SHEF-luh-ruh
Schizanthus—ski-ZAN-thuhs
Scilla—SIL-luh
Sempervivum—sem-per-VYE-vuhm
Senecio—suh-NEE-shee-oe
Sequoia—suh-QUOY-uh
Sinningia—si-NIN-jee-uh
Solandra—soe-LAN-druh
Soleirolia—soe-lee-uh-ROE-lee-uh
Spiraea—SPEYE-REE-uh
Strelitzia—stre-LIT-see-uh
Syngonium—sin-GOE-nee-uhm

T *Tagetes*—tuh-JEE-teez
Taxodium—taks-OE-dee-uhm
Thuja—THOO-yuh
Thymus—TYE-muhs
Tibouchina—tib-oo-KYE-nuh
Tigridia—tye-GRID-ee-uh
Tolmiea—tol-MEE-uh
Trachelospermum—tra-kee-lo-SPER-muhm
Tradescantia—trad-es-KAN-shee-uh
Trichostema—trik-oe-STEE-mah
Tropaeolum—tro-PEE-oh-luhm
Tsuga—TSOO-guh

V *Vaccinium*—vak-SIN-ee-uhm
Vancouveria—van-koo-VEE-ree-uh
Verbascum—vur-BAS-kuhm
Verbena—ver-BEE-nuh
Vinca—VING-kuh
Vitex—VEE-teks

W *Waldsteinia*—wahld-STYE-nee-uh
Weigela—wye-JEE-luh

X *Xylosma*—zye-LOZ-muh

Z *Zantedeschia*—zan-tuh-DES-kee-uh
Zephyranthes—zef-i-RAN-theez
Zizyphus—ZIZ-uh-fuhs
Zoysia—ZOY-see-uh

GARDENERS' LANGUAGE

Acid soil, Alkaline soil, Neutral soil. Acidity and alkalinity describe one aspect of the soil's chemical reaction: the concentration of hydrogen ions (an ion is an electrically charged atom or molecule). The relative concentration of hydrogen ions is represented by the symbol pH followed by a number. A pH of 7 means that the soil is neutral, neither acid nor alkaline. A pH below 7 indicates acidity; above 7 indicates alkalinity. Many plants will grow well over a range of pH from slightly acid to slightly alkaline; some garden favorites are more particular.

Actual. That part of the formula for any product, containing several ingredients, which refers to a specific ingredient and its actual per-pound part of the total. For example, a 5-pound bag of 10-10-10 fertilizer would have 10% nitrogen, 10% phosphate, and 10% potash. 10% of 5 lbs. is ½ pound. Therefore, the actual content of each ingredient is ½ pound.

Aeration. The process of loosening or puncturing the soil by mechanical means in order to increase water and air permeability.

Alkaline soil. See Acid soil.

Annual. A plant that completes its life cycle in a year or less. Seed germinates and the plant grows, blooms, sets seed, and dies—all in one growing season. The phrase "grow as an annual" or "treat as an annual" refers to technically perennial plants that are most attractive only during their first year—hence are better grown as new plants each year.

Backfill. Soil that's returned to a planting hole after a plant's roots have been positioned.

Balled and burlapped (sometimes abbreviated B and B). Shrubs and trees that are dug from the growing field with a large *ball* of soil around the roots, wrapped in *burlap* to hold the soil together.

Bare root. Deciduous shrubs and trees, as well as some perennials, with all soil removed from their roots; sold in winter and early spring. These are dormant plants dug from growing fields, trimmed and freed of soil, and then protected against drying out.

Bedding plants. Plants suitable for massing in beds for their colorful flowers or foliage. Most are annuals.

Biennial. A plant that completes its life cycle in two years. Typically you plant seeds in spring, set out the seedling plants in summer or fall. Plants bloom the following spring, then set seed and die.

Blanching. The process of tying outer leaves over the inner head or leaves of a plant to produce a milder color or flavor.

Bloom stalk. The stem that bears a plant's flower or flowers.

Bolt. Annual flowers and vegetables that grow too quickly to flowering stage at the expense of developing well are said to *bolt.* This happens when hot weather rushes growth—either when it comes too early or when plants are set out too late.

Bonsai. A Japanese term for one of the fine arts of gardening: growing carefully trained, dwarfed plants in containers selected to harmonize with the plants. The objective is to create in miniature scale a tree or landscape.

Broad-leafed. The phrase "broad-leafed evergreen" refers to a plant that has green foliage all year but does not have the needlelike or scalelike foliage of evergreen conifers such as juniper. A broad-leafed weed is any weed that is not a grass.

Bud. This word has several meanings. A flower bud is one that develops into a blossom. A growth bud may be at the tip of a stem *(terminal)* or along the sides of a stem *(lateral).* Finally, *to bud* a plant is to propagate by a process similar to grafting.

Bud union. The part of a plant where top growth joins with the understock, generally 1 to 3 inches above the roots. It is an enlarged "knob" from which all major stems grow.

Bulb. In everyday conversation, any plant that grows from a thickened underground structure is referred to as a "bulb." But a true bulb is one particular type of underground stem. (Others defined in this glossary are Corm, Rhizome, Tuber, and Tuberous root.) The true bulb is more or less rounded and composed of fleshy scales (actually modified leaves) that store food and protect the developing plant inside. The outer scales dry to form a papery covering. Typical example is an onion.

Caliche. A deposit of calcium carbonate (lime) in a layer beneath the soil surface, found in arid areas of the Southwest.

Chlorosis. A condition (usually iron deficiency) in which the body of a leaf is paler or yellower than normal and the veins remain green. The soil may lack iron, or the iron may be chemically "tied up" and unavailable to the roots. For corrective measures, see Iron chelate, Iron sulfate.

Clay soil. (Also called adobe, or just "heavy.") A soil composed of microscopically small mineral particles that are flattened and fit closely together; spaces between particles for air and water also are small. When clay soil gets wet it dries out slowly because downward movement of water—drainage—is slow.

Cold frame. A low structure to protect plants from cold temperatures—in effect, a simple greenhouse. It may be a simple frame or box covered with plastic, cheese cloth, or glass sash; or a more elaborate structure.

Cole crops. A group of vegetables belonging to the cabbage family: broccoli, Brussels sprouts, cabbage, kohlrabi, cauliflower. They perform best under cool growing conditions.

Companion crops. Crops which have different harvest dates but are grown in the same area at the same time. One crop is harvested and removed by the time the other crop requires the growing space.

Complete fertilizer. Any plant food that contains all three of the primary nutrient elements—nitrogen, phosphorus, potassium.

Composite family. The enormous family of plants that includes all the flowers known as daisies. To name only a few of the most popular: dahlias, marigolds, zinnias.

Compost. An organic soil amendment or mulch made by gardeners from organic waste materials (dead leaves, some kitchen scraps, etc.). The materials are assembled in a pile where moisture and heat partially decompose them in a matter of months.

Conifer. Plants such as juniper, cypress, fir, and pine that are sometimes called evergreens. Several are not green all year round, but all produce seeds in a conelike structure. Leaves on most are narrow and needlelike or tiny and scalelike.

Cool-season crops. Vegetables which thrive in cool weather: cole crops, lettuce, spinach, peas.

Corm. A thickened underground stem that produces roots, leaves, and flowers during the growing season. Gladiolus and crocus are two familiar plants that grow from corms. A corm differs from a bulb in that food is stored in the solid center tissue, whereas in bulbs food is stored in scales.

Cover crop. Sometimes referred to as "green manure," this is a crop dug into the soil in early spring to return valuable organic material and nitrogen to soil. Most used are legumes such as clover, cow peas, vetch.

Crown. Portion of a plant at the juncture of the root and stem or trunk.

Cultivate. To break up the soil surface, often removing weeds as you go.

Cuttings. Portions of stem or root, sometimes called "slips," that can be induced to form roots and develop into new plants if placed in a suitable rooting medium.

Daisy flower. See Composite family.

Damping off. A plant disease, caused by fungi in the soil, that makes small seedlings wilt, rot, and die, just before or soon after they break through the soil.

Deadheading. The process of removing faded flowers to prevent seed formation.

Deciduous. Any plant that sheds all of its leaves at one time each year (typically in autumn).

Dethatch. The process of removing dead stems (thatch) that build up beneath certain ground covers and lawn grasses.

Dieback. Death of a plant's stems for a part of their length, beginning at the tips. Causes are various.

Dividing. A method for increasing plants (such as bulbs and perennials) that spread by developing roots and tops in clumps (e.g., dahlias, iris, daylilies). Accomplished by digging up all or a portion of a plant, breaking apart the rooted sections, and replanting.

Dormancy. Annual period when a plant's growth processes greatly slow down. This occurs in many plants by the coming of winter as days grow shorter and temperatures colder.

Dormant spray. An insecticide or fungicide applied to a plant during the season when it is not putting on new growth.

Double-digging. This approach has a two-fold purpose: to amend the soil on the upper level and to break up the soil on the lower level to allow roots to grow deeper. Procedure: 1. Dig a trench one spade deep; set soil aside alongside trench. 2. Dig down one spade's depth further in same trench, mixing amendments with soil in lower level. 3. Dig second trench alongside first one; mix in amendments and move amended soil to first trench. 4. In second trench, dig one spade's depth more; mix in amendments. Continue to dig trenches in same manner.

Drainage. Downward movement of water through the soil. When this happens quickly, the drainage is "good," "fast," or the soil is "well drained;" when it happens slowly, the drainage is said to be "slow," "bad," or soil is "poorly drained." Plant roots need oxygen as well as water, and soil that remains saturated deprives roots of necessary oxygen.

Drip irrigation. A system for watering at points on or just below the soil surface so that a plant's root zone is thoroughly moistened without water being wasted. The irrigation is accomplished with very low pressure over a long period of time to achieve necessary penetration.

Drip line. The circle that you would draw on the soil around a plant directly under its outermost branch tips (from which rainwater would drip). The term is used in connection with feeding, watering, and grading around existing plants.

Dust (noun or verb). A chemical product in the form of extremely fine powder, used to control insects or disease organisms. You apply by blowing the powder from a special applicator (sometimes the container is the applicator) in windless weather. It forms a cloud that settles on the plant.

Dwarf. A plant which grows smaller than the usual size for the variety or species but is nevertheless fully vigorous.

Early crop. Certain vegetable crops that mature faster than others of the same species.

Espalier. Tree or shrub trained so that its branches grow in a flat pattern—against a wall or fence, on a trellis, along horizontal wires. Espaliers may be formal and geometric, or informal.

Established. A plant firmly rooted and producing a good growth of leaves. (Remember that an established plant needs time to reestablish itself after you transplant it.)

Evergreen. A plant that never loses all of its leaves at the same time.

Eye. An undeveloped bud on a tuber, which will sprout after the tuber is planted; or any growth bud that is completely undeveloped, such as at the base of a leaf or along a bare stem.

Female plant. A plant that produces fruit or seed but does not produce pollen.

Fertilize. In popular usage, this word has two definitions: to fertilize a flower is to apply pollen (the male element) to a flower's pistil (the female element) for the purpose of setting seed (see Pollination). To fertilize a plant is to apply nutrients (plant food).

Flat. A shallow box or tray used to start cuttings or seedlings.

Forcing. The process of hastening a plant to maturity or a marketable state, or of growing a plant to flowering or fruiting stage out of its normal season, usually by growing it where temperature, humidity, and light can be controlled.

Formal. The word means "regular, rigid, and geometric." In gardening, it is variously applied to flowers, methods of training, and styles of garden design. A formal double flower, as with some camellias, consists of layers of regularly overlapping petals. Examples of formal plant training are rigidly and geometrically structured espaliers and evenly clipped hedges. Formal gardens are those laid out in precise geometric patterns, often containing formal hedges and espaliers.

French Intensive gardening. See Double-digging.

Frond. In the strictest sense, a frond is the entire leaf of a fern. Often, however, the word is also applied to the leaves of palms.

Frost-tender plant. A plant which is injured or killed by even a light frost. (Also see *Tender*.)

Fungicide. A chemical material used to retard or prevent the growth of fungi.

Germination. The sprouting of a seed.

Grafting. A method of plant propagation in which a section of one plant (called the *scion*) is inserted into a branch of another plant (the *stock*).

Ground bark. The bark of trees, ground up or shredded for use as a mulch or soil amendment.

Ground cover. Low-growing plants (usually of one kind) planted close together to create an attractive, even mass of foliage, to prevent soil erosion, or to discourage invading plants.

Harden off. This process adapts a plant that has been grown in a greenhouse, indoors, or under protective shelter, to full outdoor exposure. The plant is exposed, over a week or more, to increasing intervals of time outdoors, so that when it is planted out in the garden it can make the transition with a minimum of shock.

Hardwood cuttings. Cuttings taken from deciduous shrubs and trees during their fall-to-spring dormant season, from wood of the previous season's growth.

Hardy. This term describes a plant's resistance to, or tolerance of, frost or freezing temperatures (as in "hardy to −20° F."). The word does not mean tough, pest resistant, or disease resistant. A half-hardy plant is hardy in a given situation in normal years, but subject to freezing in coldest winters.

Heavy soil. This rather imprecise term refers to dense soil made up of extremely fine particles packed closely together. The term is used interchangeably with clay and adobe.

Hedge. A fence or barrier of living plants that are planted close together. Generally, hedges are considered to be less than 12 to 15 feet tall.

Heeling in. A means of preventing roots of bare-root plants from drying out before you can set out plants in the garden. Simplest is to dig a shallow trench, lay the plant on its side so that roots are in the trench, then cover roots with soil or other moist material.

Herb. A general term for a variety of plants valued for their flavor, fragrance, or medicinal properties.

Herbaceous. A plant with soft, non-woody tissues. In the strictest sense it refers to plants that die to the ground each year and regrow stems the following growing season. In the broadest sense it refers to any non-woody plant—annual, perennial, or bulb.

Herbicide. Chemical used to destroy undesirable plants and vegetation. *Pre-emergent* herbicides, applied to bare soil, prevent germination of weed seeds.

Humus. The soft brown or black substance formed in the last stages of decomposition of animal or vegetable matter. Common usage has incorrectly applied the word to almost all organic materials that eventually would decompose into humus.

Hybrid. A plant resulting from crossing two plants of the same type which have different individual characteristics for a trait—for example, one of them a tall plant and the other short.

Insecticide. A material toxic to insects either by contact and/or stomach poisoning.

Iron chelate, Iron sulfate. Two standard remedies for plants that show signs of chlorosis. The first is a combination of iron and a complex organic substance that makes the iron readily available to roots; the second adds iron to the soil.

Irrigation. Applying water to soil when rainfall is insufficient to maintain desirable soil moisture for plant growth.

Lateral buds. Growth buds on the sides of stems.

Lath. In gardening, any overhead structure of spaced laths that reduces the amount of sunlight reaching plants beneath or protects them from frost.

Lattice. A framework or structure of crossed wood or metal strips used to protect plants from sun or to support plant growth (i.e., vines, espaliers).

Leaching. The washing out or flushing of a soluble substance from an insoluble one. Gardeners leach soil with water when they want to remove excess salts (see Salinity). In high-rainfall areas, rain water leaches good as well as harmful substances from the soil.

Leaf burn. Leaf burn occurs when there is damage or destruction to a leaf's tissues from sunlight or chemicals.

Leaf mold. Partially decomposed leaves that can be dug into the soil as an organic amendment. Most familiar is oak leaf mold.

Lifting. The digging of a plant that is to be replanted or stored.

Light soil. An imprecise term synonymous with sandy soil. (See Sandy soil.)

Loam. Gardeners' word for soil that is rich in organic material, does not compact easily, and drains well after watering; an "ideal" garden soil.

Male plant. A plant that produces pollen but does not produce fruit or seeds.

Manure. Organic material excreted from animals, used as fertilizer and organic amendment to enrich the soil.

Microclimate. The climate of a small area or locality (such as a back yard or a portion of it), as opposed to the climate of a county or state.

Miniature. A plant that is smaller in stature and in all its parts (leaves, flowers, fruits) than the standard size of its kind.

Mulch. Any loose, usually organic, material placed over the soil (such as ground bark, sawdust, straw, or leaves). The process of applying such materials is called mulching. A mulch can retard loss of moisture from soil; reduce or prevent weed growth; insulate soil from extreme or rapid changes of temperature; prevent mud from splashing onto foliage and other surfaces; protect falling fruit from injury; make a garden bed look tidy.

Nematode. A microscopic, transparent worm which decomposes organic matter. Some are parasites that infest roots, bulbs, and leaves.

Nitrogen. One of the three major nutrients in a complete fertilizer and the first one listed in the formulation on a fertilizer label (as 10-8-6, for example).

Organic matter. Any material of organic origin—peat moss, ground bark, compost, and manure, for example—to be dug into the soil to improve its condition.

Peat moss. Highly water-retentive, spongy organic soil amendment which is the partially decomposed remains of any of several mosses. It is somewhat acid in reaction.

Perennial. A non-woody plant that lives for more than two years. With most perennials, the top growth dies down each winter and regrows the following spring.

Pesticide. A substance (most often a chemical) used to control a garden pest.

pH. See Acid soil.

Phosphorus. The second element in a complete fertilizer (such as 10-8-6). Phosphorus promotes sturdy cell structure and root growth, aids in flower and fruit production.

Pinching. Basic pruning technique using thumb and forefinger to nip off the tips of branches; this forces side growth so plant will be more compact.

Planting medium. Specially formulated mixture of organic and inorganic materials for growing plants in containers.

Plastic mulch. Sheets of polyethylene plastic laid on the soil surface to function as a mulch.

Pollen. Microscopic dust-like grains, produced on the anthers of a flower, which contain male sex cells. Each pollen grain, after coming to rest on the stigma of a pistil, will produce sperm cells to fertilize an ovule—producing a seed.

Pollination. Transfer of pollen from flower stamens to pistils for development of fruit and seeds.

Potassium. Referred to as "potash," potassium is the third element contained in a complete fertilizer (such as 10-8-6).

Pre-emergent weed killer. See Herbicide.

Propagation. Reproduction of plants either from seeds (sexual reproduction) or from cuttings, division, budding, grafting, or layering (asexual reproduction).

Pruning. The judicious removal of plant parts to obtain a more desirably shaped plant.

Rhizome. A thickened, modified stem that grows horizontally along or under the soil surface. It may be long and slender, as in some lawn grasses; or thick and fleshy, as in many irises.

Rock garden. Usually a manmade landscape, often on sloping ground, that contains natural-appearing rock outcrops and rocky soil surfaces. Plants grown in a rock garden are generally low-growing, spreading or mat-forming types that conform to the rocky terrain. Many favorite rock garden plants require fast drainage and full sun, and are somewhat drought-tolerant.

Root ball. The network of roots and the soil clinging to them when a plant is lifted from the soil or removed from a container.

Rootbound. A term used to describe a plant that has remained in a container too long so that roots grow around it in a circle, and are thoroughly congested. Seriously rootbound plants are useless for planting unless you break up the root ball so roots will have a chance to reach out into the soil.

Root crop. The term used to describe crops grown for edible roots, e.g., beets, carrots, turnips.

Rooting hormone. A powder or liquid, containing growth hormones, that will stimulate root formation on cuttings.

Rootstock. The part of a budded or grafted plant that furnishes the root system and sometimes part of the branch structure.

Runner. In common usage, an imprecise term referring to either **offsets** or **stolons.** A runner is actually a slender stem sent out from the bases of certain perennials, at the end of which an offset develops and a new plant grows.

Salinity. Gardeners use this word when speaking of an excess of salts in the soil. Salinity can harm many plants, causing leaves to scorch and turn yellow, and stunting plant growth.

Sandy soil. Soils that have comparatively large particles that are rounded rather than flattened. Compared to clay soils, sandy soils contain much more soil air, drain well, and warm quickly. They also dry out quickly; the necessary frequent watering washes out valuable nutrients. Also referred to as "light" soil.

Screening. The use of plants to block out sun, wind, sound, or an undesirable view.

Shade plant. Plant which grows well in partial or even almost full shade.

Short season crop. A crop which grows and produces its harvest within one or two months.

Shrub. A woody plant, usually shorter than a tree and with major stems growing from the ground or from low on the plant.

Slip. See Cuttings.

Sod. A surface of earth covered with grass. Also it refers to a several-inches-thick layer of soil, cut from a lawn, containing roots of the grass growing in that soil.

- **Softwood cutting.** A cutting of a young shoot from a woody or herbaceous plant taken before it has hardened.
- **Soil amendment.** Organic matter added to soil to improve texture, aeration, drainage, and moisture retention.
- **Sphagnum.** Various mosses native to bogs. They are collected live, dried, and sold for use in lining hanging baskets, in air layering, and for planting certain orchids.
- **Spike.** A flowering stem on which flowers are directly attached (without any short stem to each flower) along the upper portion of its length. The flowers open in sequence, usually beginning at the bottom of the spike. Familiar examples are gladiolus and red-hot poker.
- **Spore.** A simple type of reproductive cell capable of producing a new plant. Certain plants (such as algae, fungi, mosses, and ferns) reproduce by spores.
- **Staking.** The practice of driving a stake or rod into the ground close to a plant to provide support for its stems.
- **Standard.** A plant that does not naturally grow as a tree but that is trained into a small treelike form, with a single, upright trunk topped by a rounded crown of foliage. The "tree rose" is a familiar example.
- **Stem cuttings.** See Cuttings.
- **Stigma.** The part of the pistil in the very center part of a flower that receives the pollen.
- **Stolon.** A stem that creeps along the surface of the ground, taking root at intervals and forming new plants where it roots.
- **Stone fruit.** Fruits containing a single seed in the center; e.g., peach, plum, apricot.
- **Stress.** Growing conditions that endanger a plant's health. Examples are: lack of water; too much heat, wind, or moisture; low temperatures. The stressful condition varies according to the particular plant and its needs.
- **Subshrub.** A type of plant, usually under 3 feet high and with more or less woody stems, that is sometimes grown and used as a shrub or perennial. Examples are dusty miller and cushion bush.
- **Subtropical.** A plant that has some of the characteristics of tropical zone plants and of temperate zone plants; it usually is not killed by mild frosts, although it may die back to the ground.
- **Sucker.** In a grafted or budded plant, sucker growth originates from the rootstock rather than from the desired grafted or budded part of the plant. In trees, any strong vertical shoot growing from the main framework of trunk and branches is sometimes called a sucker, although the technical term is watersprout.
- **Sunburn.** Damage to leaves, bark from sunlight. It may result from high temperature, or exposure of previously shaded bark to sun.
- **Surface roots or feeder roots.** A plant's network of roots near the soil surface through which it absorbs most nutrients and water.
- **Systemic.** A systemic is any chemical that is absorbed into a plant's system, either to kill organisms that feed on the plant or to kill the plant itself. There are systemic insecticides, fungicides, and weed killers.
- **Taproot.** A main root that grows straight down. Dandelions have taproots, so do oak trees. Taproots can go very deep if there is a lack of surface water.

- **Tender.** Tender means the opposite of hardy. It denotes low tolerance of freezing temperatures.
- **Terminal bud.** The bud at the end of a stem. Its growth continues the stem's elongation.
- **Thatch.** Dead stems that build up beneath certain ground covers and lawn grasses.
- **Thinning.** This pruning term means to remove *entire branches*—large or small—back to the main trunk, a side branch, or the ground. The object is to give the plant a more open structure.

  In growing plants from seed, thinning out means removing excess seedlings so those remaining are spaced far enough apart to develop well.
- **Tip cuttings.** See Cuttings.
- **Topdress.** To apply on the surface, usually referring to the spreading of an organic material, such as ground bark, on the soil as a mulch. Also means to apply manure or sewage sludge on a lawn as a low-grade fertilizer.
- **Topiary.** The technique of pruning shrubs and trees into formalized shapes resembling such things as animals and geometrical figures.
- **Transpiration.** The release of moisture (absorbed largely by plant roots) through the leaves. Temperature and humidity affect transpiration rate.
- **Transplant.** To dig up a plant and replant it in another location.
- **Trellis.** An open structure of lattice used to support and train plants and vines.
- **Tropical plant.** A plant that originated in the tropical regions of the world; tropical plants are usually killed by frost.
- **Truss.** A cluster of flowers, usually rather compact, at the end of a stem; rhododendrons, for example.
- **Tuber.** A thick underground stem, from which a plant grows; similar to a rhizome but usually shorter, thicker, and doesn't lengthen greatly as it grows.
- **Tuberous root.** A thickened underground food storage structure which is a modified stem. Growth buds are in the old stems at the upper end of the root. The dahlia is a familiar example.
- **Understock.** See Rootstock.
- **Variety.** In botanical language this word has a particular meaning. A variety within a species has the basic characteristics of the species, but has at least one, sometimes more, individual characteristics of its own. Man-made varieties (called *cultivars*) are developed by cross-breeding.
- **Vine.** A plant with flexible stems that climb vertically or wander horizontally, fastening to support by clinging, or by being tied.
- **Virus.** Microscopic living particles that can infect plants and reproduce in them, causing abnormalities in growth, discolored foliage, or distorted blossoms.
- **Water basin.** A ridge of soil several inches high formed around a plant at its dripline. Water applied within the basin will thoroughly moisten the plant's root zone.
- **Watersprout.** See Sucker.
- **Weed.** A wild plant that grows out of place and competes with garden plants for water, nutrients, and space. Control consists basically of preventing growth, and destroying by mechanical or chemical means.

INDEX

Problems with pests? See pages 36-48